THE WEIRD TALE

THE WEIRD TALE

ARTHUR MACHEN
LORD DUNSANY
ALGERNON BLACKWOOD
M.R. JAMES
AMBROSE BIERCE
H.P. LOVECRAFT

by S. T. Joshi

UNIVERSITY OF TEXAS PRESS   AUSTIN

First edition, 1990

Requests for permission to reproduce material from this work should be sent to Permissions, University of Texas Press, Box 7819, Austin, TX 78713-7819.

∞ The paper used in this publication meets the minimum requirements of American National Standard for Information Sciences—Permanence of Paper for Printed Library Materials, ANSI Z39.48-1984.

Library of Congress Cataloging-in-Publication Data

Joshi, S. T., 1958–
    The weird tale : Arthur Machen/Lord Dunsany/ Algernon Blackwood/M. R. James/Ambrose Bierce/ H. P. Lovecraft / by S. T. Joshi. — 1st ed.
        p.   cm.
    Includes bibliographical references.
    ISBN 0-292-79050-3(alk. paper). — ISBN 0-292-79057-0 (pbk. : alk. paper)
    1. Horror tales, English—History and criticism.
    2. Horror tales, American—History and criticism.
    3. Fantastic fiction—History and criticism.
    4. Supernatural in literature.   I. Title.
PR830.T3J67   1990
823'.0873809—dc20   89-37753
                                             CIP
                                             Rev.

To
Steven J. Mariconda

CONTENTS

ACKNOWLEDGMENTS

An earlier version of "Arthur Machen: The Mystery of the Universe" has appeared (under the title "Arthur Machen: Philosophy and Fiction") in *Discovering Classic Horror Writers*, ed. Darrell Schweitzer (Starmont House). "Lord Dunsany: The Career of a *Fantaisiste*" has appeared in *Discovering Classic Fantasy Writers*, ed. Darrell Schweitzer (Starmont House). "M. R. James: The Limitations of the Ghost Story" has appeared in *Spectral Tales*, June 1988.

S. T. J.

PREFACE

This work did not begin as a theoretical study; indeed, it appears that I have gradually evolved toward a consciously antitheoretical position. I initially wished merely to write interpretative essays on some writers of weird fiction whom I happened to like. The essays on Machen and Dunsany were originally written for some critical anthologies assembled by Darrell Schweitzer; but I very quickly realized that I might wish to follow H. P. Lovecraft's lead and discuss the other two "Modern Masters" (M. R. James and Algernon Blackwood) covered in his seminal essay "Supernatural Horror in Literature." I then decided to add an essay on Bierce and one on Lovecraft himself. These six authors represent different facets of what Lovecraft called the weird tale, and are generally regarded as among the leading practitioners in their field. I shall suggest that there is reason to question James's rank in this august company.

Lovecraft is one of the most intelligent commentators on the weird tale, and it is unfortunate that his most perceptive remarks on his fellow weird writers are to be found in little-known essays and in his correspondence. I have constantly drawn upon both Lovecraft's theoretical and practical criticism, although not always in agreement. All citations from "Supernatural Horror in Literature" are taken from my corrected edition (*Dagon and Other Macabre Tales* [1986], pp. 365–436) and abbreviated SHiL in the text.

I take some pride in my bibliographical matter, since much of it derives from original research. My primary bibliographies aim to be reasonably complete for separate publications during the author's lifetime. (I have not attempted to list any of M. R. James's voluminous scholarly and technical works.) My secondary bibliographies are perhaps a little fuller than necessary, but I wanted to indicate the significant amount of attention several of these authors received during their lifetimes. Since these authors are on the whole so little known, I have prefaced my essays with brief biographies.

If I seem less than charitable to some previous commentators, it is frankly because I feel that much scholarship in this field has been totally misconceived; by the book's conclusion I hope to suggest some ways in which work might now proceed. The fact is, of course, that most of the writers discussed here have received very negligible criticism. But lest I be accused of completely ignoring my predecessors, I have added a Critical Appendix in which I discuss some of the better contributions to the study of each author. I have numbered each item in the secondary bibliographies, and refer to items by number in the Critical Appendix. I have not felt obligated to comment on every item I list.

One last personal note: I have written this book principally because I enjoy most of these writers and wish others to enjoy them. Naive as this sounds, I cannot imagine any other reason why anyone would want to write criticism. Because I am not an academician, I am not compelled to write criticism to maintain my position; perhaps this makes a difference. Still, the bulk of recent critical work (not merely in this field but in most others) seems so cheerless, mechanical, and obfuscatory that the reader is likely to be repelled rather than attracted to the subjects of study. I hope my work does not have an analogous effect.

I have received valuable comments on parts of this book from Mike Ashley, Donald R. Burleson, Jason C. Eckhardt, T. E. D. Klein, Steven J. Mariconda, Susan Michaud, and Devendra P. Varma, and am grateful to them and to my other friends and colleagues for their advice and encouragement. I have also benefited from the proofreading and copyediting skills of Richard Fumosa.

S. T. J.

INTRODUCTION

THE WEIRD TALE AND ITS HISTORY

*I*n 1927 H. P. Lovecraft published his great treatise "Supernatural Horror in Literature."[1] In the final chapter he devoted space to four "Modern Masters"—Arthur Machen (1863–1947), Algernon Blackwood (1869–1951), Lord Dunsany (1878–1957), and M. R. James (1862–1936). This study, remarkably ahead of its time, also made some momentous pronouncements on the theory of the "weird tale"—a phrase used consistently by Lovecraft as an umbrella term for the field as a whole. Lovecraft's relatively brief study did not, of course, pretend to deal at all comprehensively with any of the authors it dicusses; and I feel it is worthwhile to devote additional space to these still largely unrecognized figures (with the addition of Ambrose Bierce—whose inclusion shall be justified shortly—and Lovecraft himself), and to see whether some general conclusions on the nature and scope of the weird tale can be drawn.

I begin my own study with a rather odd assertion: the weird tale, in the period covered by this volume (generally 1880–1940), did not (and perhaps does not now) exist as a genre but as *the consequence of a world view.* Of the six writers covered here, only Lovecraft appears to have been conscious of working in a weird tradition; the others—even Blackwood and Dunsany, nearly the whole of whose fictional work is weird— regarded themselves (and were regarded by contemporary reviewers) as not intrinsically different from their fellow novelists and short-story writers. I hope to suggest reasons for this in the course of my work. If the weird tale exists *now* as a genre, it may only be because critics and publishers have deemed it so by fiat.

I am not, as a result, prepared to define the weird tale, and venture to assert that any definition of it may be impossible. Recent work in this field has caused an irremediable confusion of terms such as horror, terror, the supernatural, fantasy, the fantastic, ghost story, Gothic fiction, and others. It does not appear that any single critic's usage even approximates that of any other, and no definition of the weird tale embraces all types of works that can plausibly be assumed to enter into the scope of the term. This difficulty is a direct result of the conception of the weird tale as some well-defined genre to which some works "belong" and others do not.

I use the term "weird tale" more or less as Lovecraft did. Lovecraft may be still the most acute theoretician of the weird tale, although it is unfortunate that many of his important utterances are buried in obscure essays and letters. There are several conceptual problems with Lovecraft's own definition of the weird tale, and I shall examine these presently; but I am still convinced that the term he coined is the most felicitous and wide-ranging. I find the term "ghost story" particularly irksome, although it has gained wide usage. To me "ghost story" can mean nothing but a story with a ghost in it; but others have thought differently. Peter Penzoldt, in his stimulating *Supernatural in Fiction* (1952), makes this astonishing claim: "For reasons of simplicity we will use the term 'ghost story' also for tales of the supernatural that do not deal with a ghost or revenant. This can be justified on the grounds that a majority of weird tales are in fact ghost stories."[2] This is simply false; of the writers covered here, Lovecraft and Machen wrote no ghost stories, Dunsany perhaps three or four (some of them jocular), Blackwood and Bierce relatively few. Only M. R. James wrote nothing but ghost stories (in the narrow sense of the term). Jack Sullivan, perhaps the most acute recent commentator, makes a similar assertion: "In using 'ghost story' as a catch-all term, I am also compromising. All of these stories [covered in his work] are apparitional, in one sense or another, and 'ghost story' is as good a term as any."[3] It is as if Sullivan cannot be bothered to find a better term. Julia Briggs flatly asserts a wider connotation for "ghost story" without justifying it: "It may already be apparent that the term 'ghost story' is being employed with something of the latitude that characterizes its general usage, since it can denote not only stories about ghosts, but about possession and demonic bargains, spirits other than those of the dead, including ghouls, vampires, werewolves, the 'swarths' of living men and the 'ghost-soul' or *Doppelgänger*."[4] I similarly find the term "Gothic fiction" very clumsy for anything written subsequent to Poe. Lovecraft makes clear in "Supernatural Horror in Literature" the vital shift in weird writing effected by Poe—principally in making the short story rather than the novel the vehicle for the weird and in his insistence on psychological realism—so that I am puzzled by David Punter's tortuous effort to account for all usages of the term "Gothic" from the late eighteenth century to the present day.[5] The term is bandied about so casually and haphazardly in both critical and publishing circles that it becomes very awkward to use it for anything but the Gothic novels of the late eighteenth and early nineteenth centuries. And I hope to show in this study how mistaken Punter is in his assertion that "many of the best-known masters of recent supernatural fiction—Algernon Blackwood, M. R. James, H. P. Lovecraft—derive their techniques of suspense and their sense of the archaic directly from the original Gothic fiction, and many of their crucial symbols of the supernatural were previously the property of these older writers."[6]

Terminology aside, there is a further problem with the weird tale—the critical disrepute into which it has fallen in the course of this century. There are, certainly, few nowadays who fail to acknowledge the greatness of Poe (Harold Bloom is perhaps a dinosaur in this regard); but of the six authors covered here, only Bierce has even a tentative foothold in critical discourse. A recent review of *The Columbia Literary History of the United States* singled out the omission of Bierce from the volume, but not Lovecraft;[7] and of the four English writers, Machen, Dunsany, and James are mere footnotes in English literature, and Blackwood not even that. Critical analysis of these figures has accordingly been left in the surprisingly able hands of nonacademicians patiently and diligently working away in obscurity.

It might almost be said that the weird tale became a definite genre only when it went "underground," an event that appears to have caused the contemptuous dismissal of all weird work on the part of academic critics. When this event occurred, it is difficult to say; but it seems to have occurred earlier in the United States than in England. At the turn of the century many "mainstream" writers, from William Dean Howells (*Questionable Shapes,* 1903) to Mary E. Wilkins-Freeman (*The Wind in the Rose-Bush,* 1903), felt no compunction in issuing collections of weird tales in the course of their careers. Robert W. Chambers (1865–1933) published several volumes of weird fiction in the 1890s before going on to write an interminable series of sentimental romances; historical novelist F. Marion Crawford's weird tales were gathered posthumously (*Wandering Ghosts,* 1911), although some of his novels are laced with the weird. The advent of the pulp magazines did not immediately banish the weird tale to a literary ghetto; *Munsey's* published horror stories but also fiction of many other types. The establishment of *Weird Tales* (1923–1954) could be said to have effectively marked a dubious watershed: from this point on, the weird disappears almost entirely from traditional "slick" or general-interest magazines. Much of the content of *Weird Tales* was inconceivably wretched, although somewhat better than some of its still worse rivals, like *Ghost Stories.* By the middle thirties the "fantasy fandom" movement had commenced, usually conducted by very young enthusiasts (R. H. Barlow began corresponding with the ageing Lovecraft when he was thirteen). Such magazines as Charles W. Hornig's *The Fantasy Fan,* Julius Schwartz's *Fantasy Magazine,* Donald A. Wollheim's *The Phantagraph,* and—a little later—Francis T. Laney's *The Acolyte* canonized some of the pulp writers and led directly to Edmund Wilson's grand condemnation of the "Lovecraft cult" as "on even a more infantile level than the Baker Street Irregulars and the cult of Sherlock Holmes."[8] He was—at this point in time—probably right.

When August Derleth and Donald Wandrei founded Arkham House in 1939, initially to publish the work of Lovecraft, I do not think they realized what a momentous—and, quite possibly, deleterious—effect this act would have on the publicaton and recognition of weird fiction. In the twenties and thirties mainstream publishers were still willing to issue weird work—Francis Brett Young's *Cold Harbour* (Knopf, 1925), Herbert S. Gorman's *The Place Called Dagon* (George H. Doran, 1927), H. B. Drake's *The Shadowy Thing* (Vanguard, 1928), and R. E. Spencer's *The Lady Who Came to Stay* (Knopf, 1931). Lovecraft himself was solicited several times—by Knopf, Putnam's, Vanguard, and Loring & Mussey—for a weird novel or a collection of tales, although these efforts came to nothing. Derleth tried—a little half-heartedly, I think—to convince his publisher, Charles Scribner's Sons, to issue a memorial omnibus of Lovecraft, and when turned down he forthwith published the book—*The Outsider and Others* (1939)—himself. The whole history and criticism of the weird tale might have been different if Derleth had convinced a mainstream publisher to issue Lovecraft. In any event, it is highly significant that Derleth felt compelled to sign up some "big names"—mostly from England—to lend prestige to his fledgling press; as a result, some early Arkham House publications included the work of

Blackwood (*The Doll and One Other,* 1946), Dunsany (*The Fourth Book of Jorkens,* 1948), and Lady Cynthia Asquith (*This Mortal Coil,* 1947).[9] And yet it is a sad fact that the vast majority of authors published by Arkham House would never have secured book publication elsewhere—such middling pulpsmiths as Henry S. Whitehead, Seabury Quinn, and Donald Wandrei, and even perhaps Clark Ashton Smith and Robert E. Howard. To date none of these authors has been published by any but specialty houses. It is also unlikely that anyone would have wanted to publish—then and now—any of Lovecraft's letters (let alone five volumes of them), even though they are, quite frankly, some of the most remarkable literary documents of the century. The problem with Arkham House (and other such hardcover houses as Gnome Press, Carcosa House, and more recently Scream/Press) is that its publications were consciously intended for an extraordinarily small audience—almost a cult following. The small print runs were so rapidly exhausted that they became collectors' items, and Derleth made very little effort to bring any of his publications to the attention of mainstream critics or book reviewers.

In England the split was achieved later. Machen, Dunsany, and Blackwood were never published by any but major houses. The pulp magazine phenomenon in weird fiction never developed in England—British versions of *Weird Tales* and other pulps were infrequent and little regarded, and people like Blackwood and Dunsany did not publish in these magazines but rather in periodicals like *Time and Tide, Westminster Review,* and the like. (Dunsany was also a rare phenomenon in publishing his weird work extensively in American magazines like *Smart Set, Atlantic Monthly, Saturday Evening Post,* and the like through the 1940s, but this was probably a result of his anomalous fame in America.) The fantasy fandom movement also took root later and to a lesser degree: Walter Gillings's *Fantasy Review* ran in the 1940s, but it had few competitors. There was no British equivalent of Arkham House (a remark to that effect by Blackwood was long displayed on Arkham House catalogues), and there seems really to be a dearth of significant British weird work between Dunsany, Tolkien, and Mervyn Peake and the emergence in the last two decades of such writers as Robert Aickman and Ramsey Campbell; but by this time the weird tale had already become principally a marketing phenomenon. The example of Campbell—perhaps the leading living weird writer—is instructive and possibly prophetic. Campbell's first several books were issued by Arkham House, and Campbell still regards Derleth as his mentor; [10] but his novels of the 1970s and his later horror collections have appeared in hardcover from Macmillan, the same publisher that issued much of Blackwood's work half a century before. Does this sort of thing presage the final emergence of the weird tale from critical contempt? I fervently hope so.

TYPES OF WEIRD TALES

The true weird tale has something more than secret murder, bloody bones, or a sheeted form clanking chains according to rule. A certain atmosphere of breathless and unexplainable dread of outer, unknown forces must be present; and there must be a hint, expressed with a seriousness and portentousness becoming its subject, of that most terrible conception of the human brain—a malign and particular suspension or defeat of those fixed laws of Nature which are our only safeguard against the assaults of chaos and the daemons of unplumbed space. [11]

This is perhaps as satisfactory a definition of the weird tale as any; it comes from "Supernatural Horror in Literature." In a letter of 1931 Lovecraft makes another suggestive remark: ". . . the crux of a *weird* tale is something which *could not possibly happen*." [12] I believe, however, there is a fundamental confusion or misconception on Lovecraft's part in the enunciation of these statements: Lovecraft cannot seem to make up his mind whether the weird tale is strictly equivalent to the tale of supernatural horror or is something wider. The very title "Supernatural Horror in Literature," in which Lovecraft uses the term "weird tale" repeatedly, suggests a narrow reading; but how then can he justify the inclusion in his study of Bierce and Dunsany, of whom the former wrote a significant body of nonsupernatural horror and the latter wrote imaginary-world fantasies? Lovecraft, indeed, seems to exclude nonsupernatural horror entirely when he says that true weird literature "must not be confounded with a type externally similar but psychologically widely different; the literature of mere physical fear and the mundanely gruesome." I think there is some justification in this, but I hope to show that such an exclusion becomes very cumbersome and even paradoxical.

As I see it, the weird tale must include the following broad divisions: fantasy, supernatural horror, nonsupernatural horror, and quasi science fiction. All these categories should be regarded as loose and nonexclusive, and there are some other subtypes that are probably amalgams or offshoots of those just mentioned.

Supernatural horror is perhaps the most copious subset of the weird tale, and in this volume the bulk of the work of Machen and Blackwood, a significant amount of Bierce, and much of the early Lovecraft will fall into it. *Supernatural* horror can exist only where the ordinary world of our daily lives is presupposed as the norm; "natural law" can, in Lovecraft's phrase, be "violated" only when it is assumed to function in the real world. This is what the French call *le fantastique,* as Maurice Lévy remarks succinctly: "It is well known that the truly fantastic exists only where the impossible can make an irruption, through time and space, into an objectively familiar locale."[13]

The *ghost story* (in the proper narrow sense) is conceptually only a subset of the supernatural horror story, but it has had a virtually independent history. I also hope to show that it is really a very rigid and inflexible form; if this is so, it is no surprise that M. R. James—with his flippant attitude toward weird writing—simultaneously perfected and exhausted it. He had no inclination to make significant changes in the traditional ghost story, and those who did (principally Walter de la Mare and Oliver Onions) on the whole transformed it into the *psychological ghost story,* philosophically a very different form.

Quasi science fiction is a development of supernatural horror in that the real world is again presupposed as the norm, but the "impossible" intrusions are rationalized in some way. It is a more advanced form because it implies that the "supernatural" is not *ontological* but *epistemological:* it is only our ignorance of certain "natural laws" that creates the illusion of supernaturalism. A few stories by Bierce and most of the later Lovecraft fall into this category; indeed, Matthew H. Onderdonk coined the felicitous term "supernormal" to describe this phenomenon in Lovecraft.[14] I cannot think of anyone but Lovecraft who exhaustively worked in this subclass; perhaps he did it so well as to deter others from competing with him.

Lovecraft felt that the inclusion of nonsupernatural horror posed certain conceptual problems, but its exclusion poses still greater ones. Much of Bierce would have to be excluded; moreover, we have to regard the tale of *psychological horror* (of which the psychological ghost story is one component) as a subset of nonsupernatural horror. Penzoldt made the extraordinarily ingenious suggestion that "the psychological ghost stories [i.e., weird tales] based chiefly on the findings of modern psychiatry and psychoanalysis are really part of science fiction."[15] He did not explain this remark, but what I presume he means is that any tales founded upon science (and psychology is a science) must belong to science fiction. I question this conception (if it is Penzoldt's) because science fiction cannot really be thought to be based on science as such but only the *science of the future*. This is why I call much of Lovecraft quasi science fiction: the implication in his stories is that we may some day be able to account for "supernormal" phenomena, but cannot do so now; and these tales are not actual science fiction because of their manifest intent to incite horror. If anything intended to inspire horror is to be classed as a subset of the weird tale (and I cannot see how else we are to regard it), then both quasi science fiction (horror) and psychological horror must be subsets of the weird tale. Psychological horror seems to have two distinct branches—what might be called the *pseudosupernatural* (where supernatural phenomena are suggested but explained away as the product of an abnormal consciousness) and the *conte cruel*, which is what Lovecraft was explicitly wishing to exclude. The borderline between the *conte cruel* and the mystery or even detective story can occasionally be very thin—such works as Robert Bloch's *Psycho* (1959), Ramsey Campbell's *The Face That Must Die* (1980), and Iain Banks's *The Wasp Factory* (1984) seem authentically in the weird tradition, but such a work as Patricia Highsmith's *Strangers on the Train* (1950) must be regarded as a suspense or mystery story. The only distinction, as I see it, is authorial intent (something we are now once more allowed to talk about): whereas Banks, for example, is interested in the systematic presentation of repulsive or disgusting images (which he does with great artistry and psychological acuity), Highsmith is more concerned with the psychology of guilt. It is certainly odd that many pure detective writers—notably Agatha Christie, John Dickson Carr, Margery Allingham, and Dorothy L. Sayers[16]—wrote actual supernatural stories; but never—except in Carr's stunning *tour de force, The Burning Court* (1937), the exception that proves the rule—did they mingle detection and supernaturalism. Still, more work could be done on the relationship between these two types of literature. No one—except Eric S. Rabkin in *The Fantastic in Literature* (1976), if I understand him correctly—would wish to classify the detective or science fiction tale as part of the weird tale, but the distinctions are sometimes nebulous.

Fantasy is the most difficult to define because it presents the most bewildering variety of forms and also seems to lack certain metaphysical ramifications present in nearly all other types of weird fiction. In an imaginary-world fantasy—like Dunsany's *Gods of Pegāna* or Tolkien's *Lord of the Rings*—there can be no such thing as supernatural horror because the real world and its laws are not assumed to exist. Works of this sort certainly present events "which could not possibly happen," but what moments of terror are in them cannot be of an ontological variety. When, in Lovecraft's *Dream-Quest of Unknown Kadath*, Randolph Carter is swept away by a night-gaunt, he and the reader feel a certain sort of fear, but since night-gaunts are a "natural" component of this imagined realm, the effect is roughly analogous to someone being kidnapped in the real world. There may, however, be a sort of pseudo-ontological horror reflected in the responses of characters: when, in Dunsany's *The Gods of the Mountain*, someone says, "Rock should not walk in the evening," we can assume that at least in one particular this imaginary realm obeys natural laws similar to our own. But Dunsany very quickly abandoned imaginary-world settings, and his subsequent works pose greater theoretical problems. Take a work like *The Strange Journeys of Colonel Polders* (1950): here the consciousness of a retired colonel is transported by an Indian member of his club into the bodies of a bewildering succession of animals. We are not to imagine that these successive incarnations are the products of some sort of hypnosis or other mental aberration—the colonel's accounts of dwelling in the body of a dog, cat, squirrel, fox, and the like ring too true for that. Now contrast this tale with Lovecraft's "The Shadow out of Time" (1934–1935), in which a modern man's consciousness is displaced into the body of an alien being living millions of years in the past while the alien consciousness occupies the man's body. In these two works nearly the same phenomenon is at work. What is the difference? It can only be that Lovecraft wishes us to feel horror at this displacement of consciousness whereas Dunsany does not. Lovecraft's work is quasi science fiction (horror), Dunsany's is fantasy, although not of the imaginary-world sort. To put it crudely, *fantasy never truly inspires the sentiment of ontological horror.* There is certainly a "violation of natural law" going on in Dunsany's novel (since the majority of us assume that metempsychosis of this sort is impossible), but Dunsany does not wish us to feel terror at the occurrence.

It is worth considering briefly some combinations or elaborations of the above patterns. *Heroic fantasy* (principally Robert E. Howard and Fritz Leiber, although they have countless imitators) seems a combina-

tion of the supernatural horror tale with the adventure story and perhaps also the historical novel. Howard's Conan typically battles supernatural entities in the dim recesses of history. Howard's evolution of this
form is strictly dependent upon his philosophical concerns—his cham-
pioning of barbarism over civilization and his belief in the moral virtues
of struggle and conflict. Leiber's work is subtler and richer, and his style
is nowhere near as egregiously slovenly as Howard's; he is worth studying. The *ambiguous horror tale,* where doubt is maintained to the end
whether events are supernatural or not, seems to me another hybrid
form. Although it has some notable examples—Henry James's *The Turn
of the Screw* among them—I do not find it broadly typical of the field as a
whole. Scarcely any tale written by any author in this volume is of this
type; Bierce's work seems to supply some examples, but a close reading
will show that in almost every case he provides sufficient clues to point
to a supernatural or nonsupernatural resolution. Indeed, I maintain that
such a distinction is critical to Bierce. (Parenthetically I may as well dispense with Penzoldt's bizarre category of the "pure tale of horror,"
which he sees as merely a shameless display of gruesome physical horror. I do not deny that there are some lower forms of popular literature
and film that engage in this sort of thing, but it is grotesque to see it
in the work of Machen, Lovecraft, and even F. Marion Crawford, as
Penzoldt does. Penzoldt's categorization is really a result of his anomalous squeamishness in the face of explicit horror.)

All this finally brings me back to my initial remark. In spite of the
schematizations just made, it should not be assumed that I have now
come to regard the weird tale as a genre with various subgenres. My
final point is this: weird writers utilize the schemas I have outlined (or
various permutations of them) *precisely in accordance with their philosophical predispositions.* My analysis will show, for example, why Lovecraft
wishes us to feel horror at the events of "The Shadow out of Time" and
Dunsany does not in *The Strange Journeys of Colonel Polders.* All the
authors I study here (with the exception of James) evolved distinctive world views, and it was those world views that led them to write the
sort of literature they did. I am convinced that we can understand these
writers' work—the whole of their work, not merely their purportedly
"weird" writing—only by examining their metaphysical, ethical, and
aesthetic theories and then by seeing how their fiction reflects or expresses these theories. In every case we shall see that each writer's entire
output is a philosophical unity, changing as the author's conception of

the world changes. Much of this philosophical investigation is a matter of philology—a study of the facts of biography, of nonfictional writings, letters, and the like—but seems a necessary preliminary to the task.

All this may be platitudinous—surely every writer's work is a philosophical unity in some fashion or other—but I believe there is more to it than that. The weird tale offers unique opportunities for philosophical speculation—it could be said that the weird tale is an inherently philosophical mode in that it frequently compels us to address directly such fundamental issues as the nature of the universe and our place in it. Actually, this may be putting the cart before the horse: certain authors develop certain types of world views that compel them to write fiction that causes readers to question, revise, or refashion their views of the universe; the result is what we (in retrospect) call weird fiction. The differing philosophical orientations of the six authors covered here led them to write differing types of weird fiction. Each author is, in effect, trying to convince us of the truth of his vision of the world. The fictional works these authors have produced may not all fit neatly into the class of the "weird tale," but to ignore some works on that ground would seriously hinder our overall understanding of the shape, direction, and purpose of their thought.

It is possible that my work may be only preliminary to an investigation of what the weird tale actually is: all I have done here is to choose six writers generally held to have written weird fiction and to seek to ascertain, quite simply, what they were philosophically trying to do. The implications for genre are left to later study.

1.

ARTHUR MACHEN
The Mystery of the Universe

*A*rthur Machen was born Arthur Llewelyn Jones at Caerleon-on-Usk, Wales, on March 3, 1863; he adopted his mother's maiden name Machen in grade school. Fascinated from youth by the Roman ruins of Isca Silurum near his birthplace, Machen would later give them an important place in his novels and tales. He attended Hereford Cathedral School, but failed the examination for the Royal College of Surgeons in 1880; he went to London as a tutor, cataloguer, and editor. Just before leaving Wales he privately printed the poem *Eleusinia* (1881) in an edition of one hundred copies; he later claimed that his systematic destruction of this early work left only two copies of the pamphlet in existence. Aside from translating the *Heptameron* of Marguerite of Navarre (1886), Machen wrote the curious pseudophilosophical treatise *The Anatomy of Tobacco* (1884) and the picaresque novel *The Chronicle of Clemendy* (1888).

The death of his father in 1887 ensured Machen economic independence for the next decade and a half, and it was during this time that he not only produced the standard translation of Casanova's *Memoirs* (1894) but wrote the supernatural tales that would bring him immediate notoriety and ultimate fame: *The Great God Pan* (1894), *The Three Impostors* (1895), and *The House of Souls* (1906). These works—as well as the heavily autobiographical novels *The Hill of Dreams* (1907) and *The Secret Glory* (1922)—were condemned as the outpourings of a diseased imagination; Machen gathered the early reviews of these works in the volume *Precious Balms* (1924).

In 1901, his inheritance depleted, Machen was forced to seek employment. He worked as a bit player in Frank Benson's Repertory Company (1901–1909), and wrote voluminously for newspapers and literary journals—*The Academy, London Evening News, T.P.'s Weekly, John O'London's Weekly, The Independent, Daily Mail,* and many others. A small amount of his journalism was collected in *Dog and Duck* (1924), *Notes and Queries* (1926), and in two volumes edited by Vincent Starrett, *The Shining Pyramid* (1923) and *The Glorious Mystery* (1924). Starrett played an influential role in introducing Machen to American readers, and Machen's work was very popular in the 1920s, thanks largely to the many reissues of his early volumes by Alfred A. Knopf.

By the late 1920s Machen had again fallen into poverty, but efforts by his friends secured a Civil List pension of one hundred pounds a year for him. In 1929 Machen finally left the London that had exercised his imagination for fifty years. He produced few notable works in his old age: the poorly received novel *The Green Round* (1933) and two collections of tales, *The Cosy Room* (1936) and *The Children of the Pool* (1936). Arthur Machen died on March 30, 1947.

At first glance the work of Arthur Machen seems diverse to the point of chaos: could one man have written both the sensitive *Bildungsroman The Hill of Dreams* and the vicious polemic against Protestantism *Dr. Stiggins*, both the tense horror tale "The White People" and countless newspaper articles for the *London Evening News?* Machen is the author of novels, tales, essays, reviews, autobiography, religious tracts, translations, and many prefaces and introductions to other authors' books; yet—with the exception of the translations and the newspaper articles—his whole work is inspired by one idea and one only: the awesome and utterly unfathomable mystery of the universe.

The matter is made clear in his pamphlet *Beneath the Barley* (1931), in which he describes the origin of his juvenile poem *Eleusinia:* "For literature, as I see it, is the art of describing the indescribable; the art of exhibiting symbols which may hint at the ineffable mysteries behind them; the art of the veil, which reveals what it conceals."[1] Similarly, his *Hieroglyphics: A Note upon Ecstasy in Literature* (1902) is, for all its questionable merits as a handbook of aesthetic theory, a transparent elucidation of his own literary goals. To be called literature (as opposed to what Machen contemptuously labels "reading matter"), a work must contain *ecstasy.* What is ecstasy? Machen admits that the term is too nebulous to define but provides representative synonyms: "Substitute, if you like, rapture, beauty, adoration, wonder, awe, mystery, sense of the unknown, desire for the unknown. . . . In every case there will be that withdrawal from the common life and the common consciousness which justifies my choice of 'ecstasy' as the best symbol of my meaning."[2] A later quotation from the same book may in fact provide us with all the background we need to understand Machen's work: "Man is a sacrament, soul manifested under the form of body, and art has to deal with each and both and to show their interaction and interdependence" (73).

The notions of ecstasy, of the veil, and of the sacrament: can these be sufficient to unlock the mysteries of Machen's entire output? I rather think so, since, in spite of the superficial variety of form and genre, Machen's work returns again and again to these basic principles; so often, indeed—especially in his staggering quantity of journalistic pieces— that the analysis of a few works will explicate them all.

I have no intention of examining Machen's philosophy—if it can be called that—in any greater detail, save to note that, in embracing the above tenets, Machen felt compelled to undertake as systematic a rearguard opposition to the course of modern civilization as it is possible to imagine. It is in fact much easier to tell what Machen hates and despises than what he loves and respects. Wesley Sweetser has made a succinct list: "To him, the enemies of the spirit were big business, industrialization, science, naturalism, democracy, Puritanism, Protestantism, atheism, and Communism."[3] Some of these—business and industrialism—are easy targets; others—religious issues—are purely matters of upbringing and temperament, although the depth and sincerity of Machen's Anglo-Catholicism can scarcely be doubted. It is precisely the fervency of his beliefs that inspired the ferocious satire *Dr. Stiggins* (1906), in which a Protestant minister condemns himself out of his own mouth, and such a work as *War and the Christian Faith* (1918), in which Machen tries to refute atheism (on the fatuous and irrelevant claim that it leads to despair) and to bolster the belief—which many at the time understandably found difficult to accept—in the omnipotence and benevolence of God.

The battle against science and materialism is one that Machen never relinquished, but his attacks on them are strangely feeble and off the mark. To Machen, science deals only with the surface of things—the body, as it were, not the soul. As he very prettily puts it in *The Secret Glory*, "Our great loss is that we separate what is one and make it two; and then, having done so, we make the less real into the more real, as if we thought the glass made to hold wine more important than the wine it holds."[4] It is an interesting analogy but a false one, since Machen has begged the question of the soul's existence. In any case, most of Machen's polemics end up attacking a ridiculously caricatured version of science and rationalism, as in the following astonishing passage from *Hieroglyphics:*

> 1. Explain, in rational terms, *The Quest of the Holy Graal.* State whether in your opinion such a vessel ever existed, and if you think it did not, justify your pleasure in reading the account of the search for it.
> 2. Explain, logically, your delight in colour. State, in terms that Voltaire would have understood, the meaning of that phrase, "the beauty of line."
> 3. What do you mean by the word "music"? Give the rational explanations of Bach's Fugues, showing them to be as (1) true as Biology and (2) useful as Applied Mechanics.
> 4. Estimate the value of Westminster Abbey in the avoirdupois measure.
> 5. "The light that never was on land or sea." What light?
> 6. "Faery lands forlorn." Draw a map of the district in question, putting in principal towns and naming exports.
> 7. Show that "heaven lies about us in our infancy" must mean "wholesome maternal influences surround us in our childhood."
> (124–125)

Or see how the richness of Frazer's anthropological speculations in *The Golden Bough* is travestied in the following:

> Of course, I am quite willing to allow that, as a general rule, an anxiety about the spring crops fully explains the origin of all painting, all sculpture, all architecture, all poetry, all drama, all music, all religion, all romance: I admit that the Holy Gospels are really all about spring cabbage, that Arthur is really arator, the ploughman; that Galahad, denoting the achievement and end of the great quest, is Caulahad, the cabbage god. I admit all this because it is so entirely reasonable and satisfactory, and, indeed, self-evident; but though all Frazerdom should rise up against me, I cannot allow that when I lit my dark lantern I was inviting the sun to help the crops.[5]

When I read passages like this, I want to look for the nearest wall to bang my head against. Machen must refute science in some fashion or other, however bungling and inept, because its truth would (so Machen

thinks) make untenable the belief in the mystery of the universe—
something he clings to with the desperation of neurosis. If science were
true, the world would be such a *dull* place; *therefore* (as Machen, like so
many other mystics, reasons), science must be wrong. What Machen
really resents is science's intrusion into fields—principally art and religion—where he feels it doesn't belong; and while few (even in Machen's
day) would claim that our enjoyment of poetry is amenable to precise
scientific analysis, the matter of religion is very much otherwise. I find
this all very tiresome and narrow-minded; if Machen had had the inclination to study contemporary advances in astrophysics, he might
have seen that science and imagination are not always in opposition and
might have come to echo the rationalist Lovecraft's remark, "The more
we learn about the cosmos, the more bewildering does it appear."[6]

Machen's remarks on naturalism—to him the literary equivalent of
prosy science—are somewhat more interesting. It could be expected of
one who could not bear to read Conrad[7] that he would oppose realism:
"The Artist with a capital A is not a clever photographer who understands selection in a greater or less degree" (*Hieroglyphics* 27). This is because what we call the "real world" is not in fact real: "We live in a
world of symbols; of sensible perishable things which both veil and reveal spiritual and living and eternal realities."[8] The only true "realism,"
therefore, is symbolism, because the symbol *is* the reality, or at least
as close to the ineffable reality as we can get. All this is very clever, and
the only flaw in it—the flaw that cripples the otherwise suggestive *Hieroglyphics*—is Machen's inability to see that writers like Austen and
Thackeray were much more than "clever photographers" whose work is
mere "reading matter." Machen's notions of ecstasy and symbolism are
sound enough, but he interprets them too narrowly. The result is not
only a critical blindness to a very wide range of literature but also a lim-
iting of the scope of his own writing.

The sole goal of Machen's philosophy is to restore the sense of wonder
and mystery into our perception of the world; everything that tended to
foster such a goal—mysticism, occultism, Catholicism, symbolism—
was to be encouraged, and everything that hindered it—Protestantism
(criticized as appealing too much to the rational intellect), science, rationalism, realism—was to be furiously combated. But Machen was no
philosopher; the telling sign of this is the fact that his views never
changed through the whole course of his long life. Unlike his admirer
H. P. Lovecraft, who progressed from doctrinaire materialism to a rea-

soned understanding of the uncertainties of modern astrophysics, from radical political conservatism to moderate socialism, from a naive and affected archaism of style and manner to a spare yet powerful modernism of tone, Machen's monolithic views remained unaffected by any new insights. He embraced not so much a philosophy as a series of prejudices that he guarded with a dogged tenacity against opposing views he could not understand or approach sympathetically.

So much for Machen's philosophy; what of his fiction? Here we find another remarkable circumstance: although he wrote novels and stories from the age of twenty to the age of sixty, nearly all his best work was produced within the single decade of 1889–1899—not coincidentally the one period in his life when, thanks to a timely inheritance, he could devote all his energies to writing. The chronology of Machen's stories does not at all correpond to their dates of publication, and it is worthwhile to have some idea of the sequence of his fiction-writing (see the appendix at the end of this chapter).

What strikes us about Machen is the number of works that can be totally dispensed with or ignored without affecting our understanding of him. Indeed, it might have been better if Machen had done a similar purging. Machen's worst flaw—over and above his insubstantial philosophy, his clumsy polemics, his complete lack of narrative skill—is that he wrote too much. We have already noted this in his nonfictional writing: *Dr. Stiggins* was not read in his day and is unreadable in ours; *The Canning Wonder* (1926) is a mind-numbingly tedious account of a strange disappearance in the eighteenth century—an account he had previously written up in at least two shorter versions;[9] and his very first work (excluding *Eleusinia* [1881], a rather able poem for a seventeen-year-old), *The Anatomy of Tobacco* (1884), is an intolerably precious attempt to mingle scholastic philosophy with Machen's fondness for tobacco. No one need criticize Machen for writing this work—it is the sort of cleverly sophomoric jeu d'esprit that many twenty-year-olds might have written; but he should have thought twice about allowing it to be published. Even *The Chronicle of Clemendy* (1888), a picaresque episodic novel derivative of Balzac and Rabelais, is seriously flawed in its very conception. Machen—like Lovecraft in his poetry—here opens the Pandora's box of conscious archaism. The problem with it is that it can now be used only parodically or ironically: any attempt to present archaism as a serious aesthetic instrument must be done on the heroic scale of a

William Morris (who, let us remember, nevertheless had very advanced political views) lest the author be accused of being either irrelevant or coy. The reason why the pseudo-archaism of the early Dunsany succeeds is that we are aware that it transparently masks a profoundly cynical and "modern" view of the world.

But the "great decade" of Machen's fictional output saw the writing of such works as "The Great God Pan," the episodic novel *The Three Impostors*, "The Inmost Light," *The Hill of Dreams*, the exquisite prose-poems later collected in *Ornaments in Jade* (1924), the short novel *A Fragment of Life*, and "The White People." (*Hieroglyphics* was also written at this time but published in 1902.) These works—plus, perhaps, the later novel *The Secret Glory*, published in 1922 but written apparently around 1907—are all the Machen fiction that anyone need read.

There are two reasons why the rest of Machen's tales can be virtually ignored: first, he had by 1907 said whatever he had to say in fiction; second, he had become a journalist. This was perhaps the single worst thing that could ever have happened to a writer like Machen. In his autobiographies Machen is endlessly fond of describing, with a sort of masochistic frisson, the infinite agonies he suffered in the writing of his early work. Draft after draft, euphoria followed by near-suicidal despair were the preliminaries to such a toilsomely wrought work as *The Hill of Dreams*. But when Machen became precisely what he did not want to become, a "literary man"—first as columnist and reviewer for *The Academy* (1907–1912), then as roving reporter for the *London Evening News* (1910–1921), and finally as columnist or voluminous contributor to *T. P.'s Weekly* (1908–1928), *The Lyons Mail* (1919–1923), *The Observer* (1926–1937), and *The Independent* (1933–1935)—he was forced to write rapidly and frequently. His earlier tormented scribbling gave way to an evil facility. And the result is that Machen no longer wrote *about* anything, he wrote *around* it. A style that had once been the jeweled distillation of anguish became the desultory meandering of a man who has grown too fond of his own literary voice. The reverence with which Machen was regarded in the twenties—especially in America, where Lovecraft, Vincent Starrett, James Branch Cabell, Carl Van Vechten (who has a charming digression on Machen in his novel *Peter Whiffle* [1922]), and others all lauded him as an ignored genius—seems to have encouraged Machen consciously to cultivate the image of his "famous obscurity." In *Dog and Duck* (1924) he tries to make himself a twentieth-century Lamb, and other collections of his essays and journalism appeared—*Dreads and Drolls* (1926), *Notes and Queries* (1926), *The Glitter of the Brook* (1932). But Machen's essays are all too discursive to merit real greatness; they never deliver the substance their themes seem to promise.

In his fiction the journalistic tinge can be seen as early as *The Secret Glory*, a strange combination of polemic and mysticism. His war stories—those collected in *The Bowmen and Other Legends of the War* (1915) and the short novel *The Terror* (1917)—all appeared first in newspapers; they are all perfectly contentless save for one curious detail we shall study later on—the gradual breakdown of the distinction between fiction and nonfiction as the fictional persona insidiously melds into the consciously autobiographical voice of the author. The novelette "The Great Return" (1915) may be the one instance in which Machen's journalistic style works in carrying forward the theme of the story. The tale—also first serialized in the *London Evening News*—tells the story of the return of the Holy Grail to a small town in Wales, and the coldly reportorial narrative voice causes the miraculous incidents to stand out in even bolder relief.

Machen's subsequent fiction deserves little consideration. He wrote several stories for Cynthia Asquith's anthologies in the 1920s; wrote *The Green Round* (1933), a drearily verbose and unfocused rehashing of old themes, for his publisher Ernest Benn; wrote "N" for his later collection *The Cosy Room* (1936); and wrote all new stories for *The Children of the Pool* (1936). "The Cosy Room" is an effective little *conte cruel*, quite unlike anything else Machen ever wrote, but for that reason quite unrelated philosophically to the rest of his work. One uncollected story, "The Dover Road" (1936), intended for *The Children of the Pool* but not published there, is perhaps the best of these last works. Although lengthy, it is a tautly written tale about the mysterious "appearance" of a man in a house when he was evidently many miles away; Machen allows the situation to remain unresolved, but again the matter-of-fact tone of the narrative convinces.

One must be constantly making apologies for Machen: so much of his work consists either of total failures or inessential items. One of the stock defenses is to argue for the "charm" of much of this inessential writing; but this attempted exoneration becomes, even in the mouths of his loyal defenders, an unintentionally patronizing condemnation. The fact is that Machen was a profoundly self-indulgent writer. This is not merely to say that he wrote what he wished to write, without thought of popular success; this is no doubt true, as it is true of Lovecraft and

Dunsany, and it is certainly a major cause of the strength and vigor of Machen's best work, from "The White People" to *The Secret Glory*. But Machen did not have the self-discipline to know when he was producing works of a totally ephemeral character (*The Anatomy of Tobacco, Dr. Stiggins*) or works that said nothing new (*The Green Round*). His torrents of journalism—which easily dwarfs the whole of his fiction combined—can actually be excused on the ground that Machen needed the money (who reads the bulk of Poe's nontheoretical critical writings and reviews, written for precisely the same motive?) and that he made little effort to save this material for posterity. But when a man writes stories as arid and tired as those in *The Children of the Pool,* one must wonder what sort of self-awareness he had.

But it is not on his poorest but his best work that the author must be judged. It is to these works that we turn our attention.

"Man is a sacrament, soul manifested under the form of body": this is the key to Machen's early horror stories, "The Great God Pan," *The Three Impostors,* "The Red Hand," "The Shining Pyramid," and "The White People." It is, in fact, interesting that Machen chose to render this notion in horrific terms, and he seems to provide the rationale for it in the celebrated passage from "The Red Hand" that Lovecraft cited as the epigraph to "The Horror at Red Hook": "There are sacraments of evil as well as of good about us, and we live and move to my belief in an unknown world, a place where there are caves and shadows and dwellers in twilight. It is possible that man may sometimes return on the track of evolution, and it is my belief that an awful lore is not yet dead."[10] The sacrament—the ritual whereby one establishes a mystic union with God—can be both sacred and sacrilegious; the breaking down of the barrier between soul and body can be both awesome and horrifying. This is the theme of "The Great God Pan": the experiment performed on the servant girl Mary is meant to span "the unutterable, the unthinkable gulf that yawns profound between two worlds, the world of matter and the world of spirit."[11] Put in these terms, the breach can only be horrific. Mary sees Pan—that is, sees the world "as it really is," reality shorn of the material world, which is nothing but a pallid symbol of reality—and promptly goes mad and later dies. Machen was quite consciously reviving, in the horrific mode, the ancient tale of Semele, who wished to see Zeus as he really was—as Hera saw him—not in the various disguises (swan, bull, shower of gold) by which he masked his awesome reality. She too is overwhelmed and transported to heaven.

But for all the powerful conceptions and symbolism Machen is suggesting here, the actual tale degenerates into a frenzied expression of horror over illicit sex. Machen's early readers knew this and reacted with the shock and disgust to be expected of late Victorian audiences. Machen, both in *Things Near and Far* and in that most unique book *Precious Balms* (in which he merely reprints the unfavorable reviews he has received over his career, with very little comment—one of the most subtly satiric ploys he ever used), is fond of citing the horrified reactions of readers and reviewers alike. But Machen's own reaction, implicit in the story, seems even more exaggerated than that of his contemporary readers: aberrant sex becomes, for Machen, a sort of "sin against Nature"— something that threatens the very fabric of the cosmos. Lovecraft, in an analysis far more acute than the panegyric of Machen he wrote in "Supernatural Horror in Literature," sensed this:

> People whose minds are—like Machen's—steeped in the orthodox myths of religion, naturally find a poignant fascination in the conception of things which religion brands with outlawry and horror. Such people take the artificial and obsolete conception of "sin" seriously, and find it full of dark allurement. . . . The filth and perversion which to Machen's obsoletely orthodox mind meant profound defiances of the universe's foundations, mean to us only a rather prosaic and unfortunate species of organic maladjustment—no more frightful, and no more interesting, than a headache, a fit of colic, or an ulcer on the big toe.[12]

What is more, "The Great God Pan" suffers from precisely the flaw which Machen correctly recognized in Stevenson's *Jekyll and Hyde:* once the secret is out, the tale falls flat: "On the surface it would seem to be merely sensationalism; I expect that when you read it you did so with breathless absorption, hurrying over the pages in your eagerness to find out the secret, and this secret once discovered I imagine that *Jekyll and Hyde* retired to your shelf—and stays there, rather dusty. You have never opened it again? Exactly. I *have* read it for a second time, and I was astonished to find how it had, if I may say so, evaporated" (*Hieroglyphics* 70–71).

Similarly, once we know that the strange woman running through the various segments of the narrative is the same person—Helen Vaughan, daughter of Mary and "no mortal father," as Lovecraft quaintly puts it—all our interest in the tale is gone. The story is in fact extremely clumsy in construction and is written in a horribly florid and stilted style that must have made Machen wince after he revamped his style in *The Hill of Dreams.* "The Great God Pan," then, is a profound failure for not actually delivering what it promises. Two stories derived from "The Great God Pan" that are considerably superior to it in the realization of their goals are Lovecraft's "The Dunwich Horror" and Peter Straub's *Ghost Story* (1979).[13]

The horror of sex is also the underlying theme of "The White People," otherwise a magnificent tale and easily Machen's most skillful horror story. Here again we are led to imagine something stupendously cosmic in the celebrated discussion of evil that introduces the tale: "'What would your feelings be, seriously, if your cat or your dog began to talk to you, and to dispute with you in human accents? You would be overwhelmed with terror. I am sure of it. And if the roses in your garden sang a weird song, you would go mad. And suppose the stones in the road began to swell and grow before your eyes, and if the pebble that you noticed at night had shot out stony blossoms in the morning?'" (*The House of Souls* 116). But it does not seem that the tale itself carries out this notion, for it is simply the (admittedly mesmerizing) story of a girl insidiously indoctrinated by her nurse into the witch cult and the orgies she eventually practices. And yet nothing could be more brilliant than the telling of this tale through the girl's perfectly ingenuous diary, with only a few telling hints—"I am going to write here many of the old secrets and some new ones; but there are some I shall not put down at all" (125)—that are both psychologically sound and shuddersomely suggestive. I wonder whether many literary historians have noted the stupendous anticipation of stream-of-consciousness represented by this diary—we are still in 1899, years before the emergence of Dorothy Richardson and Virginia Woolf. This diary is a masterpiece of indirection, a Lovecraft plot told by James Joyce.

Machen's loathing of illicit sex crops up in two later stories that have no compensating innovations to redeem them, "The Bright Boy" and "The Children of the Pool." Both tales—but particularly the former—are marred by extreme ineptitude in narration. "The Bright Boy" would have been an effective tale of a hideous old man who yet retains the appearance of a young boy (thus representing a double dichotomy of youth versus age and innocence versus corruption) if Machen had not tacked on a prosy and needless explanation at the end, completely spoiling the subtlety of the rest of the story. Machen had already indicated, by adroit hints, the nature of the situation, but could evidently not resist spelling out the situation in black and white for his less astute readers. This sort of thing mars a number of Machen's tales—notably "The Shining Pyramid," a tepid rehashing of "The Red Hand"—and points to one of Machen's greatest failings as a fiction-writer: the lack of narrative skill. Machen's whole style, even at the beginning of his career, is the style of the essayist, not the fictionist—exposition, not narrative. In a way this accounts for the chatty introductions found frequently in Machen, notably "The White People." These passages, in which two characters abstractly discuss an issue that proves (or purports) to be the theme of the story, lay the intellectual groundwork for the actual narrative, which then becomes merely an instantiation of the general truth enunciated at the beginning. The technique, ironically, is that of the empirical science Machen held in such scorn: "The Great God Pan," "The Red Hand," "The Shining Pyramid," and "The White People" all form part of an empirical fund of data proving the proposition that the "Little People" exist.

Some words should be said about this "Little People Mythos," as it may be called. It seems to consist of the tales just mentioned, along with "The Novel of the Black Seal," "Out of the Earth," and perhaps "The Bright Boy." There is, of course, no question of any systematic unity in these tales, but Machen makes it clear that he believed in the former existence of such a race: "Of recent years abundant proof has been given that a short, non-Aryan race once dwelt beneath ground, in hillocks, throughout Europe, their raths have been explored, and the weird old tales of green hills all lighted up at night have received confirmation. Much in the old legends may be explained by a reference to this primitive race. The stories of changelings, and captive women, become clear on the supposition that the 'fairies' occasionally raided the houses of the invaders."[14] This was written more than two decades before the publication of Margaret A. Murray's *The Witch-Cult in Western Europe* (1921), which gave the stamp of approval to the thesis. But Machen knew that the really adventuresome aspect of his theory—or, rather, the radical extension of it which he made for fictional purposes—was that "the People still lived in hidden caverns in wild and lonely lands," something he maintained was "wildly improbable."[15] But behind all this speculative anthropology is the symbolism of the Little People. They are horrible and loathsome, to be sure, but they have at least one advantage over modern human beings—they have retained that primal sacrament (perverted, of course, by bestiality and violence) which links them with the Beyond. There is something of awe mingled with the horror experienced by the narrators when they witness the "Pyramid of fire" summoned by the Little People in "The Shining Pyramid," and this signals the truth uttered by the protagonist of "The White People": "Sorcery and sanctity . . . these are the only realities. Each is an ecstasy, a withdrawal from the common life" (113).

It is worthwhile to linger over "The Novel of the Black Seal," since it not only is a superb horror tale but introduces another powerful symbol in the Machenian cosmos—the hieroglyph. Actually, it is merely a variant or substitute for the symbol of the veil, "which reveals what it conceals." The hieroglyph appears in this tale—in the form of the black seal itself, a small block of stone with inexplicable characters carved upon it—and also in "The Red Hand" and "The Shining Pyramid"; its meaning is not always obvious. The hieroglyph conceals because it cannot be deciphered by ordinary (we are inclined to say profane) people; it reveals itself only to those—like Professor Gregg or Dyson—who have penetrated the veil. But what it half reveals is frightening simply because it suggests dimly a whole realm of entity not known to the world at large. Just as the Chinese language hints cloudily (to those who do not know Chinese) of the whole world of Chinese literature, history, and society, so too the weird hieroglyphs on the black seal imply the existence of an evil culture on the underside (literally) of civilization. In "The White People" we have a slight variation of the hieroglyph motif— the strange references to the "Aklo letters," the "Chian language," the "Mao games," and the like. These are *verbal* hieroglyphs, and they too only hint (to the uninitiated) of an unsuspected race with its own rituals, its own language, its own civilization. The horror is not simply that this civilization seems to be barbaric and vicious but that it exists at all: how could such a culture remain an unfathomed mystery all this time? We are suddenly forced to question our own apparent dominance of the planet.

I have alluded to "The Novel of the Black Seal" and spoken of it as an independent tale; although Machen occasionally did the same we must recall that this tale as well as Machen's other famous story, "The Novel of the White Powder," were originally printed in the strange episodic novel *The Three Impostors* (1895). But this is no incoherent jumble as are, for example, many of Robert W. Chambers's episodic novels (really short stories bunglingly stitched together for marketing purposes). Although "The Novel of the Iron Maid" was written independently (and incorporated deftly into the fabric of the novel), the other "novels" ("Black Seal," "White Powder," "Dark Valley") were written as integral components of *The Three Impostors*. At this stage we need not dwell on Machen's aesthetically fatal attempt to imitate Stevenson—whose *New Arabian Nights* and *The Dynamiter* provided the episodic framework of the novel as well as the atrociously flippant narrative tone—although there is something to be said for the view of some early reviewers that Machen had "out-Stevensoned" Stevenson. The real key to the novel lies in its subtitle (irksomely omitted from the Knopf reprint), *The Transmutations*. For all four of the "novels" (here in the sense of *nouvelle*, or tale) present transmutations in various ways. On one level we are concerned with a transmutation of landscape—from the suburbs of London ("Iron Maid," "White Powder") to the "wild, domed hills" of Wales ("Black Seal") to the desolate wilderness of the American West ("Dark Valley"). The transmutation of human beings from ordinary citizens to something akin to demons occurs in "Dark Valley" and "Iron Maid," while a physical transmutation of the most hideous sort is the subject of "White Powder." But there are more profound transmutations going on here. When the narrator of "Black Seal" remarks that "I read the key to the awful transmutation of the hills,"[16] she is not talking about scenery: she is referring to the transformation of her conception of what lies behind and within those hills in light of the knowledge of the Little People unearthed by Professor Gregg. This is declared explicitly by the doctor who treats the hapless victim of "White Powder": "My old conception of the universe has been swept away" (233). This is the ultimate transmutation.

And yet we too have now been guilty of treating the tales of *The Three Impostors* as separate entities. What happens when we restore them to their contexts? The result, curiously, is not only comic but ironic. The fact is that these tales are narrated by one or another of "three impostors," whose sole purpose is to capture and kill the "young man with spectacles" who flits through the work like a frightened fawn; and in the end they succeed in disposing of him in a particularly grisly way. This means that these tales are all (in the context of the novel) complete fabrications, designed only to trick the two protagonists, Dyson and Phillipps, into leading the impostors to the spectacled young man. Machen slyly hints at this at the conclusion of "White Powder" when he says that Dyson "decided that he would abjure all Milesian and Arabian methods of entertainment" (243)—a Milesian tale being, in antiquity, what we would call a tall tale. I confess I do not know what Machen is trying to get at in undercutting his own work in this fashion. All I can fathom is that he is ridiculing the whole modern tendency of literary realism. His "novels" are certainly to be classified in the category of "supernatural realism," whereby all events are described against a background of meticulous realism of scene, character, and psychological motivation; but the fact that they are enmeshed in a perfectly ludicrous, Arabian Nights context means apparently that this realism is only a grotesque joke in light of the awesome mystery of the cosmos.

I have saved the discussion of "The Inmost Light," a relatively early story, for last since it provides a transition from Machen's tales of horror to what might be termed his tales of awe and wonder. "The Inmost Light," although it uses the mechanism of a scientific experiment like that found in "The Great God Pan" (and makes a use of coincidence even more flagrantly implausible than in that story—something Machen lamely defended in "The Red Hand" by the "theory of improbability"), is not so much horrifying as transcendental. It is true that a death occurs—the scientist's wife, the subject of the experiment—but her parting is handled with a tenderness and elegance far from the elemental expiring of Helen Vaughan. What is the nature of the experiment here? It is nothing more than the separation of soul from body; and there is awe in the success of this experiment as the soul is dislodged from the woman into an opal: "But on the table the opal flamed and sparkled with such light as no eyes of man have ever gazed on, and the rays of the flame that was within it flashed and glittered, and shone even to my heart" (*The House of Souls* 286). That light—the inmost light—*is* the soul. Light and fire are, for Machen, powerful symbols because they are the most immaterial of material objects and as such symbolize for him the union of matter and spirit, body and soul.

This dualism extends beyond the individual: in a social dimension it is symbolized by the alienation of the sensitive individual (the "soul") from a crass and materialistic society (the "body"). This sort of dualism is at the heart of some of Machen's most ethereal works, *A Fragment of Life*, *The Hill of Dreams*, and *The Secret Glory*. Some shorter tales anticipate the trend. In many of the prose-poems collected in *Ornaments in Jade* (written in 1897 but published only in 1924), we find early examples of the great loners who populate Machen's novels. "The Idealist" is the exquisite tale of a man who leads the prosy life of a clerk by day but ventures into his own world of imagination by night. The title is particularly apt in that it suggests the conventional philosophical opposition of idealism and materialism. A character in "Psychology" makes the matter explicit: "'And every day,' he went on, 'we lead two lives, and the half of our soul is madness, and half heaven is lit by a black sun. I say I am a man, but who is the other that hides in me?'" [17] In other stories in this collection the point is made in another way. In "The Ceremony," "Midsummer," and others we are presented glimpses of otherwise "normal" people who—sometimes without even being aware of it—are found to engage in the most ancient and primitive of rituals. However brutalized people are by the dominant materialism of the age, their sense of spirituality can well up in spite of themselves in the practice of these sacraments. "The White People" displays this idea in the horrific mode, but in the *Ornaments* collection the notion of ritual is nothing but an ecstasy. All these tales are vignettes, but they can be nothing more; as prose-poems they stand as some of the finest in the language.

It is worth discussing the short novel *A Fragment of Life* here since, although it was written after *The Hill of Dreams*, it carries on the sense of ecstasy in common things that typifies *Ornaments in Jade*. Some passages in the autobiographies are helpful in showing Machen's change of direction from horror to awe and wonder. Of "The Great God Pan" he remarks: "Here . . . was my real failure; I translated awe, at worst awfulness, into evil" (*Far Off Things* 123). Elsewhere we find what is the real heart of the story: "And it is utterly true that he who cannot find wonder, mystery, awe, the sense of a new world and an undiscovered realm in the places by the Gray's Inn Road will never find those secrets elsewhere, not in the heart of Africa, not in the fabled hidden cities of Tibet." [18] This remark is important not only because it relieves Machen of the charge of empty escapism in his notion of ecstasy as a "withdrawal from the common life" (which, it is now evident, really means a penetration through the ordinariness of daily existence to the spiritual realities beyond), but because it captures the essence of *A Fragment of Life* just as that work captures the essence of Machen's whole world view. And yet this would scarcely seem to be what is going on in the novel as we read its opening pages. In this story of Edward Darnell, an ordinary city clerk, and his wife we might—but for the British setting—imagine that we have stumbled into a social novel by Edith Wharton or Louis Auchincloss. But the very ordinariness of their lives—spent discussing the furnishing of the spare room, the reception of guests, the monotonous coming and going to and from work—is vital to establish the fact that, "day after day, [Darnell] lived in the grey phantasmal world, akin to death, that has, somehow, with most of us, made good its claim to be called life" (*The House of Souls* 35). To be sure, Darnell—and still more his wife— are (as we must call them in our post-Freudian age) repressed. Not merely sexually repressed, they are repressed in their very inability to communicate to each other—or even to realize clearly to themselves— their love, their awe, their ecstasy. The material world has crushed them—socially, financially, emotionally; as Machen says poignantly in another context, "It was all a very small life." [19]

But as the novel progresses Darnell imperceptibly begins to step back and realize the vacuity of this stolid material existence; he hears the call of his Welsh heritage, and at the end he and his wife return to a fuller life in Wales. But the alteration is more than that of mere scenery: through his new vision of the world even prosy London is transformed:

> London seemed a city of the Arabian Nights, and its labyrinths of streets an enchanted maze; its long avenues of lighted lamps were as starry systems, and its immensity became for him an image of the endless universe. He could well imagine how pleasant it might be to linger in such a world as this, to sit apart and dream, beholding the strange pageant played before him; but the Sacred Well was not for common use, it was for the cleansing of the soul, and the healing of the grievous wounds of the spirit. There must be yet another trans-formation: London had become Bagdad; it must at last be trans-muted to Syon, or in the phrase of one of his old documents, the City of the Cup. (103–104)

But the miracle of this novel is its absolute seamlessness: it is impossible to tell when or how this transition in Darnell has occurred; he can simply conclude that he was "filled with the thought of that far-off sum-mer day, when some enchantment had informed all common things, transmuting them into a great sacrament, causing earthly works to glow with the fire and the glory of the everlasting light" (43). This is the Machen we love and admire: the writer who can invest the ordinary with a sense of numinous wonder. We know that the material world was for Machen only the crude symbol for something greater; and he has never more flawlessly realized that conception than in *A Fragment of Life*. Without the least violence in diction or incident, it is as violent a condemnation of late Victorian social constraints as *The Way of All Flesh*; and I suspect, too, that Machen with this work was wanting to show his contemporaries how a real "social novel" should be written. But, more than mere social satire or literary polemic, *A Fragment of Life* strives to awaken us all to the beauty and mystery of things. It is Machen's most finished and satisfying work.

Both *The Hill of Dreams* and *The Secret Glory* are marred by rather oily and transparent sarcasm, a strange thing for Machen if we are to believe his condemnation of satire in art: "Art, you may feel quite assured, proceeds always from love and rapture, never from hatred and disdain, and satire of every kind *qua* satire is eternally condemned to that Gehenna where the pamphlets, the 'literature of the subject,' and the 'life-like' books all lie together" (*Hieroglyphics* 95). But the satire in both these novels is more or less integral to them, establishing the contrast between the delicate aestheticism of the protagonists and the stolid materialism of their milieu. Of *The Hill of Dreams*, that rich and disturbing book, it is impossible to say too much, and I shall concentrate on only a few features of it. Of course, the theme is that of the artist's spiritual loneliness; as Machen says in *Hieroglyphics*, "I think that real literature has always been produced by men who have preserved a certain loneliness of soul, if not of body" (159). But what strikes me as most interesting about this novel is its apparently ambiguous conclusion. Throughout the novel we are presented with Lucian Taylor's agonizing attempts to capture on paper his emotions about "the form and mystery of the domed hills."[20] And while he attempts to do so both in his native Wales and in his London garret, he seems ultimately to fail, for he dies of a drug overdose. His landlady finds the pitiful remnants of his work: "She spread the neat pile of manuscript broadcast over the desk, and took a sheet at haphazard. It was all covered with illegible hopeless scribblings; only here and there it was possible to recognize a word" (267).

Is Lucian, then, a failed artist? In a sense yes, but that failure was inevitable and brought on by his—and, by extension, all true artists'—relation to society. It is not merely that what Lucian had to say was "occult" in the literal sense of the word (that is, hidden from the mass of humanity); it is that, as Lucian's life progresses, his art compels him into a more and more profound misanthropy. Lucian cannot write coherently because he has lost the desire to communicate to his fellow creatures; "he realised that he had lost the art of humanity forever" (183). His earlier attempts at writing are instructive in this regard: as a young man he produces a manuscript and naively sends it to a publisher in London; it is tactfully rejected, but some months later a work by a celebrated novelist appears embodying much of the text of Lucian's novel. For a time this angers him, but he later shrugs it off as meaningless: "He had tried hard to write, chiefly, it is true, from love of the art, but a little from a social motive. He had imagined that a written book and the praise of respectable journals would ensure him the respect of the country people" (152). He comes to realize that all this is vanity, that "the love of art dissociated man from the race" (197).

In his way Ambrose Meyrick, the hero of Machen's other novel, *The Secret Glory*, is as misanthropic as Lucian Taylor, but his misanthropy is manifested in a wholly different manner. There are very puzzling questions as to the genesis of this work, and matters are in some ways made worse if we read Machen's "true" ending of the novel—a manuscript of 143 leaves currently deposited in the Yale University Library with instructions by Machen that it never be published. Why he should have issued such a peculiar decree is unfathomable, for without these two final chapters the novel is seriously disfigured, and Machen's hasty précis of the events of these chapters in the published epilogue to the book is worse than useless. But although this unpublished ending contains some of Machen's richest prose, it does not help much to lend any sense of unity to the novel. The work oscillates from a vicious satire on the British school system to a languid description of Meyrick's sense of wonder and mystery. In reality these are two sides of the same coin, as Machen hints in one of his articles: "Reality is only to be apprehended by the imaginative faculty; and it is because this truth is not appreciated that the whole of modern education is not only useless, but poisonous and disastrous; and even from the 'practical' point of view a hideous and expensive failure."[21] Here again what we may call Machen's "social dualism"—materialistic society against the sensitive individual—is the core of the story, but there is a deepening of the conception here. Meyrick's own native country of Wales takes on the qualities of "soul" that he denies to the horrible school of Lupton, where he drags out his unprofitable terms: Meyrick speaks of "that land where flame was the most material substance; whose inhabitants dwell in palpitating and quivering colours or in the notes of a wonderful melody" (147–148). Meyrick's misanthropy, conversely, is carried out in a more traditional fashion than Lucian's: he begins to "play the game" and do all that the crass and stolid headmaster expects of him—playing cricket and rugby, working with apparent enthusiasm on the mindless exercises. But then, after a wild vacation in London with the servant girl Nelly, he refuses to go up to Oxford and instead joins a touring acting company (Machen clearly drew upon his own experiences with the Benson Repertory Company). This—along with Meyrick's mystic return to his homeland, where he retrieves the sacred cup of Tielo Sant and suffers "Red Martyrdom" in Asia—is the substance of the two unpublished chapters of the novel.

But the work does not hang together. The book is too unfocused and too desultory in its narration, and Machen is too fond of making lengthy detours to attack the various aspects of modern civilization that offend him. The many parallels we find with *The Hill of Dreams*—Meyrick's romance with Nelly and, later, with the Welsh girl Sylvia, similar to Lucian's perfectly chaste worship of the country girl Annie; Meyrick's perception that London has an Arabian Nights atmosphere (cf. 237); his sense of detachment from humanity—give the impression that Machen's imagination is running thin. In a sense this novel is more self-indulgent than any of his other works, and we can read it only if we are entirely in sympathy with those things that Machen favors and opposed to those he randomly attacks.

Machen's fiction after *The Secret Glory* is one long succession of failures. Some think highly of *The Terror*, but it is in fact quite bad. The American magazine *The Century* printed a shortened version of the short novel—reduced to a mere quarter of its size—which is a significant improvement on the original; and it would be rather better for Machen's reputation if this version were better known. As it is, the novel contains many absurdities. The premise—animals revolting from human beings—is clever, but, as with "The Great God Pan," the tale is intolerably flat once this premise is known. At the conclusion Machen presents us with two hypotheses to account for the revolt: either the creatures were affected by a "contagion of hate" because of the war, or the animals felt that human beings had abdicated their spiritual role as "lords of creation" by sinking too deeply into materialism. Of course, Machen adopts the latter solution, in which case we are led to wonder why the creatures didn't revolt either during the heyday of Bacon and Hobbes—the founders of modern materialism—or during the Industrial Revolution. And few rationalists will be alarmed by Machen's statement that the paradox of Achilles and the tortoise (refuted 2,300 years ago by Aristotle) proves that "all science is a lie"!

As it is, the most interesting thing about Machen's later stories is what appears to be a systematic breakdown of the distinction between fiction and nonfiction. This would seem to link him to some very recent literary trends, but it hardly needs be said that the relation is accidental—or at least much more accidental than his anticipation of stream-of-consciousness in "The White People." The trend seems to begin with some of the war stories. "The Dazzling Light" begins very like one of Machen's essays, with their urbane chattiness and negligence to come quickly to the point. "Munitions of War" and "Out of the Earth" make no secret of the fact that the narrator is not a fictional persona but Machen himself—Machen the author of "The Bowmen" (mentioned in both stories), Machen the reporter. In "The Great Return" a character confronts Machen with the following:

> "I know you are a railer," he said, and the phrase coming from this mild old gentleman astonished me unutterably. "You are a railer and a bitter railer; I have read articles that you have written, and I know your contempt and your hatred for those you call Protestants in your derision; though your grandfather, the vicar of Caerleon-on-Usk, called himself Protestant and was proud of it, and your great-grand-uncle Hezekiah, *ffeiriad coch yr Castletown*—the Red Priest of Castletown—was a great man with the Methodists of his day, and the people flocked by their thousands when he administered the Sacrament."[22]

We know from Machen's autobiographies that this is all true, although for this story Machen the narrator adopts a slightly greater tone of skepticism and incredulity than he probably felt, so as to emphasize the miraculous events of the tale—events so unlike what we would expect to find in the columns of a newspaper, where this and the other tales I have mentioned appeared.

Is there a point to this mingling of author and persona, or, rather, the utter disinclination to establish a viable persona distinct from the author? One might be tempted to reply that by this time Machen, feeling himself to be an eminent literary figure, simply could not bother to create a fictional narrator different from himself—that, like Byron, he felt the force of his own personality would carry the narrative forward. This answer is unsatisfactory for two reasons: first, these stories were written in a period (1914–1915) preceding Machen's transatlantic fame as a Great Cham of Letters; second, one suspects that, for all the false modesty Machen exhibits elsewhere, he simply would not have obtruded himself into his stories out of sheer arrogance. We would be closer to the truth if we suspected that these tales—knowingly designed for newspaper publication, where the very context would augment their credibility as fact, not fiction—were consciously planned *hoaxes*. I think there is something to be said for this view; and yet, in the end, this explanation may have to give way to a broader one—one that has been implicit in much of what I have already said. In my analysis of Machen's philosophy I had no hesitation in drawing upon Machen's tales—even those in which he himself is not the obvious narrator—for examples of his views on life and letters. This can be done with relative insouciance for the simple reason that Machen's tales are not merely outgrowths of his philosophy—as Lovecraft knew his tales were—but are, like his essays, part and parcel of his grand attempt to promote his mystical view of life. The tales are as polemical as his essays, and one suspects that Machen has adopted this method of hectoring his contemporaries because he found that his actual polemics—like *Dr. Stiggins,* which fell stillborn from the press—were not proving very effective. Materialism was still on the rampage, even in the wake of the cultural devastation brought on by World War I; and so Machen would insidiously convince his readers that the strange and wonderful and nonmaterialistic things that happen in these stories—for they are hardly more than peculiar incidents not amenable to rationalistic explanation and are told with scarcely any "artistry" in the traditional sense of narrative skill, character portrayal, and mood development—actually did happen.

So Machen's later fiction reads like nonfiction; similarly, his nonfiction—we are now talking of his autobiographies, *Far Off Things* (1922), *Things Near and Far* (1923), and *The London Adventure* (1924), and certain other pieces—bears unmistakable fictional traits. We are, of course, long past the stage of being able to regard an autobiography as simply the "naked truth" about its author. The mere act of selection and the adoption of a given tone point to devices not far from fiction. And in the case of Machen it can be seen that he is carefully manipulating and molding the only character—namely, himself—he would ever portray realistically and sympathetically. I need not remark that there is no implication here of conscious deception: Machen is not trying to falsify himself. But he is being remarkably selective. In the whole of his three autobiographies, for example, we find only two fleeting mentions of his two wives and children. One mention is so oblique—"Then a great sorrow which had long been threatened fell upon me: I was once more alone" (*Things Near and Far* 175)—that we would not understand the reference (since Machen has up to this point not mentioned his wife at all) unless we knew from other sources that Machen's first wife was long afflicted with cancer and finally died in 1899. We hear randomly of Machen's friends and associates but only sporadically and anecdotally— as in the charming remark, "Oscar Wilde confessed to me once, with shame be it said, that he thought absinthe a detestable drink" (*Things Near and Far* 83). But on the whole the impression we get is of a poor, solitary man living on bread, green tea, and tobacco, and writing, in the loneliness of his attic garret, curious and eccentric works that no one wants to read.

But haven't we heard this before? Is this not Lucian Taylor of *The Hill of Dreams?* It is impossible to determine whether Machen is Lucian or Lucian is Machen; their personalities have fused. Indeed, I must admit that one of the most harrowing things Machen ever wrote is not a story at all but merely the preface of the Knopf edition of *The Hill of Dreams*. In an act that comes close to self-flagellation—and is uncannily similar to Lucian's own self-mutilation for the sake of his beloved—Machen describes in agonizing detail the painful gestation of his great novel: the long year and a half of writing and rewriting, of elation followed by the despair of having followed a false trail:

> Alas! my pride had a deep fall indeed. I read over those last three chapters and saw suddenly that they were all hopelessly wrong, that they would not do at any price, that I had turned, unperceiving, from the straight path by ever so little, and had gone on, getting farther and farther away from the true direction till the way was hopelessly lost. I was in the middle of a black wood and I could not see any path out of it.
>
> There was only one thing to be done. The three condemned chapters went into the drawer and I began over again from the end of

Chapter Four. Five and Six were done, and then again I struggled desperately for many weeks, trying to find the last chapter. False tracks again, hopeless efforts, spoilt folios thick about me till by some chance or another, I knew not how, the right notion was given me, and I wrote the seventh and last chapter in a couple of nights. Once more the thought of the old land had come to my help; the book was finished. It had occupied from first to last the labour of eighteen months. (xiii–xiv)

"The thought of the old land" is similarly what sustains Lucian through his own despair. And Machen cannot help adding that, once his book was finished, it was sent to a publisher, who rejected it politely but announced shortly thereafter a novel very like *The Hill of Dreams* by someone else (this novel, evidently, never actually appeared). If this is true, it may make one believe in the supernatural, since this whole event is a duplicate of the incident in chapter 2 of *The Hill of Dreams*.

Throughout these three autobiographies, but especially in *The London Adventure*, Machen not merely talks about his writing, but—somewhat disingenuously—admits to never fulfilling on paper the visions in his mind (the poignant "He dreamed in fire; he has worked in clay" [*Far Off Things* 101]) and also discusses works he would have liked to write. Indeed, the whole *London Adventure* is about Machen's not having written a book called *The London Adventure*. The work begins with Machen's determination to write of the magic and mystery of London; it is a refrain that structures the entire book, but at the same time Machen confesses that what he is actually writing is *not* that work but something else, similar to it but inferior. At the conclusion Machen admits to his failure: "So here ends, without beginning, *The London Adventure*; and, indeed, I have been in London all this summer of 1923. I had thought of calling the book 'The Curate's Egg,' but I have a distaste for boastful titles" (142). The self-deprecation is typical and accounts for another curious feature of the work: Machen's copious reproductions from a juvenile notebook or commonplace book. The keeping of a commonplace book is not unusual—we hardly need recall the use Lovecraft made of his— but the conscious publication of it in an autobiography is a statement of a particular sort. Machen's commonplace book is certainly intrinsically fascinating—full of hints of strange stories never written, notes for *The Hill of Dreams*, *A Fragment of Life*, and other works—but it is the more

interesting because of Machen's deliberate invitation of the reader into
his own creative process. In a certain way the displaying of his unwritten
story notes absolves Machen from actually having to write the story—
from the threat of working in clay what he dreamed in fire—since the
reader is compelled to exercise his own imagination in conceiving what
the story might have been like; in effect, the reader writes the story. At
the same time, our criticism of Machen for not having realized his vision
is disarmed by his own confessions of incompetence:

> And so I run through the old notebook, through dozens of these
> "hints" and "sketches" and "outlines" and "arguments," most of
> which led to nothing in particular. I find it all a little pathetic, and a
> little puzzling. I find my destiny a hard one. Here am I, born appar-
> ently with this itch of writing without the faculty of carrying the
> desire into execution. . . .
> I dig deep, I burrow, far under the ground, I hew out my laborious
> subterranean passages, I blast whole strata of unsuspected rocks
> which suddenly interpose themselves between me and my end, I
> dwell down in that stifling blackness of toil, month after month, year
> after year, scarcely emerging to see the light of the sun and the glow
> of the green world. At last, after all these dark and dreadful labours,
> I succeed in laying my mine. I touch the button—and there is a
> feeble pop, which would hardly make a kitten jump. (91–93)

This goes beyond the level of modesty and becomes comic exaggeration.
Lest I be misunderstood, let me make clear that I am not doubting that
Machen did indeed sincerely feel that he rarely if ever succeeded in
fulfilling his vision; but this degree of self-abasement is more than a little
puzzling. And it all contributes to a very specific image of Machen the
man and writer which he very carefully wishes us to have.

But Machen is not a liar; even though, in the passage just quoted, he
continued to fashion what must now (in 1923) be the myth of his toil-
some efforts at writing, it is because we know Machen to be in fact describing himself that these works gain their delicate poignancy. The
magic of his autobiographies lies in the seriocomic way in which he tells
of the real misery and privation he suffered in his life, as in the description of his small room at Clarendon Road in the early 1880s:

It was, of course, at the top of the house, and it was much smaller than any monastic "cell" that I have ever seen. From recollection I should estimate its dimensions as ten feet by five. It held a bed, a washstand, a small table, and one chair; and so it was very fortunate that I had few visitors. Outside, on the landing, I kept my big wooden box with all my possessions—and these not many—in it. And there was a very notable circumstance about this landing. On the wall was suspended, lengthwise, a step-ladder by which one could climb through a trap door to the roof in case of fire, and so between the rungs or steps of this ladder I disposed my library. For anything I know, the books tasted as well thus housed as they did at a later period when I kept them in an eighteenth-century bookcase of noble dark mahogany, behind glass doors. There was no fireplace in my room, and I was often very cold. I would sit in my shabby old great-coat, reading or writing, and if I were writing I would every now and then stand up and warm my hands over the gas-jet, to prevent my fingers getting numb. (*Far Off Things* 116)

These works may be as rambling and discursive as many of his tales and essays; but that is Machen's prerogative in autobiography. In a real sense they have contributed, and continue to contribute, to his endurance as a writer; it is their very vividness in depicting Machen that makes us know that he is the central character of every one of his fictions.

At this point the puzzled reader, led apparently very far away from Machen's fiction, may wonder why I have chosen to study him here at all. I have no especial answer to that if one is looking for some account of why Machen should be regarded as a weird writer at all. It does not appear that he thought himself such. He derisively dismisses *The Terror* as "a 'shilling shocker,'"[23] and in an unpublished essay he refers to *The Three Impostors* as belonging to the category of what he calls the "wonder story"—"the story of events which are beyond the ordinary range of human observation, of events which we roughly call impossible."[24] But the essay is more centrally concerned with the technique rather than the theory of the weird tale—of how one goes about convincing a reader to believe the "impossible" events being related. The 1923 preface to *The Three Impostors* is a little more interesting: it tells of certain events occurring to Machen some years after the completion of his book that seemed uncannily to mirror events in the work itself; this allows Machen to conclude (a little impishly), "It may turn out after all that the weavers of fantasy are the veritable realists."[25] But this is really nothing but another version of his battle against naturalism. Moreover, when he refers to the "general atmosphere of the book" as "the Arabian Nights aspect of London," we see how closely the fundamental message of the work echoes that of *A Fragment of Life, The Hill of Dreams*, and *The Secret Glory*, none of which can be called weird (they are certainly not supernatural) in any meaningful sense of the term.

My point is that the division between Machen's weird and nonweird fiction is arbitrary and artificial. We assign such things as "The Great God Pan," "The White People," *The Three Impostors*, and *The Terror* to the weird purely by retrospect and very largely because of their influence on subsequent weird work—notably Lovecraft, Ray Bradbury, and T. E. D. Klein.[26] It is highly significant that *A Fragment of Life* appears (along with "The Great God Pan," "The White People," "The Inmost Light," *The Three Impostors*, and "The Red Hand") in *The House of Souls* (1906) but not in the posthumous *Tales of Horror and the Supernatural* (1948); and also that the various "novels" of *The Three Impostors* have been abstracted from their contexts with such insouciance by editors, anthologists, and critics alike. It is we who are forcing these distinctions upon Machen's work. I think I have demonstrated that Machen's entire fiction is unified in the sense that it is in every way an extension of his antimaterialistic polemic; and Machen would probably find it a sad irony that we now read the bulk of his fiction to gain a few pleasant shudders rather than to renounce the modern world of science and rationalism. In this sense Machen has failed in his literary and philosophical enterprise. The fact is that much of Machen's work fails even to entertain because it is too coldly calculative and subordinate to his intellectual preoccupations. Only those works that either fulfill his purposes perfectly—*A Fragment of Life*—or through their own dynamism escape his conscious control—"The White People," *The Hill of Dreams*—really live as literature.

In the short run the care of Machen's reputation will rest in the hands of horror aficionados. Whether he will ever again attract a mainstream audience it is difficult to say; I honestly suspect not, and I also suspect that Machen would have wanted it that way. I think he enjoyed his position as a literary curiosity—in the manner of a Thomas Lovell Beddoes or a Lafcadio Hearn—and he would have wished to be read only by a small band of sympathetic followers. As the tide of materialism and technology continues to rise, religion and mysticism continue to wane, and patience with Machen's lush and richly textured style decreases, I fear that that band of readers may become smaller and smaller. Machen is a writer who will always suffer the indignity of periodic resurrection.

APPENDIX: CHRONOLOGY OF MACHEN'S FICTION

I have tried to list here all the genuine stories of Machen (for some works it is difficult to tell whether we are to regard them as fiction or nonfiction), the dates of writing (approximate or conjectural in some cases), date of first publication, and—for works not separately published—date of first appearance in a collection of Machen's works. In the latter case I have assigned numbers to the nine volumes that contain first book appearances of stories.

Title	Date Written	First Published	First Collected
The Chronicle of Clemendy	1885–86	1888	1888
"The Great God Pan"	1890	1890	1894(1)
"A Double Return"	1890	1934	1936(8)
"A Wonderful Woman"	1890	1890	1923(4)
"The Lost Club"	1890	1890	1923(4)
"An Underground Adventure"	1890?	1890	—
The Three Impostors[a]	(1890–) 1894	(1890–) 1895	1895
"The Inmost Light"	1892	1894	1894(1)
"The Red Hand"	1895	1895	1906(2)
"The Shining Pyramid"	1895	1895	1923(4)
The Hill of Dreams	1895–97	1904	1907
"The Rose Garden"	1897	1908	1924(5)
"The Holy Things"	1897	1908	1924(5)
"The Turanians"	1897	1924	1924(6)
"The Idealist"	1897	1924	1924(6)
"Witchcraft"	1897	1924	1924(6)
"The Ceremony"	1897	1924	1924(6)
"Psychology"	1897	1908	1924(6)
"Torture"	1897	1924	1924(5)
"Midsummer"	1897	1924	1924(6)

Title	Date Written	First Published	First Collected
"Nature"	1897	1908	1923(4)
"The White People"	1899	1904	1906(2)
A Fragment of Life	1899–1904	1904	1906(2)
The Secret Glory[b]	1907	1907–1908	1922
"The Bowmen"	1914	1914	1915(3)
"The Soldiers' Rest"	1914	1914	1914(3)
"The Monstrance"	1914	1915	1915(3)
"The Dazzling Light"	1914	1915	1915(3)
"The Great Return"	1915	1915	1915
"Munitions of War"	1915	1926	1936(8)
"Out of the Earth"	1915?	1915	1923(4)
The Terror	1916	1916	1917
"The Happy Children"	1920?	1920	1925(7)
"The Islington Mystery"	1927	1927	1936(8)
"The Gift of Tongues"	1927	1927	1936(8)
"The Cosy Room"	1928	1928	1936(8)
"Johnny Double"	1928?	1928	—
"Awaking"	1930	1930	1936(8)
"Opening the Door"	1931	1931	1936(8)
The Green Round	1932	1933	1933
"Compliments of the Season"	1934	1934	1936(8)
"N"	1935	1936	1936(8)
"The Exalted Omega"	1935	1936	1936(9)
"The Children of the Pool"	1935	1936	1936(9)
"The Bright Boy"	1935	1936	1936(9)
"The Tree of Life"	1935	1936	1936(9)
"Out of the Picture"	1935	1936	1936(9)
"Change"	1935	1936	1936(9)
"The Dover Road"	1935?	1937	—
"Ritual"	1937?	1937	—

Collections of Machen's Stories

The Great God Pan and The Inmost Light (1894)
The House of Souls (1906)
The Bowmen and Other Legends of the War (1915)
The Shining Pyramid, ed. Vincent Starrett (1923)
The Glorious Mystery, ed. Vincent Starrett (1924)
Ornaments in Jade (1924)
The Shining Pyramid (Secker, 1925)

The Cosy Room (1936)
The Children of the Pool (1936)

ᵃ"The Novel of the Iron Maid" was written and published in 1890 and later incorporated into *The Three Impostors.*

ᵇChapter 6 (unpublished) of the *The Secret Glory* makes extensive use of a story or article titled "The Hidden Mystery," first published in 1907 but dated 1897 by Machen when he reprinted it in *The Cosy Room.*

2.

LORD DUNSANY
The Career of a Fantaisiste

*E*dward John Moreton Drax Plunkett was born on July 24, 1878, at his family estate in County Meath, Ireland; he became the eighteenth Baron Dunsany upon the death of his father in 1899. He attended Eton and Sandhurst and served in the Boer War. Afterward he began writing short stories of exotic fantasy—*The Gods of Pegāna* (1905), *Time and the Gods* (1906), and *A Dreamer's Tales* (1910)—and in 1909 was encouraged by W. B. Yeats to write plays for the Abbey Theatre. These plays became hugely popular both in England and in America; at one time Dunsany had five plays running simultaneously on Broadway. He was to serve in World War I, but was wounded in the Dublin riots of 1916; later he joined the Coldstream Guards in Flanders.

After the war Dunsany and his wife Beatrice lived alternately in Castle Dunsany and in a home in Sevenoaks, Kent, although they traveled widely. Dunsany made extensive lecture tours in the United States in 1919–1920 and 1928 and also traveled to Africa, India, and elsewhere to pursue his ardent hobby of big-game hunting. Between the wars Dunsany was a much sought-after writer and contributed stories, essays, and poetry extensively to the *Atlantic Monthly, Saturday Evening Post, Collier's,* and other periodicals. His first novel was *Don Rodriguez* (1922), set in Renaissance Spain, but gradually he abandoned imaginary or fantastic settings and utilized his native Ireland as a backdrop, especially in *The Curse of the Wise Woman* (1933) and *The Story of Mona Sheehy* (1939). Dunsany also achieved great popularity with his five collections of tales about the clubman Joseph Jorkens, beginning in 1925 with *The Travel Tales of Mr. Joseph Jorkens.*

In 1941 Dunsany accepted the Byron Professorship of English Literature in Athens, but had to be evacuated when the Germans invaded. In 1943 he delivered the Donnellan lectures at Trinity College, Dublin, and in 1945 wrote a series of essays on the future of civilization, *A Glimpse from a Watch Tower,* in which he wrote of his reaction to the dropping of the atomic bomb: "I think that a new era started yesterday . . . henceforth we are all people with a mission, a strange mission, not to destroy the world."[1] He continued writing to the end of his life, with such late story collections as *The Man Who Ate the Phoenix* (1949) and *The Little Tales of Smethers* (1952) and such novels as *The Strange Journeys of Colonel Polders* (1950) and *The Last Revolution* (1952). Lord Dunsany died on October 25, 1957.

The career of Lord Dunsany is a peculiar one. After achieving spectacular fame with early short stories and plays about "the edge of the world," he continued to write for several decades—novels, tales, plays, articles, reviews—with considerable success but without the thundering recognition that had greeted his early work. In the 1930s and 1940s Dunsany was certainly a respected enough writer—his work appeared in *The Spectator, Life and Letters, Time and Tide,* and other distinguished journals, and his books were reviewed by Evelyn Waugh, Elizabeth Bowen, and Seán O'Faoláin—but even his admirers seemed to wish that he had continued to write more in the vein of *Gods of Pegāna* and *Dreamer's Tales.* H. P. Lovecraft, his most ardent supporter, labeled Dunsany's Jorkens tales "tripe"[2] and never stopped expressing wistful regret at what he felt was Dunsany's waning power. Lovecraft seems to have continued to read Dunsany dutifully into at least the early thirties but without much enthusiasm; other critics responded with a similarly stony silence. The articles of the teens that had marveled at the phenomenon of Dunsany ceased abruptly when he began writing novels in the 1920s; Broadway, which had once staged five of his plays simultaneously, took no interest in his dramas after *If* (1921). I know of no significant article on Dunsany from the mid-1920s until well after his death.

Now all this is both unfortunate and unfair. It is unfortunate because some of Dunsany's later work—*The Blessing of Pan* (1927), *The Curse of the Wise Woman, The Story of Mona Sheehy*—is very brilliant, and in fact there are few works of Dunsany's that do not offer something of interest to the critic and the enthusiast; and it is unfair because it is foolish and unjust to expect an author to adhere to a single style and manner over a career of fifty years. In weird fiction, the course of Dunsany's writing is in its way even more remarkable than that of Lovecraft: whereas we can see that Lovecraft's later novelettes and novels, although light-years ahead of his early tales, nevertheless are clearly similar to them in theme and substance, the work of Dunsany is constantly expanding in style, execution, and even philosophical orientation. Whether Dunsany felt oppressed by the success of his early work—and I have received no impression that he did—he was constantly experimenting with new modes of narration, new tones and manners, new ways of saying the many things he had to say. In fact, from a critical perspective it is very hard to say anything about the early work: one can simply rhapsodize over it as an unrivaled and unique body of fantasy literature. The later work is considerably more amenable to analysis, and I hope to be excused if I spend much of my time on the later novels, plays, and stories.

What we need initially, however, is a brief critical survey of Dunsany's entire career, so that the whole of his work can be put in perspective. We need only mention the early volumes of tales—*The Gods of Pegāna* (1905), *Time and the Gods* (1906), *The Sword of Welleran* (1908), *A Dreamer's Tales* (1910), *The Book of Wonder* (1912), *Fifty-one Tales* (1915), *The Last Book of Wonder* (1916), and *Tales of Three Hemispheres* (1919)— plus the two drama collections *Five Plays* (1914) and *Plays of Gods and Men* (1917) to be aware of the awesome achievement of Dunsany's first decade or so of work. Although *Tales of Three Hemispheres* postdates World War I, the tales in it seem to have been written before or during the war; whether that conflict, in which Dunsany served, had anything to do with his abandonment of this vein of writing is hard to tell, for Dunsany is one of the most reticent of all *fantaisistes*. Whatever the cause, after *Tales of War* (1918) and *Unhappy Far-Off Things* (1919), his first purely nonfantastic writings, Dunsany abandoned the short story for the novel. "Abandon" is perhaps too strong a word, for Dunsany was stupefyingly prolific and continued to write many short tales, some collected much later and many not collected; but, to be sure, he abandoned the *Gods of Pegāna* style of tale. Its swan song may be *The King of Elfland's Daughter* (1924), criticized by some contemporary reviewers precisely for its attempted maintenance of the jeweled, quasi-biblical prose of his early tales over the course of an entire novel; but on the whole the work is as successful a recapturing of that gorgeous early style as can be imagined.

Don Rodriguez (1922) and *The Charwoman's Shadow* (1926), both pseudohistorical novels set in the Spain of the "Golden Age," represent a transition from the never-never-land of Pegāna to the realities of the modern world. In fact, it is remarkable that it took Dunsany so long to discover that fantasy can also be achieved by juxtaposing the real and the dream worlds—a juxtaposition tentatively achieved in the play *If* and in *The King of Elfland's Daughter* but first exploited to the full in *The Blessing of Pan* (1927). In a sense the rest of Dunsany's career can be seen as the gradual banishing of fantasy in the ordinary sense of the term: in style Dunsany has entirely given up any attempts at pseudoarchaism, while in substance there is a greater and greater tendency to use the supernatural less for its own sake than to underscore a philosophical point. In *The Curse of the Wise Woman* (1933) there is no strict need to explain events supernaturally; the curious novel *Up in the Hills* (1935) is purely nonfantastic in its tale of a mock war among boys in the hills of Ireland; as Darrell Schweitzer has pointed out, *The Story of Mona Sheehy* (1939) is a watershed in overtly denying anything fantastic in its incidents. A similar thing occurs in many of the tales in *The Man Who Ate the Phoenix* (1949); all but one of the tales in *The Little Tales of Smethers and Other Stories* (1952) are nonsupernatural. Of the very late novels, *The Strange Journeys of Colonel Polders* (1950) is supernatural, *His Fellow Men* (1951) is nonfantastic, and *The Last Revolution* (1952) is quasi science fiction. The later plays correspond to this trend: while *The Old Folk of the Centuries* (1930) is definitely supernatural, *Mr. Faithful* (1935; written in 1922) is definitely not; *Lord Adrian* (1933; written in 1922–1923) is somewhere in between. All the *Seven Modern Comedies* (1928) and the *Plays for Earth and Air* (1937), when they use the supernatural at all, use it as a vehicle for conveying a particular point.[3]

In a sense, though, the distinction between what is supernatural and nonsupernatural in Dunsany is an artificial one: the transition from the one to the other is not systematic, and Dunsany used either whenever he felt it would best get his point across. What we can note in Dunsany is a constant sensitivity to *style* and in particular to the question of how a style that has abandoned the "crystalline singing prose" (Lovecraft's memorable phrase [SHiL 429]) of the early tales can nevertheless create that atmosphere of shimmering fantasy that we find in the whole of Dunsany. The later work also reveals a quite pervasive interest in the question of the "suspension of disbelief": how is a tale, set in the prosy world of London or the less prosy but still obtrusively real world of Ireland or (as in the Jorkens tales) Africa or the Near East and without the benefit of the quasi-biblical rhythm and imagery that so effortlessly transport us to Bethmoora or Pegāna, to convince us of the bizarre events it is relating? If the magic of the early Dunsany makes us look for feeble parallels in the fairy tales of Oscar Wilde or, later, the convoluted prose of E. R. Eddison, the later Dunsany tempts us to look for comparisons in the starkness of Hemingway or Sherwood Anderson. This problem of *belief* is a very real one that Dunsany quite knowingly posed for himself, and he solved it in ways that, I think, will make us marvel the more at his ingenuity and versatility.

NIETZSCHE IN A FAIRY TALE

One of the difficulties in studying Dunsany at all is that he has left behind remarkably few sustained statements of his motives and purposes in writing fantasy. His three autobiographies—*Patches of Sunlight* (1938), *While the Sirens Slept* (1944), and *The Sirens Wake* (1945)—tell much less about his work than about his wide-ranging travels and hunting expeditions;[4] the pieces in *The Donnellan Lectures* (1945) on poetry, fiction, and drama are very general; and of his relatively few (few, that is, in comparison with the voluminous Lovecraft and Machen) essays and reviews we can learn only very indirectly of his theory of literature. Such an essay as "Nowadays" (1912) is very pretty, even poignant, in its condemnation of industrialism and paean to the expressive powers of poetry; but it is hard to apply these dicta in any precise way to the interpretation of Dunsany's own work. Lovecraft, at the opposite extreme, has left such an ocean of philosophical and literary comment in his letters and essays that critics seem to have had a difficult time getting beyond his own views on his work; it does not help that Lovecraft is almost invariably his own best commentator. The extremes to which Dunsany went in avoiding interpretation of his own work—aside from some routine disavowals of allegory in his early fantasies—may actually be of significance from a critical standpoint; I see it as part of a rather thoroughgoing tendency on Dunsany's part to portray himself as an *ingénu,* a child of nature who wrote whatever came to mind without any thought of pointing a moral. Lovecraft, at the height of his "art for art's sake" phase, sensed this, remarking that Dunsany's tales "are fashioned in that purely decorative spirit which means the highest art," adding significantly, "About his work Dunsany spreads a quaint atmosphere of cultivated naiveté and child-like ignorance."[5] "*Cultivated* naiveté" is exactly right, for the dominant note in Dunsany's early work is the tension between his apparently artless manner of expression and the worldly, cynical, even nihilistic message underlying it.

The Gods of Pegāna is a perfect example. This book, Dunsany's first, is a fascinating farrago of biblical sonority and very advanced philosophical views—Nietzsche in a fairy tale. In what purports to be the bible of an imaginary race dwelling on the "islands in the Central Sea" we do not expect to find such conceptions—derived from nineteenth-century science—as the infinity of time (the gods "sat in the middle of Time, for there was as much Time before them as behind them") and space ("Pegāna was The Middle of All, for there was below Pegāna what there was above it, and there lay before it that which lay beyond"),[6] determinism[7] (a Greek idea, to be sure, but emphasized in the teachings of the Social Darwinists), and this very strange conception, which a god utters to a mortal: "'There is an Eternity behind thee as well as one before. Hast thou bewailed the aeons that passed without thee, who are so much afraid of the aeons that shall pass?'"[8] This exact notion is attributed to Hume, that most skeptical and "modern" of eighteenth-century philosophers, in Boswell's *Life of Johnson:* "David Hume said to me, he was no more uneasy to think he should *not be* after this life, than that he *had not been* before he began to exist."[9] It is a notion that the atheist Lovecraft is endlessly fond of citing in his polemics against the idea of life after death.

But, of course, the profoundest cynicism comes in the very hierarchy of the gods and its attendant cosmology. As the preface to *The Gods of Pegāna* states, life is only a "game" to Māna-Yood-Sushāī, the Jupiter of the gods; the other gods confess themselves to be merely the "little games"[10] of Māna-Yood-Sushāī, but they decide to "make worlds to amuse Ourselves while Māna rests."[11] The gods and all they create are nothing but the dreams of Māna-Yood-Sushāī. Nor are we comforted by the fact that the god Hoodrazai knows "the wherefore of the making of the gods" and becomes "mirthless"[12] as a result. The gods are cruel gods: "Thousands of years ago They were in mirthful mood. They said: 'Let Us call up a man before Us that We may laugh in Pegāna.'"[13] The god Slid sends death as a reward, for he "will not forget to send thee Death when most thou needest it."[14]

Later collections only hammer home this bleak message—but always in that exquisitely lyrical prose that is like a smiling goddess handing us a daisy while summoning lightning to blast us. "The Dreams of a Prophet" (*Time and the Gods*) effectively conveys the precise idea of Nietzsche's eternal recurrence. After "Fate and Chance had played their game and ended, and all was over," they decide to play it all over again: "So that those things which have been shall all be again, and under the same bank in the same land a sudden glare of sunlight on the same spring day shall bring the same daffodil to bloom once more and the same child shall pick it, and not regretted shall be the billion years that fell between." In "The Journey of the King," a lengthy tale that concludes *Time and the Gods,* a king asks various prophets to tell him what comes after death; again, every prophet speaks in the sweetest possible prose, but the core of every prophet's message is the extinction and nothingness that follow death.

Much of Dunsany's early work suggests his dim—or perhaps intentionally skewed—recollections of his classical learning. In one of his few candid moments, Dunsany seems to suggest that his failure to master the Greek language as a boy was ultimately a source for the creation of his imaginary pantheon: "It may have been the retirement of the Greek gods from my vision after I left Eton that eventually drove me to satisfy some such longing by making gods unto myself." [15] To be sure, his early collections, for all their biblical prose, bring the Greco-Roman pantheon more to mind than Jesus and the Apostles. Several early tales—"The Revolt of the Home Gods" in *The Gods of Pegāna;* "The King That Was Not" in *Time and the Gods*—are textbook cases of hubris. The gods in Dunsany also seem to have a certain Epicurean air to them: Māna-Yood-Sushāī "is the god of Having Done—the god of Having Done and of the Resting," [16] reminding one of Epicurus's ethereal gods who do nothing but seek repose in the spaces between the stars. And note this passage in "The Vengeance of Man" (*Time and the Gods*): "All feared the Pestilence, and those that he smote beheld him; but none saw the great shapes of the gods by starlight as They urged Their Pestilence on." This is, I think, an echo of the celebrated passage in book 2 of the *Aeneid* in which Venus tells Aeneas that the destruction of Troy is being caused not only by the Greeks but by the gods:

> "Look—for the cloud which, o'er thy vision drawn,
> Dulls mortal sight, and spreads a misty murk,
> I will snatch from thee utterly . . .
>   here where thou but seest
> Huge shattered fragments and stone rent from stone,
> And dust and smoke blent in one surging sea,
> Neptune with his vast trident shakes the walls,
> And heaves the deep foundations, from her bed
> O'ertopping all the city. Juno here

Storms at the entrance of the Scaean gate,
Implacable, and raging, sword on thigh,
Summons her armed confederates from the ships.
Now backward glance, and on the embattled height
Already see Tritonian Pallas throned,
Flashing with storm-cloud and with Gorgon fell. . . ." [17]

But there is more to these early tales than echoes of half-remembered classics. In fact, I think we have to ask ourselves why Dunsany chose to invent this decadent cosmology to begin with. I am not at the moment concerned with any possible literary influences: I frankly know of nothing in earlier literature that is even remotely like *The Gods of Pegāna* or *Time and the Gods;* and even if viable antecedents could be found, that would not answer the question of why Dunsany was led to create his own pantheon and give it the traits he did. The early essay "Romance and the Modern Stage" (1911) may suggest an answer, and we see Dunsany arguing for the "romantic drama" as an antidote to the modern age: ". . . all we need, to obtain romantic drama, is for the dramatist to find any age or any country where life is not too thickly veiled and cloaked with puzzles and conventions, in fact to find a people that is not in the agonies of self-consciousness. For myself, I think it simpler to imagine such a people, as it saves the trouble of reading to find a romantic age, or the trouble of making a journey to lands where there is no press." [18] What else is Pegāna and its gods but a repudiation of modernism? The archaism of style immediately banishes us from the present and engulfs us in a world where we are, to be sure, the playthings of the gods but where things are cleaner, purer, simpler, and more august than the world of workaday London. Later stories of Dunsany's early phase begin to suggest this social satire more explicitly: in the city on Mallington Moor "there was none of that hurry of which foolish cities boast, nothing ugly or sordid so far as I could see. I saw that it was a city of beauty and song" (*The Last Book of Wonder*). But the city on Mallington Moor is imaginary.

Another uncollected story or prose-poem, "Jetsam" (1910), encapsulates another possible motive for Dunsany's early work:

. . . the cliffs of destiny wholly hem us in, they are beautiful in the morning lit by the rising sun, but they grow darker and darker as evening falls behind them. And therefore let us run swiftly along the shore and gather pretty things or build sand castles and defy the sea, for those mutable waves are coming up the beach and sweeping away the children's paper ships and sweeping away the navies of the nations and curving their beautiful crests and calling for us.[19]

We seem to have heard this all before—"*Après nous le deluge*"; "Let us eat and drink, for tomorrow we die." But this is Dunsany at his most nihilistic, and I do not think we are to take him quite at his word here. The view that Dunsany is—exaggeratedly—expressing might be adequately summed up as the *aesthetic* interpretation of life. The aesthete lives for beauty; beauty and ugliness, not good and evil, are the aesthete's opposites. We all know that Dunsany the aesthete does not believe, and does not expect us to believe, in the literal reality of the Pegāna pantheon (in this sense his repudiation of allegory becomes somewhat disingenuous, for it is either as allegory or symbolism or parable that we must interpret his work); but we believe aesthetically because Dunsany, while capturing perfectly the tone of naive earnestness that characterizes all primitive religious writing, is hammering home a profoundly "modern" message.

It is, I think, the aesthetic interpretation of life that is at the bottom of what turns out to be a systematic criticism or mockery of conventional religion. This is a tendency that can be traced through the whole of Dunsany's career, and it may be well to pursue this entire thread here. What Dunsany's actual religious beliefs were, I have no idea: I suspect he was an atheist, but he never says so. Perhaps he need not have bothered, for his antireligious (or, at the very least, anticlerical) polemic lies very close to the surface of much of his work. We have already seen the cruel and capricious nature of the gods of Pegāna; in *Time and the Gods* they continue to play out "the game of the gods, the game of life and death" ("When the Gods Slept"). "The Sorrow of Search" is a transparent allegory about the quest for truth and the inability of religion to satisfy it. King Khanazar "would know somewhat concerning the gods," and a prophet tells him a parable: there is a long road with temples all along its course, and the keeper of each temple believes that the road ends there; but one traveler walks past them all:

"It is told that the traveller came at last to the utter End and there was a mighty gulf, and in the darkness at the bottom of the gulf one small god crept, no bigger than a hare, whose voice came out in the cold:

"'I know not.'

"And beyond the gulf was nought, only the small god crying."

In "For the Honour of the Gods," we find that the only happy people are those with no gods; all the other folk are ruled by capricious gods who compel them to fight and kill in their name. In "The Relenting of Sardinac" a lame dwarf comes to be hailed as a god: this is no retelling of the Greek story of lame Hephaestus (he was not a dwarf) but a vicious jab at (morally) deformed gods.

Some of the plays enforce the antireligious diatribe in a different way. King Argimēnēs, now a slave of King Darniak, remarks mournfully: "I have no . . . hope, for my god was cast down in the temple and broken into three pieces on the day they surprised us and took me sleeping." How fragile are the gods! But Argimēnēs' fellow slave speaks of Darniak's god: "'Yet is Illuriel a very potent god. . . . Once an enemy cast Illuriel into the river and overthrew the dynasty, but a fisherman found him again and set him up, and the enemy was driven out and the dynasty returned'" (act 1). *The Glittering Gate,* Dunsany's first play, makes the point even more bluntly. Jim and Bill, both criminals who have died, are at the Gate of Heaven; Bill, who has just arrived, thinks there may be a way to break in (he is a master lock-picker), but Jim, who has been there a long time, has no hope. Bill manages to pick the lock and finds nothing but an abyss: "Stars. Blooming great stars." Bill concludes: "There *ain't* no Heaven, Jim." At this, the "faint and unpleasant laughter" that has been heard constantly in the background bursts forth into a "cruel and violent laugh" which "increases in volume and grows louder and louder." Actually Dunsany leaves open the question of whether we are really to imagine this as the gate of a nonexistent Heaven or the gate of a very real Hell.

Dunsany's novels, both early and late, continue the antireligious polemic. *The Blessing of Pan* presents a clear-cut confrontation of conventional religion and paganism. Tommy Duffin's Pan pipes ultimately lure the inhabitants of an entire village to revive ancient pagan rituals, until finally even the vicar, Elderick Anwrel, submits. But Anwrel is not the butt of the attack, and at one point Dunsany even extends sympathy toward his quest to preserve his religion: "The old ways were in danger;

something strange had come and was threatening the old ways, and they were gathered there to defend the things they knew, the old familiar ways that were threatened now by this tune that troubled the evenings" (chap. 14). The real satire is directed at the bishop and his underlings who refuse to believe what is going on and rest comfortable in their pious conventions. The rector Hetley, sent to replace Anwrel when he is forced by the bishop to take a vacation, never hears the pipes at all: he is deaf to the spiritual plight of the community. After even his wife deserts him to join the others in the hills, Anwrel's resistance is undermined and he comes to lead the ceremony.

The nonfantasy novel *His Fellow Men* (1952) is Dunsany's last exhaustive statement on religion. Here we are presented with a hopelessly naive and idealistic young man, Mathew Perry, who roams the world searching for a religion that practices "tolerance"; of course, he finds it nowhere—certainly not in the Ireland he is compelled to flee because he cannot accept the conventional enmity of Catholic and Protestant, and not in Africa, Arabia, India, or England. Although Dunsany commits the aesthetic mistake of supplying a contrived happy ending, we are left with the impression that Perry's quest was doomed to failure.

We have reached the end of Dunsany's career, but we have by no means finished discussing his early work. In particular we must demolish the notion that all his early collections, from *The Gods of Pegāna* to *Tales of Three Hemispheres*, represent a uniform body of work. It is not merely that the Pegāna mythos is not sustained after *Time and the Gods*; it is that Dunsany's attitude toward his work changes and does so rather early on. I think it would have been impossible for Dunsany to have maintained his biblical prose or his otherworldly subject matter for very long, and sure enough we find exceptions as early as the third collection, *The Sword of Welleran* (1908). "The Kith of the Elf-Folk" is the first tale that actually acknowledges the existence of the "real" world and presents the conflict between the "Wild Thing" of the title and the conventional human beings who do not understand what she is. "The Highwayman," later in the collection, is Dunsany's first tale set entirely in the "real" world.

Further curious things happen in *A Dreamer's Tales* (1910). By now much of the biblical archaism of style has slipped away, and the sense of fantasy is created almost wholly by exoticism of setting ("Idle Days on the Yann," "Bethmoora"). "The Hashish Man" is a somewhat disturbing tale, and not entirely for the reasons Dunsany intended: it is

a conscious sequel to "Bethmoora" and signals the beginning of a
strain of self-cannibalization that would reach a height in *Tales of Three
Hemispheres*.

With *The Book of Wonder* and *The Last Book of Wonder* something disastrous has occurred. Dunsany can no longer summon the perfect naiveté
that made us marvel at *The Gods of Pegāna*, and his growing sophistication (or, more likely, his increasing disinclination to suppress his sophistication) leads him to mar his creations with ever-increasing doses of
whimsy, irony, and deflation. The first two paragraphs of "The Quest of
the Queen's Tears" (*The Book of Wonder*) tell it all:

> Sylvia, Queen of the Woods, in her woodland palace, held court,
> and made a mockery of her suitors. She would sing to them, she
> said, she would give them banquets, she would tell them tales of
> legendary days, her jugglers should caper before them, her armies
> salute them, her fools crack jests with them and make whimsical
> quips, only she could not love them.
>
> This was not the way, they said, to treat princes in their splendour
> and mysterious troubadours concealing kingly names; it was not in
> accordance with fable; myth had no precedent for it. She should
> have thrown her glove, they said, into some lion's den, she should
> have asked for a score of venomous heads of the serpents of Lican-
> tara, or demanded the death of any notable dragon, or sent them all
> upon some deadly quest, but that she could not love them—! It was
> unheard of—it had no parallel in the annals of romance.

I think it is passages like this that led Lovecraft to rue the passing of
Dunsany's early manner: "As he gained in age and sophistication, he
lost in freshness and simplicity. He was ashamed to be uncritically naive,
and began to step aside from his tales and visibly smile at them even
as they unfolded. Instead of remaining what the true fantaisiste must
be—a child in a child's world of dream—he became anxious to shew
that he was really an adult good-naturedly pretending to be a child in a
child's world."[20]

Lovecraft is, I suspect, right as to the result but wrong as to the motive: I believe Dunsany simply found the *Gods of Pegāna* vein running
dry, so that the only thing to do was to poke fun at it. This comes out
especially well in an exquisite self-parody, "Why the Milkman Shudders
When He Perceives the Dawn" (*The Last Book of Wonder*), where we are

never given the answer to the question implied in the title. In both "The City on Mallington Moor" and "The Long Porter's Tale" we find that it is possible to get to the Edge of the World with a ticket from Victoria Station—a ticket "that they only give if they know you." There is complete deflation at the end of "The Long Porter's Tale," where we are told flatly that the "grizzled man" who told it is "a liar"; while the interminable "A Story of Land and Sea" concludes with a pompous "Guarantee to the Reader," whose final paragraph reads: "Meanwhile, O my reader, believe the story, resting assured that if you are taken in the thing shall be a matter for the hangman."

Tales of Three Hemispheres continues the lamentable tendency, with abrupt shattering of the atmosphere by direct addresses to the reader, transparent social satire, and, on occasion, an intentionally flat and pedestrian style used for comic effect. Self-cannibalization continues with two moderately interesting but ultimately vacuous continuations of "Idle Days on the Yann."

Accompanying this shift of attitude is a shift in Dunsany's whole conception of fantasy. In *The Gods of Pegāna,* aside from a curious mention of Olympus and Allah on the very first page, one would have no idea that the "real" world ever existed. Indeed, this mention—"*Before* there stood gods upon Olympus, or every Allah was Allah, had wrought and rested Māna-Yood-Sushāī" (my italics)—obviously states a chronological priority of Pegāna to the world. Although this conception is maintained in a few other stories—not the reference to "the days of long ago" in "The Fortress Unvanquishable Save for Sacnoth" (*The Sword of Welleran*)— it is not consistent in Dunsany. Indeed, Dunsany has singularly little concern with the relation of his invented realms to the "real" world. Babbulkund was known to Pharaoh and Araby and received gifts from Ceylon and Ind. There were Europeans in Bethmoora before its desertion. The narrator of "Idle Days on the Yann" comes "from Ireland, which is of Europe, whereat the captain and all the sailors laughed, for they said, 'There are no such places in all the land of dreams.'" So at least Yann is in a dream world. And we have seen how it is possible to get to the Edge of the World from Victoria Station. I wonder which way the route lies. North? Does Dunsany think, with Samuel Johnson, that the Hebrides are the Edge of the World? I don't know, and it hardly matters. There is, of course, no reason why Dunsany should be consistent in the establishment of his fantasy lands: he is not writing a connected epic like Eddison or Tolkien, and he would be the first to scorn the notion that trains, maps, or any such appurtenances of the rational world have any application to his realms.

But what is more important than the precise location of Pegāna is why it and similar imaginary realms gradually disappear from Dunsany's work. A glancing reference in *The Queen's Enemies* to "fairy Mitylenë," uttered by Queen Nitokris of Egypt, may be our starting point: it does not take a classical scholar to know that Mitylene was a very real city in ancient Greece, and this is our first suggestion in Dunsany that the realm of fantasy is dependent upon perspective and imagination. *The Last Book of Wonder* brings this point home emphatically. In "A Tale of London" London is spoken of in the same exotic terms as any fabled Eastern city; in "A Tale of the Equator" a Sultan finds greater satisfaction in hearing his court poets describe a wondrous city than in actually building it. "The Last Dream of Bwona Khubla," in *Tales of Three Hemispheres*, completes the circle: here again a mirage of London seen in the depths of Africa inspires all the awe and wonder that Babbulkund or Sardathrion ever did.

Later works continue to develop and enrich the idea. *The King of Elfland's Daughter*, if stylistically a striking resumption of Dunsany's early biblical manner, is thematically quite different. One would think that this tale of a mortal man winning the hand of Lirazel, the daughter of the King of Elfland, would provide an opportunity for contrasting the prosiness of the "real" world with the wonder of an imaginary realm; but in large part the reverse is the case. To be sure, Elfland is a place of magic; but the very name of the "real" country involved—Erl, the German for "elf"—already signals a very tenuous distinction between our world and fairyland. Similarly, the names of characters in Erl—Narl the blacksmith, Guhic the farmer, Oth the hunter, Vlel the ploughman (chap. 5)—remind us pointedly of certain inhabitants of Pegāna and its congeners. And to Lirazel and the other denizens of Elfland, the real world is just as much a source of wonder as their realm is to us:

> He [a troll] told of cows and goats and the moon, three horned creatures that he found curious. He had found more wonder in Earth than we remember, though we also saw these things once for the first time; and out of the wonder he felt at the ways of the fields we know, he made many a tale that held the inquisitive trolls and gripped them silent upon the floor of the forest, as though they were indeed a fall of brown leaves in October that a frost had suddenly

bound. They heard of chimneys and carts for the first time: with a
thrill they heard of windmills. They listened spell-bound to the ways
of men; and every now and then, as when he told of hats, there ran
through the forest a wave of little yelps of laughter. (chap. 24)

In *Don Rodriguez* and *The Charwoman's Shadow* Dunsany solves—or,
rather, evades—the problem by setting the tale in a half-fantastic historical time—the "Golden Age past its wonderful zenith" (*The Charwoman's Shadow*, chap. 1), whenever that is—but the matter is taken up
again in *The Curse of the Wise Woman* and later novels. *Wise Woman* is,
strangely, the first of Dunsany's novels to deal explicitly with Ireland;
and with its two companions, *Rory and Bran* (1936) and *The Story of
Mona Sheehy* (1939), we reach the culmination and resolution—a very
curious one—of Dunsany's approach to fantasy.[21] Has Dunsany here
merely replaced Pegāna with Ireland? The answer is not quite as simple
as that. Certainly Dunsany's lyric descriptions of Ireland in these novels
create a certain sense of shimmering fantasy, but his approach is really
subtler than this. In all three novels we are quite clearly dealing with a
real Ireland of farmers, tinkers, and estates. The contrast to this reality is
provided, first, by the dialect speech put in the mouths of the Irish characters and, second, by the allusions to names out of Irish folklore or topography—the half-imaginary realm of Tir-nan-og in *Wise Woman*, the
mountain Slievenamona in *Rory and Bran* and *Mona Sheehy*. The first
replaces Dunsany's archaistic prose, the second his resonant, imaginary
place-names. The Wise Woman's ponderous utterances now supply the
only escapes into prose-poetry that Dunsany allows himself:

> "We walked down the river, Mother," said Marlin.
> "Aye, the river," said she, "and one of the great rivers of the world,
> though it's small here. For it widens out on its way, and there's cities
> on it, high and ancient and stately, with wide courts shining by the
> river's banks, and steps of marble going down to the ships, and folk
> walking there by the thousand, all proud of their mighty river, but
> forgetting the wild bog-water." (chap. 10)

The Story of Mona Sheehy seems to represent a dramatic shift in
Dunsany's attitude to fantasy: here we are concerned with a young girl
who believes herself to be a child of the fairies, when in fact Dunsany

makes it abundantly—almost excessively—plain to us that she is merely the product of an illicit liaison between Lady Gurtrim and Dennis O'Flanagan. The opening and closing sentences are identical—" 'I never saw a more mortal child' "—and Dunsany never tires of reminding us that Mona's belief in her magical birth is all a delusion. It is not merely that fantasy has become relative, as in the "fairy Mitylenë" reference: fantasy here is explicitly denied. I am not sure that this novel is not the sole representative of an anomalous new class, which might be called "psychological fantasy," analogous to "psychological horror." Just as psychological horror is horrific but nonsupernatural (Bloch's *Psycho*, Campbell's *The Face That Must Die*), so in psychological fantasy the fantasy does not exist except in the mind—here, in the mind of Mona Sheehy and the many townspeople who share her delusion. Dunsany even provides some simple-minded anthropology to account for the phenomenon: ". . . the story of many a fairy, many an elf, is probably but the history of the small things dwelling in woods, altered a little by the eye of man, for he saw them in dim light, altered again by his mind as he tried to explain them, and altered again by frailties of his memory, when he tried for his children's sake to remember the stories that his grandmother told him" (chap. 20).

I think, though, that this climax to Dunsany's fantasy work has some possible antecedents. Thematically *Mona Sheehy* is very similar to Lirazel in *The King of Elfland's Daughter*: both are outcasts from conventional society, Lirazel supernaturally, Mona nonsupernaturally. In *The Curse of the Wise Woman* the role of the supernatural is highly problematical: Dunsany leaves entirely open the question of whether the titanic storm concluding the novel is a natural occurrence or the result of the Wise Woman's curses. Some highly significant passages in *Rory and Bran* also anticipate the renunciation of fantasy in *Mona Sheehy*: "The world is full of wonders, and all the wonders that our imagination paints are but the mirages of them" (chap. 2). And note the constant use of similes when fairyland is invoked: "the notes of thrushes [seemed] like notes from the horns of Elfland" (chap. 20). What in the early Dunsany would have been a bold metaphor explicitly identifying the thrushes with Elfland has now become a mere simile which precisely negates such an identification. *Mona Sheehy*, then, has its predecessors.

The shift, of course, is not irrevocable, and with many later short stories and the novel *The Strange Journeys of Colonel Polders* we are back among the supernatural; but the manner in which Dunsany now approaches the supernatural is very different and must be discussed when we study the notion of belief in Dunsany's later work.

HUMAN BEINGS VERSUS NATURE

A curious coherence can be noticed in Dunsany's novels, stories, and plays of the late twenties and thirties, a coherence whose central theme is what might be called *the nonhuman perspective of life.* The plays *The Old Folk of the Centuries* (1930), *Lord Adrian* (1933), *Mr. Faithful* (1935), and *The Use of Man* (1937) and the novels *My Talks with Dean Spanley* (1936), *Rory and Bran* (1936), and the very late *The Strange Journeys of Colonel Polders* (1950) all focus around the conflict of human beings with the animal world. But in truth the theme is broader than this, and the use of nonhuman perspective—seeing the world as, say, a dog or a fox might see it—is merely a vehicle for Dunsany's wholesale criticism of modern society and the industrialized civilization it has erected. The focal point for this criticism is nothing less than the very brief play *The Evil Kettle* (in *Alexander and Three Small Plays,* 1925).

This powerful little play asks us to imagine the young James Watt as he notices his mother's teakettle boiling and begins to realize the awesome potential of steam. Later the Devil comes to him and shows him apocalyptic visions of the future with the familiar "dark, Satanic mills" marring the natural environment. The symbolism of this play is very obvious (steam = factory smoke = the fires of Hell), but it nevertheless lays the groundwork for two fundamental and related principles in Dunsany's later work: first, the tragic and increasing separation of human beings from their natural environment; and, second (evidently the cause of the first), the dominance of the machine in modern civilization. The first theme is developed in a much more interesting and dynamic way than the second, and it is worth studying in detail.

The Blessing of Pan and *The Curse of the Wise Woman,* two of Dunsany's strongest novels, portray the cleavage between civilization and nature very poignantly. In *The Blessing of Pan* it is clear that the elfin tune played by Tommy Diffin, a tune that ultimately summons the inhabitants of an entire town to follow him up the hills and reenact ancient rituals, is a means for reintegrating himself and his listeners with primal nature. In an early scene Tommy finds it impossible to take a game of chess seriously: chess presents merely an *artificial* problem and solution. Lovecraft once remarked in a letter that games are pointless because "after I solve the problem . . . I don't know a cursed thing more about Nature, history, and the universe than I did before."[22] In Dunsany the game is a symbol for the meaningless artificiality of modern civilized life: it is too far from nature. Such a simple thing as taking off one's shoes holds great significance for Tommy: "Somehow in bare feet he felt a little closer to that mystery of which the pipes were the clue" (chap. 6). And the ending leaves no doubt of Dunsany's message: "Tommy Duffin's curious music . . . seems to have come at a time when something sleeping within us first guessed that the way by which we were then progressing t'wards the noise of machinery and the clamour of sellers, amidst which we live today, was a wearying way, and they turned from it. And turning from it they turned away from the folk that were beginning to live as we do" (chap. 35).

Similarly, *The Curse of the Wise Woman* particularizes the conflict of human beings versus nature in the struggle of the Wise Woman to defeat a development company that plans to drain an ancient bog—the precise theme, curiously enough, of Lovecraft's early story "The Moon-Bog" (1921). Here the Wise Woman herself is described as "something akin to those forces that ruled, or blew over, the bog, and that cared nothing for man" (chap. 3); and the storm that in the end destroys both her and the development project points to the bitter and perhaps mutually destructive conflict in which the human being dares to take on nature. And, however repulsive it may be to modern sensibilities, we must admit that the narrator's hunting expeditions across the face of Ireland—the bulk of the novel deals with them—reinforce the harmony that can be established between the human and the natural worlds. Yes, the narrator— he is perhaps the only significantly autobiographical character in all Dunsany—kills and kills frequently, but in some strange way he establishes a bond between himself and the world around him. Many of us perhaps find Dunsany's enthusiasm for hunting very repellent; but he never made apologies for it and never regarded it as an aberration. It is true that the narrator of *The Curse of the Wise Woman* kills principally for food, not for sport (fox hunting is defended on the ground that the fox is a menace to sheep and poultry); but, more important, his hunting compels him to learn the ways of nature, and in the end he is no more or less predatory than the animals he hunts and shoots.

From a slightly different perspective many of the plays in *Seven Modern Comedies* (1928) display "modern" attitudes only to condemn them.

In *Atalanta in Wimbledon* a girl advertises in the paper challenging prospective husbands to a table tennis game: if he wins, he marries her; if he loses, he dies. The title becomes witheringly ironic, for not only do we have a jarring juxtaposition of ancient goddess and modern suburb, but this modern Atalanta sets up a contest for herself that obtrusively lacks the profound mythic dimensions of her predecessor. In *The Raffle* a man's soul is bartered about with unbelievable cynicism by the "business mentality" of the characters—even a bishop—as they debate how much money is worth spending to buy the soul back from the Devil. In *The Journey of the Soul,* a virtual metadrama, an acting company hopelessly misconstrues a play that does not provide the frivolous amusement and titillation expected by cast and audience alike from modern plays. In *His Sainted Grandmother* the ghost of a man's "sainted grandmother" tells the man's daughter that she was by no means as straitlaced and conventional as he has imagined: here the satire is double-edged, directed both at the old fogy's pious reverence for the "old ways" and at the callowness of the younger generation. But the unifying feature of these plays—emphasized by the almost grating modernity of diction employed in them—is the greed, shallowness, and hypocrisy of the modern world: as in many of Dunsany's later plays, there is not a single admirable character in them, not a single one who is not mercilessly caricatured.

Society's alienation from the world of nature has entailed a concurrent polarization with the animal world: this is the theme of a whole series of works of the twenties, thirties, and later, and it is here that Dunsany uses the nonhuman perspective, with varying degrees of effectiveness. Curiously, an uncollected early tale or prose-poem, "From the Mouse's Point of View,"[23] anticipates the trend, picturing very prettily the towering vastness of a house and the shuddersome presence of the huge cat as seen from a mouse's perspective. The otherwise very slight play *The Old Folk of the Centuries,* in which a boy has been turned into a butterfly, does little more than show sympathy with nonhuman life forms: the boy, while being irked at his transformation, finds the situation itself comfortable and even enjoyable. It is in *Lord Adrian* (composed in 1922–1923)—in which a man, injected with the gland of an ape to rejuvenate himself, begets a son (Lord Adrian) who, although perfectly normal-looking, shows disturbing affinities to animals—that the point is first made significantly (indeed, if anything, rather too obviously). Adrian makes such utterances as "I don't love men" (act 3, sc. 1) and "I regard the domination of all life by man as the greatest evil that ever befell the earth" (act 3, sc. 2). He finally concludes: "Nature's scheme is clear enough. You see it in every bird and every flower. Every city you build, every noisy invention you make, is a step away from the woods, is a step away from Nature, is a step that is wrong" (act 3, sc. 2). There is some vicious satire in this play—at one point Adrian is trying to explain to his sweetheart Nellie his deep sense of sympathy with the animal world, and she replies with the appallingly platitudinous "I'm awfully fond of animals too" (act 2, sc. 3)—but on the whole the play lacks subtlety and comes across as naively moralistic.

Much better is the outrageously funny *Mr. Faithful* (composed in 1922), in which a man desperate for work takes on the job of a watch-dog, presenting the argument that, as an intelligent human being, he can do the job far better than a mere animal. The artificial and self-serving way in which people make use of animals is, for all the rollicking hilarity of the play, brutally underscored here; and this play is far more effective in depicting the evils of the human being's domination of beast than is *Lord Adrian*. A final play, *The Use of Man* (in *Plays for Earth and Air*, 1937), is even more viciously satirical. Here a man is transported in a dream to a meeting of the spirits of animals, who all confront the man and demand to know the "use" of people, just as the man and his friends could find no especial use—from the human perspective—of badgers. None of the animals, save the obsequious dog, speaks up for human beings: the bird hates their cages, the mouse their traps, the cat is too aloof and indifferent to their fate. Finally the mosquito speaks up— the human being is its food.

A trilogy of novels completes the human-animal dichotomy in Dunsany. *Rory and Bran* tells of a boy and a dog as they lead cattle to a fair and back; but we are never told that Bran is a dog, and through the course of the entire novel it is possible to interpret Bran as simply Rory's brother or (human) companion. But this novel is more than a vast tour de force or practical joke (although evidently some reviewers never saw through the ploy): the point Dunsany is making is the senseless artificiality of distinguishing the animal and the human. This is not a contradiction of such a work as *Mr. Faithful*, but a confirmation of it from a different perspective: the world of nature makes no distinction between human and animal—and Rory, the farmer's son, is ultimately indistinguishable from Bran because both are part of the natural landscape; it is only when people become civilized that they lose the link with nature. I am reminded of Dunsany's statement about the Irish poet AE, a statement that could apply more precisely to Dunsany himself: "He had a prophetic feeling that cities were somehow wrong."[24]

My Talks with Dean Spanley (1936) is an entertaining but rather slight work about a man who believes himself to have been a dog in a previous incarnation. Dunsany is certainly uncannily precise in depicting a dog's state of mind, but this novel ends up as simply a trial run for the more exhaustive *The Strange Journeys of Colonel Polders*. Here an Indian pundit causes Colonel Polders to experience dozens of incarnations as all manner of animals—dog, cat, eel, butterfly, stag, and on and on. Again Dunsany is enormously clever at depicting the lives and putative thoughts of various animals; but, like *Rory and Bran*, all this is more than an exercise in ingenuity. The one message hammered home again and again in Polders's account of his various incarnations is the *natural comfort* of animal life. When he is made an eel, he remarks: "'To be frank, I was perfectly comfortable. I will say that for the fellow; he always made me comfortable. No credit to him of course. It's merely that animals lead comfortable lives. And, when he sent me there, I was naturally comfortable. Not that an eel is an animal. But you know what I mean. Why animals should be any more comfortable than us I don't know. With all our conveniences, it should be the other way about" (chap. 14). Earlier Polders notes that "it takes so much money and so many drinks and smokes and comforts, and machinery of different sorts, to get [the] comfort" (chap. 8) of a fox in its den. Throughout the novel, too, infallible animal instinct—the instinct that allows geese to fly south, an eel to reach the open sea, a sparrow to return to its home—is compared invidiously to the slow-moving human reason; and the animal's immediacy of experience leads Polders to claim that the life of a dog is "a more ample life than any, I am sorry to say, that any of us can live. More full, more ample, life with a grander scope" (chap. 3). As a dog, Polders finds absolute contentment chasing a ball; as a sparrow, he finds flies "delicious" because they are a sparrow's natural food; and Polders's keenness of sight and smell as a butterfly prompts his exclamation "How blunt our senses are!" *The Strange Journeys of Colonel Polders* may seem formless, but Polders's kaleidoscopic shifting from one incarnation to the next—with each incarnation designed for maximum contrast with its predecessor—is all the form a novel of this sort needs.

The other branch of Dunsany's criticism of modern society—the dominance of machines—is not handled with nearly the richness or subtlety as the theme of the human being's alienation from nature. It is, of course, society's increasing mechanization that has initiated this alienation to begin with, and it is a notion that can be found as early as his essay "Romance and the Modern Stage" (1911). The evils of industrialism randomly and tangentially enter many of Dunsany's works, but one must wait until *The Last Revolution* (1951) before it is treated comprehensively. And yet this novel of machines developing an intelligence of their own and challenging the supremacy of human beings is not a success: the theme is handled too obviously, and Dunsany's ever-placid narrative tone never produces the requisite tensity and sense of dramatic conflict, in spite of one exciting scene in which the protagonists are besieged by the machines. It is almost as if the theme was so close to Dunsany's heart that he could never treat it except in this blunt and obvious way.

As it is, a much more successful handling of the idea occurs in a very late story, "The Ghost of the Valley" (1955), which ends poignantly:

> "Times are changing," it [the ghost] said. "The old firesides are altering, and they are poisoning the river, and the smoke of the cites is unwholesome, like your bread. I am going away among unicorns, griffons, and wyverns."
>
> "But are there such things?" I asked.
>
> "There used to be," it replied.
>
> But I was growing impatient at being lectured to by a ghost, and was a little chilled by the mist.
>
> "Are there such things as ghosts?" I asked then.
>
> And a wind blew then, and the ghost was suddenly gone.
>
> "We used to be," it sighed softly.[25]

This is a fine conceit: the disappearance of the creatures of the imagination is a powerful symbol for the disappearance of wonder and mystery in the industrial age, and it brings full circle the pensive warning that Dunsany made at the beginning of his career: "I know of the boons that machinery has conferred on man, all tyrants have boons to confer, but service to the dynasty of steam and steel is a hard service and gives little leisure to fancy to flit from field to field."[26]

JORKENS

The five volumes of tales about the clubman Joseph Jorkens must be considered as a unit. Lovecraft may not be the only to find it odd, even vaguely repellent, that Dunsany could have written these light-hearted jeux d'esprit; but again such a reaction is to deny the diversity of Dunsany's literary work. If many of the Jorkens tales are quite frivolous and "clever" in the pejorative sense of the term, many of them underscore in a lighter vein the central themes of Dunsany's work. In particular we note, in three tales in *The Travel Tales of Mr. Joseph Jorkens* (1931), the preoccupation with the human-animal dichotomy dominant in Dunsany's work of the 1930s. In "The Tale of the Abu Laheeb" Jorkens stumbles upon a species, unknown to science, that, like the human being, has learned the control of fire. Jorkens refuses to shoot the beast precisely because of this unholy but inescapable relation. One is immediately reminded of *Lord Adrian*, where Adrian is at the end killed just as he is beginning to teach animals the use of fire: the human domain must not be usurped in this way. In "Our Distant Cousins," a rather peculiar science fiction tale, a man discovers that the humanoid inhabitants of Mars are *not* the dominant species on the planet. In "The Showman" apes in Africa capture a circus showman and display him in a cage; the title becomes a pun, as it does in "Elephant Shooting" (*Jorkens Has a Large Whiskey*, 1940), in which an ancient four-tusked elephant sees through a trap and shoots a hunter with his own rifle. Two other tales reveal the fragility of our supremacy over the natural world. In "The Walk to Lingham" (*Mr. Jorkens Remembers Africa*, 1934) Jorkens is unnerved as he senses a line of poplars following him menacingly along a deserted road: he feels that these trees do not grant "the respect that is due to man"; but the trees withdraw as Jorkens approaches a town, and he remarks with a significant political metaphor—"I knew at once that there had been no revolution"—that anticipates *The Last Revolution*. Finally, in "On Other Paths" (*Jorkens Borrows Another Whiskey*, 1954) Jorkens, having angered some African gods, is given a glimpse of the state of things if human beings had not secured domination over beasts. He reflects: "It was very likely a nearer thing than we think, our getting the domination. We had to beat the mammoth and the tiger. It might easily have gone some other way."

There is less development, stylistically and thematically, in the Jorkens tales than in the rest of Dunsany's work—perhaps necessarily so, given the nature of the serial character. The trick that Dunsany has to accomplish in these tales is to amaze us with highly remarkable events and inventions and yet conclude the tale with Jorkens—and the world—not significantly different from how they were at the beginning of the story. As a result, Jorkens finds and loses many fortunes ("A Large Diamond," "The Pearly Beach," "A Nice Lot of Diamonds," and several others), he marries a mermaid but she swims away at the end ("Mrs. Jorkens"), and he is a witness to countless fantastic inventions that are either lost or destroyed. One story, "Making Fine Weather" (*The Fourth Book of Jorkens*, 1948), offers a variation on this theme. Here we are asked to believe in a man who has discovered the secret of controlling the weather and who produces a torrential rainstorm on a clear day: "You may remember that year, when all the oats in England were laid flat." But whereas the occurrence might conceivably have been real (as the Vermont floods of 1927 in Lovecraft's "The Whisperer in Darkness" were real), only Jorkens knows the "real" cause of it. A man goes to Mars in "Our Distant Cousins," but of course no one believes him; in "The Slugly Beast" the man goes back to Mars, never to return.

It would be false to say that the Jorkens tales all deal frivolously with themes dealt with seriously elsewhere in Dunsany. True enough, the later Jorkens tales begin to become parodies of themselves, as in "The Sultan, the Monkey, and the Banana," in which the strange story hinted in the title is never in fact told, or in "An Unrecorded Test Match" (*Jorkens Borrows Another Whiskey*), a shaggy-dog story in which a man claims that the Devil has given him great prowess in cricket in exchange for a single virtue—"That of always speaking the truth." This is a wry version of the "All Cretans are liars" paradox; unfortunately, Dunsany uses precisely the same punch line in another story.[27] Similarly, "The Lost Romance" is a purely nonsupernatural tale of Jorkens being outwitted by a group of clever nuns. But in at least one story the lightness of tone actually enhances the power of the message. In "A Life's Work" we are told of a man who spends thirty years single-handedly shovelling away a hill, then decides to spend thirty years shovelling it back. Behind the frivolity we get a glimpse of the monstrous futility of all human effort, and again the title becomes grotesquely ironic.

A final curious feature of the Jorkens tales is the possibility—and it is, I think, nothing more—that we are to read them sequentially. All the tales were of course written over many years, and they seem to be arranged in rough chronological order; but Dunsany is careful, in the first four of the Jorkens collections, to label each story a "chapter" and not a separate entity. I am not sure that much is really to be made of this: the first several tales in *The Travel Tales of Mr. Joseph Jorkens* are meant to be read in sequence; some stories are conscious sequels of others; but beyond this it may not be possible to go. As it is, *Jorkens Has a Large Whiskey* seems to exhibit the greatest unity of arrangement: "The Grecian Singer" is the tale of a modern Siren; "The Development of the Rillswood Estate" deals with a satyr in the suburbs; and in "A Doubtful Story" Pan talks to Jorkens in Homeric Greek and goes with him to London.

No one would want to read all five volumes of the Jorkens tales in succession; but it is remarkable how fresh and vigorous even the later tales remain. Some of these later stories are nothing but written-out jokes ("On the Other Side of the Sun," "Out West"), but Dunsany's imagination is as dynamic as ever. And it is worth serious thought whether the tone of bland casualness that, as we shall see, dominates Dunsany's later work is a result of the Jorkens tales, begun in 1925 and continued sporadically to the end of his career. The relation between the Jorkens tales and Dunsany's other work is perhaps too subtle for so simplistic an analysis, but these stories do have a place, and possibly a significant place, in Dunsany's literary output.

STYLE

Style in Dunsany is a massive issue, and we can only touch upon some central features. The magic of Dunsany's early style is close to unanalyzable, for to say that he uses the cadences of the King James Bible explains almost nothing. Certain features are very obvious—sonorous repetition, a staggeringly bold use of metaphor, just the right soupçon of archaism (much less, say, than in E. R. Eddison)—and can be illustrated by a single quotation from "A Legend of the Dawn" (*Time and the Gods*), that exquisite fable of the rising and setting of the sun:

Again the Dawnchild tossed the golden ball far up into the blue across the sky, and the second morning shone upon the world, on lakes and oceans, and on drops of dew. But as the ball went bounding on its way, the prowling mists and the rain conspired together and took it and wrapped it in their tattered cloaks and carried it away. And through the rents in their garments gleamed the golden ball, but they held it fast and carried it right away and underneath the world. Then on an onyx step Inzana sat down and wept, who could no more be happy without her golden ball. And again the gods were sorry, and the South Wind came to tell her tales of most enchanted islands, to whom she listened not, nor yet to the tales of temples in lone lands that the East Wind told her, who had stood beside her when she flung her golden ball. But from far away the West Wind came with news of three grey travellers wrapt round with battered cloaks that carried away between them a golden ball.

This passage illustrates two further aspects of Dunsany's early style: the relatively sparing use of adjectives and the exhaustive use of paratactic construction. The early Dunsany probably has significantly fewer adjectives per square inch than similar work of its kind—Wilde's fairy tales, Eddison, Lovecraft's "Dunsanian fantasies"—and Dunsany was always careful never to have mere catalogues of jeweled words and phrases. As for paratactic construction—the conscious avoidance of subordinate clauses, as contrasted with the syntactic construction of the periodic style derived from classical models—it was something Dunsany retained throughout his career and is exemplified perfectly in a passage from *The King of Elfland's Daughter:*

When Alveric understood that he had lost Elfland it was already evening and he had been gone two days and a night from Erl. For the second time he lay down for the night on that shingly plain whence Elfland had ebbed away: and at sunset the eastern horizon showed clear against turquoise sky, all black and jagged with the rocks, without any sign of Elfland. And the twilight glimmered, but it was Earth's twilight, and not that dense barrier for which Alveric looked, which lies between Elfland and Earth. And the stars came out and were the stars we know, and Alveric slept below their familiar constellations. (chap 12)

There is more to this than merely the old joke of beginning every sentence with "and": there may actually be no less imagery in this passage than in one of similar size in the syntactic construction; but the effect is one of simplicity, because the failure to subordinate clauses creates the impression of linear sequentiality. This is, incidentally, the principal reason why Lovecraft's "Dunsanian fantasies," for all their close derivation from—and in some cases near plagiarism of—Dunsany's work, never ring true: Lovecraft, nurtured from infancy on the Greco-Roman classics and their stylistic imitators of Augustan England, was too wedded to the syntactic construction to abandon it, even for the sake of imitation. Paratactic construction is really the fundamental element Dunsany himself derived from the King James Bible, and it is this element that gives to his work its distinctive air of childlike simplicity. Padraic Colum's antithesis—"We are all fictionists nowadays: Lord Dunsany, however, is that rare creature in literature, the fabulist"[28]—is exactly right as far as this feature of style is concerned.

As Dunsany's style develops, the first thing to be sloughed off is the archaism. I do not mean to imply by this either that there is anything intrinsically wrong with archaism of diction (one only has to point to Lucretius and Spenser) or that Dunsany was at all clumsy in his early use of it: *The Gods of Pegāna* could be a textbook for that sort of thing. But as early as *A Dreamer's Tales* almost all the *thee*s and *thou*s are gone. Surprisingly little is lost by this procedure, for to the end of his career Dunsany's style remained one of the most musical and subtly rhythmical in all English, and I think it is possible to assert that his is, quite simply, some of the greatest prose (qua prose) in world literature. But the loss of archaism is not immediately felt because the exoticism of setting continues to dazzle us; this carries us through Dunsany's work of the mid-1920s, at least through *The Charwoman's Shadow*.

In the plays, interestingly enough, the progression is quite otherwise. His first play, *The Glittering Gate* (1909), presents two Cockney plebeians in all their dialectic colloquialism, something one would never have expected from the author of "Poltarnees, Beholder of Ocean." But this aberration gives way to the richly melodious and atmospheric plays of Dunsany's early period—*Five Plays, Plays of Gods and Men,* and *Alexander* (written in 1912)—although even here *The Lost Silk Hat* (1913) seems an anticipation of his later work. But the real watershed seems to be *Plays of Near and Far,* whose plays were composed around 1919 and 1920. Here we have archaistic plays—*The Compromise of the King of the Golden Isles, The Flight of the Queen*—juxtaposed with plays in modern idiom: *Cheezo, A Good Bargain, If Shakespeare Lived To-day, Fame and the Poet.* There is much reason for this, for all these plays quite obviously satirize various features of the modern world. In the play *If* Dunsany can have his cake and eat it, too, for the plot allows him to go from modern

London to the Near East and back again. In fact, a large part of the success of this play is the startling contrast between modernism and archaism, as in the following bit of dialogue:

John: . . . But who is your master?
Ali: He is carved of one piece of jade, a god in the greenest mountains. The years are his dreams. This crystal is his treasure. Guard it safely, for his power is in this more than in all the peaks of his native hills. See what I give you, master.
John: Well, really, it's very good of you. (act 1, sc. 2)

This sort of device is found in diluted form in one late play—*Golden Dragon City* in *Plays for Earth and Air*—but otherwise Dunsany abandons the prose-poetry style entirely in his remaining dramas: *Mr. Faithful, Lord Adrian, Seven Modern Comedies, The Old Folk of the Centuries,* and the remaining *Plays for Earth and Air*.

In the novels and later stories a similar tendency is at work, but the break is not quite so clear-cut. *The Blessing of Pan* is one of Dunsany's most carefully written works, and its subtly modulated and understated prose is as effective in creating an atmosphere of fantasy as the most involved archaism would have been. Here Dunsany's earlier bold metaphors have given way to an equally bold and precise symbolism: "Very soon he [Anwrel] saw the trees rising over the hedges, both of which encircled the rectory and church of Rolton. Great fields lay around it, stretching far away, and the trees seemed guarding that part of the parish from the level waste of the eternal fields. A few farmhouses straggled away behind" (chap. 20). The hedges encircle the rectory and church because in the end the forces of nature, symbolized by Tommy's tunes on the Pan pipes, will overwhelm Anwrel's conventional religion and lead him to partake of the ancient rituals; the few farmhouses suggest the tenuous hold of modern civilization over the "great fields" of nature. A later reference to the music of the pipes as "that awful messenger" (chap. 26) brilliantly suggests two things at once: the messenger is "awful" in the modern sense to Anwrel but "awful" in the archaic sense ("aweful") to the rest of the community. This punning antithesis is all the more apt in that Anwrel represents the modern world and the other inhabitants the ancient world of primitive nature worship.

We have seen how, in *The Curse of the Wise Woman,* the utterances of the Wise Woman allow Dunsany a few moments of archaism and prose-poetry. The narrative itself occasionally bursts forth into restrained lyricism, and Dunsany can still coin breathtaking metaphors, as in the description of a sunset as "that unseen finger lifted to still the world" (chap. 17) or during the apocalyptic storm: "I seem to remember the sound of the crash of the strides of Time" (chap. 32). Obvious as this sort of dactylic prose is, it is yet effective in context. And one earlier passage must be quoted at length:

> So we went further into the bog. And Marlin found a place for me, and there I waited, with no thought but for the coming of the geese, while Earth darkened and the sky became like a jewel of a magician in which some apprentice to magic gazes deeply, but comprehends nothing. And while I waited the hush of the evening seemed to deepen, until quite suddenly into that luminous stillness there stepped the rim of the moon, stepped flashing like the footsteps of a princess or faery coming into our world from her own, shod in glittering silver. And, as it rose, it slowly became golden, a vast orb holding me breathless, no pallid wanderer of the wide sky now, but huge on the edge of Earth like an idol of gold on its altar. I gazed at that magical radiance, forgetting the geese. And just as the lower edge of the great disc left the horizon I turned to Marlin to say something of what I felt, but said no more than: "It's a fine moonrise, Marlin." (chap. 17)

All the features of Dunsany's earlier style—paratactic construction, boldness of metaphor and simile, utter simplicity of diction—are here but modernized; more important, the lyricism is now brought to bear in describing a very real occurrence.

Rory and Bran and *The Story of Mona Sheehy* seem more archaistic because of their greater use of Irish dialect, which—at least in Dunsany's rendition—seems, if not more archaic, at least more metaphorical than normal speech, as in Mona's memorable phrase defending her supposedly fantastic lineage: "Sure, we have nothing to do with Heaven" (chap. 9). But in Dunsany's short stories and novels of the 1930s and 1940s the modernism of tone has yielded to a positively flat and almost pedestrian style. Again, even this style is still inherently musical, but if we did not know better we would think we were dealing with an English Hemingway. The Jorkens stories are the prime examples here, but other works confirm the tendency. Dunsany remarked that the humor of *My Talks with Dean Spanley* stems from the contrast between the dean's "rather polished language"[29] and the dog's thoughts he claims to utter. This statement is interesting because, first, it points to the fact that Dunsany chose his laconic, conversational style deliberately (note that two of his last three novels, *The Strange Journeys of Colonel Polders* and *The Last Revolution,* are very largely dialogue); second, it indicates that humor has become a prime concern with Dunsany.

The role of humor in the late works will be studied later, but we can note here that virtually all his fiction of the 1940s and 1950s—the Jorkens tales, the short stories in *The Man Who Ate the Phoenix* and *The Little Tales of Smethers* (although several were written in the 1920s and 1930s), the two novels mentioned above, and many uncollected stories, especially those contributed to *Punch*—are avowedly comic; only the anomalous *His Fellow Men* stands apart among his late works. And the means Dunsany chose to convey his dry humor was the deadpan tone exemplified in the following passage from *Colonel Polders:*

> We were again in the reading-room, where I had persuaded our little party to adjourn as soon as possible, because I had seen the colonel looking too often towards the pundit; and, when one reflected that Polders had been a tiger and was but just now remembering it, while Sinadryana had caused him more than one violent death, it was easy to realize how inharmonious, and detrimental to the best interests of the club, a meeting between them might be. There was of course no guarantee that the pundit would not enter the reading-room; indeed, there was a probability that he would; but trouble in the future somehow seemed better than immediate trouble now. I think all of the colonel's little audience saw my motive, and did what they could to further it. Over our coffee and some liqueurs we sat silent awhile. And then the colonel looked up from his coffee. "Yes, I was a tiger," he said. (chap. 16)

How successful this is I have no especial interest in deciding: for my part I think *Colonel Polders* a masterpiece of comic fantasy (or fantastic comedy), and many stories in *The Man Who Ate the Phoenix* are very amusing; but Dunsany was writing a great deal in this period, and some—perhaps much—necessarily falls flat. I do not think that many of the parodic detective stories in *The Little Tales of Smethers* are particularly successful; in any case, Dunsany's style in this last decade and a half of work becomes, for once, too uniform and monotonous to be consistently effective. It is foolish to criticize Dunsany for developing this vein of writing: it was in many senses a logical development of his stylistic and aesthetic conceptions of the 1920s and 1930s, with, first, the emergence of Jorkens and, second, the repudiation of fantasy in plays and novels alike. But I think Dunsany's writing becomes rather mechanical after a while, especially in his endless *Punch* sketches (many of them neither funny nor clever) and other uncollected tales. But works like *Colonel Polders* and the wickedly funny "The Two Bottles of Relish" (1932) redeem almost any amount of routine hackwork.

DUNSANY THE DRAMATIST

Something must be said of Dunsany the dramatist. It is by the drama that he initially achieved his tremendous popular acclaim of the teens and twenties, and throughout his career Dunsany provided eminently actable plays for little theaters both in America and England. And although his playwriting career began almost by accident—Yeats casually asked him to write a play for the Abbey Theatre—Dunsany seems to have known from the beginning that a novelist or short-story writer, however successful, is not necessarily a successful playwright; and it was Dunsany's ability to adapt his skills for the stage that makes him one of the most powerful dramatists of his period. Some of his dramatic touches are mind-numbingly simple: we have observed the "faint and unpleasant laughter" that is heard in the background throughout *The Glittering Gate;* the chilling hideousness of this effect has to be heard or imagined to be perceived. Then there is the simple device, early in *Alexander,* of Alexander the Great sitting casually upon "some fallen pillar or stone" (act 1)—what a powerful anticipation of his eventual doom!

Dunsany knew that even the finest prose in dialogue could never make a successful play; indeed, he advises strongly against making fine dialogue an end in itself:

The essential thing is the drama . . . it is the sudden manifestation
of one of Destiny's ways . . . Dialogue is the means whereby such
things are shown on the stage, and is to dramatists what canvas is to
the painter, or bricks to the architect. You seldom praise the canvas

of a painter, indeed you do not see it, and one never says of a fine house that the bricks are very good, well baked and square at the ends, for a heap of bricks is not architecture. Let us be equally sure that brilliant dialogue is not drama.[30]

This is not to say that dialogue in Dunsany is not fine, but it is always subordinate to the dramatic point. The magnificently jarring opening of *King Argimēnēs and the Unknown Warrior,* in which Argimēnēs, now enslaved, says with great satisfaction, "This is a good bone; there is juice in this bone," brings home the awfulness of his fate more powerfully than pages of high-flown lament could have done. A more elaborate example is *If,* a meditation on the nature of time. John Beal, an ordinary London salesman, is offered the chance to change a single incident in his past, although this alteration will still allow him to return (in some fashion) to his present home and circumstances. Beal chooses to relive a moment ten years before when he was not permitted to board a train to work—a harmless enough incident, one supposes. The result, of course, changes his entire life and takes him to the East in company with a femme fatale, Miralda Clement. The shift in Beal's circumstances is conveyed almst entirely by language: as the play opens, Beal is the typical suburban Englishman ("By Jove!"; "Very good of you"; "Cater's rather an ass"); as the scene shifts to the East, so too does Beal:

And I will exalt myself. I have been Shereef hitherto, but now I will be king. Al Shaldomir is less than I desire. I have ruled too long over a little country. I will be the equal of Persia. I will be king; I proclaim it. The pass is mine; the mountains shall be mine also. And he that rules the mountains has mastery over all the plains beyond. If the men of the plains will not own it let them make ready; for my wrath will fall on them in the hour when they think me afar, on a night when they think I dream. (act 3, sc. 2)

But as Beal returns to London after the ten years of his altered life, so too do his old habits of language return: "I had been intended for work in the City. And then, then I travelled, and—and I got very much taken with foreign countries, and I thought—but it all went to pieces. I lost everything. Here I am, starving" (act 4, sc. 2).

This is a brilliant example of how Dunsany can use dialogue not only to enhance the drama but to draw character: the inherent weakness of

Beal's personality is signaled by these radical shifts in his speech. I think it ought to be pointed out that Dunsany is in fact one of the few *fantaisistes* who can draw character at all. Machen was never successful at portraying any character who did not resemble himself; Lovecraft sidestepped the whole issue by vaunting "phenomena" as the real characters in his stories. But Dunsany, both in his fiction and his dramas, could vivify just about any character he chose. I think one of the most delicate examples is Queen Nitokris in *The Queen's Enemies*. It seems that this sort of character—the woman who, under a guise of helplessness, masks her vengeful and ruthless nature—held a fascination for Dunsany, for we find it again in the Miralda of *If*. But the queen is even subtler than Miralda and is one of Dunsany's masterful creations: throughout the play she debases herself before her enemies as they dine in her underground chamber; but even at the end, when she lets in the Nile to carry them off, she does not relinquish her facade—after all, it was simply her sensitive nature that could not bear to have enemies. Dunsany was right to take pride in the conclusion:

> *Ackazarpses:* Illustrious Lady, the Nile has taken them all.
> *Queen (with intense devotion):* That holy river.
> *Ackazarpses:* Illustrious Lady, will you sleep to-night?
> *Queen:* Yes. I shall sleep sweetly.

Dunsany was most proud, however, of *The Gods of the Mountain:* "Was this not something new to the English stage?"[31] The absolute flawlessness of this play beggars analysis, and I shall say nothing about it save to note that both Lovecraft and Dunsany himself seem to have been mesmerized by that portentous utterance "Rock should not walk in the evening" (act 3), as a character sees the real gods of the mountain come to take vengeance on the beggars who have set themselves up as the real gods. Dunsany quite elegantly justifies this utterance by remarking, "When people are terrified they are likely to say simple things"[32]—a secret to much of the effectiveness of Dunsany's entire work. *The Gods of the Mountain,* more than any of his other plays, is magnificent in its dramatic modulation, its sense that destiny is commanding Dunsany's pen. It is as close to Greek tragedy as the twentieth century will ever get.

The Gods of the Mountain also uses what proves to be a favorite dramatic device of Dunsany's—the rapid multiple climax. This effect is seen to good advantage in the otherwise peculiar play *Cheezo*. Here we have two threads of action: the quest of an unscrupulous businessman to invent a substitute for cheese and an Anglican preacher's desire to win the hand of the businessman's daughter. Both threads are resolved brilliantly and simultaneously in the dynamic conclusion. The businessman opposes the marriage because the preacher cannot bring himself to accept the notion of eternal punishment, a stance that hinders his advancement; there seems no way round this impasse until the cleric sees that the cheese substitute, Cheezo, has indeed been eaten by some mice, but that it has killed them. (What Dunsany would have done with Cheez Whiz, I have no idea.) This unfortunate result, far from deterring the businessman, only goads him the more defiantly to market his product. It is at this point that the preacher says, "suddenly with clear emphasis": "I THINK I *DO* BELIEVE IN ETERNAL PUNISHMENT."

Alexander concludes not with a multiple climax but a deliberate anticlimax. Throughout the play we witness Alexander's growing belief, fostered by his sycophantic supporters, in his own divinity; but the climax of the play is not his lingering death from fever but the bourgeois reflections of his party after he has died. It is not merely that Alexander is mortal; it is that he must posthumously suffer the scorn and contempt that is the natural pendant to his former elevation:

> *1st Archer:* It is a hard thing, comrade, that none will bury
>   Alexander.
> *2nd Archer:* What matters it what becomes of Alexander now that we
>   are governed by plain honest men.
> *1st Archer:* Indeed you are right, comrade. And yet he was worthy
>   perhaps of burial. (act 4, sc. 2)

But Alexander remains unburied, his body ignored by all save Rhododactilos, Queen of the Amazons.

The later plays tend to be less intense—inevitably so, what with their almost abrasively modern diction and their pervasive irony and deflation—but still dramatically effective. Some of the works in *Plays for Earth and Air* were adapted from earlier short stories, one not so successful (*Golden Dragon City*, adapted from "The Wonderful Window") and one very successful (*The Bureau de Change*, from "The Bureau d'Echange de Maux"). In this latter case the play is more effective than the story—as Dunsany recognized[33]—because the play creates an almost kaleidoscopic effect as various characters discuss the exchanging of their "evils," some trivial and some quite otherwise, with each other. The dialogue is the key to this play, and the narrative prose of the story cannot come close to duplicating the effect. Similarly, the insubstantial short story "The Use of Man"[34] was turned into a magnificent little play; again the secret is dialogue, especially the dialogue of the silly young fool upon whom has been thrust the unenviable task of defending the "use" of the human race.

SATIRE AND PHILOSOPHY

Dunsany found it irksome when critics labeled his early work allegorical; he was, I suppose, right to do this, but some of his early work, if it is not allegory, must be termed parable, and there is certainly a preponderance of irony, satire, and scarcely veiled philosophy in the whole of his work. It may seem a little late in the game to discuss Dunsany as philosopher; but the fact is that he never evolved—and never claimed to evolve—a coherent philosophy and made it the foundation of his whole work, as Machen and Lovecraft did. This does not, I think, necessarily undermine my initial premise that all weird writing is the result of a world view, for it simply means that each of Dunsany's works must be studied individually for the philosophy imbedded in it. We have seen bits of philosophy come out in our previous discussions—Dunsany's aestheticism as the source for his easygoing atheism and his hatred of mechanization and advertising; his sense of our alienation from the natural world—but some works are so consciously philosophical, so endowed with an obvious "message," that they deserve to be studied separately.

The most concentrated of such works is the collection of prose-poems *Fifty-one Tales* (1915). I am not sure that this is not in the end Dunsany's finest collection, as every story is one flawless facet of Dunsany's whole approach to life and literature. In under 500 words each of these stories distills a certain essence of the Dunsanian world view: it is as close to philosophy as he ever came.

Dunsany brings all his known tools into play here—simplicity of utterance, boldness of metaphor, a sprinkling of archaism, and all the rest. Many tales deal with the concept of time—time as the foe to beauty but also as the cleanser of ugliness; time in conflict with art for supremacy and survival. In "The Raft-Builders" writing is likened to rafts, but

"Oblivion's Sea" deals mercilessly with most of them; the conclusion can only be quoted:

> Our ships were all unseaworthy from the first.
> There goes the raft that Homer made for Helen.

What can one say when faced with prose like this? Or take "The Prayer of the Flowers," one of Lovecraft's favorites: the message is heart-stoppingly simple—the flowers see the rise of great cities with their smoke and noise, but Pan calms them by saying, "Be patient a little, these things are not for long." It is this offhand way in which Dunsany can speak of the destruction of civilization that makes many of these tales so powerful; and he does not require even his understated prose to achieve the effect. In "The Workman" the ghost of a man who has fallen from a scaffolding comes to the narrator and says bluntly: "Why, yer bloomin' life 'ull go by like a wind, and yer 'ole silly civilisation 'ull be tidied up in a few centuries." The secret of this passage is "tidied up": not only is it shockingly colloquial, but it implies that civilization is some contemptible stain that must be cleaned up. One could write essays on every one of the pieces in *Fifty-one Tales:* they are all parables, devastating in their simplicity.

A somewhat anomalous use to which Dunsany puts philosophy is in a group of tales whose point is nothing less than literary criticism. Methodologically this is different from parody—Lovecraft's "Sweet Ermengarde," for example, a send-up of the Horatio Alger–type story—although the end result is the same, the emphatic underscoring of a particular critical stance. The first example seems to be the Jorkens tale "The Club Secretary" (*Mr. Jorkens Remembers Africa*), in which Jorkens stumbles upon a very exclusive club—a club for famous poets, so rigid in its membership qualifications that Pope is only a hall porter. There is no need to cite passages from Dunsany's nonfiction to show his dislike of Pope and the "school of wit" he represented. Late in his career Dunsany produced many tales of this type, most rather crude and obvious, but some quite successful, or at least mildly amusing. "Darwin Superseded"[35] displays a man who has proved that modern poetry is a sure sign that human beings have begun to reverse the course of evolution and return to primitivism; he concludes: "In fact, if my theory is sound, as I feel sure it is, this should bring us back to the trees before the end of the century." This was a theme Dunsany never tired of uttering, not only in countless articles and diatribes against what he felt was the irrationality of modern poetry but in stories like "A Fable of Moderns" (1951), a scathing attack on T. S. Eliot (never named, of course), or "The Awakening,"[36] in which a man, listening to a pianist, senses that he is finally beginning to understand modern music and spins a grandiose philosophical interpretation of the piece—but the "pianist" is only the piano tuner. Obvious as this is, it is redeemed by its unrelenting ferocity.

The issue of irony and satire in Dunsany is a large one, and I have earlier pointed out certain examples. Again much of the effectiveness of Dunsany's satire comes from the unnerving contrast between the viciousness of the irony and the mild and gentle manner of its expression. Some of the later plays exhibit this tendency brilliantly. Throughout *Seven Modern Comedies* and *Plays for Earth and Air* we look in vain for an admirable character; the success of several of these plays lies in the fact that *everyone* is the target of satire. *Golden Dragon City,* in the latter collection, portrays each of its three characters as shallow and unimaginative fools. A man has bought a window from a strange Arab and sets it up in his flat; and the window magically reveals a fantastic city under siege from an invading army. But the miracle of this sight escapes everyone—Bill, his landlady, and his sweetheart Lily—and it becomes nothing but a carnival amusement. A single bit of dialogue will be enough:

> *Bill:* Won't you take another look at your city, Mrs. Lumley?
> *Mrs. Lumley:* Not now, thank you, sir. I've a few things to do. I'll take a good look later. I'm glad we've got it down there. Come to think of it, I really am. I'll be going now, sir. (*Exit*)
> *Bill:* Well, Lily, when you've finished your muffin we'll take another look at the city.
> *Lily* (*mouth full*): Yes.

A Matter of Honour is a vicious parody of a deathbed scene, as a dying man confesses, "as a matter of honor," that he once succeeded in seducing a bishop's wife, thereby winning an old bet from his two friends. And we have seen how, in *The Raffle,* all the characters are mercilessly flayed as they bandy about the monetary value of a man's soul.

When Dunsany shifted to a lighter and more overtly humorous style in the 1940s and 1950s, the ferocity of his satire tended to wane and yielded occasionally to a wistful pensiveness that is almost reminiscent of *Fifty-one Tales*. Three tales collected in *The Man Who Ate the Phoenix* are good examples. In "The Policeman's Prophecy" (first published 1930) Dunsany uses the casual remark of a policeman to a reckless driver, "You'll kill yourself and everybody else," as a springboard to imagine a world without human beings, concluding with the reflection "What a noise we made! But it will all be forgotten." "Poseidon" (first published 1941) speaks of a man traveling in Greece who meets the ancient god of the title; but Poseidon is a weak and insubstantial god now, no longer having any worshippers, and at the end he quite literally fades away. In a more amusing vein is "The Honorary Member," in which we find the god Atlas an honorary member of a London club. The message is the same as in "Poseidon"—Atlas has no place in the world because, as he remarks, "The world's got too scientific for all that"—but the effect is achieved by the brutal yet comic juxtaposition of the incongruous. I want to single out one further example in which the lighter approach can nonetheless be devastating. I refer to the late work "The Speech" (*The Little Tales of Smethers and Other Stories*), one of the most remarkable stories in Dunsany's entire corpus. In pre–World War I days a firebrand member of the House of Commons plans a speech that will almost certainly bring war to Europe; the government is determined to let the man speak, but a shadowy group is equally determined to stop him in the interests of peace. This group resorts to nothing so crude as assassination—not, at any rate, of the M.P. Instead, they murder the man's father, Lord Inchingthwaite; the M.P. is suddenly a peer and cannot speak in the lower house. At this point the tale is merely amusingly clever; but we have not reached the end:

> "So war was averted," said one of us.
> "Well, yes," said old Gauscold. "Not that it made any difference in the end."

The Great War came anyway.

BELIEF

The question of belief is an important and complex one in Dunsany. By this I mean the manner by which Dunsany convinces us of the reality—or at least the probability—of the supernatural or fantastic events he is describing. There seem to be two fundamental ways in which this can be done in fantasy writing. One is the use of a lavish, richly textured prose style which acts almost as an incantation; the other is the minute accumulation of background details, whether accompanied by a dense prose style (Machen, Lovecraft) or by a colloquialism or flatness of diction so as to make the events more believable (M. R. James, Kipling). Dunsany of course makes extensive use of the first in his early work but never fully utilizes the second once he abandons his quasi-biblical prose; in fact, what Dunsany does in his late work is to evade the question of belief altogether. But his early prose style is so rich and lyrical as to be almost hypnotic: the effect is to convince us effortlessly, whether we are dealing with ersatz religion or folklore (*The Gods of Pegāna, Time and the Gods, The Sword of Welleran*) or parable (*Fifty-one Tales*). And yet the parables of *Fifty-one Tales* in a way prefigure the later work: no one of course is expected to believe, in "The Prayer of the Flowers," that the flowers actually have feelings or that Pan actually speaks to them: everything here is symbol.

Dunsany's early novels convince by use of a simpler, less involved lyricism of style coupled with fantastic settings. The fantastic setting is then discarded, so that in *The Blessing of Pan* we are left wondering throughout the novel whether the source of Tommy Duffin's music is supernatural or not; but this question is of no especial importance, since we are really concerned only with the conflict of the old (symbolized by the music) and the new (represented by Anwrel). All this suggests that Dunsany is beginning to use fantasy or the supernatural as a prop or mechanism to convey his message, so that the interest in the supernatural event as such dissipates. This use of fantasy in a way makes Dunsany's repudiation or renunciation of fantasy in *The Story of Mona Sheehy* more explicable: if fantasy is merely a means to an end, then it makes no difference whether the fantasy is in someone's mind (as it is in Mona's) or whether it is actually postulated to exist in the world. Dunsany elaborates upon the *Mona Sheehy* technique in a late work, the novelette "The Man Who Ate the Phoenix." Again we are informed at the outset of the nonsupernatural nature of the events: Paddy O'Hone has not killed and eaten a phoenix but merely a pheasant; and when Paddy begins to tell tales of the creatures he has seen after eating the bird—ghosts, leprechauns, banshees, witches, the living dead—Dunsany is careful to imply natural causes for all these events. The whole tale is one of comic deflation.

This story provides a suitable transition to Dunsany's late works. We have seen how the comic element comes to dominate his writings of the 1940s and 1950s. It is here that Dunsany, at least in part, evades the whole question of belief in the supernatural events being narrated. A starting point might be the avowedly humorous *My Talks with Dean Spanley*. Dunsany treads the line between belief and incredulity perfectly here, doing so by the use of what might be called the *significant detail*. This is different from what Lovecraft called "the maintenance of a careful realism in every phase of the story *except* that touching on the one given marvel"[37] because no laborious effort is made to build up this realism. It is simply that the dean's accounts of what he felt and thought as a dog are so perfectly consistent and so like what a dog might actually feel and think that they convince us willy-nilly. This tale is, for the reader, almost perverse in that we *know* Dunsany has his tongue in his cheek, and yet detail after detail hits home in an inimitable way.

This short novel's *editio maior, The Strange Journeys of Colonel Polders*, carries the notion one step further. It is not merely that, like that of *Dean Spanley*, Polders's narrative is unfailingly accurate in recording the thoughts and feelings of the animals he has supposedly been; it is that Dunsany now uses a narrative technique that almost dares us to disbelieve him. This novel is written in that bare, flat, conversational style of Dunsany's late period; but, more than this, Polders announces each new incarnation in such a blunt way as repeatedly to take us aback: "in fact I was a dog" (chap. 2); "I found that I was a fox" (chap. 7); "the next thing that fellow did was to make me a moth" (chap. 12); "I was a pig" (chap. 13); "the damned fellow made me an eel" (chap. 14); "Well, I was a tiger" (chap. 15); and on and on and on. And yet it is the significant detail that counts. When Polders is a cat, he climbs up on a kitchen table to lap a jug of cream, but the cook repeatedly puts him back on the floor; nothing could capture the serene self-centeredness of a cat better than Polders's ingenuous statement at this point: "She can't have known what she was doing" (chap. 18). Or there is the stupendous understatement in Polders's remark when, as a fox, he is being chased by hounds: "There is no other experience quite like it" (chap. 11). But Dunsany is toying with us; and when Polders finally becomes a djinn, our unwilling credulity is strained to the breaking point.

One other means Dunsany uses to evade or undermine the question of belief is tacitly to deny the credibility of the narrators of the stories. This is something we find in both early and late stories: many of the stories in *The Last Book of Wonder* are tales told by various unreliable narrators, and we have seen how, in "The Long Porter's Tale," the narrator's deceitfulness is explicitly declared. The Jorkens tales make this technique a fine art, and again we tread the line between the plausibility of what Jorkens is saying and the implausibility of his ever telling the truth. Indeed, it could be said that the one unifying feature in the stories included in both *The Man Who Ate the Phoenix* and *The Little Tales of Smethers* is the fact that nearly all of them are narrated indirectly—that is, through the voice of a character and not that of an omniscient narrator. Dunsany rarely states bluntly that we are to disbelieve these stories, but the use of the unreliable narrator absolves him from taking any stance whatever as to the veracity of what is being told.

It is worth discussing Dunsany as a science fiction writer in this context. Several works—the two Jorkens tales dealing with trips to Mars, "Our Distant Cousins" and "The Slugly Beast"; "The Possibility of Life on the Third Planet" (*The Man Who Ate the Phoenix*), about a radio message from Mars; *The Last Revolution;* and a few others—can be classified as science fiction by their subject matter; but I hesitate to call Dunsany a real science fiction writer because he makes no especial effort to convince us of the probability of any of the events he is describing. This sense of intentional incredulity is dominant in the three short stories mentioned: the spaceship used to get to Mars is described in the most perfunctory way, as is the means by which the message from Mars reached a human radio operator and was translated by him. Dunsany is not interested in the mechanism but the effect: the effect of "Our Distant Cousins" is to portray a humanoid race that is *not* the dominant species on the planet; the effect of "The Possibility of Life on the Third Planet" is again the deflation of human self-importance, since the message speaks contemptuously of the great improbability of intelligent life existing on the Earth. In *The Last Revolution* the mechanism—intelligent machine life—is not ignored but simply presented bunglingly. Dunsany has no awareness of the stupendous complexity and difficulty of artificial intelligence, and this novel—like its antecedent, "The New Master" (*The Little Tales of Smethers and Other Stories*)—is simply unconvincing either in showing how machines could think independently or how they could come to gain the human emotions of jealousy, hatred, and ambition.

While we are at it, we should consider Dunsany as a detective writer. Here we are concerned with *The Little Tales of Smethers and Other Stories,* in particular the first nine stories in that collection, which form a cycle narrated by the traveling salesman Smethers. The interest in these tales, frankly, is not from the standpoint of detection—in this regard they are merely clever, and one ("The Shooting of Constable Slugger") uses the hoary device of the bullet made of ice that melts after inflicting the fatal injury—but rather from the standpoint of narrative technique. This is the first time in Dunsany's long career that he actually adopts another persona—that of the foolish and self-effacing Smethers—to narrate a tale. The result is interesting and amusing but nothing more. Smethers constantly deprecates himself as a "small man" and stands in exaggerated awe of the detective powers of his friend Linley. The impression is that these tales are conscious parodies of the Holmes-Watson dichotomy, and perhaps we are to see the evil villain that runs through several of these tales, Steeger, as a pseudo-Moriarty. *The Little Tales of Smethers* contains several other detective tales, none especially notable; only the final tale, "The Shield of Athene," is supernatural, and it too is undistinguished.

The question of whether Dunsany is a horror writer is also worth some consideration. There are certainly horror elements all through his work: his early stories and plays hint of nameless fates for those who have offended the gods, although of course we get no Lovecraftian evocations of their reduction to "liquiescent horror" or anything of the sort; and such a tale as "The Two Bottles of Relish," with its suggestion of cannibalism, is really quite revolting, as it was intended to be. One detects a smirk behind Dunsany's ostensibly self-deprecatory remark that "my literary agent was unable to get any man in England or America to touch it."[38] But this is a rare, perhaps solitary, instance of horror or gruesomeness for its own sake; Dunsany really uses horror, as he does science fiction, only as a means and not an end. The Jorkens tale "The Walk to Lingham" has all the brooding atmosphere of Machen, but the point of the tale is to suggest the poplars' tentative questioning of the human being's domination of the planet. Another tale, "The Ghost in the Old Corridor,"[39] illustrates the difference perfectly. This tale is a variant of "The Return," in which the narrator at the end discovers that he himself is the ghost being discussed in the various places he visits along a lonely road (who cannot think of Lovecraft's "Outsider"?); but "The Ghost in the Old Corridor" is different in that the narrator, speaking to another man about the ghost, finds out that that man is the ghost. This is what the narrator says upon this discovery: "I cannot say that he vanished when he ceased; for it was by now so dark that I only saw the

outline of his face, and that no clearer than the will-o'-the-wisps that
rose far off in the night. When his voice was silent there was nothing
more to guide me to the direction in which he was, and I found my way
home alone out of the marshes." This calm, pensive ending would have
been unimaginable to Lovecraft, whose narrators flee madly and pre-
cipitately from all contact with the supernatural: as defenders of reason
face to face with the irrational, they can do nothing else. But Dunsany
finds the situation one of pathos and not of horror; and all this points
to a truth so obvious that many seem not to have realized it—that horror or fantasy is almost entirely a matter of approach rather than of subject matter.

CONCLUSION

Throughout this chapter I have discussed Dunsany's work chronologically, tracing themes, conceptions, and imagery from the beginning to
the end of his career, because I think this is the only way to understand
him. An honest reader of Dunsany must get beyond the early work,
siren song as it is; one must explore what he chose to do in the nearly
four decades of writing after *Tales of Three Hemispheres* (1919) and read
this material with the expectation that it will be significantly different
from—but not necessarily inferior to—the earlier work. I resolutely refuse to pass judgment on whether his earlier or his later writing is superior: there are times when I, like most readers, want to genuflect before
The Gods of Pegāna or *A Dreamer's Tales*, but I would never wish to part
with *The Blessing of Pan, The Curse of the Wise Woman, The Story of Mona
Sheehy,* or *The Strange Journeys of Colonel Polders.* But it is not a matter of
likes or dislikes: Dunsany, quite simply, was always evolving as a writer.

It is difficult to lay down any clear divisions in his work, especially
with the recent discovery of a mass of uncollected fiction, early and late.
Even the series of short-story collections from *The Gods of Pegāna* to *Tales
of Three Hemispheres* cannot be regarded monolithically, since such things
as *The Book of Wonder, The Last Book of Wonder,* and portions of *Tales of
Three Hemispheres* represent a significantly different attitude to his work
from that found in *Time and the Gods* or *The Sword of Welleran.* As I said
earlier, the pseudonaiveté of the *Gods of Pegāna* style was exhausted
quite early on. The shift from short stories to novels with *Don Rodriguez*
(1922) did not bring an immediate change of tone or style: of course,
the novels as a whole are less intense and concentrated than the tales,

but it would have been foolish—or at least risky—for Dunsany to have attempted to maintain the early short-story style in the novels. The real break comes, first, in the complete abandonment of archaism of both style and setting in *The Blessing of Pan*, then the use of his native Irish background in *The Curse of the Wise Woman*, and then the rejection of fantasy in *The Story of Mona Sheehy*. Overlapping this shift is the inclusion of overt humor, first with the Jorkens tales (the first one composed in 1925), then with *My Talks with Dean Spanley*, and finally the late stories and *The Strange Journeys of Colonel Polders*. In the plays the break is more straightforward, and the archaistic manner is abandoned almost completely after *Plays of Gods and Men* (1917). Lovecraft's comment is interesting in this regard: while he regarded Dunsany's comedies of manners (he must have been referring to the early *Lost Silk Hat* or to *Fame and the Poet*, since he was writing well before *Seven Modern Comedies* and the later plays) worthy of Sheridan, he nonetheless regretted the change: "A reincarnated Sheridan is precious indeed, but the Dunsany of *A Dreamer's Tales* is a wonder twice as precious because it cannot be duplicated or even approached."[40] Much as I admire Lovecraft, it is precisely this attitude—this impatience with Dunsany's growth as a writer—that I am interested in combating.

In the end the career of Lord Dunsany is both unique and edifying. Let us by all means reverence the early work, the work we unconsciously designate when we use the adjective "Dunsanian"; but let us learn that the later work is just as Dunsanian, just as representative of his temperament at a later stage. Let us marvel at his seemingly effortless mastery of so many different forms (short story, novel, play, even essay and lecture), his unfailingly sound narrative sense, and the amazing consistency he maintained over a breathtakingly prolific output. Like Lovecraft, like Machen, Dunsany claimed aesthetic independence from his time and culture, became a sharp and unrelenting critic of the industrialism and plebeianism that were shattering the beauty both of literature and of the world, wrote works almost obtrusively and aggressively unpopular in tone and import yet retained a surprising popularity—at least in terms of the sale of his work—through the whole of his career. The criticism of Dunsany is at an even more primitive level than that of Machen, Lovecraft, or M. R. James, and certainly more than that of Poe and Bierce. In part I think this is because many critics—and I will include myself in this number—find his early work so flawless of its kind as to be virtually uncriticizable, and most have not considered the later work at all. But it is also because Dunsany is seen by many simply as a *predecessor:* a dominant influence on Lovecraft, Tolkien, and others, to whom an obligatory tip of the hat and no more is necessary. Lovecraft died in 1937, the year *The Hobbit* was published; Dunsany continued to write for nearly two decades after this. I have done all I can to indicate the compelling interest in the whole of this work; later critics must continue the task of explication so that Lord Dunsany becomes more than just a hallowed name.

3.

ALGERNON BLACKWOOD

The Expansion of Consciousness

*A*lgernon Henry Blackwood was born in Shooter's Hill, Kent, on March 14, 1869, the son of Sir Stevenson Arthur Blackwood, a clerk in the Treasury and later Secretary of the Post Office. In his youth Blackwood absorbed a strict Evangelical upbringing from his father, although early on he showed signs of rebellion by surreptitiously reading the *Bhagavad Gita* and theosophy. Blackwood spent time at a series of private schools, and a year-long stay (1885–1886) at the School of the Moravian Brotherhood in Königsfeld, Germany, impressed him profoundly with its military discipline but also its "beautiful spirit of gentleness and merciful justice." He spent the summer of 1887 in Switzerland before being sent by his father to Canada on business. In 1888 Blackwood entered Edinburgh University but left the next year.

In May 1890 Blackwood went to Canada again to make his living. He attempted to start a dairy farm, but it failed and Blackwood lost much of his investment. He then engaged in a partnership to run a hotel, but found the work not to his liking and sold his share in it in 1892. After an idyllic summer in the Canadian backwoods he went to New York, where he became a reporter for the *Evening Sun*. Here he fell into the company of Arthur Bigge (disguised as Boyde in his autobiography, *Episodes before Thirty* [1923]), who as Blackwood's roommate stole much of his money and whom Blackwood finally tracked down and had arrested. Blackwood lived in desperate poverty at this time, although his circumstances improved when he became a reporter for the *New York Times* in 1895 and then a private secretary to the wealthy banker James Speyer in 1897.

By 1899 Blackwood felt the urge to return to England. He became a partner in a dried milk company, although he was little involved in its operations. Over the next several years he took various lengthy trips—to the Danube (the setting of "The Willows"), France, his old school in

Germany, and elsewhere. He became interested in paranormal phenomena, joining the Golden Dawn in 1900.

Although a voluminous reporter, Blackwood wrote only a few stories, essays, and poems until his middle thirties. A chance meeting with Angus Hamilton, an old friend from Canada, led Blackwood to submit a collection of his stories to Eveleigh Nash; it was published as *The Empty House* (1906). Blackwood became a writer of stature with the enormously popular *John Silence* (1908) and from then on devoted his life to writing. From 1908 to 1914 he lived in Böle, Switzerland, where he wrote prolifically. A trip to the Caucasus Mountains in 1910 inspired *The Centaur* (1911), the central work of his oeuvre. A trip to Egypt led to the writing of "Sand," "A Descent into Egypt," and *The Wave* (1916). *A Prisoner in Fairyland* (1913) was later adapted into the play *The Starlight Express,* with music by Elgar.

During World War I Blackwood served as an undercover agent for British military intelligence. After the war he settled in Kent, turning his attention principally to drama. By 1923 Blackwood felt that he had come to the end of his fictional career and began writing articles and reviews. *Tongues of Fire* (1924) and *Shocks* (1935) were his last collections of stories, and the novels of this period are largely children's books or whimsies—*Sambo and Snitch* (1927), *Dudley and Gilderoy* (1929), and *The Fruit Stoners* (1934). Blackwood continued to travel extensively in Europe and also visited New York briefly in 1933.

In 1934 Blackwood began a new career reading stories on BBC radio. He was enormously popular, and in 1936 he began to appear regularly on television. In 1940 the house of Blackwood's nephew was destroyed in the Battle of Britain, Blackwood surviving by accident. He retired to Bishopsteighton, Kent, where he continued preparing talks and plays for radio. This work continued after the war, leading to Blackwood's becoming a commander of the British Empire in 1949. Algernon Blackwood died on December 10, 1951.

The life and work of Algernon Blackwood are in some ways remarkably similar to those of Arthur Machen. Both self-confessed mystics, they devoted themselves to a systematic onslaught against materialism and the advance of technology. Both suffered extreme poverty in their youth as they tried to make their way as journalists, and both wrote heart-wrenchingly of their experiences in two of the most exquisite autobiographies in English, Machen's *Far Off Things* (1922) and Blackwood's *Episodes before Thirty* (1923). Both produced their greatest work in a relatively short period of their careers, Machen during his "Great Decade" of 1889–1899, Blackwood with the fifteen books of his first ten years of writing (1906–1916); and Machen and Blackwood were the authors of what Lovecraft considered the two finest weird tales ever written, "The White People" and "The Willows"—a judgment that has much to recommend it, although I might rank Blackwood's "A Descent into Egypt" even higher than "The Willows."

But a closer look at these resemblances will reveal increasingly profound differences in Machen's and Blackwood's whole approach to life, literature, and philosophy. Machen's mysticism is intimately related to his Anglo-Catholicism, and his bitterest criticism of scientific rationalism is its diffusion of skepticism and agnosticism. Blackwood's mysticism is no less religious at its base, but it is free of dogma and creed. Blackwood keenly describes his very rigid Evangelical upbringing and his early absorption of Buddhism as an antidote against it;[1] and while his later "religion of nature" has Buddhist elements in it,[2] it is really a religion of Blackwood's own making. More important, Machen's whole philosophy is negative: he was always fighting *against* something, whether it be materialism or literary realism or mechanization. Blackwood's view of the world strikes me as much more positive and constructive: he seeks to show how his philosophy can actually *work* in the world, and he seems to have lived by it as much as it is humanly possible to do. Machen's work is, accordingly, dark and brooding; he is, really, a more profound pessimist than Ambrose Bierce, since for all his furious literary activity he seems early on to have resigned himself to failure at converting the world. Blackwood, on the other hand, is quite frankly the most wholesome and cheerful horror writer I know of; in fact, his most characteristic work is not horrific but—to use a loathsome neologism—upbeat. Indeed, after reading the whole of Blackwood (and it is something one must do if one is to understand him), one wonders why he even attempted to convey fright in some of his tales, as his predominant message is optimistic in regard to human beings, their souls, and their place in the cosmos.

It is not especially profitable to study Blackwood chronologically, since there is relatively little development in the forty years of his active writing career: the goals he set for himself at the outset remained, with some modifications, to the end, and we can note only a gradual decline in intensity and vividness after about 1916, although even among the later novels and stories there are occasional items of merit. A more interesting division of Blackwood's work—one that gets closer to the heart of his philosophical purpose—is a tripartite distinction of stories by type: stories of awe, stories of horror, and stories of childhood. In reality, the first group is the core of Blackwood's writing, and the other two can be seen as facets of it; it is the first that provides the key to understanding the other two.

Blackwood, unlike Machen or Lovecraft, did not embody his philosophy in vast numbers of essays or letters; although he wrote a number of reviews and some revealing radio talks, he alone of all the writers in this volume restricted himself principally to fictional composition. But to put it this way is somewhat misleading, because Blackwood, even more than Lovecraft, wrote unashamedly philosophical fiction. Although *Episodes before Thirty* provides significant clues as to Blackwood's view of the world, it does so much less intensely than *The Centaur* (1911) and *Julius LeVallon* (1916). These two novels—the leading examples of Blackwood's "stories of awe"—provide nearly all the tools we need to interpret the rest of his work.

Let me state at the outset that I do not understand Blackwood's philosophy. By this I mean that I frequently cannot follow the courses of reasoning—if they can be called that—by which Blackwood arrives at his conclusions and attitudes. I am not a mystic and do not understand the mystical temperament. When, in *Episodes before Thirty,* Blackwood says of a friend of his youth, "His reasoning powers were slight, for like all true mystics he believed in the intuitive perception of truth" (65), he is clearly also speaking of himself. Elsewhere in his autobiography he writes engagingly of his frequent and cordial arguments with an atheist friend, who would always worst Blackwood in logical argument but who would never alter Blackwood's convictions one iota. It would be easy to claim that Blackwood's mysticism—no less than Lovecraft's materialism—was rigidly dogmatic; but I think this is to misconstrue the whole process by which one arrives at a philosophical stance. Blackwood's world view, like Lovecraft's, was gradually acquired over a lifetime of thought and experience; for either thinker suddenly to have renounced or overhauled his philosophy would have required profound psychological metamorphoses. Blackwood's is, nonetheless, a real philosophy, not a set of prejudices like Machen's; and yet I am still working under the handicap of viewing Blackwood from what is essentially Lovecraft's philosophical position. There are times when I wish I could believe as Blackwood does, but this brings me no closer to actually doing so.

AWE

To say that "nature" is at the core of Blackwood's thought does not get us very far, given the imprecision of the term—or, rather, its multiplicity of connotations. There may, at least initially, have been a similar confusion on Blackwood's part. No doubt Blackwood liked the great outdoors—wilderness, campfires, that sort of thing. But what I see as the central, almost archetypal, event in Blackwood's life—one that shaped the whole of his fictional work—is not merely his youthful rambles in the vast forests of Canada, but his sudden departure from the wilds to the phantasmagoric civilization of New York. It is this brutal juxtaposition—one moment the open spaces, the next a cheap boardinghouse full of vermin—that colored Blackwood's entire outlook. His description of New York in the 1890s could not have been surpassed by Lovecraft:

> I seemed covered with sore and tender places into which New York rubbed salt and acid every hour of the day. It wounded, not alone because I felt unhappy, but of itself. It hit me where it pleased. The awful city, with its torrential, headlong life, held for me something of the monstrous. Everything about it was exaggerated. Its racing speed, its roofs amid the clouds with the canyon gulfs below, its gaudy avenues dripping gold that ran almost arm in arm with streets little better than sewers of human decay and misery, its frantic noise, both of voices and mechanism, its lavishly organized charity and boastful splendour, and its deep corruption in the grip of heartless and degraded Tammany—it was all this that painted the horror into my imagination as of something monstrous, non-human, almost unearthly. It became, for me, a scab on the skin of the planet, brilliant with the hues of fever, moving all over with its teeming microbes. I felt it, indeed, but half civilized. (124–125)

Contrast this with Blackwood's loving and heartfelt account of what nature meant to him:

Forests, mountains, desolate places, especially perhaps open spaces like the prairies or the desert, but even, too, the simple fields, the lanes, and little hills, offered an actual sense of companionship no human intercourse could possibly provide. In times of trouble, as equally in times of joy, it was to Nature I ever turned instinctively. . . . This call sounded above all other calls, music coming so far behind it as to seem an "also ran." Even in those few, rare times of later life, when I fancied myself in love, this spell would operate—a sound of rain, a certain touch of colour in the sky, the scent of a wood-fire smoke, the lovely cry of some singing wind against the walls or window—and the human appeal would fade in me, or, at least, its transitory character became pitifully revealed. The strange sense of oneness with Nature was an imperious and royal spell that overmastered all other spells, nor can the hint of comedy lessen its reality. Its religious origin appears, perhaps, in the fact that sometimes, during its fullest manifestation, a desire stirred in me to leave a practical, utilitarian world I loathed and become—a monk! (39–40)

This tells us many important things: first, that nature worship functioned as an ersatz religion (I mean no disrespect by this phrase: Blackwood's beliefs are certainly far more intellectually acceptable than those of most conventional religions); second, that it came to outweigh—or, perhaps, helped to put into proper perspective—Blackwood's more earthy sentiments, something we will find in the very curious romances that fill his tales and novels; and third, and most important, that this perception of nature was linked—indeed, became united—with his mystical sense of the oneness of all existence. Perception, indeed, is of especial importance, for it is through a heightened or altered perception that we are given access to other, truer realms of entity. In his autobiography Blackwood quotes a passage from William James's *Varieties of Religious Experience* that he could have written himself:

One conclusion was forced upon my mind . . . and my impression of its truth has ever since remained unshaken. It is that our normal waking consciousness, rational consciousness as we call it, is but *one special type* of consciousness, whilst all about us, parted from it by the filmiest of screens, there are potential forms of consciousness entirely different. We may go through life without suspecting their existence; but apply the requisite stimulus and at a touch they are there in all their completeness; definite types of mentality which probably somewhere have their field of application and adaptation. No account of the universe in its totality can be final which leaves these other forms of consciousness quite disregarded. (249)

The expansion of consciousness—this is what Blackwood is after. The terms vary from work to work—expansion, extension, intensification, sometimes merely change—but at its heart is some mystical awareness of a broader vista than science and rationalism provide. Many things produce such an augmented consciousness—intense emotion, ritual, drugs,[3] and a number of other things.[4] Ultimately, what Blackwood seeks to accomplish by this extended consciousness is to overcome the limitations imposed upon our beings by the laws of time and space— what he refers to in *The Human Chord* as "the essential bitterness and pain that lies at the heart of all transitory earthly things—the gnawing sense of incompleteness and vanity that touches the section of transitory existence we call 'life'."[5] In this quest his goal seems superficially similar to Lovecraft's, who also speaks of the "galling limitations of time, space, and natural law which forever imprison us and frustrate our curiosity about the infinite cosmic spaces beyond the radius of our sight and analysis";[6] but the differences are in fact profound. Lovecraft's goal is purely one of intellectual understanding, while Blackwood seeks some mystical merging with the cosmos; moreover, Blackwood evidently feels that these limitations can in reality be overcome, whereas Lovecraft felt they could be only imaginatively or psychologically.

It is important to realize that the expansion of consciousness is not a mere "subjective" state. I am not sure there is any such thing as a subjective state in Blackwood, in spite of his constant—almost excessive— probing of the psychologies of his characters. On the very first page of *The Garden of Survival* the narrator proclaims earnestly that "to have my experience disbelieved, or attributed to hallucination, would be intolerable to me" (1). And when, in a late story, "Elsewhere and Otherwise" (in *Shocks*), it is stated that "as consciousness grows, the universe it perceives grows and changes with it,"[7] we suddenly realize that there is some symbiotic relationship between this changed consciousness and the world that consciousness finds itself in. The notion seems to be that we actually have some sort of direct communion with a larger sphere of entity, one where the distinctions between terrestrial—or, for that matter, cosmic—objects are seen to be illusory or nugatory.

Such a perception ordinarily requires or results in (I am not certain of the sequence of cause and effect here) a removal both from the modern age and from the concentration of modernity represented by the urban environment; this is why so many of Blackwood's tales take place in remote areas and also involve the recrudescence of forces from distant gulfs of time. This is the focus of Blackwood's *The Centaur,* his prototypical essay on the human need for unification with nature. More than *Episodes before Thirty,* it can be seen as Blackwood's true autobiography, if we are to believe what the protagonist of *The Garden of Survival* tells us: "This record deals principally with the essential facts of my life, the inner; the outer events and actions are of importance only in so far as they interpret these, since that which a man feels and thinks alone is real, and thought and feeling, of course, precede all action" (66). *The Centaur* is such a record. I cannot pretend to treat it in any depth or detail in the space I have, but certain features of it are worth singling out as patterns of thought Blackwood would maintain throughout his career. This is the tale of Terence O'Malley, who aboard ship encounters a strange Russian man and his apparent son, and is invited to follow them to the remote fastnesses of the Caucasus Mountains, where he undergoes a mystical experience that makes him aware of the "cosmic life." He returns to civilization and seeks to convert the world to his point of view, but of course fails and dies. This bald account can hardly convey the poetry and throbbing vitality of this work, the cornerstone of Blackwood's output.

Who is this strange being whom O'Malley meets? He is a "Cosmic Being . . . a little bit, a fragment, of the Soul of the World, and in that sense a survival—a survival of her youth."[8] In the modern age there is no room for such a being, and O'Malley's quest at regenerating his contemporaries was doomed to failure. But in a sense it is the transformation of O'Malley himself that is of greatest significance. At the outset he has nothing but scorn for his contemporaries: "Civilization, he loved to say, had blinded the eyes of men, filling them with dust instead of vision" (9). A later outburst is even more vicious: "'And I loathe, *loathe* the spirit of to-day with its cheap-jack inventions, and smother of sham universal culture, its murderous superfluities and sordid vulgarity, without enough real sense of beauty left to see that a daisy is nearer heaven than an airship—'" (40). Without ever renouncing these views, O'Malley comes back from his voyage with a completely new desire to help the world he despises: "'If only I can get this back to them!' passed through him, like a flame. 'I'll save the world by bringing it again to simple things! I've only got to tell it and all will understand at once—and follow!'" (228). Naive and quixotic as this is—and as Blackwood intends it to be—there is a nobility in it that testifies to the expansion, in every sense, of O'Malley's consciousness.

The culmination of O'Malley's mystical experience in the Caucasus is the sighting of a herd of centaurs. The symbolism of the centaur is explained more clearly in "Imagination" (in *Ten Minute Stories*), a story that Blackwood wrote while experiencing difficulty completing *The Centaur*. Here a man who wishes to write about "some power of unexpended mythological values strayed back into modern life" chooses the centaur as his symbol: "His Centaur was to stand for instinct (the animal body close to Nature) combined with, yet not dominated by, the upright stature moving towards deity."[9] It is this combination of reason and instinct that Blackwood sees as the optimum state of consciousness for human beings. It is what separates Julius LeVallon from his fellows: "Julius alone . . . combined Reason and Intuition in that perfect achievement towards which humanity perhaps slowly seems to be moving."[10] Very slowly, indeed; for, as we shall see, the war shattered, at least temporarily, Blackwood's sanguine hopes for the regeneration of the race.

It would perhaps be unfair to subject the arguments of *The Centaur* to rigorous philosophical analysis; no doubt Blackwood in the end would claim that if one did not feel the truths he is expounding, it would be hopeless to argue them. But unfortunately Blackwood invites such scrutiny by his constant attacks on the inadequacy of reason and science, by his bountiful quotations—both in epigraphs to chapters and in the text itself—from William James, F. H. Bradley, and other thinkers, and by the lengthy arguments on the subject conducted by O'Malley and his devil's-advocate friend, Stahl. It is very easy to refute Blackwood logically. When O'Malley says, "The Earth has a Collective Consciousness. We rise upon the Earth as wavelets upon the ocean. We grow out of her soil as leaves grow from a tree" (95), the deficiencies of the argument from analogy are revealed at their starkest.[11] A little later Blackwood makes the unfortunate mistake of trying to bring in the concept of the ether to bolster his view ("'Every element has its own living denizens. Ether, then, also has hers—the globes'" [96]); and although he supports this conception by a quotation from William James, the nonexistence of the ether is rather damaging to the argument. This sort of thing goes on throughout the novel, and aside from its philosophical ineptitude it weighs down the work to an appreciable degree. Remarkable and important as *The Centaur* is in many ways, I am not convinced that it truly succeeds as a novel: there is in the end too little dramatic interest to carry the narrative along.

It is worth pointing out that the return to nature, although often couched in language suggesting a return to an anterior stage of history—indeed, of prehistory, or at least prior to the growth of civilization—is not ultimately a return to primitivism. Voltaire, had he read Blackwood, would not have felt inclined to crawl on all fours as he claimed to do after reading Rousseau. A passage in *The Centaur*, however, does suggest the reverse, as O'Malley ponders on the return to nature as what the narrator calls "the Call of the Wild, raised to its highest power": "'The call,' he answered, without turning to look at me, speaking it into the night about us, 'the call to childhood, the true, pure, vital childhood of the Earth—the Golden Age—before men tasted of the Tree and knew themselves separate; when the lion and the lamb lay down together and a little child could lead them'" (99–100). But I think we must look to a passage at the conclusion of *The Bright Messenger* (1921) for Blackwood's true view: "'If we lived closer to nature we might get better results, I mean. Primitive man, I'm convinced, did get certain results, but he was a poor instrument. Modern man, in some ways, is a better, finer instrument to work through, only he is blind to the existence of any beings but himself. A bridge, however, might be built, I feel.'"[12] Blackwood is really looking for the same union of reason and instinct portrayed in Julius LeVallon and other characters. Primitive human beings had only instinct, modern human beings have only reason. I think Blackwood is nevertheless tempted toward primitivism, if for no other reason than for its contrast to urban civilization. This conflict figures in Blackwood's ambiguous treatment of animals—nonrational and instinctive entities par excellence. In "A Psychical Invasion" (in *John Silence*) John Silence's dog and cat are the first to detect the unearthly presence in the haunted house; indeed, Silence brought them for precisely that reason. The cat in particular feels entirely at home with the ghostly manifestation, leading Silence to reflect:

There rose in him quite a new realisation of the mystery connected with the whole feline tribe, but especially with that common
member of it, the domestic cat—their hidden lives, their strange
aloofness, their incalculable subtlety. How utterly remote from anything that human beings understood lay the sources of their elusive
activities. As he watched the indescribable bearing of the little creature mincing along the strip of carpet under his eyes, coquetting
with the powers of darkness, welcoming, maybe, some fearsome
visitor, there stirred in his heart a feeling strangely akin to awe. Its
indifference to human kind, its serene superiority to the obvious,
struck him forcibly with fresh meaning; so remote, so inaccessible
seemed the secret purposes of its real life, so alien to the blundering
honesty of other animals. (44)

But if there is something sinister in this cat's closeness to spectral phenomena, it is entirely otherwise in *A Prisoner in Fairyland* (1913), in
which the cat senses that the spirits of children leave their bodies in
sleep: "Riquette then witnessed a wonderful and beautiful thing, yet
witnessed it obviously not for the first time. Her manner suggested no
surprise. 'It's like a mouse, only bigger,' her expression said. And by this
she meant that it was natural. She accepted it as right and proper."[13] The
difference is entirely one of tone: the actual phenomena are almost
identical. Similarly, in "Ancient Sorceries" we witness all the inhabitants
of a town as cat-creatures who manifest their feline selves at night; this
alteration is presented as unutterably evil, and John Silence pontificates
at the conclusion how Vezin, a guest in the town, escaped "the degradation of returning, even in memory, to a former and lower state of development" (124). Compare this with the character in *Julius LeVallon* constantly referred to as "The Dog-Man," of whom it is said that "he was
just one degree above the animal stage" (163): here this statement is
meant in praise—or, at least, certainly not in denigration—since it signifies the man's closeness to the natural world. Still, I think Blackwood
tended to fear a wholesale return to primitivism, especially one engen-
dered by some collapse of the fabric of civilization; we shall note such a
concern in some of his later works.

If *The Centaur* is Blackwood's archetypal tale of the oneness of all nature, then *Julius LeVallon* (1916) is its pendant in reflecting another central tenet in his philosophy—the theory of reincarnation. The connection of reincarnation with nature worship is made early on in the novel,

when it is remarked that metempsychosis is "the earliest intellectual attempt of man . . . to conceive th[e] world, not as alien to him, but as akin to him" (40). This conception is not entirely clear to me, but perhaps it is clarified by a later statement: "A human being was but *one* living detail of a universe in which all other details were equally living and equally—possibly more—important" (46). When it is claimed that metempsychosis is analogous to the theory of the conservation of energy, we are evidently to understand that there are only a limited number of souls that must inhabit the successive generations of all living things; indeed, the notion that some souls are "old" and others are "new"—i.e., that some have experienced more reincarnations than others—is an important one in Blackwood, and it is his way of accounting for the stolidity and lack of spirituality of the mass of humanity: it is only young souls who are preoccupied with the surface realities of the world—it is they who become scientists, businessmen, and world leaders. The old souls have left this sort of bustle behind them, realizing its futility.

Julius LeVallon is concerned with the reenaction of a mystical ceremony by three individuals—LeVallon, his wife, and the narrator—who, in a prior life in the remote past, were interrupted in the completion of the rite. This does not sound like a vary promising premise for a novel, and it is not: although there are some exquisite and delicate touches here and there (especially in the characterization of LeVallon as subtly different from his peers), this novel too does not sustain real interest. There are, fortunately, fewer attempts at philosophical argumentation; although Blackwood again stumbles into an obvious fallacy when LeVallon remarks, "Do you expect Nature to be less intelligent than the life that she creates?" (78), where nature is misconceived as a sentient entity rather than the sum total of all natural phenomena. At the end the mystical ceremony somehow goes awry, and we are led to believe that some strange nature being has entered, not LeVallon, as was the intention, but his unborn son in his wife's womb. The novel ends curiously:

> For some weeks after the events that have been here described, Mrs. LeVallon gave birth to a boy, surviving him alas! by but a single day.
> This I heard long afterwards by the merest chance. But my strenuous efforts to trace the child proved unavailing, and I only learned that he was adopted by a French family whose name even was not

given to me. If alive he would be now about twenty years of age.
(354)

We shall see later where this leads.

The reincarnation theme is one that pervades Blackwood's work as
systematically as the nature theme; and, as with so much of Blackwood,
we have both "cheerful" and grim treatments of the idea. The former is
evident in a delicate tale, "Old Clothes" (in *The Lost Valley*), in which it is
made clear that a little girl is possessed by the spirit of a former tenant of
her dwelling: "Were I a painter I might put her upon canvas in some
imaginary portrait and call it, perhaps, 'Reincarnation'—for I have
never seen anything in child-life that impressed me so vividly with that
odd idea of an old soul come back to the world in a new young body—a
new Suit of Clothes."[14] Here a conventional dualistic metaphor is given
a twist, and the body stands for the older, possessing spirit, and the
clothes represent the present-day body that is so possessed. Curiously
for one who does not put much faith in science, Blackwood allows the
girl to be "cured" by hypnosis: "Hypnotic suggestion had wiped from
her mind the last vestige of her dreadful memories; . . . she played and
laughed with all the radiance of an unhaunted childhood, and her
imagination was purged and healed" (172). It is entirely otherwise in
the mesmerizing "The Insanity of Jones" (in *The Listener*), in which
Jones, an ordinary secretary, comes to feel that his boss is the reincarnation of a being who inflicted grievous tortures upon his own previous
incarnation: "he left the office with the certain conviction in his heart
that the time for his final settlement with the man, the time for the inevitable retribution, was at last drawing very near."[15] What is interesting is
not only the notion of retribution—that souls are compelled to redress
wrongs inflicted by or upon them in prior lives—that we find in *Julius
LeVallon*, but the fact that "The Insanity of Jones" bears a striking superficial resemblance to Dunsany's "The Finding of Mr. Jupkens" (in *The
Man Who Ate the Phoenix*). Dunsany's similar tale—in which an ordinary
individual of today ruthlessly tracks down another man because of what
he fancies to be a wrong committed "forty incarnations" ago—reads almost like a parody of Blackwood's; and this is precisely because in
Blackwood we are to believe (as Blackwood apparently believes) in the
phenomenon of reincarnation whereas in Dunsany we are to see in it
(as Dunsany apparently sees) the symptoms of a dangerous monomania.

Blackwood's very next novel after *Julius LeVallon, The Wave* (1916), also treats the reincarnation theme, but still less successfully. Here we are to understand that the odd love triangle taking place among three individuals vacationing in Egypt is the reenactment of an ancient scenario in which an Egyptian slave fell in love with a general's wife and was tortured to death, the woman then committing suicide. In the modern setting a man falls in love with a woman who first returns his affection, then finds herself infatuated with the man's dashing cousin, then finally returns to her first lover. Here too a sort of balancing or redressing of wrongs takes place; the notion strikes me as somewhat naive, as if justice will somehow be served if one is reincarnated often enough. Still, there is power and pathos in this work, and Blackwood writes with the poignancy and veracity of experience: he has felt the emotions he is describing.

Both *The Centaur* and *Julius LeVallon* deal, necessarily, with conventional religion. What is its relation to the "religion of nature" Blackwood espouses? An important passage in *The Centaur,* where the German philosopher Fechner is being quoted, provides a clue:

> "'On a certain spring morning I went out to walk. The fields were green, the birds sang, the dew glistened, the smoke was rising, here and there a man appeared; a light as of transfiguration lay on all things. It was only a little bit of the earth; it was only a moment of her existence; and yet as my look embraced her more and more it seemed to me not only so beautiful an idea, but so true and clear a fact, that she is an angel, an angel so rich and fresh and flowerlike, and yet going her round in the skies so firmly and so at one with herself, turning her whole living face to Heaven, and carrying me along with her into that Heaven, that I asked myself how the opinions of men could ever have so spun themselves away from life as to deem the earth only a dry clod, and to seek for angels above it or about it in the emptiness of the sky—only to find them nowhere.'" (103)

Materialism and conventional religion alike are misconstruals of the fundamental unity of existence. The gods, indeed, are nothing but "projections of [the Earth's] personality—aspects and facets of her divided self" (104). This sort of reasoning leads inevitably to the (somewhat platitudinous) idea that LeVallon's "tolerance and respect for all the religions of to-day were based upon the belief that each contained a portion of the truth at least" (46)—perhaps at most. LeVallon maintains that his "teaching . . . might unify the creeds, put life into the formal churches, inspire the world with joy and hope, and bring on the spirit of brotherhood by helping the soul to rediscover its kinship with a living cosmos" (79). A cheerful idea, but it does not appear as if LeVallon gets very far along in this direction.

Other works treat the religious theme more interestingly. In particular, nearly all the tales in *Incredible Adventures*—perhaps Blackwood's greatest story collection—have the conflict of conventional and "true" religion as their foundation. The very titles of some of the stories—"The Regeneration of Lord Ernie," "The Sacrifice," "The Damned"—suggest this. "The Damned" is perhaps the most philosophically straightforward, and yet it embodies one of the most novel conceptions in the history of weird fiction. A man and his sister come to visit the home of the sister's friend, whose husband—a banker who advocated an unusually intolerant form of salvation for the elect and eternal torture for all others—has just died. Everyone feels uncomfortable—the man cannot continue his writing, his sister paints loathsome and uncharacteristic pictures, the sister's friend wanders about in a daze. But this is no mere haunted house tale—or, rather, it is a haunted house tale of almost cosmic proportions. The creatures who are haunting this place are encountered by the man in an unforgettable climax:

> The throng that pressed behind me, also surged in front: facing me in the big room, and waiting for my entry, stood a multitude; on either side of me, in the very air above my head, the vast assemblage paused upon my coming. The pause, however, was momentary, for instantly the deep, tumultuous movement was resumed that yet was silent as a cavern underground. I felt the agony that was in it, the passionate striving, the awful struggle to escape. The semi-darkness held beseeching faces that fought to press themselves upon my vision, yearning yet hopeless eyes, lips scorched and dry, mouths that opened to implore but found no craved delivery in actual words, and a fury of misery and hate that made the life in me stop dead, frozen by the horror of vain pity. That intolerable, vain Hope was everywhere.[16]

They are literally the "damned" souls that have been banished to the fire and brimstone by the banker—as well as other tenants of the house, who by an evil (and, frankly, implausible) coincidence have all practiced exclusionary religious beliefs. Blackwood makes it clear that all such religions are the object of his attack: "'. . . before he came here, the house was occupied by Manetti, a violet Catholic without tolerance or vision; and in the interval between these two, Julius Weinbaum had it, Hebrew of the most rigid orthodox type imaginable . . .'" (233).

"The Sacrifice" is a still more delicate story in which a man, Limasson, having suffered a multitude of personal tragedies, is on the brink of renouncing his gods (i.e., his spirituality) when he meets two strange individuals who urge him to accompany them in climbing a mountain. What Limasson learns is that "all of life is a Ceremony on a giant scale, and that by performing the movements accurately, with sincere fidelity, there may come—Knowledge" (113). There may also come salvation, for during the mystical experience upon the mountain one of his companions informs him: "By the renunciation which seems to you as death shall you pass through the gates of birth to the life of freedom beyond" (125). What is remarkable in this story is how, with every act being a ceremony, every sentence becomes a metaphor. At the height of his experience Limasson wakes up and finds he has been in the lobby of the hotel all the time; but recall that in Blackwood there is no such thing as a "subjective" experience—the event was "real" because the experience and the revelation were real. When Limasson is helped to his room by two passersby, he remarks, "I really think—I can manage alone" (127), and so he can—for the rest of his life: "Limasson walked up the two flights to his room without faltering. The momentary dizziness had passed. He felt quite himself again, strong, confident, able to stand alone, able to move forward, able to *climb*" (127).

Then we come to the two most remarkable stories in *Incredible Adventures,* "The Regeneration of Lord Ernie" and "A Descent into Egypt." The regeneration Lord Ernie undergoes following his participation in an archaic ritual in the Jura Mountains is no mere religious conversion: throughout his life Ernie had been "without desire which is Life" (4); but following the ritual Ernie reestablishes contact with nature—for the ceremony involves the evocation of what are for Blackwood the two most potent elements in nature, wind and fire. His friend, witnessing the rite, reflects on its significance:

He saw the human faces, symbols of spiritual domination over all
lesser orders, each one possessed of belief, intelligence and will.
Singly so feeble, together so invincible, this assemblage, unscorched
by the fire and by the wind unmoved, seemed to him impressive
beyond all possible words. And a further inkling of the truth flashed
on him as he started: that a group of humans, a crowd, combining
upon a given object with concentrated purpose, possessed of that
terrific power, certain faith, may know in themselves the energy to
move great mountains, and therefore that lesser energy to guide the
fluid forces of the elements. And a sense of cosmic exultation leaped
into his being. For a moment he knew a touch of almost frenzy.
Proud joy rose in him like a splendour of omnipotence. Humanity, it
seemed to him, here came into a grand but long neglected corner of
its kingdom as originally planned by Heaven. (72–73)

The climactic scene of this long short story is as gripping as anything in
weird fiction.

"A Descent into Egypt," perhaps Blackwood's finest single work, returns in a sense to the ideas of "The Damned." Here again, in this tale set
in hoary Egypt, the power of *belief* is emphasized: "For centuries vast
multitudes, led by their royal priests, had uttered this very form and ritual—believed it, lived it, felt it. The rising of the sun remained its climax.
Its spiritual power still clung to the great ruined symbols. The faith of a
buried civilisation had burned back into the present and into our hearts
as well" (318–319). I shall not even attempt to describe the cumulative
suspense and intensity of this tale—it must be read to be experienced.
And how Blackwood can create so powerful a climax merely by depicting three characters sitting around, talking and waiting for the dawn, is
one of the mysteries of literature. Finally we learn that the past of Egypt
has literally claimed one of the three:

I witnessed the disappearance of George Isley. There was a dreadful
magic in the picture. The pair of them, small and distant below me
in that little sandy hollow, stood out sharply defined as in a miniature. I saw their outlines neat and terrible like some ghastly inset
against the enormous scenery. Though so close to me in actual space,
they were centuries away in time. And a dim, vast shadow was

about them that was not mere shadow of the ridges. It encompassed them; it moved, crawling over the sand, obliterating them. Within it, like insects lost in amber, they became visibly imprisoned, dwindled in size, borne deep away, absorbed. (331)

I suppose Lovecraft came closest to capturing the magic of this collection of stories when he wrote: "A weird story, to be a serious aesthetic effort, must form primarily a *picture of a mood*—and such a picture certainly does not call for any clever jack-in-the-box fillip. There *are* weird stories which more or less conform to this description . . . especially in Blackwood's *Incredible Adventures*."[17]

Blackwood's religion of nature postulates a very specific place for the human race in the cosmic framework. There are occasions when Blackwood seems unable to make up his mind whether certain human creations—particularly cities—really are "natural" in the sense of belonging to nature. In "The Heath Fire" (in *Pan's Garden*) one character urges another not to "limit the word ['natural'] to mean only what we understand. There's nothing anywhere—unnatural."[18] Although here the principal connotation is that all phenomena can ultimately be explained without recourse to the "supernatural," there is a corresponding notion that all phenomena are equally "natural" parts of the cosmos. Indeed, no other inference is possible from the unity of nature. But contrast this with an extremely odd utterance in a John Silence story, "The Camp of the Dog," as the protagonists leave the city for the wilderness: "We realised for the first time that the horror of trains and houses was far behind us, the fever of men and cities, the weariness of streets and confined spaces" (262). It is not usual for someone to find houses qua houses horrific, but it is statements like this that lead one to understand that Blackwood's nature is eternally and unstably balanced between the metaphysical and the real—between nature as the unity of all things and nature as the great outdoors. Logically, the latter is subordinate to, or a limited aspect of, the former, as O'Malley in *The Centaur* (99) notes when he says that the "so-called Love of Nature" (outdoors) can allow "a more intimate knowledge with [our] great Mother" (unity of all things). But Blackwood comes dangerously close to regarding those aspects of modern civilization he doesn't like as "unnatural," as when it is said of the protagonist of *The Bright Messenger* that "He believed the industrial system lay at the root of Civilization's crumbling, and that man must return to Nature" (253). Sensing the unity of existence in an industrial system should not be logically impossible, but Blackwood does not give it much of a chance.

In any case, the tales of awe stress that the human race occupies, to be sure, a small place in the cosmos, but that place is nonetheless vital and important. The protagonist of *The Human Chord* comes to such a realization: ". . . the little secretary, for the first time in his existence, saw life as a whole, and interpreted the vision, so wondrous sweet and simple, with the analogies of sound communicated to his subliminal mind by the mighty Skale. Whatever the cause, however, the fine thing was that he saw, heard, knew. He was of value in the scheme. In future he could pipe his little lay without despair" (141). The narrator of *Julius LeVallon* draws a similar conclusion: "And thus, I suppose, it was that I realised humanity as but a little portion of the whole—important, of course, as the animalculae in a drop of water are important, yet living towards extinction only if they live apart from the surrounding ocean which divinely mothers them" (298–299). The exquisite short story "The Golden Fly" (in *Pan's Garden*) is a textbook example of this idea and broadens the conception to note that all things occupy their own irreplaceable niche in nature. A stolid businessman flees to nature to escape the little tragedies of his life, but kills a golden fly in a thoughtless moment. But he senses that he has committed a grave act:

His own small world, fed by [his] senses, was after all the merest little corner of Existence. To the whole of Existence, that included himself, a golden fly, the sun, and all the stars, he must somehow answer for his crime. It was a wanton interference with a sublime and sovereign Purpose that he now divined for the first time. He looked at the wee point of gold lying still and silent in the forest of hairs. He realised the enormity of his act. It could not have been graver had he put out the sun, or the little, insignificant flame of his own existence. (379)

I think we can connect this idea with another recurrent theme in Blackwood: the notion that those entities—human or otherwise—who are close to nature are quite literally *bigger* than their fellows. O'Malley's first sight of the "Cosmic Being" embodies this conception:

For this appearance of massive bulk, and of shoulders comely yet almost humped, was not borne out by a direct inspection. It was a mental impression. The man, though broad and well-proportioned, with heavy back and neck and uncommonly sturdy torso, was in no sense monstrous. It was upon the corner of the eye that the bulk and hugeness dawned, a false report that melted under direct vision. O'Malley took him in with attention merging in respect, searching in vain for the detail of back and limbs and neck that suggested so curiously the sense of the gigantic. (21)

We will see that some of the horror tales present the converse of this idea, where the cosmic insignificance of human beings becomes a source of acute terror.

Nature as outdoors, and its gradual possession of the responsive human being, forms the basis of some of Blackwood's most ethereal yet powerful tales of awe. "May Day Eve" (in *The Listener*) may be the first such example. It tells of a man seeking the house of a friend deep in the country; but he has unwittingly chosen May Eve for the journey and finds himself surrounded by mysterious entities in a house he thinks is that of his friend:

"He asks the way to a house when he does not even know the way to his own mind!" another voice said, sounding overhead it seemed.

"And could he recognise the signs if we told him?" came in the singing tones of a woman's voice close behind me.

And then, with a noise more like running water or wind in the wings of birds, than anything else I could liken to it, came several voices together:

"And what sort of way does he seek? The splendid way, or merely the easy?"

"Or the short way of fools!"

"But he must have *some* credentials, or he never could have got as far as this," came from another.

A laugh rang round the room at this, though what there was to laugh at I could not imagine. It sounded like wind rushing about the hills. I got the impression too that the roof was somehow open to the sky, for their laughter had such a spacious quality to it, and the air was so cool and fresh, and moving about in currents and waves. (188)

The nature metaphors are obvious but effective; the creatures, of course, are elementals. After his encounter the man finds his friend's house "with the instinct of an animal" (193)—an experience like this always expands consciousness and brings one to a more intimate, more instinctive understanding of the world.

"The Man Whom the Trees Loved" (in *Pan's Garden*) stands on the borderland between a tale of awe and a tale of horror, although I am inclined to classify it among the former: the trees surrounding the estate of David Bittacy wish to "amalgamate" (26) him, but Bittacy does not react to this with horror, even though his wife—against whom much shallow satire at her conventionality is directed—does so. In the end the trees do amalgamate him, a consummation Bittacy has sought so long. The ending can only be quoted:

> And when the winter's morning stole upon the scene at length, with a pale, washed sunshine that followed the departing tempest, the first thing she saw, as she crept to the window and looked out, was the ruined cedar lying on the lawn. Only the gaunt and crippled trunk of it remained. The single giant bough that had been left to it lay dark upon the grass, sucked endways toward the Forest by a great wind eddy. It lay there like a mass of drift-wood from a wreck, left by the ebbing of a high springtide upon the sands—remnant of some friendly, splendid vessel that once had sheltered men.
>
> And in the distance she heard the roaring of the Forest further out. Her husband's voice was in it. (98–99)

A slightly different message is conveyed by another delicate tale, "The Eccentricity of Simon Parnacute" (in *The Lost Valley*), in which the character of the title finds the confining of birds in cages so unnatural that he seeks to set as many of them free as possible. The symbolism is transparent, of course—the freeing of birds from cages represents the freeing of the human spirit from the prison of the body. The point is made clear in the end, when Parnacute dies after an illness. "The human cage was empty. Some one had opened the door" (328). Dunsany could not have done better.

The truths Blackwood is seeking are of such a sort that the role of language becomes very problematical. A late story, "The Man Who Lived Backwards" (in *Shocks*), offers the archetypal utterance of this conception: "If it is true that most people have one secret they never share, it is also true that many have an experience they never tell, not so much from fear of ridicule or being disbelieved as from utter inability to describe it intelligibly. Language has grown gradually: it describes the experience of the race; anything beyond human experience exposes the poverty of language at once. No words exist" (245). From this it can be seen that the incommunicability of extramundane experience results not—as with Lucian Taylor in Machen's *Hill of Dreams*—from a lack of desire to communicate, but from the nature of the phenomena themselves. The narrator of "A Descent into Egypt" remarks with wistful regret: "There is a language of the mind, but there is none as yet of the spirit" (266). O'Malley in *The Centaur* yearns to tell the world what he has learned and felt, and tries valiantly to do so, but fails. There are more frustrated writers in Blackwood than in any writer I can think of. O'Malley himself has set down a rambling treatise of his experiences, and *The Centaur* is a fascinating medley of the narrator's discussions with O'Malley and paraphrases from this account—it is rarely quoted directly, being evidently too incoherent. Both *The Centaur* and *Julius LeVallon* offer further motives for the inadequacy of written or spoken language. O'Malley complains: "'There are no words, there are no words,' he kept saying, shrugging his shoulders and stroking his untidy hair. 'In me, deep down, it all lies clear and plain and strong; but language cannot seize a mode of life that throve before language existed'" (107). The chronological priority of cosmic consciousness, and its gradual waning in human beings precisely in accordance with the growth of language and civilization, is a potent and often-expressed notion in Blackwood; and when the narrator of *Julius LeVallon* refers to "Action— a three-dimensional language" (229), we suddenly understand the purpose and significance of the rituals and ceremonies so many characters undertake to restore themselves to a state of unity with the cosmos.

Connected with Blackwood's frustration with language is his scorn of science—language and science being the two preeminent symbols of our increasing rationality and (by Blackwood's account) decreasing spirituality. And yet Blackwood's repudiation of science is a curiously mixed affair. His own conception of cosmic consciousness is unscientific or even antiscientific in that the sciences can do little or nothing to confirm it; and Blackwood is endlessly fond of condemning the mere accumulation of information that he, like so many nonrationalists, mistakenly assumes is the function of scientific inquiry. The passing reference in "The

Temptation of the Clay" (in *Pan's Garden*) to "those few scattered details the world calls knowledge" (458) is typical. But Blackwood feels strongly obliged to come to some sort of terms with science, to the point of appropriating the terms and even the conceptions of science to bolster his own philosophy. John Silence does this repeatedly, rationalizing weird phenomena pseudoscientifically. In "Entrance and Exit" (in *Ten Minute Stories*) both a mystical and a pseudoscientific explanation are offered for a mysterious disappearance:

> "As though Nature," the physicist went on, half to himself, "here and there concealed vacuums, gaps, holes in space (his mind was always speculative; more than speculative, some said), through which a man might drop into invisibility—a new direction, in fact, at right angles to the three known ones—'higher space,' as Bolyai, Gauss, and Hinton might call it; and what you, with your mystical turn"—looking toward the young priest—"might consider a spiritual change of condition, into a region where space and time do not exist, and where all dimensions are possible—because they are *one.*" (163)

Of course, here we are to understand the second explanation as the more "plausible," but the mere fact that Blackwood feels obliged to present the pseudoscientific account is significant. In *The Human Chord* the protagonist states: "I have often felt—wondered, rather . . . whether there might be other systems of evolution besides humanity" (52). Why such extraterrestrial or cosmic beings should be subject to any sort of evolution is never explained, but the phrase recurs repeatedly throughout Blackwood's work. Again in *The Human Chord,* in order to support the notion that "Forms, shapes, bodies are the vibrating activities of *sound made visible*" (65), we are presented with this plausible-sounding (but, in truth, grotesquely unlikely) rationalization:

> "To change the form of anything," he said in his ear, "is merely to change the arrangement of those dancing molecules, to alter their rate of vibration." His eyes, even in the obscurity of the dusk, went across the other's face like flames.
> "By means of sound?" asked the other, already beginning to feel eerie.
> The clergyman nodded his great head in acquiescence.
> "Just as the vibrations of heat-waves," he said after a pause, "can

> alter the form of a metal by melting it, so the vibrations of sound
> can alter the form of a thing by inserting themselves between those
> whirling molecules and changing their speed and arrangement—
> change the outline, that is." (161–162)

What Blackwood is getting at, I suppose, is that these sorts of conceptions are really the science of the future—they are the things orthodox
science will come to prove empirically at some later date. This is the
point of Julius LeVallon's impassioned utterance: "You think it is wild
nonsense. I tell you it is in the best sense scientific" (208).

A final element in some of Blackwood's tales of awe is love. Blackwood's treatment of human love is extremely curious; in some senses his
handling of love between human and nonhuman (as in "The Man
Whom the Trees Loved") is more "natural" for him because it is obviously something he felt himself. We have already noted that Blackwood
looked to the love of nature to counterbalance disappointments in more
ordinary affairs; so perhaps it was not to be expected that this lifelong
bachelor would portray human—much less sexual—love sympathetically. He does not, it is true, reveal the hostility to it that Lovecraft and
Bierce do, but in Blackwood love among persons is always subordinate
to—and sometimes an interference of—a higher aim. And yet in "The
Regeneration of Lord Ernie" Blackwood calmly makes this statement:
"For all energy, intellectual, emotional, or spiritual, is fundamentally
one: it is primarily sexual" (52). How Blackwood harmonized this stupendous utterance with the entirety of his work, which seeks to refute
or at least downplay such a claim, I have no idea.

What we note among Blackwood's romances is that they do not occur
so often between *two* people as between *three,* usually with the scenario
of two men in love with a single woman. One could say that Blackwood
resorts to this sort of thing simply in order to avoid even the opportunity
for any sexual involvement, but there is probably more to it than that—
Blackwood's mystical belief in the power of the number three or something of the sort. Perhaps there is an autobiographical connection. In
Julius LeVallon we find such a triangle: the narrator, LeVallon, and
LeVallon's wife. What makes this interesting is that in their past lives it
was the narrator and LeVallon's wife who were the lovers, and this creates a tension that is not resolved even at the end; for it is LeVallon's wife
who, out of love for LeVallon, foils the ritual and prevents the cosmic
forces from entering him. Similarly, in *The Human Chord,* a mesmerizing

novel that probes the mystical qualities of sound and music, the love of Miriam for the protagonist Spinrobin spoils the attempts of the Faustian Philip Skale to set up a "human chord" that would potentially reorganize all matter. Just as they are about to take their places and give utterance to the chord, Miriam flees and urges Spinrobin to do the same:

> "Oh, but the heaven we're losing . . .!" he cried once aloud, unable to contain himself. "Oh, Miriam . . . and I have proved unworthy . . . small . . .!"
>
> "Small enough to stay with me for ever and ever . . . here on the earth," she replied passionately, seizing his hand and drawing him further up the hill. Then she stopped suddenly and gathered a handful of dead leaves, moss, twigs and earth. The exquisite familiar perfume as she held it to his face pierced through him with a singular power of conviction.
>
> "We should lose *this*," she exclaimed; "there's none of this . . . in heaven! The earth, the earth, the dear, beautiful earth, with you . . . and Winky . . . is what I want!"
>
> And when he stopped her outburst with a kiss, fully understanding the profound truth she so quaintly expressed, he smelt the trees and mountains in her hair, and her fragrance was mingled there with the fragrance of that old earth on which they stood. (306–307)

Touching as this scene is, I am not convinced that it reflects Blackwood's true feelings, just as I am half convinced that we are meant to side with Skale, in spite of Blackwood's repeated attempts to depict him as a dangerous man who might conceivably destroy the cosmos as we know it.

Perhaps the most exquisite—if to me perplexing—treatment of love occurs in the delicate short novel *The Garden of Survival* (1918). Here a man loses his wife, Marion, after they have been married only a month (the marriage was not consummated, remarkably enough); but she continues to haunt him with her presence, guiding his subsequent actions. The man claims that "the dead, though they do not return, are active; and those who lived beauty in their lives are—benevolently active" (76). And yet the man confesses that he never really loved his wife but only married her out of affection and pity; he senses that she realizes this, too, as her dying words indicate: "I need your forgiveness, born of love, but love lies unawakened in you still. . . . I have failed . . . but I shall try again" (87). The man experiences a mystical experience—

whose nature frankly puzzles me, so obliquely is it related—the core of which is summed up in the phrase "That beauty which was Marion lives on, and lives for me" (138). In some strange fashion his love for his wife, now awakened, is merged with a general love of beauty. Something like this seems to be going on, although I am by no means certain of it. Nevertheless, this novel is worth reading solely for its lapidary style— perhaps the best prose in Blackwood—and for its almost painful honesty of expression. It reads somehow like a confession.

"The Woman's Ghost Story" (in *The Listener*) is worth studying here not only because it is among the earliest of Blackwood's "optimistic" weird tales but because of the startling contrast it presents to certain other works superficially similar to it. Here a woman investigates a reputed haunted house and finds, poignantly, that the ghost wants nothing more than her love and affection. She provides it, and the house is haunted no more. This conclusion is jarringly different from such tales as Robert Hichens's "How Love Came to Professor Guildea" or Oliver Onions's "The Beckoning Fair One," in which a ghost's "love" for a human being is portrayed as a loathsome and unnatural abomination. It is one of the many examples of Blackwood's ability to take a potentially horrifying conception and turn it into something wholesome and even inspiring. The most remarkable instance of this is in a scene in *Julius LeVallon* in which LeVallon tries to reanimate a corpse. What Lovecraft and Bierce would have portrayed (and did portray) with a ghoulish graveyard humor becomes in Blackwood's hands almost awe-inspiring, for what LeVallon is trying to do is explained by the narrator:

> I mean, in a word, that this experiment was a poor attempt to recon-
> struct an older ritual of spiritual significance whereby those natural
> forces, once worshipped as the gods, might combine with qualities
> similar to their own in human beings. The memory of a more august
> and effective ceremony moved all the time behind the little recon-
> struction. The beauty was derived from my dim recollection of some
> transcendent but now forgotten worship. (111)

HORROR

The very precise relationship of Blackwood's tales of horror to his tales of awe—the fact that the former are, in effect, mirror images of the latter—is suggested initially by some remarks by the priest in "The Regeneration of Lord Ernie." "There's evil thinking up there [in the mountains]," he says, "but, by heaven, it's alive; it's positive, ambitious, constructive" (21). He immediately qualifies this by saying: "Evil? . . . How can any force be evil? That's merely a question of direction" (23). The sense of horror is merely a matter of perception: the phenomena may be identical, but whether one feels horror or awe will depend almost entirely upon the degree to which one is in tune with cosmic consciousness. The narrator of "Initiation" (in *Day and Night Stories*) makes this clear: "And the fear I'd felt was nothing but the little tinkling pain of losing my ordinary two-cent self, the dread of letting go, the shrinking before the plunge."[19] In the late "Elsewhere and Otherwise" (in *Shocks*), it is bluntly stated that horror is a "negative emotion" (53).

The human being's place in the cosmos undergoes a profound change in the horror tales. It is not that nature suddenly becomes malevolent— it maintains the same indifference it did in the tales of awe, as the narrator of "The Wendigo" (in *The Lost Valley*) notes when he becomes aware of "that other aspect of the wilderness: the indifference to human life, the merciless spirit of desolation which took no note of man" (84). But this perception is now suddenly a source of terror, very much as it universally is in Lovecraft. It is no surprise that so many characters in the horror tales are stolid materialists; it is they who have principally erected this artificial barrier between the human world and nature, and it is they who are shattered—mentally if not physically—when that barrier is shown to be illusory. The cocksure Dr. Cathcart in "The Wendigo" is a pattern for many characters in these tales. Of him it is said contemptuously, "like many another materialist . . . he lied cleverly on the basis of insufficient knowledge, *because* [Blackwood's italics] the knowledge supplied seemed to his own particular intelligence inadmissible" (112). When the Wendigo manifests itself, Cathcart utters an "unintelligible cry" (121)—an apt metaphor for his stupefaction at this appearance of something he cannot comprehend or fit into his limited philosophical scheme. Similarly, in "The Willows" (in *The Listener*) the narrator feels unease at his "realisation of our utter insignificance before this unrestrained power of the elements about me" (20); and at the conclusion his Swedish comrade announces harriedly: "There are forces close here that could kill a herd of elephants in a second as easily as you or I could squash a fly. Our only chance is to keep perfectly still. Our insignificance perhaps may save us" (53).

Even the expansion of consciousness, looked upon in the tales of awe

not merely as something to be sought for but as humanity's only opportunity for salvation, becomes a thing of dread. The protagonist of "Ancient Sorceries" remarks: "I got the impression that the whole town was
after me—wanted me for something; and that if it got me I should lose
myself, or at least the Self I knew, in some unfamiliar state of consciousness" (88). It is statements like this in the horror tales that underscore
the truth of what is said in *The Bright Messenger:* "To th[e] surface consciousness alone was so-called evil possible" (15).

The Empty House and Other Ghost Stories (1906) is Blackwood's first
book, and it is almost exclusively made up of horror stories. It is an odd
collection—there are some routine ghost stories ("The Empty House,"
"A Case of Eavesdropping"); one tale with the trite "It was all a dream"
conclusion ("A Suspicious Gift"), which is interesting only for its expression of one of Blackwood's phobias, his fear of being falsely accused
of a crime; and some peculiar nonsupernatural tales ("The Strange Adventures of a Private Secretary in New York" [also heavily autobiographi-
cal], "Skeleton Lake: An Episode in Camp"). Perhaps the only notable
tale is "A Haunted Island," with its mesmerizing account of the ghosts of
some Indians haunting a house "on a small island of isolated position in
a large Canadian lake."[20] The volume seems tentative and experimental,
as if Blackwood is trying a variety of styles and tones to see what works
best. After this volume the conventional ghost story appears with extreme infrequency in his work.

The Listener and Other Stories (1907) is remarkable simply for the
assurance of technique it displays, appearing only a year after its predecessor. We have seen that it contains the first genuine examples of
Blackwood's tales of awe, in "May Day Eve" and also the delicate vignette "The Old Man of Visions"; its inclusion of "The Willows" would
alone make it noteworthy. I do not know what more I can say about this
masterwork: like the best of Dunsany it seems curiously impervious to
criticism. Perhaps Lovecraft's comment—that "The Willows" is "almost
a model of what a weird tale ought to be" and that "the *lack of anything
concrete* is the *great asset* of the story"[21]—is all the commentary one
needs. No one could analyze the subtlety of this story without paraphrasing the entire narrative; and in the end we never really learn what
the bizarre entity or entities lurking behind the tale are—save that they
are a piece of the great world of nature. As with several of Blackwood's
best tales, we are inclined to echo the words of a character in "The

Nemesis of Fire" (in *John Silence*): "It's the total cumulative effect that is so—so disquieting" (139).

John Silence: Physician Extraordinary (1908) is another experimental volume, and it is just as well that Blackwood never repeated this particular experiment. The combination of the horror tale and the detective tale is about as grotesque an idea as can be imagined, especially for Blackwood. This is not merely because Silence is a repulsive character— pompous, pedantic, supercilious, patronizing; it is because Blackwood, in having the know-it-all Silence obtrude, usually at the end, with a prosy explanation of the phenomena, introduces a fatal element of rationalism into something that should not be rationalized. Several magnificent tales are nearly ruined by this procedure: "Ancient Sorceries" should have its final chapter—in which Silence, otherwise totally supernumerary, appears as an armchair detective to give the background and a makeshift "accounting" of the events—lopped off. We do not need lectures like this:

> "I suspect in this case that Vezin was swept into the vortex of forces arising out of the intense activities of a past life, and that he lived over again a scene in which he had often played a leading part centuries before. For strong actions set up forces that are so slow to exhaust themselves, they may be said in a sense never to die. In this case they were not vital enough to render the illusion complete, so that the little man found himself caught in a very distressing confusion of the present and the past; yet he was sufficiently sensitive to recognise that it was true, and to fight against the degradation of returning, even in memory, to a former and lower state of development." (123–124)

One is reminded of the similar pontification of Lovecraft's Henry Armitage in "The Dunwich Horror." In "Secret Worship" Silence appears quite literally as a deus ex machina to rescue the protagonist from the ghostly phenomena in which he has become enmeshed. More sententiousness by Silence follows: " 'It was a concourse of the shells of violent men, spiritually-developed but evil men, seeking after death—the death of the body—to prolong their vile and unnatural existence. And had they accomplished their object you, in turn, at the death of your body, would have passed into their power and helped to swell their dreadful

purposes'" (255–256). I quote these things at such length only to emphasize the rarity of these aesthetic mistakes in Blackwood. Aside from
such blunders, only Lovecraft and Dunsany could rival Blackwood in
narrative skill; and neither, I think, could equal him in the overall unity
of their work. John Silence, incidentally, returns to no especial purpose
in another tale, "A Victim of Higher Space" (in *Day and Night Stories*).

It is worth emphasizing at this point that Blackwood's entire work,
and his horror work in particular, has relatively little to do with occultism. Very nearly the first utterance of John Silence is a horrified reaction to his colleague's casual mention of his knowledge of occultism:
"Oh, please—that dreadful word!" (1). The definitive statement on this
subject occurs in "The Insanity of Jones" (in *The Listener*):

> He felt nothing but contempt for the wave of modern psychism. He
> hardly knew the meaning of such words as "clairvoyance" and
> "clairaudience". He had never felt the least desire to join the Theo-
> sophical Society and to speculate in theories of astral-plane life, or
> elementals. He attended no meetings of the Psychical Research So-
> ciety, and knew no anxiety as to whether the "aura" was black or
> blue; nor was he conscious of the slightest wish to mix in with the
> revival of cheap occultism which proves so attractive to weak minds
> of mystical tendencies and unleashed imaginations. (198)

There is, in fact, a systematic repudiation of occultism in Blackwood:
like religion and materialism, it is at best a fragmentary view of the
world; and I think Blackwood's reaction is so vehement (unlike Lovecraft's, for whom occultism was simply a nuisance or the butt of a cynical jest) precisely because his own philosophy might conceivably be
confused with it. Blackwood is unrelenting in his attacks: the satire on
the harmless and socially fashionable Prometheans in *The Bright Messenger* is as close to viciousness as he ever comes. Lovecraft, I fear, is
entirely mistaken when he criticizes Blackwood for his "credulousness
regarding 'occultism' which causes him to employ now and then a pro-
fessional mediumistic jargon of woefully weakening effect."[22] In fact, I
cannot even determine what Lovecraft had in mind by this censure, unless he is referring to *John Silence* itself, which—in spite of Silence's
objections—occasionally lapses into something akin to occultist terminology. But I think this is a case of the materialist Lovecraft not bothering
to make a proper distinction between occultism and Blackwood's very

different brand of Eastern mysticism (something he probably found equally incomprehensible).

Satire enters the horror tales in more pronounced and pungent a fashion than in the other works, and it is profitable to study it here. With a philosophy so opposed to that of the average citizen, the possibilities for satire would appear abundant; but Blackwood is only intermittently effective as a satirist, largely because he does not seem to have been of the requisite temperament. His benign optimism, naive as it may sound to many of us, was heartfelt, so that when he takes up the satirist's cudgel he wields it a little clumsily. *The Centaur* is full of rather unexpected bursts of viciousness by O'Malley, as he condemns civilization, materialism, industrialism, and the like. The effect is analogous—in a much less jarring way—to that of Machen's *Secret Glory,* that schizophrenic novel which cannot decide whether it is a satire on modernism or a treatise on mysticism. Similarly, in "The Man Whom the Trees Loved" we have this blundering attack on a doctor: "Evidently he did not care about being invited to examine patients in this surreptitious way before a teapot on the lawn, chance of a fee most problematical. He liked to see a tongue and feel a thumping pulse; to know the pedigree and bank-account of his questioner as well. It was most unusual, in abominable taste besides" (66). This sort of thing will not place Blackwood in the company of Evelyn Waugh, but in a few shorter efforts he is more effective. "The Strange Disappearance of a Baronet" (in *Ten Minute Stories*) is a powerful little vignette in which the baronet of the title dreams that he shrinks to the size of a mouse, because that is presumably his "real" size without his title and money. At one point his valet, not seeing the tiny baronet, remarks: "My little dawg's worth two of 'im all the time, and lots of spare. Tim's *real*" (41).

"An Egyptian Hornet" (in *Day and Night Stories*) opens with a startling utterance—"All men, except those very big ones who are supermen, have something astonishingly despicable in them" (159)—something so atypical of Blackwood (although a commonplace statement in the mouths of Bierce and Lovecraft) that one has to regard it as an aberration. In any case, the tale exemplifies the motto as a man, noticing a dangerous Egyptian hornet in the bathroom of a hotel, does not have the courage to dispatch it but leaves it for the next occupant, who promptly kills it with a flick of a towel and silently confronts the other with his cowardice and duplicity.

More subtle is "The Touch of Pan" (in *Day and Night Stories*), which pointedly makes a stark contrast between the lasciviousness of modern "decadent" society and the wholesome revelling of nymphs and satyrs (symbols, of course, of spirits close to nature). The narrator reflects:

> The house-party was of that up-to-date kind prevalent in Heber's world. Husbands and wives were not asked together. There was a cynical disregard of the decent (not the stupid) conventions that savoured of abandon, perhaps of decadence. He only went himself in the hope of seeing the backward daughter once again. Her millionaire parents afflicted him, the smart folk tired him. Their peculiar affection of a special language, their strange belief that they were of importance, their treatment of the servants, their calculated self-indulgence, all jarred upon him more than usual. At bottom he heartily despised the whole vapid set. (25)

That this reaction is not the result of puritanical prudishness is made evident when the narrator gets swept away by the nymphs:

> It became a riotous glory of wild children who romped and played with an impassioned glee beneath the moon. For the world was young and they, her happy offspring, glowed with the life she poured so freely into them. All intermingled, the laughing voices rose into a foam of song that broke against the stars. The difficult mountains had been climbed and were forgotten. Good! Then, enjoy the luxuriant, fruitful valley and be glad! And glad they were, brimful with spontaneous energy, natural as birds and animals that obeyed the big, deep rhythm of a simpler age—natural as wind and innocent as sunshine. (44)

Some of Blackwood's horror tales are models for what I have proposed as the distinguishing feature of all weird tales—the refashioning of the reader's view of the world. Blackwood does not merely try to convey his nature philosophy in his work; there are other tales which articulate a philosophy that is meant to hold good only for the duration of that tale and that has no direct connection with Blackwood's general thought. "The Prayer" (in *Ten Minute Stories*) is a good example. We are told at the outset that "The air is full of loose and wandering thoughts from other minds" (22), and later a Hindu tells the protagonist: "You will *see* thoughts in colour—bad ones, lurid and streaked—good ones, sweet and shining, like a line of gold light—and if you follow, you may trace them to the mind that sent them out" (28). By golly, this is just what happens. What we do not immediately notice while reading the tale is that this "philosophy" or rationale is simply asserted rather than proved, and that it is yet another instance of a purely *aesthetic* (rather than logical or empirical) foundation for a philosophical position: it would be very pretty if thoughts really were colored like this, but aside from the evidence of this tale it does not appear as if they are. Again, in "If the Cap Fits—" (in *Ten Minute Stories*) a character announces, ". . . everything, you see, has an atmosphere charged with its own individual associations. An object can communicate an emotion it has borrowed by contact with someone living" (223); there is no reason why we should believe this utterance, but sure enough, a hat taken mistakenly from a club reveals to the wearer that its original owner drowned himself.

I am frankly at a loss to explain how exactly Blackwood produces the effects he does, either in the tales of horror or the tales of awe. As I have mentioned before, in many of the "climaxes" in Blackwood's tales nothing in particular "happens"; and it becomes even more of a quandary when we add Lovecraft's comment that Blackwood labors "under the handicap of a somewhat bald and journalistic style devoid of intrinsic magic, colour, and vitality" (SHiL 428). Without taking quite so dim a view of Blackwood as a stylist—and without agreeing with the common assertion that Blackwood is habitually prolix—I must admit that I find Blackwood's style merely serviceable: it gets the job done—no more. In only a few random works—like "The Old Man of Visions" (in *The Listener*) or "The Return" (in *Pan's Garden*)—do we find Blackwood approaching anything that could be called prose-poetry. And yet Blackwood has some strange power to create an almost unbearably intense atmosphere of clutching horror or fascination, especially toward the end of his tales—"Sand," "The Regeneration of Lord Ernie," "The Willows," "The Wendigo," "A Descent into Egypt," and "Ancient Sorceries."

Perhaps "The Wendigo" offers the simplest way to analyze the *indirection* that is at the heart of Blackwood's horrific technique. It is not merely that the monster is always kept in the background; it is that the influence of the monster draws progressively closer. The first manifestation of the Wendigo is detected by *smell* ("an odour of something that seemed unfamiliar—utterly unknown" [79]). As the tale builds, the following events occur in sequence:

1. Défago, the ultimate victim, begins sobbing in his sleep for no apparent reason (94).
2. The Wendigo calls Défago ("A sort of windy, crying voice," one character says [97]); Défago leaps out of his tent with the cry "Oh! oh! My feet of fire! My burning feet of fire!" (97) and disappears into the wilderness.
3. Simpson, his tentmate, pursuing Défago, sees massive footprints which suddenly cease in the snow.
4. Examining the tracks more closely, Simpson notices an impression of *burning* around some of them.
5. Simpson hears the horrific cry of Défago—"My burning feet of fire!" (106)—coming *from the air.*
6. In an interlude, Simpson rejoins the other members of his party, and more information on the Wendigo is supplied.
7. As the hunt for Défago resumes, the party encounters him—frightfully altered; Défago makes a loathsome joke: "I'm havin' a reg'lar hell-fire kind of a trip, I am" (123).
8. The Wendigo sweeps Défago up again and he is lost forever.

Of course, this bald schematization cannot even begin to convey the excruciatingly gradual buildup Blackwood orchestrates—and without ever requiring the actual presence of the Wendigo. And this analysis brings us no closer to assessing the effectiveness of those tales in which no "monsters" are involved at all. Somehow Blackwood can invest the recreation of appallingly archaic rituals—and this is the core of his greatest tales—with not merely a sense of hypnotic intensity but a dim suggestion that the whole fabric of the universe is involved. And now and again he can pen some imperishable utterance, as in the simple statement toward the end of "Sand" (in *Pan's Garden*): "The Desert stood on end" (329).

CHILDHOOD

It should already be clear why childhood was an especially valued state for Blackwood. Our previous citation from *The Centaur* of "the call to childhood, the true, pure, vital childhood of the Earth" suggests the answer: if precivilized societies are collectively closer to nature than modern urban society, then a child is individually in a state prior to the corruptions of civilization. This is the message expressed with ineffable delicacy and grace in a series of Blackwood's works which may perhaps not be very popular with readers of "The Willows" or "The Wendigo" and to which Lovecraft seems to be alluding when he assesses one of Blackwood's flaws as "occasional insipid whimsicality" (SHiL 428) but which contain some of his most exquisite touches. These works are pure fantasies as I have defined the term; there is, aside from a few odd touches, no metaphysical horror in them. *Jimbo* (1909)—which Lovecraft referred to, along with *The Centaur,* as "too subtle, perhaps, for definite classification as horror-tales, yet possibly more truly artistic in an absolute sense" (SHiL 429)—is the first example; although if Lovecraft had read *The Education of Uncle Paul,* his praise of *Jimbo,* really a very slight novel, might well have been muted. Of Jimbo it is said that "His brothers and sisters played up to a certain point, and then put the things aside as if they had only been assumed for the time and were not real. To him they were always real."[23] Play among children is "real" because it is instinctive and unconscious; it is the gamboling of cats or the flutter of birds. Jimbo has an accident and suffers a head injury, during which we are told that he is "wandering in the regions of unconsciousness and delirium" (53); yet Jimbo's dream—taking place in an abandoned house made terrifying to him by an irresponsible governess and involving his and the governess's attempt to escape the evil guardian of the house—has a sort of never-defined quasi reality: at one point the governess in the dream tells Jimbo his temperature, 102° (82). There is certainly charm in this novel, but it is ultimately insubstantial: Jimbo's eventual escape from the dream house no doubt symbolizes both his awaking from unconsciousness and his freedom from irrational fear, but not much more can be got out of it.

It is entirely otherwise with *The Education of Uncle Paul* (1909), one of the most remarkable and heart-rending fantasies ever written. Uncle Paul—a man who has spent the bulk of his years in the wilds of Canada but who returns to tend to his sister and her children in England after her husband's death—is a prototype of Blackwood's mute, inglorious Miltons: " 'If only'—and the strange light came back for a second to his brown eyes—'I could write, or sing, or pray—live as the saints did, or do something to—to express adequately the sense of beauty and wonder and delight that lives, like the presence of a God, in my soul!' "[24]

At the core of this novel is Nixie, the eldest of the children; not only does her name suggest fairies, but Uncle Paul sees her as the embodiment of natural forces:

The eldest and most formidable of his tormentors, standing a little in advance of the rest, was Margaret Christina, shortened by her father (who, indeed, had been responsible for all the nicknames) into Nixie. And the name fitted her like a skin, for she was the true figure of a sprite, and looked as if she had just stepped out of the water and her hair had stolen the yellow of the sand. Her eyes ran about the room like sunshine from the surface of a stream, and her movements instantly made Paul think of water gliding over pebbles or ribbed sand with easy and gentle undulations. Flashlike he saw her in a clearing of his lonely woods, a creature of the elements. (52–53)

It is she who leads her uncle to the perception of the world through the eyes of children. At the very outset it is announced that children are "closer to Reality, to God" (79)—and to nature (really all the same thing to Blackwood). Because this is so, children can quite literally see things adults cannot; and in one magical passage the children and Uncle Paul sink softly under the earth and actually see the winds as they unfurl themselves from a strange subterranean forest:

> The winds moved in their sleep, and awoke.
> In loops, folds, and spirals of indescribable grace they slowly be-gan to unwrap themselves from the tree stems with a million little delicate undulations; like thin mist trembling, and then smoothing out the ruffled surface of their thousand serpentine eddies, they slid swiftly upwards from the moss and ferns, disentangled themselves without effort from roots and stones and bark, and then, reinforced by countless thousands from the lower branches, they rose up slowly in vast coloured sheets towards the region of the tree tops. (135–36)

This is something only Dunsany could have approached; and perhaps even he could not have rivaled a later passage in which children and uncle go through the "Crack"—that place where, as Nixie tells him, "all broken things and all lost things come and are happy again . . . all things that ought to happen, but never do happen, . . . all are found [there]" (191)—and see the grotesque parts of cups, saucers, dolls, and the like, "all the kittens that had to be drowned, and the puppies that died, and the collie the Burdons' motor killed, and Birthday, our old horse that had to be shot. They're all here, and all happy" (196). This sort of thing might easily become cloying, and occasionally does—one gets tired of reading "It was very wonderful" over and over again—but on the whole Blackwood manages the tone supremely well. There is no especial "point" to this novel aside from exhibiting the closeness to nature, to reality, of childhood; and it is significant that when Nixie suddenly dies, Uncle Paul "discovered that the region through the Crack . . . became more real, more extraordinarily real, than ever before" (309). I do not feel we are meant to see in this an attempt at escaping the harshness of the real world—even though Blackwood himself, in *Episodes before Thirty*, suggests it ("That crack, at any rate, became for me . . . a means of escape from unkind reality into a state of inner bliss and wonder 'where everything came true'" [140–141]); an earlier passage hints at the real meaning: "It was characteristic of him that he sought instinctively, and without cant, for the Reality that lay behind his pain; and Reality—though seas of grief may first be plunged through to find it—is always Joy. For love is joy, and joy is strength, and both are aspects of the great central Reality of the life of the soul" (304). I confess that my one disappointment with this novel is its conclusion, where Uncle Paul sees his life's work as helping his cousin Joan manage a center for homeless children. Laudable and socially acceptable as this is, it seems a flat and prosy way of ending so wistful a novel; and it almost militates against the drift of the whole work and, indeed, of Blackwood's thought. Is it really more valuable to help these "real" children than to set down his adventures in fairy tales, as Paul has begun to do? Has not Blackwood argued throughout his work that surface reality is illusory and that the life of the spirit alone is real?

If Blackwood had written no novels of childhood but *The Education of Uncle Paul*, he would perhaps not have gained his reputation for fatuous whimsicality; but unfortunately he went on to write such things as *A Prisoner in Fairyland* (1913), *The Extra Day* (1915), *The Promise of Air* (1918), *Sambo and Snitch* (1927), and *The Fruit Stoners* (1934), none of which adds anything to *Uncle Paul*. These novels are rather sad, but not in a way Blackwood intended: all the wholesome and well-adjusted children running through them are so obviously the sons and daughters Blackwood never had. In a curious passage in *Uncle Paul* (245) it is said that Paul collected the stories he had written for his nephews and nieces in a book called the *Aventures* [*sic*] *of a Prisoner in Fairyland*; and although this work is subtitled "The Book That 'Uncle Paul' Wrote," it does not seem really to be what Uncle Paul was writing. It hardly matters, for *A Prisoner in Fairyland*—Blackwood's longest novel—is an interminable and contentless exercise in benign cheerfulness. There is one passage that is worth considering: "'A friend of mine . . . once wrote a volume of ghost stories that, of course, were meant to thrill. His subsequent book, with no such intention, was judged by the object of the first—as a failure. It must make the flesh creep. Everything he wrote must make the flesh creep. One of the papers, the best—a real thunderer, in fact—said "Once or twice the desired thrill comes off, but never, alas quite comes off"'" (463). I wonder whether Blackwood was thinking of himself.

Dudley and Gilderoy (1929) may be examined from this perspective. It is a novel about a parrot and a cat who escape from their home and undertake an adventure to London before being brought home by the family butler. It is all perfectly innocuous, but with one moderately interesting feature. Blackwood goes out of his way to explain that the words he puts into the mouths of these animals are not uttered in the manner of human speech:

> Now, communication between them, be it explained once for all, was so rapid, comprehensive, adequate, that it easily surpassed the capacity of ordinary language. Human beings, having gradually invented a series of not always musical sounds to convey what they know possess none, of course, to convey what they do *not* know. For the experiences of non-humans they have no words. Hence, purring and a parrot's gurglings, since they refer to another order of experience, remain, for humans, indecipherable. Into these and other gorgeous sounds, however, these creatures project their own wisdom, their inanities, their thoughts and feelings, with consummate ease. They understand one another. Gesture and attitude, the shaking of a feather, the twitching of tail or whiskers, the cock of head or angle of neck, the flick of an ear, even the movement of agile claws and toes—these largely took the place of clumsy words. (29–30)

This is of note because of Blackwood's evident concern that this work not be interpreted allegorically, as a fairy tale: we remain just on this side of naturalism, and there is nothing in this novel—even the highly amusing incident in which Dudley commandeers two train tickets from a ticket agent by imitating the voice of his master—that could not have actually happened.

THE LATE WORK

An interesting tendency in some of Blackwood's later work is a sudden political consciousness brought on by World War I. In a sense it is strange that the work of Blackwood—who spent years as a daily reporter for New York newspapers—should be, up to 1918, so profoundly apolitical and that it should take a cataclysm like the world war to jolt him out of his carefree dreams of individual salvation and lead him to ponder the rescue of the entire race; but it is only when we read the following early in *The Bright Messenger* (1921) that we are made aware of wider horizons: "The war, above all the Peace, shook his [Edward Fillery's] optimism. If it did not wholly shatter his belief in human progress, it proved such progress to be so slow that his Utopia faded into remotest distance, and his dream of perfectibility became the faintest star in his hitherto bright sky of hope" (17).

The pattern is really begun in the insubstantial novel *The Promise of Air,* in which we are given much simple-minded sociology as to why both the political and the artistic worlds are in such turmoil: evidently all artists and intellectuals are clumsily searching for the next stage of human development. "The next stage of the world is air,"[25] Joseph Wimble utters, by which he means the development of the bird's-eye view—seeing things whole. How the music of Scriabin (mentioned by name in the novel) or the imagism of Amy Lowell can be said to be fumbling toward such a state is never adequately explained. It is only in *The Bright Messenger* that the notion is treated with anything approaching seriousness: "'The recent upheaval has been more than an intertribal war. It was a planetary event. It has shaken our nature fundamentally, radically. The human mind has been shocked, broken, dislocated'" (166). This sets the stage for the emergence of some new form of life that will help to rejuvenate human beings and perhaps lead the whole species back to the path of nature. The war may have destroyed the scientist Edward Fillery's optimism, but Blackwood could not remain a pessimist for long. Enter Julian LeVallon, a strange being raised in isolation in the Jura Mountains and brought to London by Fillery. His name, of course, is no accident; and we learn obliquely that he is the product of the mystical birth recorded at the end of *Julius LeVallon*. Will he be the means to revive the race? If not he, then no one, for we are awfully close to the edge: " [The planet] was exhausted, dying. Unless new help, powers from a new, an inexhaustible source came quickly . . ." (227). Blackwood trails off ominously. But when is this regeneration to occur? Fillery had already announced that his Utopia had "faded to the remotest distance," and later he hammers home the same conclusion: "In a hundred thousand years perhaps! Perhaps in a million!" (219). Certainly not in 1921: the novel peters out, LeVallon not having done much save perturb a few society ladies with his unearthly presence. Of course, he unites at the end with a woman who thinks and feels as he does, but the promise of their joint rescue of the world is rather dim.

Here too there is a poignancy that Blackwood did not wholly intend: it is the poignancy of an author facing the appalling refutation of his entire view of the world. The cheerfulness Blackwood tries to retain throughout this work starts more and more to appear like the grinning of a skeleton. Blackwood does not seem to understand the paradox involved in postulating humanity's rescue by this "new help": if it is something from outside—and Blackwood repeatedly claims it must be, underscoring it by his nickname for the unearthly facet of LeVallon, "N. H." (for nonhuman)—that will save human beings, how can they ever take credit for their salvation? Blackwood also calmly makes reference at the end to "Those vast Intelligences who note the fall of even a feather, watching and guarding the Race so closely that they may be said in human terms to love it" (267). Well, their guardianship of the race was evidently not very keen if they allowed the Great War to occur. Who these intelligences are is never made clear, and I am not sure they are anything but another instance of Blackwood whistling in the dark. In spite of this feebly optimistic tone, it is clear that Blackwood does not feel we can do much for ourselves. It is cold comfort if the process is going to take a million years. Indeed, if we are to believe N. H.'s boyhood prophecy, we shall get worse before we shall get better: "Entire race slips back into chaos of primitive life again. Entire Western Civilization crumbles. Modern inventions and knowledge vanish. Nature spirits reappear" (25). I find that last sentence inexpressibly pathetic: Blackwood never gives up.

But I cannot leave *The Bright Messenger* without singling out one feature that relates it in an entirely different way to the world of Blackwood's contemporaries. In one remarkable chapter we are presented with LeVallon's own thoughts—interpreted, admittedly, by Fillery—as he takes stock of the bustling London civilization he finds himself in. It is as close to stream-of-consciousness as Blackwood ever let himself come, and Blackwood does indeed convey LeVallon's unearthliness very chillingly. But is he really unearthly? Or is it not merely that he is "natural"—speaking and acting without the labored disingenuousness civilized society compels? It is understandable that LeVallon chafes at his very presence in a place like London:

> One difficulty is that my being here confuses me. Here I am already caught, confined and straitened. I am within certain limits. I can only move in three ways, three measurements, three dimensions. The space I am in here allows only little rhythms; they are coarse and slow and heavy, and beat against confining walls as it were, are thrown back, cross and recross each other, so that while they themselves grow less, their confusion grows greater. The forms and outlines I can build with them are poor and clumsy and insignificant. Spirals I cannot make. Then I forget. (87)

Speech seems to him like "monotonous tinkling"; he can read the feelings of the people around him instantly by the expressions on their faces—fear, cowardice, love, hate, lust. Blackwood cannot resist setting up, in an almost sadistic fashion, the spectacular collapse of Lady Gleeson, a lustful socialite who tries to seduce LeVallon and who after her arduous efforts receives this letter from him:

> Be sure that you are always under the protection of the gods even if you do not know them. They are impersonal. They come to you through passion but not through that love of the naked body which is lust. I can work with passion because it is creative, but not with lust, for it is destructive only. Your suffering is the youth and ignorance of the young uncreative animal. I can strive with young animals and can help them. But I cannot work with them. I beg you, listen. I love in you the fire, though it is faint and piti-ful. (266)

This LeVallon is also one of Blackwood's great characters, even though he is caught in a novel that seems not to know where it is going and, like much of the later Blackwood, suffers seriously from meandering prolixity.

Two stories in *The Wolves of God* (1921) are of relevance in this connection. "'Vengeance Is Mine'" deals with a man who is "slow . . . at first to credit the German atrocities" but who now has "a burning desire . . . that the perpetrators be fitly punished."[26] He has been shaken by the war: "Was progress, his pet ideal and cherished faith, after all a mockery? Had human nature not advanced?" (280). The man gradually becomes enmeshed in a hideous ritual that will culminate in a human sacrifice—the "vengeance" that the horrors of war require. Will the man yield to this primitive and savage act? He ponders its significance: "It was the old, old battle, waged eternally in every human heart, in every tribe, in every race, in every period, the essential principle indeed, behind the great world-war. . . . It was the battle between might and right, between love and hate, forgiveness and vengeance, Christ and the Devil" (317). Phrased in this way, there can hardly be any doubt of the result. But, in an exquisite touch in this obsessively gripping tale, very similar in its way to the conclusion of "The Regeneration of Lord Ernie," the singing of a bird causes the man to disrupt the ceremony and save the hapless victim from death. Later he "sat dreaming of his sure belief that humanity had advanced" (319–320). Well, *he* at any rate has advanced, and hence (Blackwood is presumably implying) the race. This is another tale in which Blackwood is on the edge of despair but pulls back at the last instant. It is quite otherwise in what is—for Blackwood—the strangest tale in his entire corpus, "The Man Who Found Out." This story was first published in 1912, so it cannot be used as a sign of Blackwood's postwar sentiments, but it is a remarkably atypical tale. Here we are concerned with the archaeologist Mark Ebor, who "was that unique combination hardly ever met with in actual life, a man of science and a mystic" (192). This description is important because it signifies that Ebor is not one of the undeveloped consciousnesses of the horror tales but a model in the manner of Julius LeVallon. He pontificates: "Yet what is more likely . . . than that there should have been given to man in the first ages of the world some record of the purpose and problem that had been set him to solve?" (194). Let us ignore the slipshod attempt to appropriate the rationalist's argument from probability; the conclusion outweighs this sophistical ploy. Ebor goes to the Middle East and comes back, claiming to have found the "Tablets of the Gods" wherein the human being's purpose is set down, but the truth is so horrible that he loses the will to live and wastes away. What could that truth have been? We are not told, but the inference is that humanity in fact has no purpose or aim in the cosmic scheme of things: what else could plunge a Blackwood character into such a depth of despondency? This grim little tale is much more likely to have come from a Bierce or a Lovecraft; and although Blackwood leaves himself a loophole even here by subtitling it "A Nightmare" (hence something that will dissipate into nothingness when one wakes up), it is the closest he ever came to throwing in the towel for humanity.

It appears, however, that as the memories of the war retreated into the distance, Blackwood's native optimism returned in full force, although by this time his creative powers were ebbing. Certainly there is no sign in such frivolities as *Dudley and Gilderoy* or *The Fruit Stoners* of any harrowing troubles over humanity's collective or individual soul. In the latter novel in particular Blackwood has babbled himself out into harmless senility. Blackwood lived through World War II, but his active writing career was virtually over before that conflict began: although the two stories in *The Doll and One Other* (1946) were written during the war, they do not so much as allude to it. I do not know if there is any evidence—in private correspondence, for example—of Blackwood's response to Hitler; it might be of interest. As it is, only Dunsany, of the authors in this volume, did any actual writing about World War II, although even he seemed too stunned by it to write about it effectively.

Some later tales are of interest in another respect, in that they utilize modern advances in astrophysics as the basis for Blackwood's continuing reflections on the expansion of consciousness. Einstein is mentioned in several tales in *Tongues of Fire* (1924) and *Shocks* (1935), once significantly called "the magician thinker."[27] "The Pikestaffe Case" (in *Tongues of Fire*) involves a man who uses higher mathematics to venture into another dimension; as he writes in his notes, " 'It amounts, of course, to a new direction; a direction at right angles to all we know, a new direction in oneself, a new direction—in living. But it can, perhaps, be translated into mathematical terms by the intellect. This, however, only a simile at best. Cannot be experienced that way. Actual experience possible only to *changed* consciousness.' "[28] "Elsewhere and Otherwise" (in *Shocks*) is one of Blackwood's great later tales, and at the very outset we are given to see how Blackwood has put the horrors of World War I behind him. Although the tale is set at the commencement of the war—indeed, on the very day England declares war—the narrator remarks that "this

world's affairs, even a war with Germany, seemed somehow of less account than what we had afoot" (36)—that being, of course, how a man
with a "changed consciousness . . . can function in different time" (38).
Specifically, Sydney Mantravers, at the age of sixty, looks only forty and
seems to have spent those twenty years in some different state or realm.
Mantravers then disappears for four years—exactly the period of the
war—and then returns; but in his return he feels—like Uncle Paul and
also perhaps like the character in Lovecraft's "Polaris"—that he has left
the "real" world and entered some dream world that is, moreover, ridiculously small and inhibiting. In one potent passage Mantravers expresses his sense of confinement as he rides in a taxi with his cousin, the
narrator:

> The taxi, I remember, drove dangerously fast, so that, as in the
> cinema stunt-pictures, crashes which seemed unavoidable were just
> avoided by a hair's breadth and the stream of vehicles rushed past us
> in a dreadful sequence. I was clutching for safety at everything within
> reach, when my cousin spoke. "Why doesn't the man start?" he
> asked impatiently. "He's got three directions to choose from, hasn't
> he, and the house can't come to us—down here, at any rate, it can't.
> I'm there already anyhow, if he only knew it." He gave a queer little
> gulp of laughter, turning to me with a look that set my shivers going
> again. "I knew it, knew it perfectly, you see, before I came back into
> this, but I'm losing it now, it's going again." His piercing, fiery eyes
> were full upon me; he drew a profound sigh of weariness, of disgust,
> of pity. "The cage is about me, the stupid, futile cage. It's time that
> does it, it's your childish linear time, time in a single line. In such a
> limited state it's not even being awake, just trivial dreaming, almost
> death—" and the voice died off in a whisper. He closed his eyes,
> leaning back into his corner. (60)

The cage motif is of importance in Blackwood—it is what Simon Parnacute, Julian LeVallon, and so many other of Blackwood's "cosmic"
beings sense when in the everyday world. Wherever Mantravers has
been, he has been in a realm where causation is seen to be something
more than an eternal sequence of phenomena, as the scientist Vronski
remarks: "The *why* of things, rather than the futile *how* that science
gabbles about. That's the first result of a changed, a different consciousness" (67–68). It is reality that Mantravers has experienced.

This tale, as well as "The Man Who Lived Backwards," in which a man again uses the concept of serial time to encounter a past version of himself, is of some significance in showing that Blackwood, in spite of his hostility to science and rationalism, can use modern science as a sort of intellectual backbone to his conceptions, much as Lovecraft did in "The Shunned House" and "The Dreams in the Witch House." It is something that Machen, the implacable foe of anything connected with the twentieth century, could never have done. It is of secondary importance that Blackwood may—as Lovecraft was constantly warning his associates against—have found in the discoveries of Einstein, Planck, and Heisenberg a scientific rationale for mysticism; if he did so he was not alone, and he certainly must have heard in these advances the death knell of nineteenth-century positivism.

The complete ignorance of Blackwood in the critical community is a fact that stupefies me the more I think about it. It is not, as with Dunsany, that the bulk of the material written about him is bad; it is that there is simply nothing written about him at all. Mike Ashley's very recent bio-bibliography is certainly a landmark, but it only lays the foundations for critical work. In both academic and popular criticism Blackwood is a cipher. I do not really know why this should be so; perhaps the sheer bulk of his literary work—and, aside from random short stories such as "The Willows" and "The Wendigo," the absence of any work likely to appeal to a devoted audience, as with Machen's *Hill of Dreams* or Dunsany's *Gods of Pegāna*—has daunted readers and critics alike. All this is very unfortunate, for it is now clear to me that Blackwood, Dunsany, and Lovecraft are the three principal weird writers of their time, collectively responsible for much of the best that has followed. *Incredible Adventures* may be the premier weird collection of this or any other century.

It is also worth emphasizing that Blackwood's most characteristic work is not horrific. I am not sure that even "The Willows" is truly a *horror* story, for there is as much awe as horror in it. It is interesting that Blackwood never wrote a horror novel—all his novels are either of awe (*The Human Chord, The Centaur, The Bright Messenger*) or of childhood (*Jimbo, The Education of Uncle Paul*) or something in between (*The Garden of Survival*). Perhaps Blackwood conceded the difficulty of maintaining the requisite intensity over novel length—something the modern horror novel has not solved or, in many cases, even come to terms with. In any case, Blackwood is perhaps a unique figure in stressing what might (a little fatuously) be called the *optimistic weird tale:* his cosmicism, in particular, lacks the chilling remoteness of Dunsany or the contracting horror of Lovecraft, and does so precisely because Blackwood typically sees the human being as an intimate part of the cosmos and not some minute excrescence upon it. Blackwood's psychological acuteness—parts of *The Wave* read startlingly like Henry James—should win him readers with the dominance of this branch of weird fiction in the work of Walter de la Mare, Shirley Jackson, Ramsey Campbell, and others. Blackwood's long-windedness is greatly exaggerated by critics: he requires this length not merely to build to a gradual cumulative climax (something he does better than anyone but Lovecraft) but to clarify the philosophical foundations of his work. His work is, I have maintained, more unified than Lovecraft's or Dunsany's: every story or novel contributes in some fashion to the perception of cosmic consciousness that is his aim. It is possible to maintain, too, that his work is more consistently meritorious than any weird writer's except Dunsany's: for one who wrote perhaps ten times as much fiction as Lovecraft, a certain percentage must inevitably fall flat; but a surprising residue is substantial, even among the later work. More so even than Dunsany, Blackwood is a writer waiting to be discovered. He may not belong to any recognizable school; his work may not follow the fashions of his own day or ours; he may never recruit a band of passionately devoted admirers. But his achievement is as great as any weird writer's, and we ought all to take cognizance of the fact.

4.

M. R. JAMES
The Limitations of the Ghost Story

*M*ontague Rhodes James was born on August 1, 1862, in Good-nestone, Suffolk, the son of an Anglican priest. He showed precocious antiquarian interests while at Temple Grove preparatory school at Eton, immersing himself in the study of medieval manuscripts and biblical apocrypha. He entered King's College, Cambridge, in 1882, and after graduating stayed on to become a fellow in 1887. In his distinguished career he rose to be provost of King's from 1905 to 1918 and vice-chancellor of the university from 1913 to 1915, but took greater pride in his function as director of the Fitzwilliam Museum from 1893 to 1908 and in his service on the University Press and Library syndicates. Although he never married, he played a leading role in Cambridge literary and convivial societies, and on vacations enjoyed cycling tours with friends in Britain and France.

In 1918 James was appointed provost of Eton and in later years served on several royal commissions and was appointed a trustee of the British Museum. He was made a commander of the Order of Leopold for his aid to Belgian refugees in World War I and received the Order of Merit in 1930.

James's scholarly work gained him great respect, especially in the fields of codicology, Christian art, and biblical research. He catalogued many manuscript collections, including those of the Fitzwilliam Museum, most of the Cambridge colleges, and Canterbury, and was well known particularly for his edition of *The Apocryphal New Testament* (1924). He reached a wider audience as a master of the ghost story in the volumes *Ghost-Stories of an Antiquary* (1904), *More Ghost Stories of an Antiquary* (1911), *A Thin Ghost* (1919), and *A Warning to the Curious* (1925). His *Collected Ghost Stories* appeared in 1931, and his memoirs, *Eton and King's,* in 1926. James continued as provost of Eton until his death on June 12, 1936.

M. R. James is the subject of universal respect: Lovecraft, Clark Ashton Smith, and other *fantaisistes* have paid homage to him; modern critics like Julia Briggs, Jack Sullivan, and others have discussed his work almost reverently—and acutely; James has inspired a miniature school of disciples, among them A. N. L. Munby, E. G. Swain, and perhaps Russell Kirk. The provost of Eton College, a recognized scholar on medieval manuscripts, was of such a genial temperament as to have inspired hallowed treatment in the accounts of such of his friends and associates as Stephen Gaselee and Shane Leslie. It seems difficult to say anything bad about James: he perfected the ghost story; his polished, understated, erudite style is as different as possible from either the perfumed prose-poetry of Dunsany or the dense texture of Machen or Lovecraft. Only James could successfully set a ghost story almost entirely in a library ("The Tractate Middoth"); only he would open a story with a stunning and flawless imitation of a late medieval Latin treatise, a 150-word passage in Latin followed by the narrator's tiredly casual remark, "I suppose I shall have to translate this" ("The Treasure of Abbot Thomas").[1] If I take a dimmer view of James's work than many of his devotees, it is because I am frustrated that James knowingly limited his talents to a very restricted field and was profoundly out of sympathy with related branches of the weird tale. Lovecraft could enjoy both James and Dunsany, although he realized that they were at "opposite pole[s] of genius" (SHiL 431); for James, his contemporaries Machen, Blackwood, and Lovecraft (whom he may have read) all wrote in vain, while he pays only the most frigid respect to Poe.

My first concern with James is to examine the nature of his "ghost." Curiously, it seems remarkably material, and there are actually relatively few tales in which it retains the nebulosity of the traditional specter. Many commentators have noted the *hairiness* of the James ghost; perhaps Lovecraft expressed it best when he said that "the average James ghost is lean, dwarfish, and hairy—a sluggish, hellish night-abomination midway betwixt beast and man—and usually *touched* before it is *seen*" (SHiL 432–433). This is true enough, and the prototype is the figure in "Canon Alberic's Scrap-Book":

At first you saw only a mass of coarse, matted black hair; presently it was seen that this covered a body of fearful thinness, almost a skeleton, but with the muscles standing out like wires. The hands were of a dusky pallor, covered, like the body, with long, coarse hairs, and hideously taloned. The eyes, touched in with a burning yellow, had intensely black pupils, and were fixed upon the throned King with a look of beast-like hate. Imagine one of the awful bird-catching spiders of South America translated into human form, and endowed with intelligence just less than human, and you will have some faint conception of the terror inspired by this appalling effigy. (11–12)

What such a ghost symbolizes for James—the scholar and academi-cian—is the routing of intelligence. The Jamesian ghost embodies all those traits of primitive human beings that are most frightening to the civilized and rational: not merely ignorance but aggressively violent ig-norance. The effect is achieved in remarkably subtle ways: hairiness is frequently used as a symbol for barbarity, but note the simple descrip-tion of a figure "crawling on all fours" (43) in the peculiar mezzotint in "The Mezzotint"[2] or the dog motif that crops up in "The Residence at Whitminster," "The Diary of Mr. Poynter," and "An Episode of Cathe-dral History." The dog, too, one supposes, is representative of primitive savagery.

The taint of primitivism affects even the human characters in the tale. Of the evil scholar in "Lost Hearts" it is said that he wished to reenact "certain processes, which to us moderns have something of a barbaric complexion" (33); needless to say, the victims of the "processes" return to exact ghostly revenge. Analogously, the central character in "The Treasure of Abbot Thomas" "screams like a beast" (176) when the monster embraces him in the well. The rational mind cannot endure contact with the supernormal and itself descends to barbarism. There is, in fact, only a single story—"Casting the Runes"—in which a character even attempts (here successfully) to counteract the effects of the super-natural agency; in all other instances the Jamesian figure is singularly passive and resigned.

The "eccentric composition" of some Jamesian ghosts is remarked on by Lovecraft (SHiL 433); he in particular found effective the "face *of crumpled linen*" (148), italicized in pseudo-Lovecraftian fashion, in "'Oh, Whistle, and I'll Come to You, My Lad.'" I wonder, however, whether Lovecraft or others have perceived that this tale—or, rather, the ghost at the center of it—may actually be a *parody* of the old-time ghost

story with its sheeted figure mistily floating down some centuried corridor. Here the figure materializes itself in a prosaic seaside inn where a
professor is vacationing; but I think we are to regard the jarring juxtaposition of unconventional setting and pseudoconventional ghost—
here literally manifesting itself in a bedsheet—as a bit of fun on James's
part. This is by no means to deny the unquestioned power and even
originality of the conception, for the ghost is of course not the bedsheet
itself but some invisible monster who can be seen only when embodied
behind some material substance like a bedsheet.

The loathsome creature in "The Treasure of Abbot Thomas" is initially
described as "some rounded light-coloured objects . . . which might be
bags" (175)—a hideously colloquial description. But later the monster,
more clearly seen, is said to be a "horrid, grotesque shape—perhaps
more like a toad than anything else" (179). Similarly, in "The Haunted
Dolls' House" we encounter "a frog—the size of a man" (484). I can
trace no especial symbolism behind this amphibian motif, save in its re-
pulsiveness. The Abbot Thomas ghost not merely appears, however, but
"*put its arms around my neck*" (175—those charming italics again)—a
grotesque parody of affection. It is a theme similar to that of Robert
Hichens's famous story "How Love Came to Professor Guildea" (1900),
where, I think, it is handled even better.

James reveals a virtual obsession with the mechanics of narrating the
ghost story. In many of his tales the narrator or central figure (very often
they are not the same) pieces together various documents and presents
them in artfully edited form. This method serves at least two purposes.
First, it emphasizes the fundamental rationality of the character, as it
does in Machen's "Novel of the Black Seal" and Lovecraft's "Call of
Cthulhu," otherwise tales as profoundly different from James's as can be
imagined; second, it distances the narrative, frequently by several stages.
This idea of distancing was very important to James. In his introduction
to *Ghosts and Marvels* he notes: "For the ghost story a slight haze of distance is desirable."[3] Here he refers, of course, to chronological distance,
and this accounts for another curious phenomenon in James: the setting
of many of his stories in the eighteenth or early nineteenth century.
James's method appears to require a modern setting, since he remarks in
an essay on the need for the "setting and personages [to be] those of the
writer's own day."[4] This statement appears to contradict the "haze of
distance" idea, but only superficially: for a scholar like James, accus-

tomed to dealing with the ancient and medieval world, the eighteenth or
nineteenth century would have appeared—as they did to a similar antiquarian, Lovecraft—a "fairly recent yesterday."[5] Hence "Two Doctors"
is set in 1718; "The Residence at Whitminster" begins in 1730, then advances another century or so; "Lost Hearts" is set in 1811–1812; "A
School Story" is set around 1870.

There is, however, a problem with even this pseudoremoteness. The
specificity of dates used by James compels the reader to envision a precise historical period, and the sense of familiarity with the characters
and settings is, if not destroyed, at least muted. James warns against this
by saying: "It is almost inevitable that the reader of an antique story
should fall into the position of the mere spectator."[6] This certainly ar-
gues a very elastic conception of history—and, perhaps, more elastic a
one than James could rightfully assume in his readers. He would have
been better off, I think, being a little vaguer in the dating of events. In
only one tale, the very late "Rats," does he skillfully solve the problem:
"I cannot put a date to the story, but I was young when I heard it, and
the teller was old" (610). In an entirely different way, "Martin's Close" is
a tour de force in its attempt to reproduce the actual diction of a late
seventeenth-century court case, presided over by (as we all know from
Macaulay) the redoubtable Judge Jeffreys. This is merely an extension of
a principle running through James's work: the inclusion of pseudodocu-
ments in his tales. We have already noted the lengthy Latin passage that
opens "The Treasure of Abbot Thomas," but we can also marvel at the
perfect replication of the platitudinous eighteenth-century obituary
(reputedly from *The Gentleman's Magazine*) in "The Stalls of Barchester
Cathedral" or the paraphrasing of various eighteenth-century documents in what might be James's most powerful story, "The Ash-Tree."

This finally brings us back to the role of the narrator or central figure,
who acts as "editor" of this documentary material. The degree to which
the narrator wishes to dissociate himself from the actual events is frequently remarkable: in "Count Magnus" the narrator paraphrases the
victim Wraxall's paraphrase of documents he has discovered. Perhaps
the greatest indirection occurs in "A Warning to the Curious," in which
at one point we have the principal (unnamed) narrator paraphrasing the
account of a subsidiary (unnamed) narrator who meets a traveler, Pax-
ton, who has heard a curious legend from a rector—and the rector himself has heard this legend from the "old people" (567) of the commu-

nity. This is certainly narrative distance with a vengeance! In fact, the principal narrator never returns after he has yielded to the subsidiary narrator; just as well, one supposes, as by the end we have forgotten about his existence.

James can carry this indirection too far. In "The Rose Garden" the tale is so obliquely told that it is difficult to ascertain what exactly happened; in "The Residence at Whitminster" the many layers of narration ill conceal the tale's pointlessness and prolixity. James's narrator can also be quite disingenuous: in "The Stalls of Barchester Cathedral" he remarks at one point, "I digress to put in a document which, *rightly or wrongly* [my italics], I believe to have a bearing on the thread of the story" (282). This false ignorance fools no one.

James also has a peculiar inclination to obtrude himself in the narrative at odd moments. "Canon Alberic's Scrap-Book" begins with a third-person narration about the character Dennistoun, but all of a sudden we encounter this passage: "'Once,' Dennistoun said to me, 'I could have sworn I heard a thin metallic voice laughing high up in the tower. . . .'" It is significant that this is the first intimation of the supernatural in the story, but the very abrupt distancing is clumsy. In "The Mezzotint" we have this strange interruption: "He lighted the candles, for it was now dark, made the tea, and supplied the friend with whom he had been playing golf (for I believe the authorities of the University I write of indulge in that pursuit by way of relaxation); . . ." (40). This will, no doubt, be cited by James's supporters as an example of his dry wit; dry it certainly is.

In later stories James is fond of placing the central narrative—or, at least, the portion of the narrative that definitely involves the supernatural—into the mouth of a half-educated person who tells the tale in a roundabout and colloquial fashion. Two goals are met by this method: narrative distance is achieved, and the corrupting influence of the ghostly phenomena on those closest to them is suggested. Even James, however, never—thankfully—carried this practice to the grotesque lengths that we find in the subnarrative of Zadok Allen in Lovecraft's "The Shadow over Innsmouth."

James frequently goes out of his way to avoid any suggestions of sensationalism as his climax approaches. The italics to which he succumbed in "'Oh, Whistle'" and "The Treasure of Abbot Thomas" are rare exceptions; in other stories the purported climax is handled with absolutely no fanfare. This is doubly peculiar in that James speaks of the need of a "nicely managed crescendo"[7] at the end of a tale. To be quite honest, I find no such crescendos in James; in fact, often the reverse is—quite consciously—the case. The "climax" of "The Stalls of Barchester Cathedral," the death of Archdeacon Haynes, is conveyed by a euphemistic eighteenth-century obituary; similar is the death of Eldred in "The Tractate Middoth." The curious result of this and other of James's elaborately self-conscious narrative methods is to draw attention away from the events and to focus it on the narration itself. There may also be a partial contradiction of James's principles of ghost-story writing. In speaking (presumably with Algernon Blackwood in mind) derisively of the intrusion of "psychical" theory, James writes: "I feel that the technical terms of 'occultism,' if they are not very carefully handled, tend to put the mere ghost story . . . upon a quasi-scientific plane, and to call into play faculties quite other than the imaginative."[8] While James does not indulge in occultism, this "quasi-scientific" atmosphere is exactly what we find in much of his work. I am not referring to all the pseudoscholarship (imagined medieval texts, bogus footnotes, and the like) that abounds in his writing; rather, it is more like what Lovecraft experienced when reading some of H. G. Wells's stories: "I *can't* derive a really *supernatural* thrill from matter which keeps my *mental* wheels turning so briskly; and yet when I think of some of his things *in retrospect,* supplying my own filter of imaginative colour, I am reduced to doubt again."[9] Analogously, in James the reader must frequently expend so much energy simply following the obliquely narrated plot that there is no room for the "imaginative" faculty to come into play. It is as if writing a ghost story has become an intellectual game for James.

James has profounder limitations than this, and the principal one is simply that all his tales resolve, morally, into a naive tit-for-tat vengeance motif. James is certainly right to emphasize the "malevolent or odious"[10] nature of the ghost; but in almost every one of his stories the malevolence is directed at someone who has committed some obvious moral outrage. This is a limitation, evidently, of the traditional ghost story in general and gives to James's tales a curious repetitiveness and one-dimensionality; it is simply not possible to ring many—nay, any— changes upon this one theme. In some stories, of course, we are faced with apparently hapless characters who are destroyed by what seems to be the random vindictiveness of the ghost; but what conclusion we are to draw from this is not clear. Jack Sullivan writes: "The characters are antiquaries, not merely because the past enthralls them, but because the

present is a near vacuum. They surround themselves with rarefied paraphernalia from the past—engravings, rare books, altars, tombs, coins,
and even such things as dolls' houses and ancient whistles—seemingly
because they cannot connect with anything in the present."[11] This sounds
very pretty, but there is no textual evidence to support it. James's anti-
quarians are either professionals or amateurs: they pursue the past
merely because it is their job or because it amuses them; the metaphysical
angst implied in what Sullivan calls the "'Waste Land' ambiance" of the
stories is just not there. Occasionally we have dim indications that these
characters have brought doom upon themselves: there is, in "Canon Alberic's Scrap-Book," a hint of Dennistoun's irreligiousness when he
scoffs at wearing a crucifix to protect himself ("Well, really, Dennistoun
hadn't much use for these things" [13]), while, in "'Oh Whistle,'" Par-
kins's radical disbelief in ghosts itself amounts to a religious dogma:

> "Well," Parkins said, "as you have mentioned the matter, I freely
> own that I do *not* like careless talk about what you call ghosts. A
> man in my position," he went on, raising his voice a little, "cannot, I
> find, be too careful about appearing to sanction the current beliefs
> on such subjects. . . . I hold that any semblance, any appearance of
> concession to the view that such things might exist is equivalent to a
> renunciation of all that I hold most sacred." (123)

But these hints are vague and, in the end, harmlessly jocular.

The fact is that it is simply not possible, as it is with every other author
in this volume, to derive a general philosophy out of James's stories.
They are simply stories; they never add up to a world view. The tales are
all technique, a coldly intellectual exercise in which James purposely
avoids drawing broader implications. It is not even especially fruitful to
trace themes through his work, for both the vengeance motif and the
ghost-as-savage theme remain virtually unchanged throughout his corpus. The vengeance motif is, moreover, not merely monotonous but
ultimately unconvincing: this moral accounting for supernatural phenomena will simply not work for modern readers. Some sort of pseudoscientific approach must now be used—either the quasi-scientific
method of Lovecraft or, indeed, the very occultist rationalizations so
scorned by James in the work of Blackwood: whatever we may feel
about occultism, supernatural phenomena "explained" by it at least become subsumed into a viable *Weltanschauung*.

It is also quite obvious that James's inspiration began to flag very early on. If we concede that the eight tales in *Ghost-Stories of an Antiquary* (1904) are nearly perfect examples of the form, we must also add that the rest of James's work does little but ring increasingly feeble changes upon those tales. James's first collection is all that anyone need read of his work. It is particularly unfortunate to see James spin such an incredibly tedious tale as "Mr. Humphreys and His Inheritance" (avowedly written to "fill up"[12] his second volume); all the later tales are dogged by hints of this sort of prolixity.

As it is, perhaps James is rather more interesting as a critic and theorist of the form. We are now concerned with three documents: the preface to *More Ghost Stories of an Antiquary* (1911), the introduction to *Ghosts and Marvels* (1924), and the lengthy essay "Some Remarks on Ghost Stories" (1929). The first two are principally theoretical, and impeccable as far as they go; they prove that James had clear principles for ghost-story writing (Sullivan makes much too much of James's apparent coyness and indefiniteness in this regard) and that he followed them closely enough, with the exceptions noted above. The final essay is a fascinating history of the ghost story—fascinating precisely because it is so bizarre. Admittedly, James seems to be narrowly restricting himself to the avowed "ghost story" so that perhaps it is understandable that such figures as Machen or Dunsany have no place in his account. But James's highly ambiguous stance toward Poe is of interest. The editor of *Ghosts and Marvels* had selected Poe's "Ligeia" for inclusion, and James was forced to comment upon it. His cautious remark, "Evidently in many people's judgments it ranks as a classic," scarcely conceals his distaste. "Some Remarks on Ghost Stories" is more ambivalent, as he speaks of "some Americans" (i.e., the pulp writers) who fancy that they "tread . . . in the steps of Edgar Allan Poe and Ambrose Bierce (himself sometimes unpardonable),"[13] but the hint of disapproval is strong. What offended James so much? Clearly it was the concentration on what he felt was the merely physically gruesome, as can be inferred in his slap at Bierce and also in his comment on E. F. Benson: "He sins occasionally by stepping over the line of legitimate horridness."[14] Certainly he has nothing good to say about the American pulp writers: "The[y] are merely nauseating, and it is very easy to be nauseating."[15] This is really an unprovoked attack, since the pulp writers never considered themselves "ghost-story writers" and should therefore not even have been mentioned in James's essay. I think James's squeamishness prevented him from appreciating the fact that there is a lot more to the work of Poe, Bierce, Machen, and Lovecraft than merely loathsome physical horror; James's idol LeFanu can be just as revolting, but evidently his indirection appealed to James.

I have studied James here not because I have much enthusiasm for him—this much is obvious from my discussion—and not even because I think him an especially good writer overall. I sincerely believe he is much inferior to the other writers I am studying here, largely because his work is ultimately thin and insubstantial. James showed little development over his career; if anything, there is a decline in power and originality and a corresponding preoccupation—bordering upon obsession—with technique. I discuss him here because he is clearly the perfecter of one popular and representative form of the weird tale; but in his very perfection of that form he showed its severe limitations in scope. I have nothing to say about his disciples; only Russell Kirk—if we are even to consider him a "disciple" of James—has escaped these limitations to write work that is vital and significant. The ghost story as such does not allow very much room for expansion or originality; when some writers attempt to do so, they either fail (James's followers) or, in succeeding, produce tales that can no longer be called ghost stories (Oliver Onions). It is quite possible that James came to realize this and that this is the reason for the very peculiar, self-reflexive nature of his later work: with *Ghost-Stories of an Antiquary* James had already exhausted the form and could do nothing but move his limited number of components into various permutations to create an illusory sense of newness. But it didn't work, and few of his readers—even his valiant supporters, if they would only admit it—were taken in.

5

AMBROSE BIERCE
Horror as Satire

*A*mbrose Gwinnett Bierce was born on June 24, 1842, in Meigs County, Ohio, one of thirteen children of Marcus Aurelius and Laura Bierce. He attended Kentucky Military Institute and saw distinguished service in the Union army in the Civil War, participating in such important battles as Chickamauga and Shiloh and rising to the rank of lieutenant. He later wrote graphically of his war experiences in stories and articles, the latter collected in *Bits of Autobiography* (in the first volume of his *Collected Works* [1909]).

After the war Bierce served briefly as a Treasury aide in Alabama, then joined General William B. Hazen's expedition through the Indian territory before settling in San Francisco. At that time Bierce began to contribute articles and sketches to California papers, becoming editor of the *News-Letter and California Advertiser* in 1868. His first short story, "The Haunted Valley," was published in 1871.

On Christmas Day, 1871, Bierce married Mollie Day, by whom he had two sons, Leigh and Day, and a daughter, Helen. The marriage was stormy: the couple separated in 1888 and divorced in 1905. Day was killed in a duel in 1889; Leigh died of pneumonia in 1901.

In 1872 Bierce and his wife went to England, where Bierce produced his first book, a collection of humorous pieces entitled *The Fiend's Delight* (1872). Most of these pieces were contributed to Tom Hood's magazine *Fun* or to *Figaro,* and two other humor collections appeared in 1872 and 1873. Returning to San Francisco in 1875, Bierce took a job at the U.S. Mint and then became associate editor of *The Argonaut,* where he began his famous "Prattle" column. With Thomas A. Harcourt he produced the curious hoax *The Dance of Death* (1877), purporting to condemn the immorality of dancing. In 1880 Bierce entered into a venture to mine gold in the Black Hills, but it failed disastrously and Bierce returned to San Francisco.

In 1881 Bierce became editor of the newly founded *Wasp*. Here he continued "Prattle" and began a new column, "The Devil's Dictionary"; the latter was eventually collected as *The Cynic's Word Book* (1906), a title supplied by the publisher. In 1887 Bierce began to write for William Randolph Hearst's *San Francisco Examiner* and later lobbied for Hearst interests in Washington. This was his most prolific period: his vast output included his two principal short-story collections, *Tales of Soldiers and Civilians* (1891) and *Can Such Things Be?* (1893), *Fantastic Fables* (1899), two collections of poetry, and voluminous essays and reviews.

From 1900 to 1913 Bierce lived in Washington, D.C., where he wrote for *Cosmopolitan* and other journals. In 1908 Walter Neale conceived the idea of publishing Bierce's *Collected Works,* and Bierce settled down to the onerous task of editing; the series came out in twelve volumes from 1909 to 1912, although it is by no means complete—an enormous amount of his journalism remains uncollected. In 1913 Bierce left to travel through the South, visiting Civil War battlefields and heading toward Mexico. One of his last recorded utterances is in a letter to Samuel Loveman on September 10, 1913: "I am going away to South America, and have not the faintest notion when I shall return." He vanished without a trace. It is presumed that he was caught up in the Mexican Civil War.

One of my favorite comments about Ambrose Bierce is by Clifton Fadiman:

> Bierce's nihilism is as brutal and simple as a blow, and by the same token not too convincing. It has no base in philosophy and, being quite bare of shading or qualification, becomes, if taken in overdoses, a trifle tedious. Except for the skeleton grin that creeps over his face when he has devised in his fiction some peculiarly grotesque death, Bierce never deviates into cheerfulness. His rage is unselective. The great skeptics view human nature without admiration but also without ire. Bierce's misanthropy is too systematic. He is a pessimism-machine. He is a Swift minus true intellectual power, Rochefoucauld with a bludgeon, Voltaire with stomach ulcers.[1]

As Bierce himself once said in an entirely different context, "This is so fine as to be mostly false."[2] It is false because, first, it attributes an unwavering and uniform pessimism to Bierce; second, it claims that that pessimism is philosophically unfounded; and, third, it carries the implication that pessimism can never be a philosophically viable position. Then there are other Bierce critics (in particular his latest and most diligent biographer, Paul Fatout) who are inclined to attribute all Bierce's pessimism, whether manifested in his life or in his work, to personal and environmental factors. There is reason to question all these assertions. Lovecraft once noted indirectly that it may be a mistake to see in a writer's creative work the *totality* of his view of the world,[3] and it seems clear that Bierce simply preferred to depict the darker side of life in his tales; I see no reason to doubt Bierce when he says, "I like many things in this world and a few persons."[4] But Bierce's pessimism and misanthropy were dominant traits of his thought, and it may be worthwhile to see whether he managed to justify them with intellectual rigor.

The fact of Bierce's pessimism can hardly be questioned, and I think one quotation in particular is all we need. In "To Train a Writer" (1899) he wrote that an author ought always to keep in mind that "this is a world of fools and rogues, blind with superstition, tormented with envy, consumed with vanity, selfish, false, cruel, and cursed with illusions—frothing mad!" (10.77). Well, that settles that. But *why* did Bierce feel this way? Yes, he participated in the Civil War; yes, he had many personal tragedies and disappointments. But to say that these things alone caused Bierce's misanthropy is both naive and insulting because it robs Bierce of the ability to think independently of his time and circumstances; and no writer insisted upon clarity, objectivity, and rationality—both in thought and in writing—more than Bierce. Of course, it is easy to say that Bierce valued these qualities precisely because he lacked them himself, but this is an evasion.

Bierce had no overarching view of the world. He once remarked: "We human insects, as a rule, care for nothing but ourselves, and think that is best which most closely touches such emotions and sentiments as grow out of our relations, the one with another. I don't share the preference, and a few others do not, believing that there are things more interesting than men and women."[5] This is close to Lovecraft's "cosmic indifferentism," as is the phrase that Bierce claimed summed up his entire outlook—"Nothing matters."[6] But this is schoolboy philosophy, and in any case I am not certain that Bierce maintained this sort of aloofness with any consistency. He was an atheist but not an especially vociferous one, and it would be simplistic to suppose that the bleakness of his stories could only have been produced by a man who had lost (or never found)

God. In truth, the closest he came to uttering a real philosophy is in a
newspaper column of 1872:

> The Town Crier does not seek a wider field for his talents. The only
> talents that he has are a knack of hating hypocrisy, cant, and all
> other shams, and a trick of expressing his hatred. . . . Be as decent
> as you can. Don't believe without evidence. Treat things divine with
> marked respect—don't have anything to do with them. Do not trust
> humanity without collateral security; it will play you some scurvy
> trick. Remember that it hurts no one to be treated as an enemy en-
> titled to respect until he shall prove himself a friend worthy of
> affection. Cultivate a taste for distasteful truths. And, finally . . . en-
> deavor to see things as they are, not as they ought to be.[7]

Although the last phrase significantly anticipates his definition of "Cynic"
in *The Devil's Dictionary* ("A blackguard whose faulty vision sees things
as they are, not as they ought to be"), the whole passage is nothing
more than a series of unsupported assertions. And yet had Bierce been
asked point-blank why he was a pessimist, cynic, and misanthrope, perhaps his reply would simply have been this: it works. Maybe the world
just is a wretched place to be. Maybe people just are, by and large, fools,
scoundrels, and hypocrites.

Perhaps a more profitable approach may be offered by a body of
Bierce's fiction that has gone almost totally unnoticed by critics—the
Swiftian satires that fill much of volume 1 of his *Collected Works*, especially the short novels *Ashes of the Beacon* and *The Land beyond the Blow*.
The latter in particular, a sort of combination of *Gulliver's Travels* and
Montesquieu's *Persian Letters*, presents scathing critiques of American
social and political institutions. But more, these works lead one to the
view that Bierce's pessimism may have been triggered—or, at least, re-
inforced—by his observation of political phenomena, where, of course,
"hypocrisy, cant, and all other shams" have their widest play. If there is
any strain of consistency in Bierce's life and work, it is his role as witness
to—and occasionally participant in—political events. *Ashes of the Beacon*
offers an obvious but still unanswerable refutation of democracy: "An
inherent weakness in republican government was that it assumed the
honesty and intelligence of the majority, 'the masses,' who were neither
honest nor intelligent" (1.61).

Interestingly, one of the societies encountered in *The Land beyond the Blow* appears to be Epicurean in the original sense of the term: they regard death as utter annihilation and assert that "There is no such thing as dying" (1.110), by which they (and Epicurus) mean that at any given point one is either alive or dead.[8] In this way the fear of death is presumably abolished. This argument is used by the captured spy Parker Adderson in "Parker Adderson, Philosopher," who likewise claims: "There is really no such thing as dying" (2.138), although at the end he loses his philosophic composure when faced with the actual prospect of death. But the bulk of *The Land beyond the Blow* is a blunt but powerful and frequently vicious condemnation not merely of political abuses—bribe-taking, special interests, monopolies—but the very foundations of republican government: the party system, popular election, the Supreme Court. I am inclined to believe that much of Bierce's dim view of humanity was therefore rooted in his discontent with American political ideals and practice, which he viewed at first hand for the thirty or forty years of his journalistic career. Whether he found the English system any better, in his lengthy English stay of 1872–1875, is hard to say; perhaps not, since he felt that "selfishness . . . is the dominant characteristic and fundamental motive of human nature and human action respectively" (1.18).

If Bierce was not a systematic philosopher—and never pretended to be—he had very pronounced views on writing, in particular on writing the short story. Here we are concerned with three essays—"The Novel" (1897), "The Short Story" (1897), and "To Train a Writer." One passage from the first will suffice:

> The novel bears the same relation to literature that the panorama bears to painting. With whatever skill and feeling the panorama is painted, it must lack that basic quality in all art, unity, totality of effect. As it can not be seen at once, its parts must be seen successively, each effacing the one seen before; and at the last there remains no coherent and harmonious memory of the work. It is the same with a story too long to be read with a virgin attention at a single sitting. (10.18)

This sounds very much like a mechanical adaptation of Poe's theory of poetry and probably is; but it is Bierce's view, and he stuck to it. Certain other of Bierce's remarks—his contempt for literary realism ("imagination chained to the perch of probability"—10.19), his preference for the romance (Scott, Hawthorne) over the novel, and his implicit scorn of Edgar Fawcett's criticism of the short story because " 'it can not express the one greatest thing in all literature—intercommunication of human characters'" (10.234)—are, taken together, all we need to know of Bierce's literary theory.

Of greater interest is what Bierce's views may have been on the theory of weird fiction. His remarks on romance are suggestive, but we can learn much more on this matter in a rather unusual way—by examining his remarkable and radical reorganization of the contents of his two principal collections of horror tales, *Tales of Soldiers and Civilians* and *Can Such Things Be?* This act of rearrangement has apparently gone almost entirely unnoticed by Bierce scholars, but it is of vital importance to Bierce's aesthetic of horror, for the dominant motive at work is the segregation of his supernatural and his nonsupernatural tales.

The first edition of *Tales of Soldiers and Civilians* (San Francisco: E. L. G. Steele, 1891) contained the following tales: Soldiers: "A Horseman in the Sky"; "An Occurrence at Owl Creek Bridge"; "Chickamauga"; "A Son of the Gods"; "One of the Missing"; "Killed at Resaca"; "The Affair at Coulter's Notch"; "A Tough Tussle"*; "The Coup de Grâce"; "Parker Adderson, Philosopher"; Civilians: "A Watcher by the Dead"; "The Man and the Snake"; "A Holy Terror"; "The Suitable Surroundings"; "An Inhabitant of Carcosa"*; "The Middle Toe of the Right Foot"*; "Haïta the Shepherd"*; and "An Heiress from Red Horse." The reissue of 1898 (New York: G. P. Putnam's Sons), now titled *In the Midst of Life* (taken from the British edition of 1892), adds the following three tales: "An Affair of Outposts"; "The Damned Thing"*; and "The Eyes of the Panther." When, however, the collection was reprinted as volume 2 of the *Collected Works* (1909), the tales I have marked with an asterisk were removed and placed in volume 3 (*Can Such Things Be?* 1910), and "The Boarded Window" was added. It is obvious that Bierce wished to exclude any overtly supernatural tales from this collection—hence the exclusion of the two otherworldly fantasies, "An Inhabitant of Carcosa" and "Haïta the Shepherd," and the definitely supernatural "Middle Toe of the Right Foot"; "The Damned Thing" might be considered supernatural, but more on this later.

Two stories—"The Boarded Window" and "The Eyes of the Panther"—hint of the supernatural but do not actually involve it. Let us consider the former. A man and his wife live in an isolated cabin near Cincinnati. The wife falls ill and, in spite of attempts by her husband to nurse her back to health, lapses into unconsciousness and "apparently" (2.368) dies after three days. The man is prostrated with shock and falls asleep. He is awakened in the dark by the sound of a scuffle, and learns that a panther has crawled through a window and is dragging the woman's body away. The man shoots his rifle at the animal and scares it away. Although the woman's body is now mutilated by lacerations at her throat, "between [her] teeth was a fragment of the animal's ear" (2.372). Probably we are to understand that the woman was not in reality dead but merely in a sort of coma, from which she revived when the animal attacked her—otherwise a "pool of blood" (2.372) could not have issued from her throat at the animal's attack.

"The Eyes of the Panther" is an extraordinarily difficult tale, and many (including Peter Penzoldt and Jason C. Eckhardt) have declared flatly that this is the story of a shape-changer, and hence supernatural; but there are suggestions to the contrary. Jenner Brading wishes to marry Irene Marlowe; she loves him but claims that she cannot marry him because she is insane. She tells him a story in which her mother, left alone in a cabin by her husband, was frightened to madness by the "luminous orbs" (2.394) of a panther looking into the window. Irene was born a few months later, and she maintains that these circumstances warrant the belief that she is insane. Jenner, who has heard stories of a panther peering into people's houses at night, believes that Irene is indeed insane, but that she has fantasized her own past from these accounts. Jenner withdraws, letting it be known that he has been rejected in matrimony by the daughter of the recluse Old Man Marlowe. One evening he sees at his window "two gleaming eyes that burned with a malignant lustre inexpressibly terrible!" (2.401). He shoots the object with a gun and of course finds that it is Irene.

The key is what we are to make of all these shining eyes. Does Irene's mere possession of such eyes imply that she is herself a sort of werewolf—sometimes human, sometimes a panther? This is possible, for details like this are frequently used in weird tales to signal the supernatural. But Bierce on two occasions goes out of his way to emphasize that, although shining eyes were seen, no actual panther was present. First, when Irene departs after her last meeting with Jenner, he "caught a quick, brief glimpse of shining eyes"; but "no panther was visible" (2.399). Second, after Jenner shoots Irene and follows her as she drags her fatally wounded body into the forest, he comes upon the victim: "But it was no panther" (2.402). The bluntness of these utterances seems to suggest that Bierce is signaling a nonsupernatural resolution to the story.

But if the tale is nonsupernatural, is it that Irene is simply insane? that she *fancies* herself occasionally a panther? This is the solution I had adopted until Susan Michaud suggested to me an entirely different interpretation: *it is Jenner who is insane.* He had been incensed at Irene's rejection of his proposal, to the point that he wished to strangle her. When Jenner sees the shining eyes at his window, he may be playing out some subconscious desire to kill Irene—and he in fact does so. Michaud believes that Irene refused to marry Jenner because she did not wish to abandon her reclusive father and therefore made up the tale about her mother and the panther; she came to Jenner's window not to harm him but out of genuine love and concern. I like this reconstruction because it makes the tale fall into a pattern of several Bierce works involving the central irony of individuals talking and acting at cross-purposes, whereby each party is unaware of the other's real motivations. We shall see this exemplified supernaturally in "The Moonlit Road."

The only thing that puzzles me about the tales omitted from *In the Midst of Life* is the removal of "A Tough Tussle," a perfectly good (nonsupernatural) war story. I can only suppose that Bierce thought it too similar in basic plot to "A Watcher by the Dead," although other such parallelisms ("The Affair at Coulter's Notch" is very close in conception to "A Horseman in the Sky," and "The Man and the Snake" bears resemblances to "One of the Missing") do not seem to have bothered him.

The case with *Can Such Things Be?* is considerably more complicated. The first edition (New York: Cassell, 1893) contained "The Death of Halpin Frayser"; "The Mocking-Bird"*; "My Favorite Murder"**; "One Officer, One Man"*; "The Man out of the Nose"*; "An Occurrence at Brownville"*; "Jupiter Doke, Brigadier-General"**; "The Famous Gilson Bequest"*; "The Story of a Conscience"*; "The Secret of Macarger's Gulch"; "The Major's Tale"**; "A Psychological Shipwreck"; "One Kind of Officer"*; "The Applicant"*; "One of Twins"; "The Night-Doings at 'Deadman's'"; "The Widower Turmore"**; "George Thurston"*; "Three Episodes in the Life of a Brave Man"; "John Bartine's Watch"; "The Realm of the Unreal"; "A Baby Tramp"; "Some Haunted Houses"; "Bodies of the Dead"; and "Mysterious Disappearances." The stories marked with one asterisk were transferred to volume 2 of the *Collected Works* (*In the Midst of Life*), and for fairly obvious reasons: "The Mocking-Bird," "One Officer, One Man," "The Story of a Conscience," "One Kind of Officer," and "George Thurston" are war stories; "The Man out of the Nose," "An Occurrence at Brownville" (retitled "An Adventure at Brownville"), and "The Applicant" are clearly nonsupernatural. "The Famous Gilson Bequest" seems to involve a ghost at its conclusion, but it is probable that the apparition is in the mind of the protagonist, Mr. Brentshaw: Bierce lets himself off the hook by noting that Brentshaw "could . . . perceive, or think he perceived" (2.278) the ghost. In any case, the ghost—if it is that—is not central to the plot, which involves a purely human feud between Brentshaw and Gilson.

The four stories marked with two asterisks were transferred from *Can Such Things Be?* to volume 8 of the *Collected Works* (1911), containing Bierce's obviously farcical or grotesque tales, now grouped under the headings "Negligible Tales," "The Parenticide Club," "The Fourth Estate," and "The Ocean Wave" (also included in this volume are an odd series of sketches called "'On with the Dance!' A Review," which ironically recommends dancing as morally uplifting, and a long string of epigrams). Again, the reason for the transfer of these tales is very clear, as they are all more obviously humorous than the other tales in the collection.

In addition, the following tales were added to volume 3 of the *Collected Works:* "One Summer Night"; "The Moonlit Road"; "A Diagnosis of Death"; "Moxon's Master"; "The Haunted Valley"; "A Jug of Sirup"; "Staley Fleming's Hallucination"; "A Resumed Identity"; "Beyond the Wall"; "John Mortonson's Funeral"; "The Stranger"; The Ways of Ghosts (including "Present at a Hanging," "A Cold Greeting," "A Wireless Message," and "An Arrest"), Soldier-Folk (including "A Man with Two Lives," "Three and One Are One," "A Baffled Ambuscade," and "Two Military Executions").

The final contents of volumes 2, 3, and 8 of the *Collected Works* represent virtually the totality of Bierce's short stories. Volume 2 (*In the Midst of Life*) contains Soldiers: "A Horseman in the Sky"; "An Occurrence at Owl Creek Bridge"; "Chickamauga"; "A Son of the Gods"; "One of the Missing"; "Killed at Resaca"; "The Affair at Coulter's Notch"; "The Coup de Grâce"; "Parker Adderson, Philosopher"; "An Affair of Outposts"; "The Story of a Conscience"; "One Kind of Officer"; "One Officer, One Man"; "George Thurston"; "The Mocking-Bird"; Civilians: "The Man out of the Nose"; "An Adventure at Brownville"; "The Famous Gilson Bequest"; "The Applicant"; "A Watcher by the Dead"; "The Man and the Snake"; "A Holy Terror"; "The Suitable Surroundings"; "The Boarded Window"; "A Lady from Red Horse"; and "The Eyes of the Panther."

Volume 3 (*Can Such Things Be?*) contains "The Death of Halpin Frayser"; "The Secret of Macarger's Gulch"; "One Summer Night"; "The Moonlit Road"; "A Diagnosis of Death"; "Moxon's Master"; "A Tough Tussle"; "One of Twins"; "The Haunted Valley"; "A Jug of Sirup"; "Staley Fleming's Hallucination"; "A Resumed Identity"; "The Night-Doings at 'Deadman's'"; "Beyond the Wall"; "A Psychological Shipwreck"; "The Middle Toe of the Right Foot"; "John Mortonson's Funeral"; "The Realm of the Unreal"; "John Bartine's Watch"; "The Damned Thing"; "Haïta the Shepherd"; "An Inhabitant of Carcosa"; "The Stranger "; "The Ways of Ghosts"; "Soldier-Folk"; "Some Haunted Houses" (now incorporating "Bodies of the Dead" and "'Mysterious Disappearances'").

Volume 8 contains Negligible Tales: "A Bottomless Grave"; "Jupiter Doke, Brigadier-General"; "The Widower Turmore"; "The City of the Gone Away"; "The Major's Tale"; "Curried Cow"; "A Revolt of the Gods"; "The Baptism of Dobsho"; "The Race at Left Bower"; "The Failure of Hope & Wandel"; "Perry Chumly's Eclipse"; "A Providential Intimation"; "Mr. Swiddler's Flip-Flap"; "The Little Story"; The Parenticide Club: "My Favorite Murder"; "Oil of Dog"; "An Imperfect Conflagration"; "The Hypnotist"; The Fourth Estate: "Mr. Masthead, Journalist"; "Why I Am Not Editing 'The Stinger'"; "Corrupting the Press"; "'The Bubble of Reputation'"; The Ocean Wave: "A Shipwreckollection"; "The Captain of 'The Camel'"; "The Man Overboard"; "A Cargo of Cat"; "'On with the Dance!' A Review"; and various epigrams.

I have gone into all this at some length and tedium to show that Bierce put an unusual amount of thought into this process of rearrangement. The finalized *In the Midst of Life* does not contain a single supernatural tale; the finalized *Can Such Things Be?* contains almost no nonsupernatural tales (for the one exception, see below); volume 8 of the *Collected Works* contains nothing but farces, most nonsupernatural. I think that Bierce was planning such a distinction all along but perhaps was compelled to violate it when first putting his collections together simply to fill the volumes. "The Night-Doings at 'Deadman's,'" a clearly supernatural tale, had been published as early as 1877, but Bierce did not include it in *Tales of Soldiers and Civilians* (1891), instead reserving it for

Can Such Things Be? (1893). "The Damned Thing" was first published in a magazine in 1893, the same year as the first edition of *Can Such Things Be?* But that volume, not nearly as popular as its predecessor, was never reprinted until the *Collected Works,* and so Bierce evidently felt he might as well include the story in the revised *In the Midst of Life* (1898), since the chance to include it in a collection might never occur otherwise. The case of "Soldier-Folk," a series of four brief tales, is interesting. This is the only instance of overt supernaturalism combined with the war story. I do not know when these stories were written, but it is interesting that Bierce chose to include them in the finalized *Can Such Things Be?* rather than the finalized *In the Midst of Life:* the supernatural aspect of these tales evidently took precedence over the war aspect in Bierce's mind.

Certain curious remarks in some stories we have hitherto deemed supernatural shed further light on Bierce's theory of weird fiction. In an attempt to account for the phenomena observed in "The Damned Thing," a character remarks: "'We so rely upon the orderly operation of familiar natural laws that any seeming suspension of them is noted as a menace to our safety, a warning of unthinkable calamity'" (3.287). And, at the end:

> "At each end of the solar spectrum the chemist can detect the presence of what are known as 'actinic' rays. They represent colors— integral colors in the composition of light—which we are unable to discern. The human eye is an imperfect instrument; its range is but a few octaves of the real 'chromatic scale.' I am not mad; there are colors that we cannot see.
>
> "And, God help me! the Damned Thing is of such a color!" (3.296)

This attempt at a quasi-scientific explanation of seemingly supernatural phenomena, apart from being a startling anticipation of a cardinal tenet in Lovecraft's theory of weird fiction, is of momentous significance because it removes the tale from the rubric of supernaturalism altogether and places it in the realm of science fiction. This is not an isolated reference in Bierce: in "The Boarded Window" we again find mention of the "suspension of familiar natural laws" (2.368), and in "One of Twins" we read of "the natural laws of which we have acquaintance." Bierce adds, as if the implication were not obvious, that "perhaps we have not all acquaintance with the same natural laws" (3.121). This stupendous notion that "natural laws" are in the domain of epistemology, not ontology, is a startling antidote to the positivism of the late nineteenth century and in a dim way even anticipates Heisenberg's Indeterminacy Principle.

Although such tales as "The Realm of the Unreal" (in which the bizarre incidents are explained away by hypnosis) and "A Diagnosis of Death" (in which a pseudoscientific air is maintained throughout in the discussion of whether it is possible to forecast a person's death) approach science fiction, Bierce comes closest to it in "Moxon's Master," which must be one of the earliest tales (Poe's "Maelzel's Chess-Player" not excluded) genuinely to deal with the question of artificial intelligence. Moxon, the inventor, reveals himself to be a vitalist in the extreme:

> "Doubtless you do not hold with those (I need not name them to a man of your reading) who have taught that all matter is sentient, that every atom is a living, feeling, conscious being. *I* do. There is no such thing as dead, inert matter: it is all alive; all instinct with force, actual and potential; all sensitive to the same forces in its environment and susceptible to the contagion of higher and subtler ones residing in such superior organisms as it may be brought into relation with, as those of man when he is fashioning it into an instrument of his will. It absorbs something of his intelligence and purpose—more of them in proportion to the complexity of the resulting machine and that of its work." (3.93–94)

He finds Herbert Spencer's definition of life ("Life is a definite combination of heterogeneous changes, both simultaneous and successive, in correspondence with external coexistences and experiences") as applicable to machines as to people. (It apparently does not occur to Moxon, or to Bierce, that this may be because the definition is flawed rather than because machines are in fact not different in kind from people.) And although the ending is predictable—the machine, an automaton chessplayer, kills Moxon after being defeated by him in a match—the way in which Bierce gradually and subtly hints at the machine's acquisition of human emotions (the shuddersomely suggestive remark that the machine moved the chess pieces "with a slow, uniform, mechanical and, I thought, somewhat theatrical movement of the arm" [3.101]) is masterful. Written more than fifty years before Dunsany's very similar novel, *The Last Revolution* (1952), "Moxon's Master" is much more effective and intellectually sound. And yet I suspect that the point of the tale is principally satiric or even misanthropic: if machines are people, then people are machines. La Mettrie is vindicated.

I want to return to the distinction between supernaturalism and non-supernaturalism and its possible importance to Bierce, because I think it will help to explain why Bierce's war tales can be regarded as authentic horror stories. I cannot believe that Bierce, in arranging *Tales of Soldiers and Civilians,* wished us to regard the two groups of tales as discrete entities, although the title might be thought to suggest it. I am afraid that Lovecraft is (along with many others) almost entirely wrong when he says in passing of the war stories that they "form the most vivid and realistic expression which [the Civil War] has yet received in fiction" (SHiL 406): vivid they are, but realistic they are not—Bierce was not a realist and did not wish to be. In particular, his characters are not "realistic" in any meaningful sense of the term. Edmund Wilson—whether in praise or censure I cannot quite tell, although I suspect the latter—remarked aptly that "in all Bierce's fiction, there are no men or women who are interesting as men or women—that is, by reason of their passions, their aspirations or their personalities. They figure only as the helpless butts of sadistic practical jokes, and their higher faculties are so little involved that they might almost as well be trapped animals."[9] But all this is precisely in accord with Bierce's aesthetic of fiction: this is how Bierce *wanted* to portray men and women. What "realism" there is in Bierce is the higher realism of romance—the realism, say, of "A Horseman in the Sky" or "The Affair at Coulter's Notch," in which the tragedy of the Civil War in splitting up families into enemy factions is unforgettably etched; but the characters and incidents Bierce uses to convey this realism are, quite frankly, highly artificial.

Even more artificial—or, perhaps, artificial in a different way—would be the intrusion of supernaturalism into the war story. Yes, he did just this in the "Soldier-Folk" section of *Can Such Things Be?* but these stories are slight and not especially effective. In all the war stories in *Tales of Soldiers and Civilians* it was important to Bierce to establish that the events are *not* supernatural, that nothing in them happens contrary to nature—either cosmic nature or human nature. Peyton Farquhar's arduous escape from the execution committee at Owl Creek Bridge is only a hallucination in the split second before he dies by hanging. An air of dreamlike fantasy pervades "Chickamauga," even when the boy protagonist comes into contact with the grotesque band of men coming out of the forest: "He now approached one of these crawling figures from behind and with an agile movement mounted it astride. The man sank upon his breast, recovered, flung the small boy fiercely to the ground as an unbroken colt might have done, then turned upon him a face that lacked a lower jaw—from the upper teeth to the throat was a great red gap fringed with hanging shreds of flesh and splinters of bone" (2.52). But they are nothing but the (very real) survivors of one of the bloodiest battles of the Civil War. Carter Druse in "A Horseman in the Sky" seems to see the horseman flying through the air:

> Straight upright sat the rider, in military fashion, with a firm seat in the saddle, a strong clutch upon the reins to hold his charger from too impetuous a plunge. From his bare head his long hair streamed upward, waving like a plume. His hands were concealed in the cloud of the horse's lifted mane. The animal's body was as level as if every hoof-stroke encountered the resistant earth. Its motions were those of a wild gallop, but even as the officer looked they ceased, with all the legs thrown sharply forward as in the act of alighting from a leap. But this was a flight! (2.24)

I would not be surprised if Lovecraft were influenced by this in his own description of fantastic horsemen in "Celephaïs":

> Just as they galloped up the rising ground to the precipice a golden glare came somewhere out of the east and hid all the landscape in its effulgent draperies. The abyss was now a seething chaos of roseate and cerulean splendour, and invisible voices sang exultantly as the knightly entourage plunged over the edge and floated gracefully down past glittering clouds and silvery coruscations. Endlessly down the horsemen floated, their chargers pawing the aether as if galloping over golden sands . . .[10]

But Lovecraft's tale is an otherworldly fantasy; in Bierce it is only Carter Druse's mind that has slowed the horseman's crash from the cliff to the woods below, since he knows he has killed his own father. In "A Tough Tussle" Brainerd Byring feels "a sense of the supernatural" (3.113) as he obsessively stares at an enemy body he has come upon—but it is only a corpse, and it is Byring's fear of death that kills him.

Many critics have noted the principal feature of all the war stories— the isolation of the central characters. But there is more to it than that:

they are not merely isolated but in a state of *compulsion*. It is because they are placed in intolerable situations, and are unable to escape them, that they meet their doom, whether it be death or madness. Carter Druse cannot abandon his post as a sentry lest he betray his entire army: he has no choice but to kill his father, a scout on the enemy side. In a very similar tale, "The Affair at Coulter's Notch," Coulter is placed inescapably in an excruciating position: he must man the tiny pass single-handedly and destroy the house on the other side, even though it is his house and his wife and child are inside. In "An Occurrence at Owl Creek Bridge" Peyton Farquhar, although surrounded by enemy soldiers, is hideously alone as the hangman's noose slips around his neck; and it is significant that virtually the last image in his delusion of escape is the sight of his wife, "looking fresh and cool and sweet" (2.44), on the verandah of his house. Farquhar yearns to return to his family, but it is all an illusion. In "One of the Missing" Jerome Searing is physically immobile as he is caught in the collapse of a house, his gun falling in such a position that its barrel is pointing directly at his forehead. But, as with all these tales, this physical fixity is a thin symbol for the psychological paralysis that overcomes the characters in the face of death. This is made explicit in "A Tough Tussle," in which Byring can simply walk away from the corpse at his feet, but his mind will not let him.

It is worth establishing that in several of Bierce's war stories the actual war element is not intrinsic to the plot—this is what makes them non-supernatural horror tales rather than war tales. To be sure, the crazy sort of bravery we find in "A Son of the Gods" or "Killed at Resaca" could only be exhibited in war, while we have already noted the tragic splitting of families caused by the Civil War portrayed in "A Horseman in the Sky" and "The Affair at Coulter's Notch"; but in several other tales the war is only a phantasmagoric backdrop. Once again I point to the similarity in plot of "A Tough Tussle" and "A Watcher by the Dead"—the former a "soldier" tale, the latter a "civilian" tale. Peyton Farquhar could be any criminal convicted of a capital crime. Jerome Searing could have been a huntsman caught in a shanty where he was camping out.

The degree to which characters in the war stories *observe* phenomena in a strangely objective way—Carter Druse observing his father on the cliff; Peyton Farquhar noting carefully all the paraphernalia of his execution; Jerome Searing taking minute stock of the detritus all around him in the shack—links them in a suggestive way to another body of Bierce's work that has gone relatively unnoticed, *Bits of Autobiography*

(1.225–402). These sketches of his years during and slightly after the war are similarly filled with observation, but it is Bierce who finds himself suddenly stepping back and looking at a war in which he is supposed to be participating:

> My regiment having at last been relieved at the guns and moved over to the heights above this ravine for no obvious purpose, I obtained leave to go down into the valley of death and gratify a reprehensible curiosity. (1.261)
>
> Looking across the fields in our rear (rather longingly) I had the happy distinction of a discoverer. What I saw was the shimmer of sunlight on metal; lines of troops were coming in behind us! (1.275)
>
> I observed this phenomenon at Pickett's Mill. Standing at the right of the line I had an unobstructed view of the narrow, open space across which the two lines fought. (1.291–292)
>
> As a member of Colonel Post's staff, I was naturally favored with a good view of the performance. (1.316)

I suspect that Bierce—both as a soldier and later as a journalist—rather liked this role as objective spectator upon the anthill of life. We are not, I think, to understand that, because of this, Bierce's characters in the war stories are autobiographical, especially since they do not retain their objectivity very long; but it is an interesting phenomenon. As it is, probably more work could be done in tracing links between *Bits of Autobiography*—which, incidentally, contains some of Bierce's finest writing, especially the poignant and kaleidoscopic "What I Saw of Shiloh"—and the war tales.

In all Bierce, but especially in these war stories, we cannot help feeling that coincidence has been used a little too neatly in setting up these artificially dramatic situations. One of the most powerful and shocking of Bierce's tales is "The Coup de Grâce." Captain Downing Madwell is a devoted friend to Caffal Halcrow, but Caffal's brother Creede maintains a furious hatred of Madwell. During a battle Caffal falls at Madwell's feet, evidently mortally wounded. It does not seem that Madwell can do anything but put him out of his misery. He places his gun next to Caffal's forehead and fires; it is empty. In desperation he takes his sword and finally dispatches his friend.

At that moment three men stepped silently forward from behind the clump of young trees which had concealed their approach. Two were hospital attendants and carried a stretcher.

The third was Major Creede Halcrow. (2.132)

This is undeniably effective, but there is a suggestion of authorial trickery here—we have been manipulated in some O. Henry–like fashion. How would Bierce respond to this charge? I am not sure that he would, save again to assert his freedom, as a romancer, from the mechanical conventions of realism. But there are hints of another answer in some of the tales. I suspect that Bierce adhered to the view (expounded first by Democritus) that we are not merely creatures of fate, but that what we call chance or coincidence is nothing but fate itself working in ways we do not perceive or understand. A very long and curious passage to this effect in "One of the Missing" is worth quoting in this regard:

But it was decreed from the beginning of time that Private Searing was not to murder anybody that bright summer morning, nor was the Confederate retreat to be announced by him. For countless ages events had been so matching themselves together in that wondrous mosaic to some parts of which, dimly discernible, we give the name of history, that the acts which he had in will would have marred the harmony of the pattern. Some twenty-five years previously the Power charged with the execution of the work according to the design had provided against that mischance by causing the birth of a certain male child in a little village at the foot of the Carpathian Mountains, had carefully reared it, supervised its education, directed its desires into a military channel, and in due time made it an officer of artillery. By the concurrence of an infinite number of favoring influences and their preponderance over an infinite number of opposing ones, this officer of artillery had been made to avoid punishment. He had been directed to New Orleans (instead of New York), where a recruiting officer awaited him on the wharf. He was enlisted and promoted, and things were so ordered that he now commanded a Confederate battery some two miles along the line from where Jerome Searing, the Federal scout, stood cocking his rifle. Nothing had been neglected—at every step in the progress of both these men's lives, and in the lives of their contemporaries and ancestors, and in the lives of the contemporaries of their ancestors, the right thing had been done to bring about the desired result. Had anything in all this vast concatenation been overlooked Private Searing might have fired on the retreating Confederates that morning, and would perhaps have missed. As it fell out, a Confederate captain of artillery, having nothing better to do while awaiting his turn to pull out and be off, amused himself by sighting a field-piece obliquely to his right at what he mistook for some Federal officers on the crest of a hill, and discharged it. The shot flew high of its mark. (2.76–77)

There is, certainly, a bantering or even parodic tone to this passage; but the idea it expresses—and this is what makes Edmund Wilson's criticism of Bierce for his failure in characterization irrelevant—is found in more compressed form in all Bierce's stories: we are pawns in the hands of fate.

The same sort of compulsion that we found in the war tales can be found in the "civilian" tales. The corpse-watcher in "A Watcher by the Dead" is affected in very much the same manner as Byring in "A Tough Tussle" while "The Man and the Snake," in which Harker Brayton is frightened to death by what proves to be a toy snake, is one of Bierce's most carefully written tales. Here again the compulsion is entirely psychological: Brayton can simply walk out of the room if he wishes—but he cannot. Bierce's mastery both of style and of psychological perception is encapsulated in a single paragraph: "The snake had not moved and appeared somewhat to have lost its power upon the imagination; the gorgeous illusions of a few moments before were not repeated. Beneath that flat and brainless brow its black, beady eyes simply glittered as at first with an expression unspeakably malignant. It was as if the creature, assured of its triumph, had determined to practise no more alluring wiles" (2.320). Here nearly every other phrase alternates between what is in fact realistic description of the toy snake (it does not move because it is not alive; its eyes glitter because they are made of shoe buttons) and Brayton's erroneous perception of it. The snake really is "brainless," but Brayton does not know that. Only at the end do all the pieces fall into place, and we come to realize the significance of the telltale phrases ("appeared," "illusions," "it was as if") that reveal what Brayton's imagination is adding to the stuffed snake.

In the tales in *Can Such Things Be?* Bierce is just as careful in using the supernatural as he is in avoiding it in *Tales of Soldiers and Civilians*. We have already noted the tales that approach science fiction: what they represent is an extension of the boundaries of the natural world to encompass what, given our current state of scientific knowledge, appear to be supernatural events. Many other tales—perhaps the most effective is "The Middle Toe of the Right Foot," although "Staley Fleming's Hallucination," "The Night-Doings at 'Deadman's,'" and "Beyond the Wall" all fit the pattern—are simply tales of revenge in which the supernatural is a scarcely veiled metaphor for the conscience of the guilty.

Perhaps Bierce's most remarkable supernatural tale is the much-discussed "Death of Halpin Frayser." Recently a controversy has arisen over what actually happens in this tale and whether the supernatural comes into play at all. In a brilliant and ingenious essay, Robert C. Maclean[11] has argued that it is possible to explain all the events of the tale naturally, with the conclusion that the murderer of Halpin Frayser is his own father, disguised as the private detective Jaralson. Maclean's work is too involved to discuss in detail here,[12] but both he and William Bysshe Stein, who discussed the problem earlier,[13] reject the obvious supernatural "explanation" of the events of the tale—that Frayser is killed by his own deceased mother. But I sense that they and other critics do so because they are unwarrantedly embarrassed at the mere existence of the supernatural, which in any case does not preclude other (e.g., psychoanalytical) interpretations. Bierce leaves hardly any doubt of Frayser's incestuous love for his mother (a love that she reciprocates), and it appears—thus far Maclean is correct—that we are to understand that Frayser and his mother fled separately west and lived as man and wife. Frayser kills his wife/mother, but she comes back from the dead and murders her son as he lurks by her grave. Any other reconstruction of events will make the epigraph—a passage from the sage Hali—inexplicable: "Whereas in general the spirit that removed cometh back upon occasion, and is sometimes seen of those in flesh (appearing in the form of the body it bore) yet it hath happened that the veritable body without the spirit hath walked. And it is attested of those encountering who have lived to speak thereon that a lich so raised up hath no natural affection, nor remembrance thereof, but only hate" (3.13). Frayser's mother is the "lich so raised up." The phrase "natural affection" is interesting; for the mother it suggests merely the blind destructiveness of the undead, but for Frayser it is meant to convey his profoundly unnatural love of his mother. At the end of the story the detective and a sheriff, standing over the murdered body of Halpin Frayser as it lies atop his mother's grave, hear "the sound of a laugh, a low, deliberate, *soulless* laugh . . . a laugh so *unnatural,* so *unhuman,* so devilish, that it filled those hardy man-hunters with a sense of dread unspeakable!" (3.43). Now unless Bierce is deliberately trying to deceive us (something he never does in this precise way) or is suggesting that the two characters are victims of a collective hallucination, this can only be the laugh of the "body without the spirit" that is Halpin Frayser's mother. To say that this is merely a tale about "zombies" (as Mary Elizabeth Grenander does in dismissing the supernatural interpretation) is both to imply that there is something inherently subliterary about zombies (itself a questionable assertion) and to misconstrue the role of the supernatural here. What we have is a *double* irony: Halpin Frayser is killed by his own murder victim, not out of simple revenge (for his mother has no "remembrance" of the crime), but by sheer chance—the same sort of chance that trapped Cthulhu in the sinking R'lyeh in Lovecraft's "The Call of Cthulhu." It is the haplessness (and hopelessness) of human beings against the inexorable course of fate that is at the heart of this story.

The clarity and precision, both of diction and imagery, that are central to Bierce's actual methodology of writing—his scorn of slang and dialect is too well documented for citation—frequently augment and in some senses even create the sense of horror in his work. Lovecraft censures Bierce for his "prosaic angularity" (SHiL 408), remarking that "many of the stories are . . . marred by a jaunty and commonplacely artificial style derived from journalistic models" (SHiL 406). I regret to say that the entirety of this statement is false. Oh, Lovecraft is free to regret the lack of "atmosphere" in Bierce, but he seems not to have understood that the harrowing and pitiless clarity of Bierce's images is the secret to much of his effectiveness. More surprisingly, Lovecraft appears to have been unaware that Bierce's style is, fundamentally, modeled upon the same eighteenth-century idiom that served as the basis for his own style. But whereas Lovecraft's Asiatic, densely textured prose drew from Addison and Johnson, the spare, laconic, Attic style of Bierce derives from Swift and Gibbon. Clarity was Bierce's hallmark. There is never an imprecise sentence or image in his work, never a time when we do not know exactly what is going on. One tale in particular, "The Moonlit Road," emphasizes this tendency in an especially satisfying way. Jack Sullivan remarks—rather oddly, I think—that the story "achieves an almost mind-numbing complexity by emerging from three fragmented points of view,"[14] but Sullivan is mistaken if he thinks obfuscation is Bierce's aim. Each character—even the murdered Julia Hetman, "through the medium Bayrolles" (3.74)—tells his or her side of the story, and only by combining these three accounts can we arrive at the truth of the matter. Joel Hetman, Julia's son, begins the tale. He has been summoned home from college because, as his father says, his mother has been murdered by an intruder who was seen entering the house but escaped undetected. Later, as he and his father walk along a moonlit road, the father sees an apparition but the son sees nothing; the father then disappears. The father (under the pseudonym Caspar Grattan) then takes up the narrative. He is a jealous man and wishes to test his wife's faithfulness. He tells his wife he will be away until the next afternoon, but returns home in the evening to see someone enter through the back door. Enraged, he bursts in and kills his wife, who is cowering in a corner of a room. It is the apparition of his wife that he sees on the moonlit road, and he flees in terror. Julia Hetman now reports that the intruder was just that—not a lover but a burglar who was frightened away by the return of her husband. But she, imagining that the burglar has returned, tries to hide in the dark. She does not know who killed her, and when her spirit meets her husband and son on the moonlit road it is to express her "great love and poignant pity" (3.78), not her hatred or revenge. Here again the supernatural is used in almost a clinically precise way to fill in the missing gaps in the story. And yet this tale finally becomes a testament to Bierce's authorial supremacy: only he (and, now, the reader) knows the true circumstances of the story; each of the characters is missing some vital element of the picture, even the deceased Julia Hetman, since "the sum of what we know at death is the measure of what we know afterward of all that went before" (3.77).

Clarity of expression is the key to another story, "An Occurrence at Owl Creek Bridge." This tale is a masterwork because of the almost mathematically exact way in which the style leads us to reverse the period of waking and dreaming in Peyton Farquhar. The first section of the tale is the "waking" part, with the grim preparations for an all too real execution; but Bierce presents it almost as if it were a dream (or nightmare) of Farquhar's: we are not told here the crime for which he is being executed; Farquhar's sensations seem both dulled ("A piece of dancing driftwood caught his attention and his eyes followed it down the current. How slowly it appeared to move! What a sluggish stream!"—2.30) and preternaturally heightened (the ticking of his watch sounds like "the stroke of a blacksmith's hammer upon the anvil"—2.31). But in the brief second section we learn that Farquhar was convicted of passing on information to the enemy, and in the third section (Farquhar's delusion) every image is crystal clear: he feels a "sharp pain in his wrist" (2.36) from the ropes; as he struggles in the water to free himself "his whole body was racked and wrenched with an insupportable anguish!" (2.37). Freed, he finds himself

> now in full possession of his physical senses. They were, indeed, preternaturally keen and alert. Something in the awful disturbance of his organic system had so exalted and refined them that they made record of things never before perceived. He felt the ripples upon his face and heard their separate sounds as they struck. He looked at the forest on the bank of the stream, saw the individual trees, the leaves and the veining of each leaf—saw the very insects upon them: the locusts, the brilliant-bodied flies, the gray spiders stretching their webs from twig to twig. He noted the prismatic colors in all the dewdrops upon a million blades of grass. The humming of the gnats that danced above the eddies of the stream, the beating of the dragon-flies' wings, the strokes of the water-spiders' legs, like oars which had lifted their boat—all these made audible music. A fish slid along beneath his eyes and he heard the rush of its body parting the water. (2.37–38)

And it goes on—in the split second before his death Farquhar's mind conjures up images far more lucid and precise than in the minutes before his execution.

Bierce was a satirist, and a great one. In the final analysis, I am not sure that Bierce's satire—or any satire—requires a philosophical justification: it will be valid insofar as it is skillfully manipulated. For Bierce, satire *is* philosophy; his whole world view can be inferred from it. More, it is satire that links the whole of his literary work—war stories, Swiftian satires, supernatural tales, journalism, poetry, and those two masterpieces of wit, *Fantastic Fables* and *The Devil's Dictionary.* This overarching satiric tendency may help to explain certain anomalies in the horror tales as well as to redeem certain of Bierce's lesser stories. But first a curiosity about Bierce's satiric method: all Bierce's satire has an undercurrent of violence. In a sense, of course, this may be said of satire generally, but even to call Bierce's satire Juvenalian is a little mild. Note the degree of viciousness in even so harmless a thing as a parody of conventional greetings in *The Land beyond the Blow:*

> The tigerherd having perceived me, now came striding forward, brandishing his crook and shaking his fists with great vehemence, gestures which I soon learned were, in that country, signs of amity and good-will. But before knowing that fact I had risen to my feet and thrown myself into a posture of defense, and as he approached I led for his head with my left, following with a stiff right upon his solar plexus, which sent him rolling on the grass in great pain. After learning something of the social customs of the country I felt extreme mortification in recollecting this breach of etiquette, and even to this day I cannot think upon it without a blush. (1.131)

Bierce's satire is always of this sort: it is just on this side of gratuitous nastiness. When, in "An Occurrence at Owl Creek Bridge," Peyton Farquhar is struggling in his mind to free himself from his bonds, Bierce obtrudes this incredible aside: "What splendid effort!—what magnificent, what superhuman strength! Ah, that was a fine endeavor! Bravo!" (2.36). This would be bad enough for one who is actually fighting for his life but is particularly unnerving for one who is only hallucinating. "The Applicant," in *Tales of Soldiers and Civilians,* is neither a war story nor a horror tale but a satire: it paints the grim picture of a man turned away from a "Home for Old Men" ("'The trustees,' Mr. Tilbody said, closing more doors than one, and cutting off two kinds of light, 'have agreed that your application disagrees with them'"—2.287), for the man is the once-prosperous benefactor of the home. The mere inclusion of this tale may point to the fact that satire is the real underlying body of unity in this collection.

Two tales in *Can Such Things Be?* illustrate Bierce's graveyard humor at its best. One is supernatural, the other nonsupernatural; but the horror is produced by satire, not the supernatural or the lack of it. "One Summer Night" tells the grisly tale of two graverobbers who plunder the tomb of the recently deceased Henry Armstrong. Armstrong, however, refuses to acknowledge the fact of his death and sits up in his grave when it is unearthed. One robber flees, but the other "was of another breed": he kills the corpse again with his shovel, takes it to the local medical college that uses his services, and calmly demands his pay. In

"John Mortonson's Funeral" (actually a tale by Bierce's son Leigh, but one which Bierce extensively polished and prepared for publication) the somber obsequies of Mortonson are rudely interrupted when the mourners flee in terror at the sight of the deceased's face. The coffin falls over and the glass shatters: "From the opening crawled John Mortonson's cat, which lazily leapt to the floor, sat up, tranquilly wiped its crimson muzzle with a forepaw, then walked with dignity from the room" (3.254). There is nothing supernatural about this; it is merely a macabre joke. This lone exception to the supernaturalism of *Can Such Things Be?* is again explicable only if we regard satire as the unifying feature of the volume. "One Summer Night" is also a macabre joke, but the supernaturalism is not an important component of it. Or, rather, while the supernatural itself is significant (the joke depends on the double death of Henry Armstrong), there is no need—and Bierce makes no attempt—to account for the supernaturalism, either pseudoscientifically or in any other way.

But Bierce has gained the greatest notoriety—and, indeed, opprobrium—for the graveyard humor of the four tales included in volume 8 of the *Collected Works* under the heading "The Parenticide Club." Perhaps the most amusing thing about them is the outrage they have elicited among some of Bierce's critics.[15] But we will not understand these tales unless we ascertain whom the satire is directed against. "My Favorite Murder" opens with "Having murdered my mother under circumstances of singular atrocity . . ." (8.147); in "Oil of Dog" we learn that the narrator "was born of honest parents in one of the humbler walks of life, my father being a manufacturer of dog-oil and my mother having a small studio in the shadow of the village church, where she disposed of unwelcome babies" (8.163); and so on. Who is being satirized here? Who but the reader? It is as if Bierce is daring us to find these things funny. Bierce can't lose: if we are revolted, then he can merely chuckle and heap contempt upon us for our squeamishness; if we laugh, we stand self-condemned as sadists. I do not know whether any other works of literature offer an experience parallel to this. It could even be said that this sort of thing—in milder (or subtler) form—colors the whole of Bierce's fiction. What varies, of course, is tone. The bizarre authorial intrusion we noted in "An Occurrence at Owl Creek Bridge" is unusual in its bluntness; in the other war tales Bierce's ice-cold style alone produces shock and horror. Perhaps the trick ending we noted in "The Coup de Grâce," and which in various forms occurs frequently in

Bierce, can be accounted for by appealing to his satiric intent: all Bierce is interested in is a certain type of tableau in which a character is pitilessly placed in a grotesque or unbearable position. This is why so many of Bierce's tales—whether of war or of the supernatural—have irony as their central feature: the irony of a man killing his own father in battle; the irony of a husband killing his wife on a false suspicion of adultery; the irony of a man frightened to death by a stuffed snake. It is clear that these are the focal images which came to Bierce's mind at the moment of inspiration; and he concocted a scenario of events—whether plausibly or not—to work these images into a narrative.

If Bierce is to be termed a misanthrope, it will not be from his avowedly philosophical utterances but from the philosophy that is implicit in his tales. When faced with a crisis, his characters always fail; they fear what should not be feared, act with irrational violence, and collapse in weakness when they should hold firm. If this is Bierce's picture of humanity, then it is a sufficiently bleak one, and the rapier strokes of his prose seem to take a perverse glee in augmenting the horror of his conceptions. Bierce's importance in weird fiction rests upon his role as a satiric horror writer—or a horrific satirist. As such he simultaneously founded and closed a genre; he has no successors.

6.

H. P. LOVECRAFT
The Decline of the West

*H*oward Phillips Lovecraft was born on August 20, 1890, in Providence, Rhode Island. When he was three his father suffered a paralytic attack, dying five years later. The boy's upbringing was left to his overprotective mother, his two aunts, and his grandfather, Whipple Van Buren Phillips, a wealthy industrialist. A precocious boy, Lovecraft was reading at two, writing poems and horror stories at seven, and learning Latin and Greek at eight.

The family's fortunes suffered a reversal in 1904, and Lovecraft and his mother were forced to move into smaller quarters in Providence. Distressed at the loss of his birthplace, the young Lovecraft immersed himself in intellectual pursuits. His formal education was sporadic because of chronic ill health, and in 1908 he apparently suffered a nervous breakdown which prevented him from graduating from high school and enrolling at Brown University. The next five years were spent in relative hermitry, as Lovecraft continued to pursue an impressive self-education in literature, science, and philosophy.

In 1914 Lovecraft joined the amateur journalism movement, plunging into the literary and political activities of the United Amateur Press Association and, later, the National Amateur Press Association. He produced thirteen issues of his own journal, *The Conservative* (1915–1923), filling it with poems, essays, and commentary. Gradually, at the urging of friends, Lovecraft recommenced the writing of horror tales: "The Tomb" (1917) is the first story of his mature period.

For years Lovecraft had no thought of publishing his work professionally. In 1923, however, he was urged to contribute to the fledgling pulp magazine *Weird Tales*. Over the next fifteen years the bulk of his fiction appeared in the pages of that magazine. Still, Lovecraft's genteel upbringing rendered him persistently diffident about commercially marketing his writing, and several attempts by book publishers to issue his work between hard covers came to nothing.

In May 1921 Lovecraft's mother died; a few months later he met Sonia Greene (later Davis), a Russian Jew several years his senior. In 1924 they married, and Lovecraft moved to Brooklyn. Their marriage, however, was not a success; Lovecraft was unable to find a regular job, Sonia's health quickly gave way, and financial troubles forced her to seek a job in the Midwest. Lovecraft was left alone in a city he had come to loathe for its noise, decadence, and "foreigners." He wrote few stories during this period but did the bulk of work on his study "Supernatural Horror in Literature" (1927). In April 1926 he returned to Providence, essentially ending the marriage, and proceeded to write his greatest work—such tales as "The Call of Cthulhu" (1926), "The Colour out of Space" (1927), "The Whisperer in Darkness" (1930), *At the Mountains of Madness* (1931), and "The Shadow out of Time" (1934–1935), as well as the sonnet cycle *Fungi from Yuggoth* (1929–1930). He traveled widely on various antiquarian excursions—to Quebec, Richmond, Charleston, and St. Augustine—and became a stunningly voluminous letter-writer, corresponding with such *fantaisistes* as August Derleth, Donald Wandrei, Clark Ashton Smith, Robert E. Howard, Frank Belknap Long, Robert Bloch, and others.

By the 1930s Lovecraft, although still unknown to the literary world, had become a legend both in the realm of amateur journalism and among the budding community of modern fantasy writers and critics. He continued selling stories sporadically, supporting himself in penury by extensive ghost-writing. Upon his death in Providence on March 15, 1937, his friends set about rescuing his work from the oblivion of the fantasy pulps. In 1939 an omnibus of his tales, *The Outsider and Others,* was published by Derleth and Wandrei under the imprint of Arkham House, a firm founded to publish the work of Lovecraft and his fellow weird writers. Many other volumes have followed, including the landmark publication of his *Selected Letters* (1965–1976) in five volumes.

The problems confronting the study of H. P. Lovecraft are different from those of any other writer in this volume. Like Ambrose Bierce, Lovecraft has received a torrent of criticism from many hands, even though much of this material, even now, does not derive from formally academic sources. As with a number of other genre writers (J. R. R. Tolkien and

Arthur Conan Doyle are merely two that come to mind), Lovecraft's work has been sifted and scrutinized from more angles than one might have thought possible; how much of this criticism—particularly that concerning Lovecraft's unique myth cycle or "Cthulhu Mythos"—is of any especial value is not entirely to the point, although much recent criticism continues to be negative in simply clearing up misconceptions fostered by earlier critics, particularly Lovecraft's self-styled publisher, publicist, biographer, and all-around drum-beater August Derleth.

A more important consideration is the volume and nature of the work left behind by Lovecraft himself. Here was a man who wrote, "There is no field other than the weird in which I have any aptitude or inclination for fictional composition" (SL 3.395), but who, while generally adhering to that dictum as far as fiction was concerned, wrote hundreds of essays and poems and tens of thousands of letters, many of them longer than most of his short stories; and much of this writing—especially the letters—provides invaluable information on the understanding of Lovecraft's thought and, hence, his fiction. This material has, through the diligence of enthusiasts, been published in many editions, and now the sheer bulk of Lovecraft's nonfictional writing threatens to dwarf into insignificance the very fiction it is principally designed to explicate. Let us admit that Lovecraft will never gain much recognition purely for his essays and certainly not for his poetry; and while I maintain that his letters may ultimately be his greatest accomplishment, in the short term all this other matter will really serve as fodder for the analysis of his fiction. Moreover, since Lovecraft never wrote a formal full-length autobiography or philosophical treatise, his life and views must be inferred or collated from an enormous number of disparate sources—not merely his own writings but the countless memoirs written by those friends who knew him either for many years or for a few hours. The amount of interest generated by a man whose collected fiction can fit into only three hefty volumes—a fraction of that left by Blackwood or Dunsany—is unprecedented.

THE PHILOSOPHY OF A MATERIALIST

Lovecraft is the only writer studied here—indeed, the only writer of weird fiction generally, not excluding Poe—whose world view is of interest in itself. Although an amalgam of his wide reading in the ancient atomists and Epicureans, nineteenth-century positivism, Nietzsche, and, later, Spengler, Russell, and Santayana, Lovecraft's thought can be regarded as at least an original compound, its principle feature being an unswervingly "cosmic" point of view whereby all human actions are judged on the scale of both the temporal and spatial infinity of an unknown and aimless cosmos. His world view is worth examining in some detail so that we can then see how precisely and systematically the fiction is an expression of it.

Lovecraft maintained that he was "a mechanistic materialist of the line of Leucippus, Democritus, Epicurus, and Lucretius—and in modern times, Nietzsche and Haeckel" (SL 2.160). Let us ignore the fact that neither Nietzsche nor Haeckel would have been comfortable with the label "materialist"; but that Lovecraft—as with all materialists from the seventeenth century to the nineteenth—founded his materialism upon the atomism of Democritus and Epicurus is certain. Lovecraft had studied ancient materialism thoroughly, especially in Lucretius's *De Rerum Natura,* and he felt that his early studies in astronomy and chemistry only confirmed the tenets of the ancient theories, with such necessary modifications as Laplace's nebular hypothesis and Dalton's analysis of the atom. The dominant belief of the nineteenth century—emphasized by Macaulay, Grote, Spencer, and Thomas Henry Huxley—that atomism represented the keenest thought in antiquity was shared by Lovecraft.

Two fundamental principles are involved in mechanistic materialism: (1) all entity is material (the proposition is more important in what it denies—i.e., the existence of spirit or the immaterial soul—than in what it affirms) and (2) causality is uniform to such a degree that free will is a myth. Lovecraft was not so naive as to conceive of determinism as something external to human action (as many opponents of determinism seem inclined to do) but rather as a phenomenon pervading human life as it pervades everything else: "Determinism—what you call Destiny— rules inexorably; though not exactly in the personal way you seem to fancy. We have no specific destiny against which we can fight—for the fighting would be as much a part of the destiny as the final end. The real fact is simply that every event in the cosmos is caused by the action of antecedent and circumjacent forces, so that whatever we do is unconsciously the inevitable product of Nature rather than of our own volition" (SL 1.132).

The central modern influence upon Lovecraft's metaphysical thought was, as he freely admitted, Ernst Haeckel's *Riddle of the Universe* (English translation 1900). This landmark of thought—the summation of nineteenth-century thinking in biology and physics—incorporated the theory of evolution as the trump card against the theological assertions of both the argument from design and the existence of the soul; for—as Lovecraft echoed in some recently published essays[1]—if we have souls and beasts have none, at what point in the course of our evolution from apes to human beings did we gain this mysterious quality? But Haeckel's great edifice, at least in physics, was seriously damaged only a few years later by Einstein's introduction of the relativity theory, initially in 1905; that theory met with only limited acceptance until the early 1920s—hence the virtual ignoring of Einstein in another work which influenced Lovecraft, Hugh Elliot's *Modern Science and Materialism* (1919)—but observations on the speed of light conducted during an eclipse in 1923 made relativity a virtually certain proposition. Lovecraft's initial reaction was that of many intellectuals of the day: "All is chance, accident, and ephemeral illusion—a fly may be greater than Arcturus, and Durfee Hill may surpass Mount Everest—assuming them to be removed from the present planet and differently environed in the continuum of space-time" (SL 1.231). This of course is nonsense, if nothing else because the condition is unreal and fantastic; but Lovecraft quickly snapped out of these naive and mystical impressions of Einstein, remarking on the discovery that matter is simply another form of energy:

> Matter, we learn, is a definite phenomenon instituted by certain modifications of energy; *but does this circumstance make it less distinctive in itself, or permit us to imagine the presence of another kind of modified energy in places where no sign or result of energy can be discovered?* It is to laugh! The truth is, that the discovery of matter's identity with energy—and of its consequent lack of vital intrinsic difference from empty space—is *an absolute coup de grace to the primitive and irresponsible myth of "spirit." For matter, it appears, really is exactly what "spirit" was always supposed to be.* Thus it is proved *that wandering energy always has a detectable form*—that if it doesn't take the form of waves or electron-streams, *it becomes matter itself;* and that the absence of matter or any other detectable energy-form indicates *not the presence of spirit, but the absence of anything whatever.* (SL 2.266–267)

As for quantum theory and indeterminacy, there is good evidence that Lovecraft came to terms with them as well in the 1930s; the matter is too complicated for exposition here.[2]

If in metaphysics Lovecraft gradually learned to wean himself away from the rigid materialism and unwavering causality that had been the pillars of nineteenth-century science and adopt a more tentative but still predominantly materialistic scheme (thereby finding himself in the company of not only such thinkers as Russell and Santayana but also such disparate creative artists as Theodore Dreiser[3] and James Branch Cabell[4]), in his ethics little such adjustment was necessary. Lovecraft's ethical thought is an amalgam of Epicureanism and Nietzscheism, although an earlier stage of pessimistic Schopenhauerianism was passed through.[5] Rational pleasure is not merely the aim of existence, but in the form of the eighteenth-century standard of "good taste" serves as the actual foundation for ethics:

So far as I am concerned—I am an aesthete devoted to harmony, and to the extraction of the maximum pleasure from life. I find by experience that my chief pleasure is in symbolic identification with the landscape and tradition-stream to which I belong—hence I follow the ancient, simple New England ways of living, and observe the principles of honour expected of a descendant of English gentlemen. It is pride and beauty-sense, plus the automatic instincts of generations trained in certain conduct-patterns, which determine my conduct from day to day. But this is *not ethics,* because the same compulsions and preferences apply, with me, to things wholly outside the ethical zone. For example, I never cheat or steal. Also, I never wear a top-hat with a sack coat or munch bananas in public on the streets, because a gentleman does not do these things either. I would as soon do the one as the other sort of thing—it is all a matter of harmony and good taste—whereas the ethical or "righteous" man would be horrified by dishonesty yet tolerant of coarse personal ways. (SL 2.288–289)

Nietzsche enters into Lovecraft's dismissal of the concept of justice as an empty illusion (Epicurus also maintained the notion, but Lovecraft derived it more directly from *On the Genealogy of Morals*) and the corresponding scorn of democracy. Art is itself made subject to the pleasure principle, and Lovecraft both refutes a correspondent's naive conception of art as spiritual uplift and distinguishes good art from bad precisely by the extent of its authentic pleasure-giving capacity:

> Certainly, life can have no greater gift than emotional contentment during the aimless years from nothingness to nothingness again! However—this is not to imply that the business of acquiring contentment is an easy or frivolous matter. Only the psychology of Victorian illusion and hypocrisy tries to invest trivial and meaningless things with the insipid glamour of a pretended jollity and happiness. In stern fact, the relentless demands prompted by our glandular and nervous reactions are exceedingly complex, contradictory, and imperious in their nature; and subject to rigid and intricate laws of psychology, physiology, biochemistry, and physics which must be realistically studied and familiarly known before they can be adequately dealt with. So real and fixed is this state of things, that we may easily see how futile it is to expect anything to procure emotional satisfaction—or to pretend that it does—unless all the *genuine* laws of emotion and nerve-reaction are recognised and complied with. False or insincere amusement is the sort of activity which does not meet the real psychological demands of the human glandular-nervous system, but merely affects to do so. Real amusement is the sort which is based on a knowledge of real needs, and which therefore hits the spot. *This latter kind of amusement is what art is*—and there is nothing more important in the universe. (SL 3.21)

Related to this stance is what, for better or worse, we have labeled the "art for art's sake" attitude. For Lovecraft this attitude implied not only a totally uncommercial view of literary work—much to the irritation of Lovecraft's latest biographer, L. Sprague de Camp, who would have liked to see Lovecraft be more self-promotional than he was or could have been—but also the notion of "self-expression" as the only logical goal of art. This is why Lovecraft found the amateur journalism movement, which dominated his attention from 1914 to 1925 and persisted sporadically for the rest of his life, so congenial. Here was an organization of writers who thought of no monetary rewards but only the capturing of ideas and images clamoring for expression (so, at any rate, Lovecraft liked to believe). It is also, I believe, part of the reason for Lovecraft's adoration of Lord Dunsany, the aristocrat who could write whatever he wished without thought of audience or sales. This view of Lovecraft's persisted even as he started selling his work professionally.

Lovecraft summed up his philosophical thought by the apt term "cosmic indifferentism." This is at once a metaphysical and ethical stance; or, rather, the ethics is inherent in the metaphysics. Modern science tells us that—whatever may be the actual "stuff" of nature—the earth is but a tiny inkblot in the vast expanse of the cosmos. The whole history of human life is a momentary incident in the ceaseless churning of electrons that makes up an eternal and infinite universe. The ethics implicit in such a view is, first, the minimization of human self-importance and, second, the application of the pleasure principle as the only viable alternative to the loss of cosmic direction and purpose once supplied by the comforting teleology of the Judeo-Christian religion.

Lovecraft's general hostility to religion brings to mind not so much the great thinkers of the nineteenth century—most of whom deliberately downplayed the extent to which their findings made traditional religion untenable—as the anticlericalism of some of the Enlightenment thinkers, especially Holbach, La Mettrie, and Condorcet. We have already seen how Lovecraft used evolution to dispense with the notion of the soul; he likewise found his cosmicism a strong weapon against the notion of godhead and teleology: "A mere knowledge of the approximate dimensions of the visible universe is enough to destroy forever the notion of a personal godhead" (SL 1.44). Lovecraft also felt that important anthropological work of the late nineteenth century—by E. B. Tylor (*Primitive Culture*), John Fiske (*Myths and Myth-Makers*), J. G. Frazer (*The Golden Bough*), and others—had accounted for the origin of religious belief in an entirely satisfactory way:

Since to the untutored mind the conception of impersonal action is impossible, every natural phenomenon was invested with purpose and personality. If lightning struck the earth, it was wilfully hurled by an unseen being in the sky. If a river flowed toward the sea, it was because some unseen being wilfully propelled it. And since men understood no sources of action but themselves, these unseen creatures of imagination were endowed with human forms, despite their more than human powers. So rose the awesome race of anthropomorphic gods, destined to exert so long a sway over their creators. Parallel illusions were almost innumerable. Observing that his welfare depended on conformity to that fixed course of atomic, molecular, and mass interaction which we now call the laws of Nature, primitive man devised the notion of divine government, with the qualities of spiritual right and wrong. Right and wrong indeed existed as actualities in the shape of conformity and non-conformity to Nature; but our first thinking ancestors could conceive of no law save personal will, so deemed themselves the slaves of some celestial tyrant or tyrants of human shape and unlimited authority. Phases of this idea originated the monotheistic religions.[6]

As for religious ethics, Lovecraft showed that he had read Gibbon and Nietzsche well: "Half the tragedies of history are the result of expecting one group to conform to the instinctive reactions of another, or to cherish its values. One of the worst examples of this is the cringing Semitic slave-cult of Christianity which became thrust upon our virile, ebullient Western stock through a series of grotesque historical accidents" (SL 3.45). Religion's sole use, for Lovecraft, was as a palliative for the ignorant masses, a sort of lollipop at day's end for those too uncritical to realize the paradoxes and contradictions to known facts involved in most religious systems. Lovecraft nevertheless felt no need to become evangelically atheistical, remarking that his "only animus toward the church concerns its deliberate inculcation of demonstrable untruths in the community" (SL 1.65). Late in life he came to feel that the indoctrination of the young into a rigid religious dogma was a crime of the first order:

> If religion were true, its followers would not try to bludgeon their young into an artificial conformity; but would merely insist on their unbending quest for *truth*, irrespective of artificial backgrounds or practical consequences. With such an honest and inflexible *openness to evidence*, they could not fail to receive any *real truth* which might be manifesting itself around them. The fact that religionists do *not* follow this honourable course, but cheat at their game by invoking juvenile quasi-hypnosis, is enough to destroy their pretensions in my eyes even if their absurdity were not manifest in every other direction. (SL 3.390–391)

Truly, Lovecraft leaves little place for religion in the thinking person's life, although he (like Santayana) was the first to appreciate, purely aesthetically, the sonority of the Latin Mass or the poetry of a Georgian church steeple.

THE RENUNCIATION OF SUPERNATURALISM

The course of Lovecraft's fiction-writing shows a systematic improvement and broadening of scope unparalleled in weird literature and rarely to be met with in literature generally. All this is especially remarkable in that Lovecraft's mature fictional career spanned less than two decades, from 1917 to 1935.[7] His early work—up to 1926—is entirely routine and conventional, utilizing supernatural or macabre elements with occasional competence but without transcendent brilliance. Nothing—not even "The Rats in the Walls" (1923), a model short story but really nothing more than a supremely able manipulation of Poe-like elements—could have prepared us for the quantum leap in power and range revealed suddenly in "The Call of Cthulhu" (1926). All Lovecraft critics are right to see in this tale the commencement of Lovecraft's strongest and most typical vein of writing; but they may be right for the wrong reasons. Yes, of course, this is where we are first given a glimpse of Lovecraft's ever-evolving myth cycle; but, more important, it is his first truly "cosmic" work and one in which many of his principal concerns—our position in the cosmos; the state of civilization; the role of history in human and cosmic affairs—are adumbrated. From here Lovecraft's work keeps getting better and better, and his subsequent stories are a roll call of weird masterpieces—*The Case of Charles Dexter Ward* (1927), "The Colour out of Space" (1927), "The Dunwich Horror" (1928), "The Whisperer in Darkness" (1930), *At the Mountains of Madness* (1931), "The Shadow over Innsmouth" (1931), "The Shadow out of Time" (1934–1935), "The Haunter of the Dark" (1935). In the early thirties Lovecraft struggled somewhat—perhaps because of the rejection by *Weird Tales* of *At the Mountains of Madness* in late 1931, an incident that, as Lovecraft later testified, "did more than anything else to end my effective fictional career" (SL 5.224)—and "The Dreams in the Witch House" (1932) and "The Thing on the Doorstep" (1933) are two surprisingly inferior tales of his late period; but "The Shadow out of Time" would have redeemed a dozen failures.

There are two transcendently important statements of Lovecraft's theory of weird fiction that every critic must grasp in order to come to terms

with his achievement. The first, significantly, was written when Lovecraft submitted "The Call of Cthulhu" to *Weird Tales* in July 1927:

> Now all my tales are based on the fundamental premise that com-
> mon human laws and interests and emotions have no validity or
> significance in the vast cosmos-at-large. . . . To achieve the essence
> of real externality, whether of time or space or dimension, one must
> forget that such things as organic life, good and evil, love and hate,
> and all local attributes of a negligible and temporary race called
> mankind, have any existence at all. Only the human scenes and
> characters must have human qualities. *These* must be handled with
> unsparing *realism, (not* catch-penny *romanticism)* but when we cross
> the line to the boundless and hideous unknown—the shadow-
> haunted *Outside*—we must remember to leave our humanity and
> terrestrialism at the threshold. (SL 2.150)

This not only states the cosmic perspective emphatically but suggests the
amoralism that is at the heart of Lovecraft's most typical work. A second
statement, made a few years later, is worth citing at some length:

> Fantastic literature cannot be treated as a single unit, because it is a
> composite resting on widely divergent bases. I really agree that *Yog-
> Sothoth* is a basically immature conception, & unfitted for really se-
> rious literature. The fact is, I have never approached serious literature
> as yet. But I consider the use of actual folk-myths as even more
> childish than the use of new artificial myths, since in employing the
> former one is forced to retain many blatant puerilities & contradic-
> tions to experience which could be subtilised or smoothed over if the
> supernaturalism were modelled to order for the given case. The only
> permanently artistic use of Yog-Sothothery, I think, is in symbolic or
> associative phantasy of the frankly poetic type; in which fixed dream-
> patterns of the natural organism are given an embodiment & crys-
> tallisation. . . . But there is another phase of cosmic phantasy (which
> may or may not include frank Yog-Sothothery) whose foundations
> appear to me as better grounded than those of ordinary oneiroscopy;
> personal limitation regarding the *sense of outsideness*. I refer to the
> aesthetic crystallisation of that burning & inextinguishable feeling of
> mixed wonder & oppression which the sensitive imagination experi-
> ences upon scaling itself & its restrictions against the vast & provoca-

tive abyss of the unknown. This has always been the chief emotion in my psychology; & whilst it obviously figures less in the psychology of the majority, it is clearly a well-defined & permanent factor from which very few sensitive persons are wholly free. . . . Superadded to this simple curiosity is the galling sense of *intolerable restraint* which all sensitive people (except self-blinded earth-gazers like little Augie Derleth) feel as they survey their natural limitations in time & space as scaled against the freedoms & expansions & comprehensions & adventurous expectancies which the mind can formulate as abstract conceptions. . . . The time has come when the normal revolt against time, space, & matter must assume a form not overtly incompatible with what is known of reality—when it must be gratified by images forming *supplements* rather than *contradictions* of the visible & mensurable universe. And what, if not a form of *non-supernatural cosmic art*, is to pacify this sense of revolt—as well as gratify the cognate sense of curiosity? (SL 3.294–296)

This is perhaps the most important utterance ever made by Lovecraft, and I shall revert to it constantly throughout this chapter. At the moment it is worth emphasizing that Lovecraft has, by 1931, renounced pure supernaturalism as a viable outlet for weird writing: the majority of his pre-1926 stories are more or less conventionally supernatural, and this vein reached its apotheosis in *The Case of Charles Dexter Ward*. But from 1926 on, Lovecraft's work can only be called quasi science fiction—not merely the few stories ("The Colour out of Space," *At the Mountains of Madness*, "The Shadow out of Time") generally regarded as such, but nearly the whole of his later work. This tendency had, of course, certain dim anticipations in "Dagon" (1917), "Beyond the Wall of Sleep" (1919), and even "Facts concerning the Late Arthur Jermyn and His Family" (1920), but only with "The Call of Cthulhu" did the pattern become systematically established.

This sort of evolution—from supernaturalism to science fiction—was really inevitable given Lovecraft's world view. I am not saying that all science fiction writers are materialists or even empiricists, although I suspect a large number of them are; it is that the sort of work Lovecraft came to write, beginning with "The Call of Cthulhu," was something he gradually realized was as in tune with his materialism as anything could possibly be.

I want to juxtapose two further statements by Lovecraft on the weird tale in order to dissipate the doubts of certain critics as to whether Love-craft really expresses thoroughgoing materialism in his tales and how faithful his renunciation of supernaturalism was in even his late work. The first comes from his essay "Notes on Writing Weird Fiction," written probably around 1932 or 1933: "I choose weird stories because they suit my inclinations most—one of my strongest and most persistent wishes being to achieve, momentarily, the illusion of some strange suspension or violation of the galling limitations of time, space, and natural law which forever imprison us and frustrate our curiosity about the infinite cosmic spaces beyond the radius of our sight and analysis."[8] The sus-pension of natural law—or, rather, its depiction in fiction—appears to be a supernatural conception. But the utterance is clarified in a letter of 1931: ". . . the crux of a *weird* tale is something which *could not possibly happen*. If any unexpected advance of physics, chemistry, or biology were to indicate the *possibility* of any phenomena related by the weird tale, that particular set of phenomena would cease to be *weird* in the ultimate sense because it would become surrounded by a different set of emotions" (SL 3.434). What this means is that natural law is a mental construct based upon current scientific knowledge; any defiance or sus-pension of it is only a defiance of our (incomplete and limited) concep-tions of what is or is not possible in the universe.

Lovecraft is enormously careful to make this clear in all his utter-ances: even in the passage quoted above, Lovecraft speaks of "the illu-sion" of violating natural law. "The Shunned House" (1924) is of su-preme importance in enunciating this notion at length:

We were not . . . in any sense childishly superstitious, but scientific study and reflection had taught us that the known universe of three dimensions embraces the merest fraction of the whole cosmos of substance and energy. . . . To say that we actually believed in vam-pires or werewolves would be a carelessly inclusive statement. Rather must it be said that we were not prepared to deny the possi-bility of certain unfamiliar and unclassified modifications of vital force and attenuated matter; existing very infrequently in three-dimensional space because of its more intimate connexion with other spatial units, yet close enough to the boundary of our own to furnish us occasional manifestations which we, for lack of a proper vantage-point, may never hope to understand.

In short, it seemed to my uncle and me that an incontrovertible array of facts pointed to some lingering influence in the shunned house; . . . still operative through rare and unknown laws of atomic and electronic motion. (M 251–252)

The contrast drawn between vampires and werewolves (pure or conventional supernaturalism) and the entity in the tale is to be noticed. Of the strange meteorite in "The Colour out of Space" it is said: "It was nothing of this earth, but a piece of the great outside; and as such dowered with outside properties and obedient to outside laws" (DH 59). Passing references in *At the Mountains of Madness* to the mind's "accustomed conception of external Nature and Nature's laws" (M 28) and "alien natural law" (M 61) suggest the purely epistemological nature of the conception. In a sense, of course, Lovecraft is cheating by having so many of his creatures come from the far reaches of the cosmos, or even from outside the space-time continuum: it thus becomes very easy to escape the rubric of supernaturalism by saying that these creatures obey various unspecified "outside laws." But let us give Lovecraft credit: his extraterrestrials are never gratuitously inserted into a tale, and an enormous amount of thought has been expended in depicting their anatomy, physiology, psychology, aesthetics, and even politics.

Even pure supernaturalism is handled in occasionally novel and ingenious ways in the early tales. "The Alchemist" (1908), really a juvenile work, is more complex in this regard than many seem to realize. The apparently supernatural curse hanging over the Comtes de C———, whereby each dies around his thirty-second birthday, seems to resolve into a natural solution when it is learned that all the comtes have been killed by human agency as vengeance for the ancient murder of Michel Mauvais by the first comte; but supernaturalism returns from a different perspective, since all the deaths have been caused by a single figure, Charles Le Sorcier, Michel's son, who has prolonged his life unnaturally for hundreds of years through alchemy.

"The Temple" (1920) is a rather odd case. The narrator first declares, "It is only the inferior thinker who hastens to explain the singular and the complex by the primitive short cut of supernaturalism" (D 69); but when he perceives light and chanting in the temple of the vast underwater city, he flatly states that "the events transcend natural law" (D 71). There is no especial reason why the existence of the underwater city (a clear anticipation of the one in "The Shadow over Innsmouth") should strike anyone as contrary to natural law; but for all this the tale cannot be considered quasi science fiction, since there have previously been many other obviously supernatural incidents—some, indeed, not very well integrated into the framework of the narrative.

Before resuming my examination of the dominance of cosmicism and materialism in Lovecraft's fiction, I want to make a detour to his "Dunsanian" fantasies—largely because I see them as detours themselves in the course of Lovecraft's fiction and because they may also help us to understand why and how Lovecraft virtually abandoned both supernaturalism and pure fantasy in his later work.

DUNSANIANISM AND ITS END

What is remarkable about Lovecraft's involvement with Dunsany is not its duration (Lovecraft's intensive Dunsanian phase was really over with "The Other Gods," written less than two years after his first reading of Dunsany) nor the extravagance of his praise of the Irish *fantaisiste* (this was a commonplace amongst Dunsany's enthusiasts), but the degree to which Lovecraft was self-deluded into fancying some close aesthetic tie between Dunsany and himself. It is hard to find two more different writers of weird fiction—Dunsany's atheism is implicit, Lovecraft's explicit; even Dunsany's cosmicism, which first attracted Lovecraft to him, is of an entirely different sort from Lovecraft's: Dunsany's cosmos, enclosed in his pretty imaginary realm, entirely lacks (and is meant to lack) the clutching ontological terror of Lovecraft's void. And yet as late as 1923 Lovecraft could soberly assert that "Dunsany *is myself*" (SL 1.234) and that ". . . Dunsany has influenced me more than anyone else except Poe—his rich language, his cosmic point of view, his remote dreamworld, & his exquisite sense of the fantastic, all appeal to me more than anything else in modern literature. My first encounter with him—in the autumn of 1919—gave an immense impetus to my writing; perhaps the greatest it has ever had" (SL 1.243). Both statements were written just about the time of his discovery of Machen and prior to his discovery of Blackwood and James, but they are nevertheless remarkable. I think C. L. Moore perfectly captured the siren song of Dunsany when she wrote: "No one can imitate Dunsany, and probably everyone who's ever read him has tried."[9] Certainly Lovecraft did so.

I cannot see Lovecraft's Dunsanian stories as anything but an aberration: they deflected him from employing a contemporary time frame (as

he had already done with "Dagon") or developing his topographical realism (already dimly evident in "The Tomb" and "The Statement of
Randolph Carter"). What is more, Lovecraft wasn't even very good at
imitating Dunsany. For one who so frequently stressed the cosmicism of
Dunsany's work, Lovecraft's own imitations are singularly uncosmic,
even in intention. Rather, they aim at reproducing the "type of legend-
ary lore"[10] to which a certain part of Dunsany's work belongs. What is
also curious is that the bulk of Lovecraft's Dunsanian tales do not take
place in an imaginary realm but in the distant past of the earth—the
evidence, too cumbrous to cite here, seems conclusive.[11] "The Tree" (if
it is Dunsanian) is set in ancient Greece, a setting Dunsany almost
never used.

Most of Lovecraft's Dunsanian tales are extremely boring and add
nothing to his total achievement. "The Doom That Came to Sarnath,"
although stylistically a very slavish imitation, is interesting for its subtle
hints that the proud town of Sarnath has brought doom upon itself by its
greed and artificiality. Sarnath itself was founded "at a spot where precious metals were found in the earth" (D 44). The city waxes great and
powerful after it destroys the neighboring "grey stone city" (D 43) of Ib,
and in the midst of Lovecraft's bejeweled descriptions of Sarnath one can
detect its unnaturalness: "And in most of the palaces the floors were
mosaics of beryl and lapis-lazuli and sardonyx and carbuncle and other
choice materials, so disposed that the beholder might fancy himself
walking over beds of the rarest flowers. And there were likewise foun-
tains, which cast scented waters about in pleasing jets arranged with
cunning art" (D 46). The flowers are not real flowers but jewels; the
water does not come from the sea but a fountain.

"The Quest of Iranon" (1921) is perhaps the most effective of his
Dunsanian tales. The eternal youth that Iranon, prince of Aira, preserves
as he seeks his lost homeland is a symbol for the hope that keeps people
alive. But when he finds that he is only a beggar's boy and that Aira is a
mere daydream, he can do nothing but walk calmly to his death in a
marsh, "a very old man"; "That night something of youth and beauty
died in the elder world" (D 117).

By the time Lovecraft came to write *The Dream-Quest of Unknown Kadath*, he had already commenced his "cosmic" phase with "The Call of
Cthulhu," written several months before. The novel is not only his farewell to Dunsanianism but his repudiation of it—or, perhaps, what he

fancied it to be. In this sense the early "Celephaïs" (1920) is of great significance—not intrinsically, but in how Lovecraft recasts the events of that tale in the novel. In "Celephaïs" Kuranes ("when awake he was called by another name" [D 83]) flees the unbearable reality of London and, through drugs, enters the world of his childhood imaginings, where one afternoon he dreamed the town of Celephaïs in the Valley of Ooth-Nargai. Celephaïs is a perfectly pretty sort of place, and in this tale it is all Kuranes wants: ". . . he beheld the glittering minarets of the city, and saw the graceful galleys riding at anchor in the blue harbour, and watched the gingko trees of Mount Aran swaying in the sea-breeze" (D 85). But in *The Dream-Quest,* where Kuranes is encountered again, Celephaïs proves not so attractive:

> He himself had dreamed and yearned long years for lovely Celephaïs and the land of Ooth-Nargai, and for the freedom and colour and high experience of life devoid of its chains, conventions, and stupidities. But now that he was come into that city and that land, and was the king thereof, he found the freedom and the vividness all too soon worn out, and monotonous for want of linkage with anything firm in his feelings and memories. He was a king in Ooth-Nargai, but found no meaning therein, and drooped always for the old familiar things of England that had shaped his youth. All his kingdom would he give for the sound of Cornish church bells over the downs, and all the thousand minarets of Celephaïs for the steep homely roofs of the village near his home. (M 356)

This single passage portrays the renunciation of Dunsanianism—conceived here (mistakenly, I think) as a realm of pure imagination with no connection to the real world—as succinctly as possible. It is why Kuranes tries to dissuade Carter from pursuing his "sunset city," since Kuranes imagines that it is simply a counterpart of his own Celephaïs and will prove ultimately unsatisfying to Carter. I think this conception of Dunsanianism also explains why all the imaginary beings, places, and events created here, with a sort of feverish prodigality, touch no chord in us—they are not meant to. It is all very charming—cloud-hung Serannian, the enchanted wood, Hatheg-Kla, the gugs and ghasts and night-gaunts and cats—but it signifies nothing and is intended to signify nothing. And when Nyarlathotep finally tells Carter what his "sunset city" really is, it is something quite different from what we have been led to expect. I cannot refrain quoting at length one of the most exquisite passages in all Lovecraft, one in which he finally achieves Dunsanian delicacy and pathos:

> "For know you, that your gold and marble city of wonder is only the sum of what you have seen and loved in youth. It is the glory of Boston's hillside roofs and western windows aflame with sunset; of the flower-fragrant Common and the great dome on the hill and the tangle of gables and chimneys in the violet valley where the many-bridged Charles flows drowsily. These things you saw, Randolph Carter, when your nurse first wheeled you out in the springtime, and they will be the last things you will ever see with eyes of memory and of love. And there is antique Salem with its brooding years, and spectral Marblehead scaling its rocky precipices into past centuries, and the glory of Salem's towers and spires seen afar from Marblehead's pastures across the harbour against the setting sun.
>
> "There is Providence, quaint and lordly on its seven hills over the blue harbour, with terraces of green leading up to steeples and citadels of living antiquity, and Newport climbing wraith-like from its dreaming breakwater. Arkham is there, with its moss-grown gambrel roofs and the rocky rolling meadows behind it; and antediluvian Kingsport hoary with stacked chimneys and deserted quays and overhanging gables, and the marvel of high cliffs and the milky-misted ocean with tolling buoys beyond." (M 400–401)

What Carter knows and loves is not, as with Kuranes, an imaginary city dreamed up on an idle afternoon, but the memories of his native land developed over years of living and dreaming. For a very long time I was puzzled by why the mythical towns of Arkham and Kingsport are mentioned here—but I think I and others have been distracted by the patently autobiographical nature of the passage. Lovecraft of course can have no memories of these places, but Carter presumably does. No doubt the novel is obviously autobiographical at this point—a grand and poetic reflection of Lovecraft's return to Providence from two years of misery in New York; but more, it is an indication that realism will now dominate the remainder of his literary work. Lovecraft must draw upon his own memories for artistic creation, and it is scarcely a surprise that his very next work is that paean to Providence, *The Case of Charles Dexter Ward*.

COSMICISM AND MATERIALISM

Lovecraft's Dunsanian stories express some of his ethical concerns—the aesthetic pursuit of beauty ("The Quest of Iranon"); the dangers of a headlong quest for knowledge ("The White Ship"); the supremacy of the imagination ("Celephaïs")—but, because they are not set in the real (or, at any rate, the contemporary) world, they cannot reflect Lovecraft's principal metaphysical tenets of cosmicism and materialism. We have noted that, for whatever reason, Lovecraft chose not to portray cosmicism in his Dunsanian tales, even though he attributed this very quality to Dunsany. It is possible that the sort of cosmicism possible in imaginary-world tales was not the cosmicism he wanted: the cosmicism of Dunsany is not so much horrifying as picturesquely remote; for the metaphysical horror Lovecraft sought, cosmicism must be manifested in the real world.

Cosmicism and materialism so color Lovecraft's work from one end to the other that it is impossible to treat the subject at all comprehensively. It is the medical intern's materialism that, in "Beyond the Wall of Sleep," allows him to construct a machine that can read Joe Slater's thoughts: "It had long been my belief that human thought consists basically of atomic or molecular motion, convertible into ether waves of radiant energy like heat, light, and electricity" (D 31). Crawford Tillinghast in "From Beyond" has some fun implicitly ridiculing Descartes's metaphysics when he notes that the pineal gland "is the great sense-organ of organs" (D 93); it is what allows Tillinghast to construct a machine to see things beyond the scope of the five senses. In "The Shunned House" the vampiric entity is destroyed not by driving a stake through its heart but by sulphuric acid. There is never an entity in Lovecraft that is not in some fashion material.

"Herbert West—Reanimator" is an interesting case in this perspective. West himself seems to adhere as rigidly to materialistic principles as Lovecraft: "Holding with Haeckel that all life is a chemical and physical process, and that the so-called 'soul' is a myth, my friend believed that artificial reanimation of the dead can depend only on the condition of the tissues" (D 134). The narrator, on the other hand, is not quite so convinced: "I, myself, still held some curious notions about the traditional 'soul' of man, and felt an awe at the secrets that might be told by one returning from the dead" (D 137). But it appears that each is only partially right: to be sure, West succeeds in reviving the dead, and thus far he is vindicated; but there are dim hints that his reanimated corpses may not have enjoyed the oblivion Lovecraft felt was our only condition after death. One specimen screams, and the narrator remarks: "Not more unutterable could have been the chaos of hellish sound if the pit itself had opened to release the agony of the damned" (D 137). Both the language and the event it is describing suggest that the corpse is terrified at some loathsome thing he has seen in death. Similarly, another specimen "actually opened its eyes, but only stared at the ceiling with a look of soul-petrifying horror" (D 141). The adjective is of note: how can the soul be petrified if it doesn't exist? But I think this sort of "refutation" of West's (and Lovecraft's) materialism is meant purely in a jocular vein and underscores the parodic humor of the whole story.

Less explicable are certain remarks found in "The Call of Cthulhu." The narrator goes out of his way to stress his materialism and rationalism, noting the "ingrained scepticism then forming my philosophy" (DH 130), his "callous rationalism" (DH 132), "the rationalism of my mind" (DH 142), and so on. Then all of a sudden we read: "My attitude was still one of absolute materialism, *as I wish it still were*" (DH 144; Lovecraft's italics). What is Lovecraft suggesting here? I can only believe that he is criticizing any sort of dogmatic or doctrinaire materialism: his own had by this time become modified by Einstein, Santayana, and modern advances in astrophysics. Still, I find these remarks a little bothersome, especially since nothing in "The Call of Cthulhu" need be impossible to harmonize within a system of modified materialism.

Examples of cosmicism are also too numerous for full citation. The second story of Lovecraft's maturity, "Dagon," already hints it and shows that one of the principal ways Lovecraft chooses to suggest cosmicism is, quite simply, the stupendous *bulk* of his entities. The vampiric entity in "The Shunned House," first described as a "doubled-up human figure" (M 239), turns out to be the "titan *elbow*" (M 261) of an incalculably greater figure. This is particularly felicitous because the prior suggestions of a human shape convey our inability to conceive of any animate entity except in human terms. A similar creature is featured in "Under the Pyramids," a surprisingly powerful tale in spite of the fact that its opening descriptions of the Egyptian countryside read like a travelogue and were probably pillaged from museum handbooks on the subject.

But cosmicism truly and permanently enters Lovecraft's fiction with "The Call of Cthulhu." Of Cthulhu himself we are told, in one of Lovecraft's most memorable lines: "A mountain walked or stumbled" (DH

152). The entity (or entities) in "The Colour out of Space" is never clearly described—much to the advantage of the tale. This is perhaps the most nearly perfect story Lovecraft ever wrote, and like several other works—Dunsany's *Gods of the Mountain,* Blackwood's "The Willows"—becomes nearly uncriticizable for that reason. We seem here, however, to encounter for the first time a cosmic being of an entirely amoral character: even Cthulhu has evil cult followers, and he himself is obviously motivated by a sort of mindless violence and destructiveness. In "The Colour out of Space" Lovecraft manages to suggest that all the effects of the entity—the withering of the landscape, the loathsome crumbling of human beings and animals—are purely the product of contact between this creature and the environment it finds itself in.

"The Dunwich Horror" represents a backward step. Here we are faced not with a god like Cthulhu but with the offspring of a god—Yog-Sothoth—and a human being. This creature too is of great size, and it possesses a furious malevolence; but Lovecraft curiously diminishes the scope of the horror well before the tale is over. The death of Wilbur Whateley foils his plan to let loose the entity (his own twin brother) upon the world. It escapes and ravages the countryside, but really can cause only a certain amount of annoying physical damage. Henry Armitage announces pompously: " 'It's a frightful thing to have alive, but it isn't as bad as what Wilbur would have let in if he'd lived longer. You'll never know what the world has escaped. Now we've only this one thing to fight, and it can't multiply. It can, though, do a lot of harm; so we mustn't hesitate to rid the community of it'" (DH 191). This sounds as if he is talking about some irksome nuisance or pest; and sure enough, Armitage and his friends mutter some spells and send the creature back where it came from. There are several further problems with this story. I have never found a satisfactory explanation of—indeed, it does not even seem to have occurred to anyone to wonder—why Armitage concocts his powder so that the invisible creature can be seen for an instant. What is to be gained by such a procedure? It merely provides Lovecraft an opportunity to indulge in much florid description of ropy tentacles and the like. A greater problem is the figure of Henry Armitage. He is the prize buffoon in all Lovecraft, and I would love to agree with Donald R. Burleson that he is meant in satire, but I am now finding this increasingly hard to accept. Oh, I agree that we are to read this tale as only a temporary halting of the efforts of cosmic entities to destroy or supersede the human race—this much is made clear from the celebrated passage from the *Necronomicon:* "Man now rules where They ruled once; They shall soon rule where man rules now. After summer is winter, and after winter summer. They wait patient and potent, for here shall They reign again" (DH 170). But I now cannot find much evidence that we are to laugh at Armitage. Armitage is really an elaboration of the character of Dr. Willett in *The Case of Charles Dexter Ward,* and there are startling parallels between the two: Willett and Armitage both suppress the horrors in the end and do so by incantations; they exhibit a tendency to take matters into their own hands rather than calling in authorities like the police; and both tales seem to involve Yog-Sothoth in some fashion or other, although his role in *The Case of Charles Dexter Ward* is somewhat nebulous. Unfortunately, Willett is just as given to making self-important utterances as Armitage: "'I can answer no questions, but I will say that there are different kinds of magic. I have made a great purgation, and those in this house will sleep the better for it'" (M 228). And his concluding confrontation with Curwen, where the two trade insults like two stand-up comics trying to outdo each other, nearly ruins an otherwise magnificent novel. But in this regard Willett cannot hold a candle to Armitage: "'It was—well, it was mostly a kind of force that doesn't belong in our part of space; a kind of force that acts and grows and shapes itself by other laws than those of our sort of Nature. We have no business calling in such things from outside, and only very wicked people and very wicked cults ever try to'" (DH 197). I wince every time I read this—Lovecraft makes so few mistakes of this sort that they stand out in greater relief.

Subsequent tales rarely involve entities of cosmic dimensions—rather, we are concerned with whole civilizations of entities, whether from outside or not, and they are best studied in the context of Lovecraft's political views. But it is noteworthy that these entities are frequently vastly superior to human beings—principally in intelligence—and, although some have come from the depths of space, they now allow *us* to dwell on the planet by *their* sufferance. Of the fungi from Yuggoth in "The Whisperer in Darkness" it is said: "They could easily conquer the earth, but have not tried to so far because they have not needed to. They would rather leave things as they are to save bother" (DH 218). It is not even worth their while to destroy us. The hybrid entities of "The Shadow over Innsmouth" feel superiority to humans: "They seemed sullenly banded together in some sort of fellowship and understanding—despising the world as if they had access to other and preferable spheres of entity"

(DH 321). And Zadok Allen lets us know of their power: "'They cud wipe aout the hull brood o' humans ef they was willin' to bother'" (DH 331). Lovecraft never passes up an opportunity to diminish human accomplishments. The planet Pluto—the only new planet discovered in Lovecraft's lifetime—has been found by earthly scientists only because the fungi let them discover it; "and I shiver when I try to figure out the real reason *why* its monstrous denizens wish it to be known in this way at this especial time" (DH 264–265). But the ultimate touch is in "The Shadow out of Time." The Great Race has collected the histories of all the entities in the cosmos, but those for humanity are on the "lowest or vertebrate level" (DH 396). Here not only humanity but nearly all earthly life is seen to occupy a derisively inferior status in the realm of cosmic entity.

GODS AND PLACES

The most distinctive feature of Lovecraft's fiction is its elaborate system of imaginary gods, places, and other paraphernalia which makes its debut in "The Call of Cthulhu" and which is articulated more or less systematically throughout much of Lovecraft's work thereafter. Lovecraft claimed in 1933 that it was Dunsany "from whom I got the idea of the artificial pantheon and myth-background represented by 'Cthulhu,' 'Yog-Sothoth,' 'Yuggoth,' etc." [12] Although there were probably many other sources, the Dunsanian connection is worth pursuing briefly. What Lovecraft presumably means by attributing the inspiration of his myth cycle to his reading of Dunsany is, of course, the artificial pantheon featured in *The Gods of Pegāna* and *Time and the Gods* and in these books alone: subsequent works by Dunsany utilize imaginary gods from time to time, but no longer in a systematic and interrelated manner. But Lovecraft's stupendous achievement was to transfer his pantheon from Pegāna to the real world. The momentousness of this transference cannot be overemphasized: Lovecraft's own "Dunsanian" fantasies evolve their own series of interconnected gods and places—Ulthar, Sarnath, and the like—but they remain in an otherworldly never-never land with dim and insubstantial relations to the real world; these tales accordingly remain pure fantasies. When Cthulhu suddenly emerges from the depths of the Pacific, he effects an unprecedented union of horror and science fiction unlike anything that went before. Cthulhu is a real entity—it may be a symbol, as Nyarlathotep and Azathoth are very largely symbols (and as Dunsany's gods, caught in their imagined universe, are entirely symbols), but it is first and foremost a real, dangerous, and malignant entity. It is also material, albeit with certain anomalous properties such as the ability to recombine disparate parts of itself. And yet its mere existence is more horrifying than its actions or attributes, for by manifesting itself in the real world it embodies the quintessential phenomenon of the weird tale—the shattering of our conception of the universe: "The Thing cannot be described—there is no language for such abysms of shrieking and immemorial lunacy, such eldritch contradictions of all matter, force, and cosmic order" (DH 152). Cthulhu's existence means that we have somehow horribly misconstrued the nature of the cosmos and our place within it; our reaction can only be horror and madness.

Lovecraft's "gods" are not, of course, the sort of gods one finds in conventional religions. In the first place, they tend, like Cthulhu, to be generally material, although usually in some peculiar way—Yog-Sothoth's offspring in "The Dunwich Horror" is invisible; the avatar of Nyarlathotep in "The Haunter of the Dark" cannot stand light and is destroyed (with ironic fortuitousness) by a bolt of lightning. And although they tend to be worshipped either by crazed human beings scattered around the world or by extraterrestrials (the fungi in "The Whisperer in Darkness" revere Nyarlathotep), they seem neither to require nor to benefit from such worship: Cthulhu's sunken city R'lyeh rose from the waves because of an earthquake, and sank because the "stars were not right"; his worshippers neither caused the first event nor could forestall the second. In what are considered other major tales of Lovecraft's myth cycle no "gods" are involved at all, or are involved tangentially. There are none in "The Shadow over Innsmouth" and perhaps none in "The Whisperer in Darkness"—unless one assumes that the strange being disguised as Henry Akeley is Nyarlathotep, something I am now inclined to doubt. But fundamentally these tales are about material entities, although again of an odd sort—the fungi from Yuggoth cannot be photographed with an ordinary camera, and the denizens of Innsmouth, although the appalling product of miscegenation with loathsome fish-frogs, have developed virtual physical immortality once they return to their ocean lairs.

But, as Robert M. Price has proved,[13] even Lovecraft's "gods" do not remain gods for long. Price makes it clear that, in his later work—notably *At the Mountains of Madness* and "The Shadow out of Time"—Love-

craft "demythologized" his gods and reduced them to mere extraterrestrials. This is one of the most important conclusions in the history of
Lovecraft studies, although Price in his brief article did not draw all the
inferences possible from it. For our purposes we should note that this
"demythologizing" renders Lovecraft's "gods" still more amenable to a
materialistic system than before. Of the Old Ones who established their
vast civilization on this planet millennia ago, it is stated that "They were
. . . the originals of the fiendish elder myths which things like the
Pnakotic Manuscripts and the *Necronomicon* affrightedly hint about" (M
59). Their latter-day worshippers are pitiable fools for attributing deific
properties to them: true, they "created all earth-life" (M 22), but they
were merely a race of creatures not fundamentally different from human
beings, albeit of vastly superior intellect. The Old Ones, the fungi from
Yuggoth, the Cthulhu spawn, and the Great Race all battled one another
on this planet in the dim recesses of time—this may suggest, perhaps,
the battles of the Greek or Norse gods, but it is all entirely material and
belongs more to the realm of history than to myth.

In effect Lovecraft's gods or extraterrestrial species all exemplify what
Lovecraft called "*supplements* rather than *contradictions* of the visible &
mensurable universe": they are all logically possible. In a metaphorical
way I believe we can analogously account for the other appurtenances
of Lovecraft's myth cycle, in particular his creation of an elaborate fictional topography superimposed upon or juxtaposed to the real world. I
refer, of course, to such sites as Arkham, Innsmouth, Dunwich, Kingsport, and the like. There is nothing intrinsically odd in creating a mythical
town for the duration of a single tale; but the way Lovecraft built up, bit
by bit, his mythical New England in tale after tale—a phenomenon that
began much earlier than the introduction of his artificial pantheon in
"The Call of Cthulhu"—calls for notice and explication. Any creative
artist will tell you that places are usually invented because no single
locale is likely to have all the features necessary for its function in a
given work, and there is something of this motivation in Lovecraft also:
much work has been done on the real sources for his mythical cities, and
invariably they turn out to be amalgams of places he has seen or read
about. But there is more to it than that: each town develops its own history, and this history is deftly—even insidiously—woven into the real
history of the region. The "old gentry" (DH 157) of Dunwich came there
from Salem in 1692, just as Joseph Curwen came to Providence to escape the witch trials. The *Necronomicon* can be found both at the Wide-

ner Library of Harvard and at the Library of Miskatonic University in Arkham.

These mythical books are a final important component of the myth cycle. Here again real works of demonology and witchcraft would simply not have served Lovecraft's purpose: an ersatz religion needs ersatz bibles and commentaries, and Lovecraft and his friends have supplied plenty. There is occasionally considerable subtlety in the mixture of real and mythical titles, as in one passage in "The Festival": "The books . . . included old Morryster's wild *Marvells of Science* [lifted from Ambrose Bierce], the terrible *Saducismus Triumphatus* of Joseph Glanvill [real], published in 1681, the shocking *Daemonolatreia* of Remigius [real], printed in 1595 at Lyons, and worst of all, the unmentionable *Necronomicon* of the mad Arab Abdul Alhazred [Lovecraft's invention]" (D 211). Olaus Wormius, the Latin translator of the *Necronomicon*, is a real figure, although Lovecraft (whether by error or design I have never been certain) places him in the thirteenth instead of the seventeenth century; John Dee is made the English translator of the work. Gradually, of course, the proliferation of titles defeated its own purpose and became predictable; and one simply skips over passages like this: "He had himself read many of them—a Latin version of the abhorred *Necronomicon*, the sinister *Liber Ivonis*, the infamous *Cultes des Goules* of Comte d'Erlette, the *Unaussprechlichen Kulten* of von Juntz, and old Ludvig Prinn's hellish *De Vermis Mysteriis*" (DH 100).

I believe we must still regard this whole elaborate myth cycle—which is really more akin to a saga in the weird mode—as Lovecraft's greatest achievement. It is what makes Lovecraft's work different from that of any of his predecessors, even Dunsany and Machen from whom he drew so much; and if it is futile to distinguish cleanly which tales do or do not utilize this framework of gods, places, and books, it is nevertheless the case that the subtle links between nearly all the stories of Lovecraft's later period allow them to build upon one another and derive a cumulative power they could not have achieved as separate units.

HISTORY

No reader of Lovecraft can have failed to note the remarkable *specificity* of Lovecraft's work. It is something that goes beyond mere realism, although realism is at its foundation. Realism is not an end but a function in Lovecraft: it heightens the weird by contrast.

In writing a weird story I always try very carefully to achieve the right mood and atmosphere, and place the emphasis where it belongs. One cannot, except in immature pulp charlatan-fiction, present an account of impossible, improbable, or inconceivable phenomena as a commonplace narration of objective acts and conventional emotions. Inconceivable events and conditions have a special handicap to overcome, and this can be accomplished only through the maintenance of a careful realism in every phase of the story *except* that touching on the one given marvel. ("Notes on Writing Weird Fiction" 138)

Something akin to this appears to be happening in Lovecraft's very complex treatment of history. There is such a plethora of dates and events (real and imaginary) in Lovecraft that Peter Cannon has been able to compile an entire booklet of them.[14] We know that the events of "The Picture in the House" took place in November 1896; the events in "Dagon" and "The Temple" occur at very exact points during World War I; we know so precisely the births and deaths of the residents of "The Shunned House" that the tale reads like a radically compressed horrific parody on the generational sagas of Trollope and Galsworthy. What is going on here? Perhaps one other citation from a letter is illuminating: "My own rule is that no weird story can truly produce terror unless it is devised with all the care & verisimilitude of an actual *hoax*" (SL 3.193). There is, certainly, something of the hoax idea in Lovecraft's insertions of so many horrible events into the real history of the ancient and contemporary world; but I keep coming back to the notion of "*supplements* rather than *contradictions*," for what Lovecraft seems to be suggesting is that *more* things have happened in history than we suspect. In precisely the way that the existence of Cthulhu or Yog-Sothoth compels us to revise and expand our notions of entity, the existence of nameless events in Western history—or, in some cases, secret *motivations* for those events—brings us face to face with a past over which we have suddenly lost control. Peaslee's dreams force him into a revision of history: "Traditional facts took on new and doubtful aspects, and I marvelled at the dream-fancy which could invent such surprising addenda to history and science" (DH 396). A passing comment in "Under the Pyramids" (1924) is of interest: "Germans were in charge of the work [of excavating the Temple of the Sphinx], and the war or other things may have stopped them" (D 222–223). I have no doubt that this is what actually happened, but that phrase "or other things" suddenly suggests some loath-some *cause* for their cessation not known before. In one ingenious pas-sage in "The Haunter of the Dark" we get a slight variant of the idea: "The Pharaoh Nephren-Ka built around it [the Shining Trapezohedron] a temple with a windowless crypt, and did that which caused his name to be stricken from all monuments and records" (DH 106). Here is an imaginary person deftly inserted and simultaneously obliterated from history.

Lovecraft's greatest meditation on the nature of history is *The Case of Charles Dexter Ward*. This novel is, quite simply, a detective story; it may be the greatest supernatural detective story ever written. We need not be told that Ward's father is at one point "driven by some vague detective instinct" (M 173) to understand that the whole style and construction of the novel is that of a detective tale. Lovecraft is as rigorously fair to the reader as John Dickson Carr. One example will suffice. At one point we encounter a body, fifty years dead, seen running madly through the town before falling into the frozen river: he is a being Joseph Curwen has raised from the dead, and has singular properties: "The digestive tracts of the huge man seemed never to have been in use, whilst the whole skin had a coarse, loosely knit texture impossible to account for" (M 137). But where have we read this before? Did not Charles Dexter Ward himself, described at the outset of the novel in an asylum, exhibit these features?

> Respiration and heart action had a baffling lack of symmetry; the voice was lost, so that no sounds above a whisper were possible; digestion was incredibly prolonged and minimised, and neural reac-tions to standard stimuli bore no relation at all to anything here-tofore recorded, either normal or pathological. The skin had a morbid chill and dryness, and the cellular structure of the tissue seemed ex-aggeratedly coarse and loosely knit. (M 108)

If we had been paying attention, we could have concluded that the being in the asylum is not Ward at all but Joseph Curwen, dead for a century and a half before being resurrected by Ward. Every line of the novel is written in a way that tells only the surface events of a given incident but suggests something sinister beneath them.

In the great historical digression that forms the long second chapter of the novel we are plunged into the very real history of Providence and

New England: only Curwen and his cohorts are imaginary. Even minor figures like "Dr. Checkley the famous wit" (M 120) and John Merritt, who pay brief visits to Curwen, are real: Merritt's tomb can still be seen in St. John's Churchyard in Providence, and Lovecraft read of Checkley in one of the many books about Providence history he secured during his New York years. Here too we are given hints of the "real" motivations behind certain real events: Curwen once queries someone he has resurrected "about the Black Prince's massacre at Limoges in 1370, as if there were some hidden reason which he ought to know" (M 131); and of course, after the band of Providence worthies dispatch Curwen, they seek to drown their memories in action: "Every man of those leaders had a stirring part to play in later years, and it is perhaps fortunate that this is so. Little more than a twelvemonth afterward Capt. Whipple led the mob who burnt the revenue ship *Gaspee,* and in this bold act we may trace one step in the blotting out of unwholesome images" (M 146). This enormously clever stroke again underscores Lovecraft's whole conception of history—that conventional political and social history masks something so nameless and sinister that it can only be dimly hinted. In this sense the technique of the novel itself, whereby we are forced constantly to read between and *under* the lines of the superficially ordinary events, exemplifies the very point it is making.

Later stories raise this conception to a cosmic level. The successive waves of extraterrestrials that have established civilizations on this planet millions of years in the past make our human conquest of the world—a matter of a few thousand years at most—seem ludicrously infinitesimal. And it is not merely what happened before us but what will follow that gives us cause for unease. We have already seen how, in "The Dunwich Horror," according to the *Necronomicon,* the Old Ones (whoever they are in this particular instance) will take over control of the earth. Peaslee, in the body of his captor, encounters minds from earth's past and future, including "the hardy coleopterous species immediately following mankind" (DH 395). Our rulership of the earth is sandwiched between dinosaurs and insects.

We cannot even claim to have evolved by ourselves to our present state. Lake, when first discovering the Old Ones, recalls myths of "Elder Things supposed to have created all earth-life as jest or mistake" (M 22). This conception is disturbingly confirmed by the bas-reliefs in the Old Ones' city, where "a curious variety of primitive vertebrates" are seen:

These vertebrates, as well as an infinity of other life-forms—animal and vegetable, marine, terrestrial, and aërial—were the products of unguided evolution acting on life-cells made by the Old Ones but escaping beyond their radius of attention. They had been suffered to develop unchecked because they had not come in conflict with the dominant beings. Bothersome forms, of course, were mechanically exterminated. It interested us to see in some of the very last and most decadent sculptures a shambling primitive mammal, used sometimes for food and sometimes as an amusing buffoon by the land dwellers, whose vaguely simian and human foreshadowings are unmistakable. (M 65)

This is probably one of the most fiercely cynical and misanthropic utterances ever made: the degradation of humanity can go no further. It is of no especial importance that, in Lovecraft's very next story, "The Shadow over Innsmouth," an entirely different origin of the human race is supplied, as Zadok Allen notes: "'Seems that human folks has got a kind o' relation to sech water-beasts—that everything alive come aout o' the water onct, an' only needs a little change to go back again'" (DH 331). The guiding principle is the same: the utter decimation of human self-importance by the attribution of a grotesque or contemptible origin of our species.

What is remarkable about Lovecraft's treatment of history is that there is frequently an enormously elaborate effort—amounting to a virtual conspiracy—to suppress hideous facts. Nearly all mentions of Joseph Curwen are expunged from existing documents, and Lovecraft draws a significant parallel with a character in Dunsany's "The King That Was Not": "It can be compared in spirit only to the hush that lay on Oscar Wilde's name for a decade after his disgrace, and in extent only to the fate of that sinful King Runazar in Lord Dunsany's tale, whom the Gods decided must not only cease to be, but must cease ever to have been" (M 147–148). It is as if a sort of revision of history has taken place. This sort of thing occurs elsewhere. We have noted it briefly in the glancing citation of the Pharaoh Nephren-Ka in "The Haunter of the Dark." After the Dunwich horror has wreaked its havoc, "all the signboards pointing toward [the town] have been taken down" (DH 157). Like Joseph Curwen, the town of Dunwich is not acknowledged to exist, just as Lovecraft says (twice) that some people "do not admit that Arthur Jermyn ever existed" (D 82). The government hushes up the events of "The Shadow over Innsmouth," and even the press acquiesces: "Complaints from many liberal organisations were met with long confidential discussions, and representatives were taken on trips to certain camps and prisons. As a result, these societies became surprisingly passive and reticent. Newspaper men were harder to manage, but seemed largely to coöperate with the government in the end" (DH 304). There will be no Watergate or Iran-Contra here. The Great Race erects psychological barriers to prevent displaced minds from recalling their experiences, although in the case of Peaslee these barriers are increasingly worn down through his dogged and almost maniacal pursuit of the truth. What we have, therefore, is a sort of rewriting or plastering over of history, so that certain events are (almost) obliterated. Things are discovered only by chance—the "piecing together of dissociated knowledge" (DH 125) that causes such mental perturbation to the narrator of "The Call of Cthulhu." Better to leave history alone—or, indeed, actively to conceal certain things in the past—than to come face to face with our own fragility, both temporally and spatially, in the cosmos.

HUMANITY AND KNOWLEDGE

In Lovecraft's cosmic scheme humanity occupies a very specific place and function. The human being is an atom in infinity—nothing more but also nothing less. What this means is that the alien, the subhuman, and the superhuman all come under condemnation in Lovecraft. There is a fourth class of abnormal beings—hybrids—but they are better studied in the context of his racialism.

We have seen that, in "The Alchemist," Charles Le Sorcier has literally extended his stay on earth by alchemy. He is the first of Lovecraft's supernaturally aged beings, a type that stalks through many of his tales, especially those of a less intensely cosmic variety. In "The Picture in the House" (1920) the loathsome central figure has prolonged his life by cannibalism: he is at once superhuman in being preternaturally aged and subhuman in the barbarism of his nature and habits. The archaic gentleman of "He" (1925) has lived centuries beyond his allotted span by gaining some sort of mastery over nature:

"To—my ancestor—" he softly continued, "there appeared to reside some very remarkable qualities in the will of mankind; qualities having a little-suspected dominance not only over the acts of one's self and of others, but over every variety of force and substance in Nature, and over many elements and dimensions deemed more universal than Nature herself. May I say that he flouted the sanctity of things as great as space and time, and that he put to strange uses the rites of sartain half-breed red Indians once encamped upon this hill?" (D 271)

These same Indians supernaturally dispatch him hideously. Dr. Muñoz of "Cool Air" (1926) uses science to prolong his existence after death; but the crudeness of his method of artificial preservation condemns him to an unutterable death. Joseph Curwen, of course, in *The Case of Charles Dexter Ward* is one of Lovecraft's greatest creations, and his combination of necromancy and science triumphs over death again and again. Born in 1663, he is done away with—temporarily—in 1771 by a robust band of Rhode Island colonials (although at one point [see M 147] there is a suggestion that Curwen really brought death upon himself by summoning up something he could not control). But he is revived by Charles Ward, his lineal descendant, in 1927, and himself kills Ward before being finally destroyed—for good, presumably—by Dr. Willett. I am inclined to believe that it is not merely the duration of Curwen's life but the very time in which he chose to live that summons Lovecraft's condemnation. Curwen did the bulk of his esoteric studies in the seventeenth century (see M 157); his handwriting is surrounded by the "general aura of the seventeenth century" (M 161): is his very existence so far into Lovecraft's beloved Age of Reason a sort of insult to rationalism?

From the opposite perspective the subhuman is something Lovecraft finds equally loathsome. The very title of "The Beast in the Cave" (1905) suggests that the man who became lost in Mammoth Cave is no longer human. Joe Slater, in "Beyond the Wall of Sleep" (1919), is a denizen of the Catskill Mountains whose primitivism is meant to inspire repulsion in us. Slater is possessed or occupied by some cosmic entity; as a result, the visions he sees in sleep "were assuredly things which only a superior or even exceptional brain could conceive" (D 30). This unusual mental capacity is seen as a virtually supernatural phenomenon. Finally the cosmic being, liberated by Slater's death, says in what strikes me as astonishing contempt: "He is better dead, for he was unfit to bear the active intellect of cosmic entity" (D 34). The mercilessly cruel portrayal of Slater reveals one of Lovecraft's least admirable traits—a sort of intellec-

tual fascism that spares no abuse of mental inferiority. Later stories handle
the idea more subtly but no less viciously. In "The Rats in the Walls" we
see how, as in "The Picture in the House," the human can become the
subhuman through uncouth and primitive practices; but here, of course,
the decline occurs spectacularly fast, in one of the most gripping climaxes in all Lovecraft.

Aliens in Lovecraft—extraterrestrials for the most part—naturally inspire horror (at the outset, at any rate) largely for their mere physical
difference from human beings—tentacles, rugose cones, and the like.
But Lovecraft reserves his greatest sense of loathing when he finds aliens
doing the sort of thing only human beings should do. One suggestive
remark is found in "The Call of Cthulhu": "There are vocal qualities peculiar to men, and vocal qualities peculiar to beasts; and it is terrible to
hear the one when the source should yield the other" (DH 137). Here
the context is that of a depraved band of cultists in a Louisiana bayou;
the notion is that these beings have renounced their humanity and de-
scended to a bestial level. But what horrifies Lovecraft's characters most
is seeing aliens calmly performing activities commonly thought to be
"human" by reason of the high level of intellect and psychological sophistication they require. This is what disturbs Peaslee so much about
the Great Race:

> Their actions, though harmless, horrified me even more than their
> appearance—for it is not wholesome to watch monstrous objects
> doing what one had known only human beings to do. These objects
> moved intelligently about the great rooms, getting books from the
> shelves and taking them to the great tables, or vice versa, and some-
> times writing diligently with a peculiar rod gripped in the greenish
> head tentacles. The huge nippers were used in carrying books and in
> conversation—speech consisting of a kind of clicking or scraping.
> (DH 392–393)

The Great Race has usurped all those qualities that distinguish us as
"human"—speech, reading, writing. Indeed, they do these things much
better than we. Of the fungi from Yuggoth it is said that they had "voices
like a bee's that tried to be like the voices of men" (DH 123). It is as if the
mere attempt to mimic humanity's most distinctive emblem of rationalism is blasphemous.

It is from this context that *At the Mountains of Madness* should be studied. When Lake's subexpedition is destroyed by the Old Ones, Dyer and Danforth survey the damage and remark with loathing: "I have said that the bodies were frightfully mangled. Now I must add that some were incised and subtracted from in the most curious, cold-blooded, and inhuman fashion" (M 37). The word "inhuman" is to be noted. But did not Lake perform a similar crude bisection of an Old One? How is this act any less "inhuman" from the Old Ones' perspective? Dyer and Danforth bury the human and canine remains of the party, just as the Old Ones buried their own dead in that "row of insane graves with the five-pointed snow mounds" (M 39). But the Old Ones are not evil, because they are led by the same spirit of scientific inquiry that brought the whole Miskatonic party to the Antarctic in the first place. When Dyer and Danforth find the sledges abandoned by the Old Ones in their city, they react initially with horror at what they find: "It seems that others as well as Lake had been interested in collecting typical specimens; for there were two here, both stiffly frozen, perfectly preserved, patched with adhesive plaster where some wounds around the neck had occurred, and wrapped with patent care to prevent further damage. They were the bodies of young Gedney and the missing dog" (M 86). The "patent care" is to be observed, for it absolves the Old Ones of any nefariousness in their actions; and it leads directly to Dyer's impassioned utterance: "They were men!" (M 96).

What Lovecraft seems to be saying by the creation of alien, super-human, and subhuman types is that the "normal" human being is so much the norm that any deviations from it will summon an entirely deserved destruction. This notion can be extended even to those human characters who do not in themselves defy normal human physiology. The principal notion here is that of knowledge. The attainment of super-human power is, in Lovecraft, almost exclusively the result of super-human knowledge (the individual in "The Picture in the House" is the only exception). Other characters aspiring to this sort of knowledge suffer equally spectacular dooms. In "The Other Gods" (1921), a very simple-minded tale of hubris, Barzai the Wise penetrates the secret of the gods: "'The wisdom of Barzai hath made him greater than earth's gods, and against his will their spells and barriers are as naught'" (D 130); he is snatched up by the gods and never seen again. In an equally inept tale, "From Beyond" (1920), Crawford Tillinghast has contrived a machine that reveals sights beyond what the five senses can perceive; up to this point nothing is wrong, but what Tillinghast seeks to do with this knowledge bodes ill for him: "'I tell you, I have struck depths that your little brain can't picture! I have seen beyond the bounds of infinity and drawn down daemons from the stars. . . . I have harnessed the shadows that stride from world to world to sow death and madness. . . . Space belongs to me, do you hear?'" (D 96). Tillinghast is perhaps the first example of an excessive or misdirected pursuit of knowledge; but there are many others. The nebulous figure in "Hypnos" (1922) "had designs which involved the rulership of the visible universe and more; designs whereby the earth and the stars could move at his command, and the destinies of all living things be his" (D 166); but this is no proper role for a mere mortal, and he is destroyed (for our purposes it is of no especial importance whether he was a product of the narrator's imagination or not). Charles Dexter Ward writes that Joseph Curwen's plans involve "all civilisation, all natural law, perhaps even the fate of the solar system and the universe" (M 181–182). I am somewhat at a loss to understand how this is possible merely from the resurrection of the "essential saltes" of human beings: even the combined knowledge and powers of the world's greatest thinkers—for it is they whom Curwen and his cohorts are resurrecting—would not seem to have any *cosmic* ramifications. It is true that Curwen also raises nameless entities from "outside spheres," but their function is never clarified.

Knowledge does not always appear in so dismal a light in Lovecraft, and it would be wrong and even paradoxical to call Lovecraft anti-intellectual; indeed, pure intellection not only becomes something to be desired but serves as a *justification* of various characters' behavior, even if they go on to suffer death or madness. The simple and poignant utterance, "I did it for the sake of knowledge" (M 182), exonerates Charles Dexter Ward of any complicity in the resurrection of Joseph Curwen. The central figure of "The Temple," a German submarine commander, is subjected to the most fatuous sort of propagandistic satire ("my iron German will" (D 59]; "He was a German, but only a Rhinelander and a commoner" [D 68]), but actually becomes a fairly admirable character by his pursuit of knowledge even in the face of his desperate situation: "Though I knew that death was near, my curiosity was consuming" (D 68).

In the later, cosmic tales this idea is elaborated at considerable length. A transitional work seems to be "The Whisperer in Darkness" (1930), in which Lovecraft cannot quite bring himself to admit that human penetration of the unknown gulfs of the cosmos is anything but an appalling aberration. In this tale entities from outer space—variously called the Outer Ones or the fungi from Yuggoth—have come to the earth principally, it seems, to mine a metal not available on their planet, but also to take the minds of certain human beings on infinitely vast voyagings throughout the cosmos. This is virtually identical with what, several years later, the Great Race would do in "The Shadow out of Time," and the idea is portrayed there as, certainly, a little disconcerting but ultimately one in which the fascination of cosmic knowledge outweighs the displacement of one's personality. Such a position has yet to be reached in "The Whisperer in Darkness," and the fungi are presented as loathsome abominations. A letter written by the fungi to Albert Wilmarth, the narrator, is of interest:

> All that the Outer Ones wish of man is peace and non-molestation and an increasing intellectual rapport. This latter is absolutely necessary now that our inventions and devices are expanding our knowledge and motions, and making it more and more impossible for the Outer Ones' necessary outposts to exist *secretly* on this planet. The alien beings desire to know mankind more fully, and to have a few of mankind's philosophic and scientific leaders know more about them. With such an exchange of knowledge all perils will pass, and a satisfactory *modus vivendi* be established. The very idea of any attempt to *enslave* or *degrade* mankind is ridiculous. (DH 239)

This idea sounds perfectly rational, but in context it is presented as part of an elaborate deception whereby Wilmarth himself will be taken off the planet to prevent his disseminating information about the entities. Later Wilmarth himself speculates: "To shake off the maddening and wearying limitations of time and space and natural law—to be linked with the vast *outside*—to come close to the nighted and abysmal secrets of the infinite and the ultimate—surely such a thing was worth the risk of one's life, soul, and sanity!" (DH 243). This exact utterance, stated less hyperbolically, can be found in "Notes on Writing Weird Fiction"; but Wilmarth draws back in horror and flees.

By the time we come to *At the Mountains of Madness* the pursuit of knowledge has become an unalloyed good. Both the aliens—the starheaded Old Ones—and the human protagonists are fired with a thirst for knowledge and understanding. Dyer, in speaking of how he maintained his equilibrium when exploring the millennia-old city of the Old

Ones in Antarctica, states: "In my case, ingrained scientific habit may have helped; for above all my bewilderment and sense of menace there burned a dominant curiosity to fathom more of this age-old secret—to know what sort of beings had built and lived in this incalculably gigantic place, and what relation to the general world of its time or of other times so unique a concentration of life could have had" (M 47). Toward the end the Old Ones themselves cease to be horrifying, since they are inspired by the same scientific spirit as their human counterparts; I must now quote the entire passage whose conclusion I cited earlier: "Scientists to the last—what had they done that we would not have done in their place? God, what intelligence and persistence! What a facing of the incredible, just as those carven kinsmen and forbears had faced things only a little less incredible! Radiates, vegetables, monstrosities, star-spawn—whatever they had been, they were men!" (M 96).

"The Shadow out of Time" completes the pattern. The Great Race, a group of disembodied minds who have flitted from body to body over the eons, are the universe's greatest intellects: the race "had learned all things that ever were known or ever would be known on the earth, through the power of its keener minds to project themselves into the past and future, even through gulfs of millions of years, and study the lore of every age" (DH 385). They have no function but intellection; even the Old Ones of *At the Mountains of Madness* maintained an empire of sorts for a time, and it was this that indirectly led to their fall. Nathaniel Wingate Peaslee's mind is displaced by a mind of the Great Race, and he is flung back into the body of his displacer. At one point he remarks: "Sight and sound are the only senses I have ever exercised" (DH 392) during the dreams in which he recalls his experiences. This is interesting because it is, again, almost exactly the state the minds in "The Whisperer in Darkness" would find themselves in: "There was a harmless way to extract a brain, and a way to keep the organic residue alive during its absence. The bare, compact cerebral matter was then immersed in an occasionally replenished fluid within an ether-tight cylinder of a metal mined in Yuggoth, certain electrodes reaching through and connecting at will with elaborate instruments capable of duplicating the three vital faculties of sight, hearing, and speech" (DH 257). But again the notion is presented there as horrific.

Somewhere between the two extremes of pure knowledge and knowledge used for evil purposes is a sort of *aesthetic* quest for knowledge in which certain characters engage. Note the remark of the protagonist of

"Dagon" as he explores the strange terrain revealed by a volcanic erup-
tion: "Dazed and frightened, yet not without a certain *thrill* of the scientist's or archaeologist's *delight* . . . " (D 17). The narrator of "The Nameless City" (1921) states: "I was more afraid than I could explain, but not
enough to dull my *thirst for wonders*" (D 101)—it is wonders, not knowledge, that he thirsts for. The narrator of "The Lurking Fear" (1922) confesses, a little pompously, to a "love of the grotesque and the terrible
which has made my career a series of quests for strange horrors in literature and in life" (D 179)—a slightly more rational version of the quest
for new sensations indulged in by the characters of "The Hound"
(1922), but still not a pursuit of knowledge in any abstract way. These
characters end up not dead but psychologically shattered, and the suggestion is that their impure approach to intellection has brought this
about.

And yet Lovecraft seems to have had an extraordinarily low opinion
of people's ability to deal with certain types of knowledge. As early as
1918 he wrote: "All rationalism tends to minimise the value and importance of life, and to decrease the sum total of human happiness. In many
cases the truth may cause suicidal or nearly suicidal depression" (SL
1.65). This sort of thing—a highly exaggerated sense of the power of the
intellect in human affairs—is understandable in one who himself so
consistently led the life of the mind. It leads not only to grandiose utterances like the one quoted earlier ("a mere knowledge of the approximate dimensions of the visible universe is enough to destroy forever the
notion of a personal godhead" [SL 1.44]—would that it were so!), but
to such things as the celebrated opening of "Arthur Jermyn": "Life is a
hideous thing, and from the background behind what we know of it
peer daemoniacal hints of truth which make it sometimes a thou-
sandfold more hideous. Science, already oppressive with its shocking
revelations, will perhaps be the ultimate exterminator of our human
species—if separate species we be—for its reserve of unguessed horrors
could never be borne by mortal brains if loosed upon the world" (D 73).
(Parenthetically it is to be wondered whether this rousing oration is actually borne out by the events of the tale: Arthur Jermyn learns that *he*
has a white ape in his very recent ancestry, but this was merely an isolated case of miscegenation. Does Lovecraft mean us to feel horror, by
extension, at the truth of the Darwin theory? Surely even Lovecraft did
not expect people to find evolution psychologically unbearable.) And
we cannot refrain from quoting the opening of "The Call of Cthulhu":

The most merciful thing in the world, I think, is the inability of the human mind to correlate all its contents. We live on a placid island of ignorance in the midst of black seas of infinity, and it was not meant that we should voyage far. The sciences, each straining in its own direction, have hitherto harmed us little; but some day the piecing together of dissociated knowledge will open up such terrifying vistas of reality, and of our frightful position therein, that we shall either go mad from the revelation or flee from the deadly light into the peace and safety of a new dark age. (DH 125)

The word *merciful* is of extreme frequency in Lovecraft and applies most often to instances in which characters just fail to learn some cataclysmic truth which would destroy their equilibrium—principally by revealing their appallingly trivial place in the cosmic scheme of things. Peaslee, speaking of his failure to bring back the scroll that would have proven the truth of all the events of "The Shadow out of Time," remarks: "For an instant I half regretted having lost a certain awesome object in my stark fright—but now I know that the loss was merciful" (DH 411–412). Its loss allows Peaslee to maintain—pitiably—the comforting belief that all his experiences were a dream; it is a prime instance of what Lovecraft elsewhere calls "the desperation of mental self-defence" (M 44).

One final aspect of the role of knowledge in Lovecraft is the notion of curiosity. This too seems to have its positive and negative sides (although principally the latter), and the guiding principle is again the manner in which curiosity is manifested. When, in "The Tomb," the narrator states that "in that instant of curiosity was born . . . madly unreasoning desire" (D 5), his fate is sealed. The narrator of "The Nameless City" confesses that "the tangible things I had seen made curiosity stronger than fear" (D 101). The narrator of "The Music of Erich Zann" (1921) notes, "I had a curious desire to look out of that window" (DH 87), suggesting simultaneously a sense of curiosity and an admission that there is something a little anomalous—even unwholesome—in such curiosity. The lounger who was to have supplied ice to Dr. Muñoz "had fled screaming and mad-eyed . . . perhaps as a result of excessive curiosity" (DH 206). At one point the narrator of "The Shadow over Innsmouth" notes: "Curiosity flared up beyond sense and caution" (DH 327). What Gilman, in "The Dreams in the Witch House," learns about Keziah Mason "fascinated [him] beyond all reason" (M 263). There are surprisingly few instances of what might be called restrained or rational curiosity—we have noted it in "The Temple" and *At the Mountains of Madness,* where it is also stated that "human curiosity is undying" (M 35). Nevertheless I am disinclined to attribute too much to this phenomenon—I cannot imagine that Lovecraft means us, for example, to think that the narrator of "The Shadow over Innsmouth" brought doom upon himself merely by excessive or unwise curiosity: his ultimate transformation into a monster is a function of his own heredity, hence something over which he has no control.

As it is, the notion that knowledge, while in itself morally neutral, can cause profound psychological trauma is something Lovecraft is endlessly fond of expressing. The narrator of "Dagon" will kill himself after telling of his harrowing experience. The narrator of "The Call of Cthulhu" confesses to permanent psychological disturbance: "I have looked upon all that the universe has to hold of horror, and even the skies of spring and the flowers of summer must ever afterward be poison to me" (DH 154)— and this after not even seeing Cthulhu but merely reading of that entity from Johansen's narrative. "The Outsider" is perhaps the most poignant example of this idea. At the outset the creature states that "my longing for light grew so frantic that I could rest no more" (DH 47). Here the surface reference is to the light of the sun, since the creature has lived in an underground castle his entire life; but by a transparent symbolism we are to understand that he seeks the light of knowledge, in particular knowledge of himself and his relation to the world. He finds this knowledge, discovers that he is a monster, and concludes: "I know that light is not for me" (DH 52).

PSYCHOLOGY

Lovecraft rarely engages in the sort of intense psychological analysis that distinguishes the work of Blackwood. He attempted to explain this feature of his work (I am not yet ready to call it a deficiency) by claiming that "phenomena" and not individuals are at the heart of his tales. Indeed, the cosmicism of Lovecraft's outlook, minimizing human beings to atoms in infinity, would have made vivid characterization actually detrimental to his philosophical goal. But in truth all this strikes me as an elaborate rationalization for Lovecraft's profound unconcern with individuals qua individuals (not as representatives of civilization); he admitted as much in a candid moment: "Individuals and their fortunes within natural law move me very little. They are all momentary trifles bound from a common nothingness toward another common nothingness. Only the cosmic framework itself—or such individuals as symbolise principles (or defiances of principles) of the cosmic framework—can gain a deep grip on my imagination and set it to work creating. In other words, the only 'heroes' I can write about are *phenomena*" (SL 5.19). There really are relatively few memorable characters in Lovecraft, and like Milton's Satan they tend to be more flamboyantly evil ones, like Joseph Curwen or Keziah Mason.

Lovecraft's concern with individual human psychology is generally restricted to that of his narrators: it is they who, by their perception of and reaction to phenomena, will convey to the reader the sense of cosmic insignificance that is at the heart of Lovecraft's fictive aim. Peaslee's discovery of the document he must have written 150,000,000 years ago is perhaps the most mind-shattering moment in all literature. Dyer and Danforth constantly engage in the "desperation of mental self-defence" as they explore the hoary city of the Old Ones, trying not to think that an alien civilization vastly antedating the human race and vastly superior to it erected the place.

There are only two aspects of psychology in Lovecraft that I want to discuss here, because they dovetail nicely with both his materialism and his political concerns over the decline of the West. One is what might be called the *integrity of consciousness.* By this I mean the notion that the mind or consciousness is logically separable from the body. On the face of it, this sounds like some sort of naive dualism and hence a refutation of materialism, but in fact the reverse is the case: since, for Lovecraft, the mind is precisely equivalent to the (material) brain, thought and consciousness became nothing more than epiphenomena of brain function. It may be odd to assert that minds in Lovecraft are more often than not impervious to infiltration—that they, like the old conception of the atom, retain their integrity even when displaced from the body—but such seems to be the case, even—perhaps especially—when mind transference is involved.

Consider "The Thing on the Doorstep." Asenath Waite has developed the power of casting her mind into the body of another person, while that person's mind occupies her own body. Throughout the story it becomes essential that this transference occur cleanly—there is, and can be, no intermingling of minds, merely a sort of mental musical chairs whereby minds leap from one body to another. Daniel Upton, the friend of Asenath's husband Edward Derby, can tell precisely (although he refuses to admit it to himself) when Edward is occupying his body and when Asenath has forced him out:

> Then the thing happened. Derby's voice was rising to a thin treble scream as he raved, when suddenly it was shut off with an almost mechanical click. I thought of those other occasions at my home when his confidences had abruptly ceased—when I had half fancied that some sort of obscure telepathic wave of Asenath's mental force was intervening to keep him silent. This, though, was something altogether different—and, I felt, infinitely more horrible. The face beside me was twisted almost unrecognisably for a moment, while through the whole body there passed a shivering motion—as if all the bones, organs, muscles, nerves, and glands were readjusting themselves to a radically different posture, set of stresses, and general personality. (DH 289–290)

And when Derby asks harrowingly, "Asenath . . . *is there such a person?*" (DH 289), he is in effect defining a human being solely by consciousness: there is no (longer) such a person as Asenath, because Asenath is really the mind of her father Ephraim, who displaced the consciousness of his own daughter at his death. And similarly there ceases to be an Edward Derby when Asenath does the same to him, flinging his mind into her decaying body after Derby has killed her. This is why Upton can announce at the beginning: "It is true that I have sent six bullets through the head of my best friend, and yet I hope to shew by this statement that I am not his murderer" (DH 276): the body he riddled with bullets was Derby's, to be sure, but the mind was Asenath's (or Ephraim's). Therefore the *person* is Asenath or Ephraim.

Exactly analogous is "The Shadow out of Time," in which a similar shuttling back and forth of minds occurs, although this time over vast gulfs of space and time. I must add parenthetically that this method is an extraordinarily ingenious way of escaping the pitfalls and paradoxes of conventional time travel: since it is only the mind that travels, there is no alien body to disrupt the events of the future or past. Lovecraft even alludes to this phenomenon at one point:

> When a captive mind of alien origin was returned to its own body in the future, it was purged by an intricate mechanical hypnosis of all it had learned in the Great Race's age—this because of certain

troublesome consequences inherent in the general carrying forward
of knowledge in large quantities.

The few existing instances of clear transmission had caused, and
would cause at known future times, great disasters. (DH 388)

Perhaps the only flaw in the conception of this tale is Lovecraft's failure
to explain—or even to conjecture plausibly—*how* the Great Race had
developed the ability to cast their minds into the future and past. Mind
transference of the Asenath Derby variety is at least conceivable; but to
say only that the Great Race performed their feat with "suitable mechanical aid" (DH 386)—presumably the "queer mixture of rods,
wheels, and mirrors" (DH 374) seen in Peaslee's home just prior to the
end of his "amnesia"—is worse than useless. It is the one weak link in
an otherwise stupendous story.

"The Whisperer in Darkness" also implicitly identifies the person
strictly with mental activity, since the premise is that the "prodigious
surgical, biological, chemical, and mechanical skill" (DH 257) of the
fungi makes it possible for them to carry the living brains of human (and
other) beings in canisters and bear them off on unthinkable voyages
through the cosmos. Wilmarth reacts to this idea with horror, but Peaslee has evidently reconciled himself to it.

Real interpenetration of a human mind or consciousness does occur
in Lovecraft, but it is infrequent and generally incomplete. In "The
Tomb" a modern-day character is possessed by the spirit of his ancestor,
and the latter causes him to perform highly uncharacteristic acts like
uttering a bawdy drinking song when he himself appears to be a shel-
tered teetotaller. I am unsure of the degree of interpenetration of the
cosmic entity into the mind of Joe Slater in "Beyond the Wall of Sleep":
as Steven J. Mariconda has pointed out, there is a jarring discontinuity
between Slater's conceptions (originating from the cosmic entity) and
his speech, which is simply "the debased patois of his environment" (D
27). The vampiric entity of "The Shunned House" performs a limited
possession of his victims, making them shriek in French when they do
not know the language. Cthulhu, of course, is attributed with a "mastery of dreams" (DH 147); although, interestingly enough, this mastery
extends only to those who are aesthetically sensitive—just as the Great
Race selects for mind transference only "a person of keen thoughtful-
ness" (DH 377). This is the same sort of intellectual exclusivity we saw

earlier in "Beyond the Wall of Sleep," handled here with less offensive crudity.

The Case of Charles Dexter Ward is the most ambiguous example. Recent critics have ridiculed Barton L. St. Armand's notion that "Charles Dexter Ward is . . . literally possessed by the past, which in the form of his ancestor Joseph Curwen reanimates itself in his body, usurps his mind, and plunges him fully into an alien and evil world." [15] This is, indeed, not exactly what happens in the novel, but St. Armand may be more correct than he himself—or his opponents—realized. There is no literal possession of Ward by Curwen: Ward simply unearths Curwen's grave and resurrects him through his "essential saltes"; and Curwen ultimately murders Ward when the latter proves too "squeamish" in carrying out Curwen's grand plans for the rulership of the universe (or whatever he has in mind). The crux of the matter is what causes Ward to commence researching his ancestor's life and work so compulsively. We have seen that for much of the novel Ward is activated by a purely academic quest ("I did it for the sake of knowledge"); and at one point the omniscient narrator provides an entirely sound rationale for Ward's delvings: "Charles Ward . . . first learned in 1918 of his descent from Joseph Curwen. That he at once took an intense interest in everything pertaining to the bygone mystery is not to be wondered at; for every vague rumour that he had heard of Curwen now became something vital to himself, in whom flowed Curwen's blood. No spirited and imaginative genealogist could have done otherwise than begin an avid and systematic collection of Curwen data" (M 148). But there are faint suggestions that Curwen is somehow exercising an influence beyond the grave so that Ward is compelled to resurrect his ancestor without really knowing what he is doing. Why else does Curwen marry and, at the birth of a daughter, "welcome [the event] with a fervour greatly out of keeping with his usual coldness" (M 127)? Why does he write in a letter: "*And of ye Seede of Olde shal One be borne who shal looke Backe, tho' know'g not what he seeks*" (M 151)? And somehow Yog-Sothoth is involved. In this same letter Curwen notes that "I laste Night strucke on ye Wordes that bringe up YOGGE-SOTHOTHE," and later: "ye Thing will breede in ye Outside Spheres." Whether Yog-Sothoth *is* the "Thing" that will so breed or something else, I am not certain; probably they are separate. In any case, Curwen then writes in a memo: "I am Hopeful ye Thing is breed'g Outside ye Spheres. It shall draw One who is to Come" (M 162); and

Willett challenges Curwen at the end: "I know how you wove the spell that brooded outside the years and fastened upon your double and descendant" (M 232–233). I still have no idea what Yog-Sothoth is in this story; I am not sure Lovecraft did, either. But the point still remains that Ward (pace St. Armand) is not responsible for his own actions, since in some fashion or other something from outside seized him and caused him to resurrect Curwen. If there were real psychic possession involved, it is strange that Curwen had to kill Ward instead of controlling him mentally.

True interpenetration of minds occurs in only a single story, "The Haunter of the Dark." Here there is no question that Robert Blake's mind is possessed—fleetingly, at any rate—by the avatar of Nyarlathotep; his diary entry makes it clear:

> "My name is Blake—Robert Harrison Blake of 620 East Knapp Street, Milwaukee, Wisconsin. . . . I am on this planet. . . .
>
> "Sense of distance gone—far is near and near is far. No light—no glass—see that steeple—that tower—window—can hear—Roderick Usher—am mad or going mad—the thing is stirring and fumbling in the tower—I am it and it is I—I want to get out . . . must get out and unify the forces. . . . It knows where I am. . . ." (DH 115)

Incidentally, this passage and the whole scenario are rather obviously derived from Hanns Heinz Ewers's "The Spider" (which Lovecraft read in Dashiell Hammett's 1932 anthology, *Creeps by Night*). In Ewers's tale a man is similarly fascinated by a presence in a building across from his hotel room; he similarly keeps a diary and writes at the end:

> My name—Richard Bracquemont, Richard Bracquemont. Richard— oh, I can't go any farther—Richard Bracquemont—Richard Bracquemont—now—now—I must look at her . . . Richard Bracquemont—I must—no—no, more—more . . . Richard . . . Richard Bracque—[16]

I am not sure Lovecraft has improved on Ewers in this tale.

The other aspect of psychology I wish to treat is the notion of madness. An unusually large number of Lovecraft's characters go mad at some point or other, and many others have madness imputed to them. The narrator of "The Tomb" feels obliged to make this admission right at

the outset: "In relating the circumstances which have led to my confinement within this refuge for the demented, I am aware that my present
position will create a natural doubt of the authenticity of my narrative"
(D 3). The narrator of "Dagon" is no more assuring: "I am writing this
under an appreciable mental strain, since by tonight I shall be no more"
(D 14). But there are more interesting cases; in particular, there are
many tales in which characters, in the "desperation of mental self-
defence," merely attribute madness either to themselves or to others in
order not to acknowledge certain horrible truths about the universe. In
this sense madness becomes a type of *excuse*—a means whereby we can
preserve our own precarious mental equilibrium. Madness means that
there is something wrong with the perceiver, not the universe perceived.
From this perspective madness is at once metaphysical and political—
metaphysical because it is a way of shielding ourselves from certain
truths too painful to endure, and political because civilization at large
can use madness as a way of covering up these same unpleasant truths.

"It was so much simpler—so much more normal—to lay everything
to an outbreak of madness on the part of some of Lake's party" (M 36),
Dyer writes when encountering the horror of Lake's decimated subexpedition. When Derby tells Upton of Asenath's powers of mind exchange, Upton ponders: "Could I accept an explanation as insane as
this?" (DH 294). Later on he wonders whether he himself is mad but is
forced to conclude: "No madness of mine could account for *all* the evidence" (DH 299). Recall also Dyer's remark about the "row of insane
graves" (M 39) of the Old Ones—they are "insane" only on the pre-
sumption that human beings dug them; the truth—that living Old Ones
buried their dead—is at this point too incredible for Dyer to accept. The
entirety of "The Shadow out of Time" is one long attempt by Peaslee to
pass off his experiences as dream or delusion: "There is reason to hope
that my experience was wholly or partly an hallucination" (DH 368).

Madhouses in Lovecraft are habitually places housing those who have
glimpsed some truth about existence too horrible to bear. It is not necessarily the case that the inmates of asylums are actually mad; it is that a
civilization based upon rationalism is compelled to do away with those
of its members who threaten its stability. Even the narrator of "The
Tomb" may be of this sort, for he is certainly rational in the telling of his
tale. The cousin of the narrator of "The Shadow over Innsmouth" has
been locked away for years in a madhouse, presumably because he has
"the Innsmouth look." Joseph Curwen, after he has killed Ward and

tries to take his place, is placed in a madhouse, even though it seems as if his maladies are more physiological than psychological. "The Thing on the Doorstep" is an enormously ingenious example of this conception. Derby is placed in an asylum because of his (true) belief that Asenath is really Ephraim and is trying to take over his mind. But this notion is so "insane" to the world at large that he is locked away. Later Upton hears that "Edward's reason had suddenly come back" (DH 298); he hastens to the sanitarium "in a flood of delight" (DH 298), but what he finds is a being who is outwardly entirely rational but who entirely lacks all Edward's traits of character. It is Asenath, of course, in Edward's body: "He spoke affably of arrangements for release—and there was nothing for me to do but assent, despite some remarkable gaps in his recent memories. Yet I felt that something was terribly, inexplicably wrong and abnormal. There were horrors in this thing that I could not reach. This was a sane person—but was it indeed the Edward Derby I had known?" (DH 298). These same "gaps in his recent memories"—memories of Charles Ward's boyhood—are exactly what banish the disguised Curwen to the asylum.

THE POLITICS OF A MATERIALIST

Hitherto I have studied Lovecraft philosophically; but the tendency to study Lovecraft from a political perspective is very strong, not merely because certain types of political considerations—notably racialism—enter into his work at a very early stage and persist throughout his career, but because during at least the last seven or eight years of his life Lovecraft appeared to pay more attention to matters of politics, economics, and social reform than to any other issue. Lovecraft's conversion from monarchism to socialism appears to be the most spectacular turnabout in his entire philosophy, although perhaps we shall find it less so. In any case, a political interpretation of some of his tales not only is mandated by the nature of those tales themselves but will highlight Lovecraft's lifelong concern with the fate of civilization.

As with his philosophy, a brief analysis of the nature and, even more important, the development—of his political philosophy is a necessary prelude to a political interpretation of the stories. His letters and essays allow us to trace the course of his thought with some precision.

Lovecraft was born in the presidency of Benjamin Harrison; Victoria would still reign for more than a decade in England. Lovecraft's responses to the political and social issues of the 1890s and 1900s remain unknown: we do not know what—if anything—he thought of the Populists or the Progressives (when Theodore Roosevelt died in 1919 Lovecraft wrote an elegy on him, but his praise of Roosevelt as a strong leader is platitudinous), of the female suffrage movement, of the curtailing of the power of the House of Lords (1911), and other important developments. Lovecraft's attention was instead fixed on matters closer to home. His views were initially shaped, almost passively, by familial and societal influence and by his early reading. I wonder whether Lovecraft, when he remarked how he nostalgically read James Thomson's *Seasons* in Quinsnicket Park (SL 1.90), was aware that this harmless indulgence in antiquarianism might also have been a reflection of that longing for the rural landscape that is still a part of the American myth and that the Populists—a movement of the American farming class against the urban moneyed interests—used as the symbol for their campaign. The rapid urbanization of the United States was something of which Lovecraft was virtually an eyewitness, as he saw his own birthplace, then on the outskirts of the town and bordering the open country, gradually swallowed up by the encroaching suburbs of Providence.

Lovecraft's first real political consciousness is evinced in the matters of racial purity and the influx of foreigners to his native land. I have no interest either in condemning or defending Lovecraft's views on this matter; it is of greater importance to ascertain their origin and purpose. Lovecraft's opinions have been aired widely by hostile critics, but they were relatively commonplace to the majority of educated people at the turn of the century. Moreover, the intent of Lovecraft's racial views changed—although not as radically as some apologists think—over the course of his life, so that in the 1930s he could tentatively embrace Hitler but not for the same reasons that he had trumpeted "Aryan supremacy" twenty years before.

Where did his ideas originate? Clearly they were triggered initially by familial influence: in Lovecraft's youth his family had four black servants, whom Lovecraft later remembered fondly. New England long remained the most politically and socially conservative area of the nation, and the upper-class Bostonian's notions of aristocracy could easily lead to segregationalism. But Lovecraft also began an early investigation of the matter himself: his juvenile poem "De Triumpho Naturae" (1905) is dedicated to William Benjamin Smith, author of *The Color Line: A Brief in Behalf of the Unborn* (1905). Some of his early essays on the matter are clearly influenced by Thomas Henry Huxley, Spencer, and other Social Darwinists. But to Americans the issue of racial purity was at this time no longer an abstract one: the unprecedented influx of immigrants at the turn of the century—by 1910, 13,345,000 foreign-born persons were settled in the United States[17]—was a source of great concern to "old Americans," especially since the immigrants came this time not from Ireland, Germany, and Scandinavia but from Eastern Europe, Asia, and Latin America. The key to Lovecraft's racialism—and, indeed, to the whole of his political and social thought—is not biology (save in the case of the Negro, who was—as Lovecraft and many leading scientists of the day believed—demonstrably inferior biologically to the "Aryan") but the concept of *culture*.

We have seen, in our study of Lovecraft's ethics, that he derived greatest pleasure from "symbolic identification with the landscape and tradition-stream to which I belong." Lovecraft was a great conservative (hence the aptness of the title of the journal he edited as a young man), even when he adopted socialism at the end of his life. His great desire—a desire exacerbated by the accelerated rate of change in the age in which he lived—was to preserve as much of the past as possible in the name of culture. It is easy to say that this position was a mere rationalization of his early influences—his upbringing in a town filled with reminiscences of colonial days; his learning Latin and Greek at a time when these accomplishments were already becoming uncommon among the educated classes; his reading eighteenth-century books in the dusty attic of his birthplace; his early sense of dislocation from his own age—but, if so, the rationalization was a singularly persuasive and intellectually challenging one.

Of course, his early views on blacks, Jews, and foreigners are very naive and dogmatic and are merely the products of bookishness, sequestration, and an ignorance of the world. It is easy (and perhaps justifiable) to laugh when Lovecraft speaks of the "pan-Teutonic ideal" (SL 1.54); it is less comforting to hear Lovecraft supporting the Ku Klux Klan. And his early Anglophilia (initially inspired purely by literature and the trappings of royalty and aristocracy so tempting to certain uncritical Americans) led him to condemn the Sinn Fein and Irish Home Rule movements and, as late as 1921, to make the astonishing statement that "the early 'English oppression' [of Ireland] . . . was never as severe as is popularly stated."[18] But his views on race and culture steadily grew more thoughtful with the years, so that toward the end of his life he could justify segregation in the name of cultural autonomy: "A real friend of civilisation wishes merely to make the Germans *more German*, the French *more French*, the Spaniards *more Spanish*, and so on" (SL 4.253).

In his preferences for political organization Lovecraft again made it clear that the preservation of a rich and thriving culture was all that concerned him.

> All I care about is *the civilisation*—the state of development and organisation which is capable of gratifying the complex mental-emotional-aesthetic needs of highly evolved and acutely sensitive men. Any *indignation* I may feel in the whole matter is not for the woes of the downtrodden, but for the threat of social unrest to the traditional institutions of the civilisation. The reformer cares only for the masses, but may make concessions to the civilisation. I care only for the civilisation, but may make concessions to the masses. (SL 2.290)

Initially Lovecraft felt that a frank hereditary aristocracy was the only political system to ensure a high level of civilization; but as the prosperous twenties gave way to the Depression of the thirties, he began to realize that a restoration of the sort of aristocracy of privilege, cultivation, and civic-mindedness advocated (and embodied) by Henry Adams was highly unlikely, in the days of labor unions, political bosses, and crass plutocrats of business who did not have sufficient refinement to be the leaders of any civilization Lovecraft cared about. The solution for Lovecraft was socialism. This is not nearly as much an about-face as it is sometimes conceived; for both aristocracy and Lovecraft's brand of "fascistic socialism" would eliminate what were for Lovecraft the two great threats of culture—capitalism (because it brought to the fore the false values of money, speed, and calculativeness) and democracy (because it inculcated the illusion of justice and illegitimately extended the principle of equality from the legal to the social and intellectual realm): "What I used to respect was *not really aristocracy, but a set of personal qualities which aristocracy then developed better than any other system . . . a set of qualities, however, whose merit lay only in a psychology of non-calculative, non-competitive disinterestedness, truthfulness, courage, and generosity fostered by good education, minimum economic stress, and assumed position,* AND JUST AS ACHIEVABLE THROUGH SOCIALISM AS THROUGH ARISTOCRACY" (SL 5.321). The "fascistic" element in Lovecraft's system (he had welcomed

Mussolini's rise to power in 1922) would really be what he called an "aristocracy of intelligence": [19] the vote would be restricted to those who could pass certain intellectual and psychological tests, and the actual government run not by "geniuses"—for there is no guarantee that an Einstein would make a good head of state—but specialists in political science and economics. While real political power would be restricted to the few, economic wealth would be spread to the many, through government control of important utilities, social security, old-age pensions, and fewer working hours so that all who were capable of working could have an opportunity to work. The increased leisure time accruing from such a program would be spent in increased educational and cultural activity, so that more people than ever before could enjoy the fruits of civilization.

It all sounds very utopian; did Lovecraft actually think it could come about? Or was it the case that he—like the many others, from T. S. Eliot to Arnold Toynbee, who were strongly influenced by Oswald Spengler's monumental *Decline of the West*—felt that he was on a sinking ship, that the coming decades and centuries would bring only an ultimate collapse of civilization and a return to barbarism? This view was certainly dominant in Lovecraft's thinking in the 1920s, and he arrived at it years before he read Spengler in 1926; in 1921 he had already written: "No civilisation has lasted for ever, and perhaps our own is perishing of natural old age. If so, the end cannot well be deferred." [20] The major culprit, which evilly united with capitalism and democracy, that "catchword and illusion of inferior classes, visionaries, and dying civilisations" (SL 1.207), was (and here too he anticipated Spengler and many others) mechanization:

> But nothing good can be said of that cancerous machine-culture itself. It is not a true civilisation, and has nothing in it to satisfy a mature and fully developed human mind. It is attuned to the mentality and imagination of the galley-slave and the moron, and crushes relentlessly with disapproval, ridicule, and economic annihilation, any sign of actually independent thought and civilised feeling which chances to rise above its sodden level. It is a treadmill, squirrel-trap culture—drugged and frenzied with the hasheesh of industrial servitude and material luxury. It is wholly a material body-culture, and its symbol is the tiled bathroom and steam radiator

rather than the Doric portico and the temple of philosophy. Its denizens do not live or know how to live. (SL 2.304)

But again, by the 1930s Lovecraft finally admitted that the technological
age was here to stay; and his socialism, with its plan for fewer working
hours for all, took account of the fact that mechanization had made it
possible for a few to do as much work as it had taken many to do before.
This whole shift in attitude can be traced quite precisely in some of his
later stories: in the ghost-written tale "The Mound" (1929–1930), *At
the Mountains of Madness* (1931), and "The Shadow out of Time"
(1934–1935) Lovecraft depicts various alien races and describes their
political and social structure with some exactitude. I have elsewhere[21]
described this progression of thought—from an initial attempt to turn
back the clock and return to the rural-based aristocracy of the eighteenth century to a frank (if resigned) acceptance of the radical changes
affecting modern society and the hammering out of a political system
that might ensure both the comfort and sustenance of all and a sufficiently high grade of culture for those able to appreciate it. It was not a
system Lovecraft lived to see, for World War II—which Lovecraft had in
a nebulous way predicted as early as 1917 (cf. SL 1.53)—changed the
course of history once again and made his solution farther from realization than ever by temporarily bolstering precisely those forces of democracy and capitalism which he felt were the harbingers of barbarism.

THE DECLINE OF THE WEST

The emphasis Lovecraft put on *civilization* means that he—like the Machen who for fifty years engaged in a love-hate relationship with London—came to regard a particular type of *urban* civilization as the norm
and model; this in spite of his tongue-in-cheek longing to be the country
squire of a hereditary estate. The eighteenth century in England was
manifestly focused around London—at least the eighteenth century
Lovecraft cared about, the century of Addison, Steele, Johnson, and
Gibbon. One of his remarks about the eighteenth century is highly significant in this connection: "What the eighteenth century really was,
was the *final* phase of that perfectly unmechanised area which as a
whole gave us our most satisfying life" (SL 3.50). In this fashion Lovecraft could champion civilization over barbarism (as he did, for example,

in a lengthy correspondence with Robert E. Howard) but also condemn mechanization without abandoning the city for the country as Dunsany and Blackwood did.

Indeed, the first aspect of Lovecraft's treatment of civilization in his fiction that I wish to discuss is his attitude to nature. Here we are referring not to the sum total of all existence but the outdoors, the countryside, the nonurban. Lovecraft's reaction to it is highly ambiguous. The very famous opening of "The Colour out of Space"—"West of Arkham the hills rise *wild,* and there are valleys with deep woods that *no axe has ever cut*" (DH 53)—signifies that nature is some uncontrollable beast whose almost active resistance to human attempts to tame it is somehow sinister and even suggestive of cosmic alienage. Blackwood might have begun a tale in exactly the same manner, but it would have led to some delicate prose-poem on the glories of the natural world. Similarly, in "The Dunwich Horror," "the planted fields appear *few and barren;* while the sparsely scattered houses wear a surprisingly uniform aspect of age, squalor, and dilapidation" (DH 156). One of my favorite lines in "The Lurking Fear" refers to "certain overnourished trees whose very existence seemed an insult to sanity" (D 199). This sentiment, even if uttered less hyperbolically, would have been impossible for Blackwood. "The Whisperer in Darkness" is Lovecraft's great exploration of the theme, and on a single page we find references to a "half-abandoned railway track," "virgin granite," "untamed streams," and "half-concealed roads" (DH 247). Roads and railways cannot endure the hostility of nature; civilization is defeated. It is no surprise that this is where the alien chooses to house itself.

The passage we quoted from "The Dunwich Horror" also touches upon the notion of *decadence.* This is perhaps the most complex and pervasive idea in all Lovecraft, and it takes a bewildering variety of forms: decadence of individuals, of races, of societies, of civilizations, even of the solar system and the universe. Frequently there is a combination of several types of decadence in a single work; and it may be noted that the specimens of subhumanity we cited earlier—the creature in "The Beast in the Cave"; Joe Slater in "Beyond the Wall of Sleep"; the old man in "The Picture in the House"; Walter de la Poer in "The Rats in the Walls"—are all located in wild or decadent environments. Of Slater's kinsmen it is said that their "isolation for nearly three centuries in the hilly fastnesses of a little-travelled countryside has caused them to sink to a kind of barbaric degeneracy, rather than advance with their more fortunately placed brethren of the more thickly settled districts" (D 26). No clearer contrast between the wholesomeness of the city and the dangers of the country could be had. In "The Picture in the House" the old man's decaying house mirrors his own decline, and the few old books he possesses are ironic glimpses of the civilization that once was his. The setting of "The Beast in the Cave" is particularly ironic in this regard, although perhaps Lovecraft was not aware of it: Mammoth Cave, a bustling tourist attraction, is an example of the futile—and, as it turns out, dangerous—attempt to control wild nature; but nature has the last laugh. Perhaps it is no surprise that one of Arthur Jermyn's ancestors was killed by a circus ape. "The Rats in the Walls" appears to be an exception but really is not: de la Poer's laborious and costly restoration of his ancestral mansion becomes a pitifully ludicrous attempt to paper over the decadence at the heart of his own family tree.

It is now time to study Lovecraft's hybrids. If subhuman creatures are cases of individual decadence, hybrids are symbols of a racial degeneracy still more horrible because vastly more widespread. There are, of course, some pure hybrids in Lovecraft—hybrids that are not the result of miscegenation. Those in "Under the Pyramids" are of a very entertaining variety: "*Hippopotami should not have human hands and carry torches . . . men should not have the heads of crocodiles . . .* " (D 240). This is quite effective in its way, but these entities, being merely artificial concoctions of "decadent priestcraft" (D 234), have no broader philosophical significance. Arthur Jermyn is perhaps a bridge between the subhuman and the hybrid, for here the miscegenation affects only a single family. It is perhaps because the whole Jermyn line was generally a studious and even noble clan that Arthur Jermyn himself is accorded a sympathy few of Lovecraft's other hybrids receive: Maurice Lévy rightly declares that up to his death Jermyn "maintains an entirely British dignity."[22]

The hybrids in "The Lurking Fear" are not treated so kindly. Here too only a single family—the cursed house of Martense—is involved, but its decadence has been much severer, and the members exhibit a loathsome fecundity in spite of (and this seems a particularly gratuitous detail) their cannibal inclinations. The tale bears many conceptual similarities to "Beyond the Wall of Sleep." Here too we encounter a milder decadence around the principal decadence—the colony of squatters, who are called "gentle animals . . . gently descending the evolutionary scale because of their unfortunate ancestry and stultifying isolation" (D 186).

This is nothing but a benign version of what is plaguing the Martense family.

From a single family decadence and hybridism affect entire communities. This is the burden of "The Horror at Red Hook" and "The Shadow over Innsmouth." At this point it may be noted that Lovecraft's preference for urban civilization does not include the particular type of urban civilization that is New York—it has already suffered a decline (principally through the incursion of foreigners) and has lost the right to be called a model. As Lovecraft says in "He" (and echoes frequently in letters): ". . . this city of stone and stridor is not a sentient perpetuation of Old New York as London is of Old London and Paris of Old Paris, but . . . it is in fact quite dead, its sprawling body imperfectly embalmed and infested with queer animate things which have nothing to do with it as it was in life" (D 267). What has happened to New York is a breakdown of cultural continuity. But it was not always so; when the central figure of "He" shows the narrator a vision of New York in its prime, it could be modern-day Providence that Lovecraft is describing: "It was Greenwich, the Greenwich that used to be, with here and there a roof or row of houses as we see it now, yet with lovely green lanes and fields and bits of grassy common. The marsh still glittered beyond, but in the farther distance I saw the steeples of what was then all of New York; Trinity and St. Paul's and the Brick Church dominating their sisters, and a faint haze of wood smoke hovering over the whole" (D 273). In "The Horror at Red Hook" it is clear that foreigners are at the root of New York's decline:

> The population is a hopeless tangle and enigma; Syrian, Spanish, Italian, and negro elements impinging upon one another, and fragments of Scandinavian and American belts lying not far distant. It is a babel of sound and filth, and sends out strange cries to answer the lapping of oily waves at its grimy piers and the monstrous organ litanies of the harbour whistles. Here long ago a brighter picture dwelt, with clear-eyed mariners on the lower streets and homes of taste and substance where the larger houses line the hill. (D 247–248)

All this is very similar to Lovecraft's early tale "The Street" (1920), perhaps the most fatuous story he ever wrote (barring his revisions and collaborations, many of which are even more contemptible), where a street in a colonial New England town gradually sees itself being abandoned by blue-eyed Anglo-Saxons and filled with uncouth foreigners. What is happening in "The Horror at Red Hook" is that a city whose urbanism has gotten out of control actually *generates* decadence: "Modern people under lawless conditions tend uncannily to repeat the darkest instinctive patterns of primitive half-ape savagery in their daily life and ritual observances" (D 248). The future is not safe: ". . . here lay the root of a contagion destined to sicken and swallow cities, and engulf nations in the foetor of hybrid pestilence" (D 260).

Lovecraft no doubt felt great satisfaction at relieving himself of his race hatred in this story; "The Shadow over Innsmouth" is considerably more subtle and carefully worked out and is one of his great stories. The worst thing about Innsmouth is its fall from a prior period of grace, dignity, and civilization: the city was "a seat of great marine prosperity in the early nineteenth century" (DH 310); and for one of Lovecraft's sensitivity to architecture no sight could be more poignant—or dimly ominous—than "the decaying remains of three once beautiful Georgian steeples" (D 320). How low has the grandeur of the eighteenth century fallen! Here again miscegenation is at the heart of the tale—a spectacular miscegenation with appallingly alien creatures, which corrupts an entire town and not, as in "The Horror at Red Hook," some small section of it. Everything is affected—skin, voice, even bone structure. And yet there are times when the narrator, in the midst of his disgust, reflects a paranoia that appears to have been Lovecraft's. He overhears some men who "exchanged some faint guttural words with a loafer in a language I could have sworn was not English" (DH 341). This is evidently supposed to be horrific or at least disturbing. A little later, in the hotel he hears "horrible croaking voices exchanging low cries in what was certainly not English" (DH 350). A "babel of sound and filth" is okay for a decadent New York suburb, but it is a nameless horror in this placid-seeming New England backwater. In a sense it is the converse of the "*indisputably English*" (DH 196) words uttered by the Dunwich horror at its death: language here signifies a loathsome intermingling of human and alien elements.

What makes "The Shadow over Innsmouth" so poignant, of course, is the narrator's own evolution, through heredity, into one of the denizens he had fled so arduously. I now find the whole elaborate chase scene, in which the narrator uses great ingenuity to escape capture, somewhat ridiculous. (Just what the Innsmouth folk would have done with him if they had caught him is another matter—it is likely that they recognized him and merely wished to bring him back into the fold.) But what Lovecraft appears to be trying to do here is to convey that the narrator can certainly flee from his pursuers, but he cannot flee so easily from his own past. "I began to acquire a kind of terror of my own ancestry" (DH 364), he says toward the end—and in this sense he is very akin to de la Poer of "The Rats in the Walls." I think, however, that his metamorphosis has not been entirely understood: we may be inclined to feel pity at his lot, as we do that of "The Outsider"; but Lovecraft surely means us to see his transition as an augmentation, not a diminution, of the horror—a seemingly "normal" person (and an Anglo-Saxon, at that) has become an alien! What could be more fiendishly evil? The narrator's acceptance of his fate, and his yearning to rejoin his kin in the deep, is in loathsome contrast to the reaction of Arthur Jermyn and is meant to signal the character's complete degradation—a degradation that now affects his mind and personality as much as his body.

What is even more sinister about the Innsmouth denizens is that, unlike the inhabitants of Red Hook, they have come to represent a *counter-civilization* in the heart of Anglo-Saxon culture. The jewelry made by the Innsmouth folk "belonged to some settled technique of infinite maturity and perfection" (DH 311); and beneath the sea they have erected splendid cities in no way inferior in scope and lavishness to those on the surface. This artistic faculty is always, in Lovecraft, a sign of some level of civilization, and this is why they pose such a threat to humanity. Analogously, the statue of Cthulhu found in a Louisiana bayou is of "exquisitely artistic workmanship" (DH 134); and although it has been fashioned not by Cthulhu's savage worshippers but by the Cthulhu spawn itself ("They had . . . come themselves from the stars, and brought Their images with Them" [DH 140]), it still points to a level of culture that makes the whole cult the more dangerous. All Lovecraft's alien civilizations—even the extraterrestrial ones—have some sort of intellectual or aesthetic superiority to human beings. The fungi from Yuggoth have developed medicine to an astonishingly high degree. The Great Race, of course, is superior to the human race in nearly every respect. *At the Mountains of Madness* is a particularly interesting example from this perspective. Of the Old Ones' bas-reliefs Dyer reports: "The technique, we soon saw, was mature, accomplished, and aesthetically evolved to the highest degree of civilised mastery; though utterly alien in every detail to any known art tradition of the human race" (M 56). When, however, Dyer and Danforth reach the very depths of the Old Ones' city, they notice something quite different: "This new and degen-

erate work was coarse, bold, and wholly lacking in delicacy of detail"
(M 92). It is the work, of course, of the shoggoths; and their *aesthetic*
inferiority to the Old Ones seems to suggest an analogous *moral*
inferiority.

Part of the reason why there are no memorable characters in some of
Lovecraft's greatest stories is that the tales present conflicts, not of individuals, but of cultures: the Old Ones versus the shoggoths; the Great
Race versus the Blind Beings; the fungi from Yuggoth versus human beings (symbolized by Wilmarth and Akeley); the Innsmouth denizens
versus human beings (symbolized by the narrator). The horror of the
last story, of course, rests in the fact that the dichotomy proves to be illusory; it is as if Lovecraft is saying that our efforts to preserve civilization are foredoomed to failure by the sins—or blunders—of our
ancestors.

Cults are seen by Lovecraft to be especially dangerous because their
fanatical, frequently quasi-religious zeal conjoins with their hatred of
civilization to be a menace. The Innsmouth denizens seem to be a cult
linked by the Esoteric Order of Dagon. The Red Hook mongrels congre-
gate at a deconsecrated church. The Cthulhu cult makes no secret of its
threat to civilization:

> That cult would never die till the stars came right again, and the
> secret priests would take great Cthulhu from His tomb to revive His
> subjects and resume His rule of earth. The time would be easy to
> know, for then mankind would have become as the Great Old Ones;
> free and wild and beyond good and evil, with laws and morals thrown
> aside and all men shouting and killing and revelling in joy. Then the
> liberated Old Ones would teach them new ways to shout and kill
> and revel and enjoy themselves, and all the earth would flame with
> a holocaust of ecstasy and freedom. (DH 141)

The political metaphors of liberation and freedom (echoed in a later passage in which Cthulhu and his followers would induce "the faithful to
come on a pilgrimage of liberation and restoration" [DH 150]) suggest
that the Cthulhu cult feels the earth to be its rightful domain and the
current civilization an upstart usurper. It is no wonder that the narrator
of "The Call of Cthulhu" mutters nervously at the end: "Loathsomeness
waits and dreams in the deep, and decay spreads over the tottering cities
of men" (DH 154).

The future of civilization, and the ever-present threat of its collapse, is a leitmotiv in Lovecraft's fiction from one end to the other. As early as "Dagon" we read, in a passage startlingly similar to that just quoted from "The Call of Cthulhu": "I dream of a day when they [the fish-creatures] may rise above the billows to drag down in their reeking talons the remnants of puny, war-exhausted mankind—of a day when the land shall sink, and the dark ocean floor shall ascend amidst universal pandemonium" (D 19). This was written, it should be noted, in the middle of World War I, at a time far from its conclusion and even from the prospect of its conclusion. The prose-poem "Nyarlathotep" (1920) is, pure and simple, a parable for the decline of the West. I see Nyarlathotep here as a symbol for the misuse of science—he was "always buying strange instruments of glass and metal and combining them into instruments yet stranger," to the point that the narrator, during one of Nyarlathotep's highly theatrical presentations, "mumbled a protest about 'imposture' and 'static electricity.'" But "shadowed on a screen" the narrator sees "the world battling against blackness; against the waves of destruction from ultimate space; whirling, churning; struggling around the dimming, cooling sun." The West's decline heralds the decline of the whole planet with the extinction of the sun. Later the world seems to be falling apart: "Once we looked at the pavement and found the blocks loose and displaced by grass, with scarce a line of rusted metal to shew where the tramways had run. And again we saw a tram-car, lone, windowless, dilapidated, and almost on its side. When we gazed around the horizon, we could not find the third tower by the river, and noticed that the silhouette of the second tower was ragged at the top."[23] People begin milling about irrationally; and when one group "filed down a weed-choked subway entrance," I wonder whether we are to read some hint that we have been doomed by our own technology. "Nyarlathotep" is one of Lovecraft's most powerful vignettes—and the fact that he *dreamed* it makes us realize how deeply rooted his anxiety for civilization was.

Later stories continue the trend. The figure in "He" shows the narrator visions of past, present, and future New York. The last is arresting:

I saw the heavens verminous with strange flying things, and beneath them a hellish black city of giant stone terraces with impious pyramids flung savagely to the moon, and devil-lights burning from unnumbered windows. And swarming loathsomely on aërial galleries I saw the yellow, squint-eyed people of that city, robed horribly in orange and red, and dancing insanely to the pounding of fevered kettle-drums, the clatter of obscene crotala, and the maniacal moaning of muted horns whose ceaseless dirges rose and fell undulantly like the waves of an unhallowed ocean of bitumen. (D 273–274)

There are those yellow people again: "Evil is embodied only by coloured people," as Maurice Lévy wrote in a nasty pun that lays bare Lovecraft's racialism.[24] "The Horror at Red Hook" ends on a transparently ironic note: hundreds of the evil Red Hook denizens have been rounded up or killed, but the cult still lingers on and will one day regain strength: "Age-old horror is a hydra with a thousand heads, and the cults of darkness are rooted in blasphemies deeper than the well of Democritus. The soul of that beast is omnipresent and triumphant" (D 265). The horrors of "The Shadow over Innsmouth" are scarcely over, despite massive federal intervention: "The Deep Ones could never be destroyed, even though the palaeogean magic of the forgotten Old Ones might sometimes check them. For the present they would rest; but some day, if they remembered, they would rise again for the tribute Great Cthulhu craved. It would be a city greater than Innsmouth next time" (DH 367). Which city, I wonder? New York? London? It is unbearable to think about it. Of the two alien civilizations in *At the Mountains of Madness*, the more repulsively alien—the shoggoths—alone remains to menace the world: "It is absolutely necessary, for the peace and safety of mankind, that some of earth's dark, dead corners and unplumbed depths be let alone; lest sleeping abnormalities wake to resurgent life, and blasphemously surviving nightmares squirm and splash out of their black lairs to newer and wider conquests" (M 105). Lovecraft does not offer humanity much hope in the end: we shall either be wiped out by those unassimilable nuclei of aliens on the fringe of our civilization or destroy ourselves through repeated miscegenation. Through it all, the ideal of a certain type of urban civilization—one very like Providence, as it happens—remains as a vision and a goal. Late in life Lovecraft saw socialism as a means to this end; but there is an irony, deeper perhaps than Lovecraft knew, in his depiction of such a model socialist state in the civilization of the Great Race: they are so spectacularly superior to human beings that it is to be wondered whether our untidy culture could ever aspire to that sort of perfection. Perhaps it is simply the old paradox of socialism: human beings must first become superhuman for socialism to work, at which point there would be no need for socialism or any other form of government.

CONCLUSION

I have studied Lovecraft last in this volume not merely because he chronologically follows the other five writers studied here but because, while being influenced by all five, he took some of their best features and made them his own—Machen's notion of evil cults lurking on the underside of civilization; Dunsany's artificial pantheon and cosmicism; Blackwood's sense of transcendent awe; James's structural complexity and verisimilitude; and Bierce's cynicism, concision, and narrative tensity. This is to assert neither that Lovecraft is better in every respect than his predecessors (each does some things better than he, and Dunsany and Blackwood are surely his equals overall as weird writers) nor that Lovecraft has done nothing but rework old formulas better. No one but he could have written *At the Mountains of Madness* or "The Shadow out of Time." But Lovecraft does culminate certain trends in weird writing of the previous fifty years: most important, the shift from supernaturalism to quasi science fiction, dimly evident in Bierce and perhaps Blackwood. The subsequent history of weird fiction is at the moment very confused: science fiction has broken off from it, and no clear trend has emerged among later weird writers. Lovecraft's countless inept imitators have only muddied the waters further.

I want to return to the startling amount of work done on Lovecraft, especially in recent years. Most of this material, indeed, has been written by a fairly small circle of devoted Lovecraft scholars but is no less perceptive for that. I hope I have shown that it is very difficult to exhaust Lovecraft even with a lengthy discussion: subjects I have treated in a few paragraphs really need the space of a whole essay for comprehensive analysis. I am convinced that there is simply *more* to Lovecraft than to nearly any other weird writer, Poe perhaps not exempted. But I hasten to add that the reasons for this lie not only in the intrinsic nature of Lovecraft's work but also—perhaps predominantly—in the staggering amount of ancillary material (letters, essays, poems) he has left behind as well as what his friends and associates have generated in the form of memoirs and biographies. It is precisely because many critics not in the inner circle of Lovecraft studies have failed to examine this material—

indeed, in some cases have not even been aware of its existence—that their analyses, when not wildly erroneous, are for the most part thin and insubstantial. The failure to read Lovecraft's letters has in particular caused problems for certain critics. They have misconstrued his philosophy or even been unaware that he has one; they have not paid attention to his pervasive self-deprecating humor or his extraordinarily keen observation of and commentary on the literary, political, and social events of his time. But most of this vacuous criticism has by now been laughed out of existence.

The bulk of Lovecraft's nonfictional work not only is very difficult to assimilate but threatens to reduce all criticism of him to mere biography or philology. It is easier to annotate a Lovecraft story than to understand it. To be quite honest, I no longer have any interest in much of the nuts-and-bolts work that takes up so much time in Lovecraft scholarship—where, for example, Lovecraft heard of the (real) artist Anthony Angarola mentioned in "Pickman's Model." Ant-industry of this sort (to use Spengler's phrase) certainly keeps many people pleasantly occupied, but unless some broader conclusion is made, it is all so much useless intellectual baggage—and brings us no closer to what Lovecraft's stories are really about. Whereas mainstream critics must struggle to absorb Lovecraft's letters and essays to understand the fiction, it may be advisable for the inner circle of Lovecraft scholars momentarily to forget this body of peripheral material and read again the stories as stories. This is what they are, and this is what Lovecraft wanted them to be; it is a historical accident that all that other matter survives.

Lovecraft is, more than any other author in this volume save Bierce, on the brink of critical and academic recognition. Machen and James are considerably farther behind, and the case seems almost hopeless for Dunsany and Blackwood. Whether such attention would be an unalloyed good is another matter; there is, after all, much to be said for writers who are more read than studied.

EPILOGUE
Criticorum in Usum

A. E. Housman subtitled his edition of Juvenal "Editorum in Usum" ("For the Use of Editors"). This irked conventional classicists, implying as it did that only Housman knew the theory and practice of textual criticism and was in effect preparing a tutorial manual for his fellow scholars. In using my own subtitle for this epilogue I have no intention of following Housman's playful arrogance; on the contrary, I wish humbly to offer an antidote to certain grandiose theorizings by some of my predecessors. The fact is that I am not sure we are even ready for a theory of the weird yet.

My own program in this book closely follows that of Maurice Lévy in his work on Lovecraft: "The object of this study is limited. Our goal is not to give the 'case' of Howard Phillips Lovecraft an exhaustive analysis; his personality is too rich, too complex for that. . . . What we modestly wish to do is to add to the thick file of this literary genre an exemplary work and to draw from it some conclusions, which must be taken for what they are." [1] Aside from the term "genre," this expresses my sentiments exactly. I have not pretended to give any writer in this volume an "exhaustive analysis": it is foolish to suppose that one can comprehensively discuss authors of forty or fifty books in as many pages. What I have tried to do is to give a picture of the totality of their work, its overall substance and philosophical direction. This involves doing something most critics seem in too much of a hurry to do: actually reading everything an author wrote and trying to understand how (or whether) it forms a unity.

It may strike some critics that my readings are a little plodding and unadventurous; to this charge I have no especial response, save that I am attempting to follow a rather old model—Leslie Stephen, the philosophical critic who cheerfully declared himself a member of the "pedestrian school of criticism." But if my approach is not very inspiring, I still feel that something analogous to it is a necessary preliminary to more theoretical treatments. In order for the nature, intentions, parameters, and even history of the weird tale to be properly determined, we must first have a much better idea of what each weird writer (so called) was trying to do. This requires initially examining each writer almost in isolation so that his philosophical purpose can be ascertained; only then can questions of literary influence and the persistence of given themes or patterns be intelligently posed and answered. My own study has, I trust, shown how different authors can use a single theme for antipodally opposite ends; and these ends are governed strictly by the philosophical goals each author has evolved. I am confident that further philosophical investigations of such authors as William Hope Hodgson, L. P. Hartley, Clark Ashton Smith, Robert E. Howard, E. R. Eddison, M. P. Shiel, Oliver Onions, Walter de la Mare, Shirley Jackson, Ramsey Campbell, and T. E. D. Klein, among many others, can and should be performed. If such study also helps to rid mainstream critics of their (largely ignorant) hostility and contempt toward works that are capable of enormously powerful effects—effects that apocalyptically reshape our conception of the universe and of our place in it—then so much the better.

NOTES

INTRODUCTION

1. First published in *The Recluse* 1 (1927): 23–59; subsequently revised in an abortive serialization in *The Fantasy Fan* (October 1933–February 1935); first complete appearance of the revised text in *The Outsider and Others* (1939); most accurate text in *Dagon and Other Macabre Tales* (rev. ed. 1986). The Ben Abramson (1945) and Dover (1973) editions are very corrupt.

2. *The Supernatural in Fiction* (London: Peter Nevill, 1952), p. 12 n.12.

3. *Elegant Nightmares: The English Ghost Story from LeFanu to Blackwood* (Athens: Ohio University Press, 1978), p. 9.

4. *Night Visitors: The Rise and Fall of the English Ghost Story* (London: Faber & Faber, 1977), p. 12.

5. *The Literature of Terror* (London: Longmans, 1980), pp. 5–9.

6. Ibid., p. 3.

7. Robert W. Adams in *New York Times Book Review,* January 24, 1988, p. 6.

8. "Tales of the Marvellous and the Ridiculous" (1945); rpt. in my *H. P. Lovecraft: Four Decades of Criticism* (Athens: Ohio University Press, 1980), p. 49.

9. Derleth had early on arranged with Machen to republish *The Green Round,* but for some reason did not do so until 1968.

10. See the introduction to Campbell's *Cold Print* (New York: TOR, 1987).

11. *Dagon and Other Macabre Tales* (Sauk City, Wis.: Arkham House, 1986), p. 386.

12. Lovecraft to August Derleth, November 20, 1931; *Selected Letters* (Sauk City, Wis.: Arkham House, 1971), 3: 434.

13. *Lovecraft: A Study in the Fantastic,* trans. S. T. Joshi (Detroit: Wayne State University Press, 1988), pp. 36–37.

14. "The Lord of R'lyeh" (1945); rpt. *Lovecraft Studies* 2 (Fall 1982): 8–17.

15. *The Supernatural in Fiction,* p. 53.

16. Random supernatural tales can be found in Agatha Christie's *The Hound of Death* (1933), John Dickson Carr's *The Door to Doom* (1980), and Margery Allingham's *The Allingham Minibus* (1969). Dorothy L. Sayers wrote one supernatural story ("The Cyprian Cat") and one *conte cruel* ("Suspicion"); both can be

found in *In the Teeth of the Evidence* (1939). A good proportion of Patricia High-smith's short fiction can be classified as supernatural (notably the title story in *The Snail-Watcher* [1970]) or even pure fantasy, as in *The Animal Lover's Book of Beastly Murder* (1975) or *Little Tales of Misogyny* (1977).

1. ARTHUR MACHEN: THE MYSTERY OF THE UNIVERSE

After the first citation, references to Machen's works will appear parenthetically in the text.

1. *Eleusinia and Beneath the Barley* (West Warwick, R.I.: Necronomicon Press, 1988), p. [10].

2. *Hieroglyphics* (New York: Knopf, 1923), pp. 18–19.

3. "Machen: A Biographical Study," in *Arthur Machen,* ed. Brocard Sewell (Llandeilo: St. Albert's Press, 1970), p. 13.

4. *The Secret Glory* (London: Martin Secker, 1922), p. 186.

5. *Far Off Things* (London: Martin Secker, 1922), pp. 104–105.

6. Lovecraft to Natalie H. Wooley, November 27, 1933; *Selected Letters* (Sauk City, Wis.: Arkham House, 1976), 4:324.

7. Letter to Munson Havens, 1924; *A Few Letters from Arthur Machen* (Cleveland: Rowfant Club, 1932), p. 25.

8. "Farewell to Materialism," *American Mercury* 36 (September 1935): 51.

9. "Our Betty's Day Out," *The Graphic,* March 14 and 21, 1925, pp. 404, 425; "The Mystery of a Century," *T.P.'s and Cassell's Weekly,* June 27 and July 3, 1926, p. 311–312, 351.

10. *The Three Impostors* (New York: Knopf, 1923), p. 255.

11. *The House of Souls* (New York: Knopf, 1922), p. 172.

12. Letter to Bernard Austin Dwyer, 1932; *Selected Letters,* 4:4.

13. Straub has admitted the Machen influence on his novel in an interview in *Twilight Zone,* May 1981, p. 13.

14. "Folklore and Legends of the North," *Literature,* September 24, 1898, p. 272.

15. "On Re-reading *The Three Impostors* and the Wonder Story," unpublished ms., August Derleth Papers, State Historical Society of Wisconsin, Madison, Wisconsin.

16. *The Three Impostors* (London: John Lane, 1895), p. 154.

17. *Ornaments in Jade* (New York: Knopf, 1924), p. 27.

18. *Things Near and Far* (New York: Knopf, 1923), p. 81.

19. *The London Adventure* (London: Martin Secker, 1924), p. 51.

20. *The Hill of Dreams* (New York: Knopf, 1923), p. 47.

21. "True Comfort," *Academy and Literature,* May 25, 1912, p. 647.

22. *Tales of Horror and the Supernatural* (New York: Knopf, 1948), p. 219.

23. In his notes to Henry Danielson's *Arthur Machen: A Bibliography* (London: Henry Danielson, 1923), p. 47.

24. "On Re-reading *The Three Impostors*."

25. Introduction to *The Three Impostors* (New York: Knopf, 1923), p. xix.

26. Klein's great novel *The Ceremonies* (1984) is as monumental a tribute to Machen as can be imagined: its entire framework is derived from "The White People," while many individual scenes and images bear a definite Machenian influence. And yet the work remains a vital, original embodiment of Klein's own world view.

2. LORD DUNSANY: THE CAREER OF A *FANTAISISTE*

Throughout this chapter, in order to keep footnotes to a minimum, I cite Dunsany's tales (most of which are quite short) merely by the collection in which they appear (*The Gods of Pegāna* is cited by the page numbers of the Luce edition; uncollected stories, of course, are cited fully); plays are cited by act and scene (the one-act plays, being very short, receive no especial citation) and novels by chapter.

1. *A Glimpse from a Watch Tower* (London: Jarrolds, 1946), pp. 41, 43.

2. Letter to Fritz Leiber, November 15, 1936; *Selected Letters* (Sauk City, Wis.: Arkham House, 1976), 5:354.

3. I should note here that I have no intention of discussing Dunsany's poetry at all. Meritorious as some of it is, it is on the whole clearly inferior to his prose work, and when fantastic it rarely expresses ideas better than his tales, novels, and plays. It is astonishing that Dunsany could allow himself to commit such aesthetic disasters as *A Journey* (1944) and *The Year* (1946), two perfectly contentless "epic" poems in Byronic stanzas (something Dunsany found apparently as easy to write as Lovecraft did heroic couplets).

4. A tendency unfortunately echoed in Mark Amory's *Biography of Lord Dunsany* (London: Collins, 1972).

5. "Lord Dunsany and His Work" (1922), in *Marginalia* (Sauk City, Wis.: Arkham House, 1944), pp. 151, 155.

6. *The Gods of Pegāna* (Boston: Luce, n.d.), p. 5.

7. Ibid., p. 21.

8. Ibid., p. 81.

9. *Life of Johnson* (London: Oxford University Press, 1970), p. 426.

10. *The Gods of Pegāna*, p. 11.

11. Ibid., p. 5.

12. Ibid., pp. 46–47.

13. Ibid., p. 76.

14. Ibid., p. 17.

15. *Patches of Sunlight* (London: Heinemann, 1938), p. 30.

16. *The Gods of Pegāna,* p. 16.

17. *Aeneid,* trans. James Rhoades (London: Oxford University Press, 1921), pp. 44–45.

18. "Romance and the Modern Stage," *National Review* no. 341 (July 1911): 831.

19. "Jetsam," *Saturday Review* (London), June 25, 1910, p. 819.

20. *Selected Letters,* 5 : 354.

21. I avoid discussion here on the peculiar nonfantasy novel *Up in the Hills* (1935), since the point of this novel appears to be merely to make fun of the Irish, a tendency found also in many of Dunsany's humorous sketches for *Punch* in the 1940s and 1950s. I also have nothing to say about the rather dour war novel *Guerrilla* (1944).

22. Lovecraft to James F. Morton, February 3, 1932; *Selected Letters* (Sauk City, Wis.: Arkham House, 1976), 4 : 13.

23. *The Open Window* 2 (September–October 1911): 327–331.

24. "Four Poets" (1957), in *The Ghosts of the Heaviside Layer and Other Fantasms,* ed. Darrell Schweitzer (Philadelphia: Owlswick Press, 1980), p. 157.

25. Ibid., p. 96.

26. "Romance and the Modern Stage," p. 830.

27. "Told under Oath" (1952), in *The Ghosts of the Heaviside Layer,* pp. 33–45.

28. Introduction to *A Dreamer's Tales* (New York: Modern Library, 1917), p. xvii.

29. *The Sirens Wake* (London: Jarrolds, 1945), p. 24.

30. *The Donnellan Lectures* (London: Heinemann, 1945), p. 46.

31. *Patches of Sunlight,* p. 158.

32. Ibid., p. 74.

33. *The Sirens Wake,* p. 22.

34. "The Use of Man," *Harper's Bazaar* no. 2626 (August 1931): 85, 108.

35. *Spectator,* October 3, 1952, pp. 420–441.

36. *Poetry Review* 44 (July–September 1953): 375–377.

37. "Notes on Writing Weird Fiction" (c. 1932), in *Marginalia,* p. 138.

38. *The Sirens Wake,* p. 6.

39. In *The Ghosts of the Heaviside Layer,* pp. 97–102.

40. "Lord Dunsany and His Work," pp. 159–160.

3. ALGERNON BLACKWOOD: THE EXPANSION OF CONSCIOUSNESS

After the first citation, reference to Blackwood's works appear parenthetically in the text. I apologize for the inconsistency of my citations—sometimes from English editions, sometimes from American editions, sometimes from paperback reprints: the scarcity of much of Blackwood's work has compelled me to use whatever editions have come to hand.

1. *Episodes before Thirty* (New York: Dutton, 1924), pp. 23–27.

2. See *Episodes before Thirty,* p. 10, for Blackwood's early Buddhist readings.

3. A drug has "rendered [Pender] ultra-sensitive and made [him] respond to an increased rate of vibration" in "A Psychical Invasion" (*John Silence: Physician Extraordinary* [New York: Dutton, 1920], p. 27).

4. Even the otherwise insignificant *Dudley and Gilderoy* (London: Ernest Benn, 1929) contributes an example, whether flippant or not: "The stimulus of danger, added to the educational drive of London life, produced, as it were, an intensification of consciousness" (198). In *The Garden of Survival* (New York: Dutton, 1918) it is noted that "Beauty, I suppose, opens the heart, extends the consciousness" (154).

5. *The Human Chord* (London: Macmillan, 1910), p. 318.

6. "Notes on Writing Weird Fiction" (c. 1932), in *Marginalia* (Sauk City, Wis.: Arkham House, 1944), p. 135.

7. *Shocks* (New York: Dutton, 1936), p. 51.

8. *The Centaur* (Harmondsworth: Penguin, 1938), p. 58.

9. *Ten Minute Stories* (New York: Dutton, 1914), p. 89.

10. *Julius LeVallon* (New York: Dutton, 1916), p. 297.

11. Curiously, in a much later tale, "Elsewhere and Otherwise" (in *Shocks*), Blackwood came to understand this deficiency: "'It is only an analogy, of couse,' he reminded me, 'and it has the fallacy that all analogies must hold'" (44).

12. *The Bright Messenger* (London: Cassells, 1921), p. 313.

13. *A Prisoner in Fairyland* (London: Macmillan, 1913), pp. 102–103.

14. *The Lost Valley and Other Stories* (London: Nash & Grayson, 1931), p. 141.

15. *Tales of Terror and the Unknown* (New York: Dutton, 1965), p. 206. All tales in *The Listener* are included in this volume, and they will hereafter be cited from this edition.

16. *Incredible Adventures* (New York: Macmillan, 1914), p. 207.

17. Lovecraft to R. H. Barlow, May 11, 1935; *Selected Letters* (Sauk City, Wis.: Arkham House, 1976), 5:160.

18. *Pan's Garden* (London: Macmillan, 1912), p. 153.

19. *Day and Night Stories* (New York: Dutton, 1917), p. 140.

20. *The Empty House* (London: Eveleigh Nash, 1906), p. 32.

21. Lovecraft to J. Vernon Shea, October 30, 1931; *Selected Letters* (Sauk City, Wis.: Arkham House, 1971), 3:429.

22. Lovecraft to Fritz Leiber, November 9, 1936; *Selected Letters* 5:341.

23. *Jimbo* (London: Macmillan, 1909), p. 21.

24. *The Education of Uncle Paul* (London: Macmillan, 1909), p. 10.

25. *The Promise of Air* (New York: Dutton, 1918), p. 9.

26. *The Wolves of God and Other Fey Stories* (New York: Dutton, 1921), p. 279.

27. "Elsewhere and Otherwise," in *Shocks,* p. 45.

28. *Tongues of Fire and Other Sketches* (London: Herbert Jenkins, 1924), pp. 106–107.

4. M. R. JAMES: THE LIMITATIONS OF THE GHOST STORY

1. *Collected Ghost Stories* (New York: Longmans, Green; London: Edward Arnold, 1931), p. 151. All subsequent references to the tales in this volume will be cited parenthetically in the text.

2. The description is repeated in the late story "Wailing Wall," p. 638.

3. Introduction to *Ghosts and Marvels,* ed. H. V. Collins (Oxford: Oxford University Press, 1924), p. vi.

4. "Some Remarks on Ghost Stories" (1929), in *The Book of the Supernatural,* ed. Peter Haining (London: W. Foulsham, 1979), p. 23.

5. Letter to James F. Morton [c. 1937], *Selected Letters* (Sauk City, Wis.: Arkham House, 1976), 5:431.

6. Introduction to *Ghosts and Marvels,* p. vii.

7. Ibid., p. vi.

8. Preface to *More Ghost Stories of an Antiquary* (1911), p. v.

9. Lovecraft to Vincent Starrett, Dec. 6, 1927, *Selected Letters* (Sauk City, Wis.: Arkham House, 1968), 2:210.

10. Preface to *More Ghost Stories,* p. v.

11. *Elegant Nightmares: The English Ghost Story from LeFanu to Blackwood* (Athens: Ohio University Press, 1978), p. 75. Illuminating as I found Sullivan's treatment, I think he wildly overstates the case for James. His comparisons of James to Yeats, Eliot, Pound, and Waugh are so grotesquely inapposite that I can only assume his enthusiasm got the better of him.

12. Preface to *Collected Ghost Stories,* p. ix.

13. *The Book of the Supernatural,* pp. 26–27.

14. Ibid., p. 26.

15. Ibid., p. 27. It would be interesting to know if Lovecraft is covered by this judgment, since James is commenting on the *Not at Night* anthologies of the late twenties, in which Lovecraft was included.

5. AMBROSE BIERCE: HORROR AS SATIRE

1. "Portrait of a Misanthrope," *Saturday Review,* October 12, 1946, p. 12.

2. "The Ravages of Shakspearitis" (1903), in *Collected Works* (Washington: Neale Publishing Co., 1909–1912), 10:110. Subsequent references to works by Bierce will, unless otherwise noted, be cited from this edition and will occur parenthetically in the text.

3. A. H. Bullen, upon reading several of Lovecraft's stories, deprecated the apparent absence of humor in them. He wrote: "The essence of a man's whole work (noticeable in these contributions) generally presents itself more or less in the form of a view of the universe. Can a view of the universe which does not take humour into consideration be complete or correct?" Lovecraft replied that "I would suggest that none of my narratives aims at scientific accuracy and inclusiveness, each being rather a mere transcript of an isolated mood or idea with its imaginative ramifications." See my edition of Lovecraft's *In Defence of Dagon* (West Warwick, R.I.: Necronomicon Press, 1985), pp. 5, 22.

4. Letter dated July 31, 1892, *The Letters of Ambrose Bierce*, ed. Bertha Clark Pope (San Francisco: Book Club of California, 1922), p. 5.

5. Letter to George Sterling, July 10, 1902, ibid., p. 59.

6. Letter to George Sterling, September 12, 1903, ibid., p. 75.

7. Cited in Paul Fatout, *Ambrose Bierce: The Devil's Lexicographer* (Norman: University of Oklahoma Press, 1951), p. 94.

8. Unfortunately Bierce attributes this view to Schopenhauer (*Collected Works*, 1:114).

9. Edmund Wilson, "Ambrose Bierce on the Owl Creek Bridge," *Patriotic Gore* (New York: Oxford University Press, 1962), p. 622.

10. *Dagon and Other Macabre Tales* (Sauk City, Wis.: Arkham House, 1986), p. 88.

11. "The Deaths in Ambrose Bierce's 'Halpin Frayser,'" *Papers on Language and Literature* 10 (1974): 394–402. I am grateful to Steven J. Mariconda for bringing this paper to my attention.

12. Victoria Eckhardt has suggested to me one possible means of refuting Maclean's argument. Maclean makes much of the fact that Jaralson has an acquaintance with the poet Myron Bayne, an ancestor of Halpin Frayser; Bierce remarks that "a Frayser who was not the proud possessor of a sumptuous copy of the ancestral 'poetical works' . . . was a rare Frayser indeed" (*Collected Works*, 3:22), and that Jaralson admits that "I have his collected works" (Ibid., p. 42). But of course the fact that all Fraysers have Bayne's poetical works does not imply that *only* Fraysers have them. Perhaps Maclean would reply that it is stretching coincidence too far that two unrelated characters would have the works of this obscure poet.

13. "Bierce's 'The Death of Halpin Frayser': The Poetics of Gothic Consciousness," *ESQ* 18 (1972): 115–122.

14. *Elegant Nightmares: The English Ghost Story from LeFanu to Blackwood* (Athens: Ohio University Press, 1978), p. 138 n. 15.

15. Stuart C. Woodruff (*The Short Stories of Ambrose Bierce* [Pittsburgh: University of Pittsburgh Press, 1964], p. 117) proclaims that these tales are examples of "pointless sadism"; sadistic they are, but pointless they are not. Fatout (*Ambrose Bierce*, p. 168), in carrying out his wish to track down everything in Bierce's tales

to biographical sources, unearths an obscure uncle whom Fatout supposes is the model for the Uncle William so roundly abused in "My Favorite Murder" and concludes, with evidently a straight face: "Ambrose could sustain a grudge for a long time, and when he took revenge, he was like the boy who dreamed of cutting throats."

6. H. P. LOVECRAFT: THE DECLINE OF THE WEST

I use the following abbreviations in the text: D = *Dagon and Other Macabre Tales* (rev. ed. 1986); DH = *The Dunwich Horror and Others* (rev. ed. 1984); M = *At the Mountains of Madness and Other Novels* (rev. ed. 1985); SL = *Selected Letters* (1965–1976; 5 vols.).

1. *In Defence of Dagon,* ed. S. T. Joshi (West Warwick, R.I.: Necronomicon Press, 1985), p. 37.

2. See my "Topical References in Lovecraft," *Extrapolation,* vol. 25, no. 3 (Fall 1984): 247–265.

3. Cf. Eliseo Vivas, "Dreiser, an Inconsistent Mechanist," *Ethics,* July 1938, pp. 498–508.

4. Cf. Arvin R. Wells, *Jesting Moses: A Study in Cabellian Comedy* (Gainesville: University of Florida Press, 1962).

5. The essay (actually a collection of letter excerpts) entitled "Nietzscheism and Realism" (1921) ought rather to have been called "Schopenhauerianism and Realism," as it derives many ideas from the *Studies in Pessimism.* I am inclined to think that the otherwise curious statement in "The Music of Erich Zann"—"my metaphysical studies had taught me kindness" (*The Dunwich Horror and Others,* ed. S. T. Joshi [Sauk City, Wis.: Arkham House, 1984], p. 87)—is an incredibly cryptic reference to Schopenhauer, whom Lovecraft quotes in "Nietzscheism and Realism" as saying: "The conviction that the world and man is something which had better not have been is of a kind to fill us with indulgence toward one another" (*To Quebec and the Stars* [West Kingston, R.I.: Donald M. Grant, 1976], p. 85).

6. "Idealism and Materialism: A Reflection" (1919), *The Shuttered Room and Other Pieces* (Sauk City, Wis.: Arkham House, 1959), pp. 86–87.

7. Lovecraft wrote a number of revisions and collaborations subsequent to "The Shadow out of Time" (1934–1935), but I am not considering them here.

8. *Marginalia* (Sauk City, Wis.: Arkham House, 1944), p. 135. All citations from this essay are taken from this edition.

9. C. L. Moore to H. P. Lovecraft, January 30, 1936, H. P. Lovecraft Papers, John Hay Library, Brown University.

10. "Lord Dunsany and His Work" (1922), *Marginalia* (Sauk City, Wis.: Arkham House, 1944), p. 151.

11. See my "Dream World and the Real World in Lovecraft," *Crypt of Cthulhu*, vol. 2, no. 7 (Lammas 1983): 4–15.

12. "Some Notes on a Nonentity" (1933), *Beyond the Wall of Sleep* (Sauk City, Wis.: Arkham House, 1943), p. xiii.

13. "Demythologizing Cthulhu," *Lovecraft Studies*, vol. 3, no. 1 (Spring 1984): 3–9, 24.

14. *The Chronology out of Time: Dates in the Fiction of H. P. Lovecraft* (West Warwick, R.I.: Necronomicon Press, 1986).

15. "Facts in the Case of H. P. Lovecraft" (1972), rpt. in *H. P. Lovecraft: Four Decades of Criticism*, ed. S. T. Joshi (Athens: Ohio University Press, 1980), p. 178.

16. *Creeps by Night*, ed. Dashiell Hammett (New York: John Day Co., 1932), p. 184.

17. Richard Hofstadter, *The Age of Reform* (New York: Vintage Books, 1955), p. 177.

18. "Lucubrations Lovecraftian" (1921), *Uncollected Prose and Poetry*, ed. S. T. Joshi and Marc A. Michaud (West Warwick, R.I.: Necronomicon Press, 1978), 1:23.

19. See "Some Repetitions on the Times" (1933), first published in *Lovecraft Studies*, vol. 5, no. 1 (Spring 1986): 13–25.

20. *In Defence of Dagon*, p. 30.

21. "Lovecraft's Alien Civilisations" (1985), rpt. in my *Selected Papers on Lovecraft* (West Warwick, R.I.: Necronomicon Press, 1989).

22. Maurice Lévy, *Lovecraft: A Study in the Fantastic* (1972), trans. S. T. Joshi (Detroit: Wayne State University Press, 1988), p. 77.

23. *Beyond the Wall of Sleep*, pp. 6–7.

24. Lévy, *Lovecraft*, p. 22.

EPILOGUE: CRITICORUM IN USUM

1. *Lovecraft: A Study in the Fantastic*, trans. S. T. Joshi (Detroit: Wayne State University Press, 1988), p. 11.

CRITICAL APPENDIX

Parenthetical numbers refer to numbered items in Bibliography.

ARTHUR MACHEN

Bibliographical: Henry Danielson's early bibliography (4) lists only books, but it is invaluable for Machen's own notes and comments on his work, some of which are very enlightening and not to be found elsewhere. The bibliography itself has been completely superseded by the definitive work of Goldstone and Sweetser (6), a model of organization and precision, although with a very few slight errors and an inadequate index.

Biographical: Early memoirs of note are those by John Gunther (8) and Robert Hillyer (9), each of which relates original anecdotes about Machen. Anthony Lejeune's memoir (included in 18 and 25) is by far the best of the later accounts. Full-length biographies are curiously scarce for a man whose life is almost more remarkable and romantically alluring than his work; perhaps biographers have been intimidated by the charm and poignancy of Machen's own three autobiographies. But the account by Aidan Reynolds and William Charlton (16) is one of the pleasantest books one could ever read.

Critical: The early articles by Vincent Starrett (20), Carl Van Vechten (27), Paul Jordan-Smith (11), the weird writer M. P. Shiel (19), and St. John Adcock (1) are now mere exercises in hyperbole; Starrett's is particularly fatuous, complaining of the "dearth of wit and humor" in *The Hill of Dreams!* The odd digression on Machen in Van Vechten's novel *Peter Whiffle* (28) is an entertainment. R. Ellis Roberts's article (17) is the only early item of note.

Several substantial reviews of Machen's work are worth citing. Joseph Wood Krutch (12) stresses that Machen compels his readers to share his mystical outlook in order to appreciate him at all. Robert Hillyer (10) calls Machen "both mystic and humanist," the former in *The Hill of Dreams* and the latter in *Things Near and Far.* Herbert S. Gorman (7) finds a "strangeness of imagination" even in Machen's essays.

Among later articles Helen Lynch (13) praises Machen principally for his verbal magic; the detective writer John Dickson Carr (2) finds Machen's work very close to the detective tale; J. M. Cohen (3) declares Machen's autobiographies "one of the best pieces of autobiographical writing of the century" (although he berates the "lurid prose" of *The Hill of Dreams*); Robert L. Tyler (24) sees Machen's central value in "his ability to attract a votive cheering section" and maintains that his mysticism "actually weakened his fiction"; Robert S. Matteson (14), after a tedious biographical section, finally settles down to analyze *The Hill of Dreams* and *A Fragment of Life*, but his few interesting observations are not worth the space he occupies.

Of the two book-length critical studies, that by William Francis Gekle (5) promises much but delivers little. Half biography and half critical study, it does neither adequately, resorting to anecdote and paraphrase instead of research and analysis. Wesley D. Sweetser's book (21) is certainly distinguished, but its study of Machen's work becomes more philological than critical; nevertheless, it is still the only sustained discussion of Machen's entire work.

As with Lovecraft, recent Machen scholarship is being done largely by non-academic devotees; much of it, though humble, is of substantial value. Brocard Sewell put together a small booklet of criticism (18), of which the best piece is probably Wesley D. Sweetser's, a succinct account of Machen's philosophy and its relation to his fiction. More recently, Mark Valentine and Roger Dobson have assembled two anthologies of criticism (25, 26), containing material both old and new. In the first, Dobson provides a sound bio-critical sketch and Andy Sawyer gives a very sensitive reading of *The Hill of Dreams* ("A minor classic? Yes, I think so"). In the second, much rare work by Machen is reprinted, and Ron Weighell studies the role of theosophy and alchemy in Machen's work.

LORD DUNSANY

Biographical: Most of the articles on Dunsany are mere panegyrics, but some are more interesting than others. Clayton Hamilton (16) has recorded a substantial interview with Dunsany, and both of Gogarty's articles (13, 14) are worth reading, the latter in particular for its keen analyses of Dunsany's ostracism from the Irish Renaissance and Yeats's rivalry or envy of him. Nancy Price's memoir (30) is surprisingly disappointing for one who knew Dunsany for nearly fifty years. Patrick Mahony's memoir (25) is both touching and amusing. But far and away the best of the memoirs is Hazel Littlefield's slim book (22), which does for Dunsany what W. Paul Cook's memoir does for Lovecraft. Dunsany visited her several times at her California home in the 1950s, and her recollections of him are keen, poignant, and affectionate. Conversely, Mark Amory's biography (1), produced with the cooperation of Dunsany's heirs, is curiously wooden and fails to bring Dunsany to life; it is also remarkable for being a biography about a writer which fails to say anything significant about the literary work; for all we would know from Amory, Dunsany was nothing but a soldier and a huntsman.

Critical: W. B. Yeats's piece (40) is one of the earliest summations of Dunsany's work and is still among the best. Yeats understands why Dunsany did not use real Irish legendry in his early work; he praises Dunsany's bold metaphors and imagery; and he concludes: "Yet say what I will, so strange is the pleasure that they give, so hard to analyse and describe, I do not know why these stories and plays delight me. Now they set me thinking of some old Irish jewel work, now of a sword covered with Indian Arabesques that hangs in a friend's hall, now of St. Mark's at Venice, now of cloud palaces at the sundown; but more often still of a strange country or state of the soul that once for a few weeks I entered in deep sleep and after lost and have ever mourned and desired."

Other early articles are amusing in their rhapsodic attempts to imitate Dunsany's style; but Emma Garrett Boyd (4) suggests some interesting parallels with Maeterlinck, although she, unlike many early critics, vaunts the tales over the plays. Montrose J. Moses (26) seeks to temper the enthusiasm of Dunsany's ardent supporters; he believes that Dunsany's "plays are lacking in the essential humanity that marks our greatest dramas" and that Dunsany as a playwright is accordingly not to be ranked above Maeterlinck, Synge, or Yeats. Edward Hale Bierstadt's book (2) is a disappointingly superficial study of the plays, and its only value is in providing, in its second revised edition (1919), a number of interesting documents by and about Dunsany. Ernest Boyd's landmark article (5), aside from introducing the word *fantaisiste* into English usage, was the first to deal exhaustively with Dunsany's work up to 1916. Although more descriptive than analytical, the article did much to establish Dunsany (fleetingly) in critical circles. Frank Harris's piece (19) is comical for its sober propounding of a ludicrous revision of the ending of *The Gods of the Mountain.* Cornelius Weygandt's piece on the dramas of Dunsany (39) is an exhaustive treatment of the early plays with some speculations on their meaning and symbolism. Odell Shepard (36), writing very prettily, claims that Dunsany's principal merit is in completely banishing the "Here and Now," although he is aware that "glints of modernity" shine through his tales. He devotes some good pages to Dunsany's prose rhythms.

Josephine Hammond's article (18), one of the lengthiest early treatments, begins with some acute observations ("his simplicity, being cosmic, is extraordinarily complicated for the sophisticated to understand"), but descends rapidly into mere description. She finds Dunsany's plays lacking in compassion and well-rounded characters but sees in *Tales of War* an inkling of a warmer side to his work. AE's article (32) is essentially a review of *The King of Elfland's Daughter* and *The Charwoman's Shadow;* of the former he says, "It is a highly sustained piece of fantasy, written in a prose whose melody never fails and never tires." Benjamin De Casseres's charmingly hyperbolic article (11) states resoundingly: "He is a splendid literary immoralist—one who works beyond the trenches of Good and Evil in the No Man's Land where the Greeks placed the Furies and the Fates and where Blake housed Urizen and the Four Zoas." Reviews by Elizabeth

Bowen (3), Graham Greene (15), Ludwig Lewisohn (21), Seán O'Faoláin (28), J. B. Priestley (31), and Evelyn Waugh (38) are all insubstantial but reveal Dunsany's continuing importance through the 1930s.

After a long drought—although Louis-Paul Dubois's French article (29) is of note—Dunsany criticism began to reappear in the fan magazines. A. Bertram Chandler wrote an appreciative review of *The Fourth Book of Jorkens* (7), emphasizing Dunsany's lightness of touch, and Arthur C. Clarke (9) added an article, notable more for its scarcity and for the mere fact that he wrote it than for its critical acuteness. George Brandon Saul (33) is one of the few academicians to treat Dunsany, and the result is not especially fortunate: his ignorance of the rhetoric of fantasy causes him to be evidently baffled at the symbolism of Dunsany's early tales, which Saul dismisses to vaunt the Jorkens tales instead. It appears that Saul sees Dunsany as nothing more than an occasionally adept storyteller who did well to leave the jeweled prose of his early tales behind and adapt the flat matter-of-factness of his later period. Seamus Heaney (20), reviewing the Collins reprints of Dunsany, indulges in some foolish snipes at Dunsany the man (whom he knows only through Amory's biography) but has kind things to say about *The Curse of the Wise Woman*.

Darrell Schweitzer has written several significant articles on Dunsany and has now summed up his views in the first full-length critical study of Dunsany's entire work (35).

ALGERNON BLACKWOOD

Reading through the meager writing on Blackwood is a sad task. Almost no serious work was done on him during his lifetime, and in the last thirty-odd years only Peter Penzoldt and especially Mike Ashley have discussed him with anything approaching depth or comprehensiveness.

The early articles by Colbron (6), Lawson (11), Reeves (14), and Walters (15) are all contentless panegyrics and seem designed principally to drum up interest—vainly, as it turned out—in a completely unrecognized author. Stuart Gilbert's article (9) starts out promisingly but ends up being confused and discursive. I am astonished that Gilbert can claim that Blackwood is not didactic, that "he neither formulates a belief nor points a moral": to my mind this is all he does, although he does so subtly and unobtrusively. Somewhat better, but still ultimately insubstantial, is the chapter from Arthur Compton-Rickett's *Portraits and Personalities* (7), which provides a few new biographical details and also seems to echo my division of Blackwood's work: "Roughly speaking, Blackwood's work falls under three headings: Occult stories, Nature stories, and Children's stories"; but he does not link these categories in any meaningful way. He also states, remarkably, that "There is plenty of mystery but little mysticism in

Blackwood's stories." His very brief comparison of Blackwood to Thoreau and George Borrow may be worth pursuing.

Peter Penzoldt's chapter in *The Supernatural in Fiction* (12) is really the first intelligent discussion of Blackwood. Penzoldt, a personal friend of Blackwood, recognizes Blackwood's principal goal as the expansion of consciousness (hardly a great achievement, since Blackwood stated it plainly in a letter to Penzoldt), and then emphasizes the sincerity of his work and gives a close analysis of Blackwood's style and horrific technique. He also points out (perhaps too harshly) Lovecraft's failure to understand Blackwood because of his materialist stance. Penzoldt's analysis is limited by its treatment of a very few works and by some dubious psychoanalytical speculation—something, of course, that is at the heart of Penzoldt's entire work.

Derek Hudson's article (10) is merely an appreciative survey but includes some poignant memories at the end. J. Russell Reaver's article (13) is a very close reading of *The Centaur.*

The most recent critical discussion of Blackwood is in Jack Sullivan's *Elegant Nightmares* (15). Unfortunately, it is almost certainly the weakest chapter in his otherwise distinguished book. I wonder why Sullivan even chose to treat Blackwood, since he wrote very few true "ghost stories"; but as I have remarked in the Introduction, Sullivan's use of "ghost story" as a generic term is very unfortunate, and especially curious in that all the other writers he discusses wrote "ghost stories" in the more restricted sense. Sullivan's reading of Blackwood is so selective that he totally misconceives the goal of his writing. He remarks casually that Blackwood wrote several "forgotten fantasy novels"—they certainly are, at least by Sullivan. Alone of Blackwood's critics he fails to realize the central importance of *The Centaur* and as a result does not understand that the horror story as such is a very limited facet of Blackwood's aim; it is no wonder that he jeers at Penzoldt's fundamentally correct statement that "Nature is good, beautiful, right and healing" in Blackwood. If Sullivan had actually read the bulk of Blackwood instead of merely citing it in his bibliography, he would have come away with a very different picture. Sullivan also dwells excessively on Blackwood's supposed stylistic infelicities, much of which are merely a result of Blackwood's difference from (but not inferiority to) Sullivan's paragon, M. R. James. There is also a flippancy in Sullivan's whole treatment—as if Blackwood were not worth the bother—which I find rather offensive.

It is unquestionable that Mike Ashley, aside from his many other accomplishments, is the leading authority on Blackwood. He has written two articles (1, 5) that are models of biographical research: one exhaustively treats Blackwood's little-known involvement with the Golden Dawn and its influence upon his work, especially in *John Silence* and *The Human Chord;* the second deals with Blackwood's early uncollected articles and stories and shows that Blackwood may have been a little disingenuous in claiming that his emergence as a writer was a sudden and unexpected occurrence. Two further articles by Ashley (3, 4) extensively discuss Blackwood's influence on Lovecraft. Ashley's work has now been summed up in a massive bio-bibliography (2), whose introductory section provides as sustained and detailed a biography of Blackwood as we shall see until Ashley completes his full-length biographical treatment; but Ashley has regretfully announced that this project will not come to fruition for some years.

M. R. JAMES

Biographical: Stephen Gaselee's obituary (7) is a moving and detailed memoir with some brief words on James's scholarship. The ghost stories are never mentioned. S. G. Lubbock's chatty memoir (9) is very pleasant, although nearly half of it is devoted to an impressive bibliography of James's scholarly publications (his ghost stories are relegated to a "Miscellaneous" section) by A. F Scholfield. Shane Leslie (8), reviewing *Eton and King's,* uses it as a springboard for some charming recollections. At the end he reports asking James whether he believed in ghosts. James's reply: "Yes, we know there are such things—but we don't know the rules." This may come as a surprise to those critics (including myself) who stress James's detachment from the implications of his weird writing; but Leslie does not elaborate on the idea.

I am incapable of judging the relative merits of the two full-length biographies of James: that by R. W. Pfaff (11) is more exhaustive (with a very complete bibliography of James's publications), but Michael Cox's (4) is a bit more readable and more attuned to James's weird writing. Neither offers literary criticism of any substance.

Critical: Mary Butts (2) has written a vapid panegyric, while Peter Fleming's piece (5) is an entertaining but insubstantial brief review of the *Collected Ghost Stories.* Peter Penzoldt's chapter on James from *The Supernatural in Fiction* (10) seems to anticipate my criticism of James for the dearth of a world view in his work when he writes, "His stories are straightforward tales of terror and the supernatural, utterly devoid of any deeper meaning"; but Penzoldt paradoxically finds this a virtue, feeling that James's "technique" redeems the tales' shallowness. Probably Penzoldt also likes James because he does not exhibit the unpleasant neuroses Penzoldt attributes (rightly or wrongly) to Machen and Lovecraft. J. Randolph Cox's article (3) is largely biographical, with a few unremarkable comments on James's horrific technique. Austin Warren's article (14) is a disappointment from an otherwise distinguished critic of mainstream literature. After a biographical introduction Warren discusses James's scholarly writing with a view to tracing thematic connections between it and his ghost stories; more perhaps can be done in this direction. His treatment of the ghost stories themselves is more descriptive than analytical.

Of the three most recent critical treatments, that in Julia Briggs's *Night Visitors* (1) presents her usual plodding and meandering analysis of James's themes, characters, and technique. She announces at the outset that a ghost story was for James "simply a bagatelle for an idle hour," but like so many of James's admirers she finds nothing wrong with such a flippant artistic stance. She never asks why we should take James's stories any more seriously than he did. I have voiced my disagreements with Jack Sullivan's chapter on James in *Elegant Nightmares* (12), although I admit that it is still the single most penetrating study of James's work. Devendra P. Varma's succinct overview (13) is one of the most sensitive appraisals of James, stressing his "spare and unadorned prose" and his ability to allow his horrors to enter insidiously into prosaic existence. Varma concludes aptly: "The balance between scholarly reticence and malignant manifestation remains perhaps the characteristic quality of the antiquarian ghost story."

AMBROSE BIERCE

Of all the authors in this volume, Bierce has received the most voluminous attention from academic sources. My secondary bibliography is very selective, concentrating on important biographies and critical studies of the fiction. There is, remarkably, no adequate bibliography of Bierce, either primary or secondary— that by Vincent Starrett (38) is no more than a checklist. I understand, however, that Elken Osher is working on a comprehensive bibliography.

Biographical: Of the four biographies of Bierce published in 1929, only Carey McWilliams's (27) is really substantial; it remained standard until Paul Fatout's work twenty years later. Walter Neale's (32) is merely a chatty memoir by Bierce's friend and publisher but contains valuable anecdotes and insights. C. Hartley Grattan (18) attempts an "intellectual biography," but his study of Bierce's thought is too discursive and superficial to be of much use. The memoir by Adolphe de Castro (13), Bierce's former collaborator Adolphe Danziger (he changed his name during World War I), is an unintentionally hilarious account principally relating de Castro's attempts to find traces of Bierce after his disappearance in Mexico. Lovecraft's colleague Frank Belknap Long prepared the work for publication after Lovecraft refused to do so. Bierce's friend George Sterling wrote a number of articles (including a long and thoughtful preface to *The Letters of Ambrose Bierce*); perhaps the best is his article in *American Mercury* (40), a piece both biographical and critical in which Sterling calls Bierce "easily the foremost American wit." Joseph Noel's book (33) is more an account of his recollections of Jack London and Sterling than of Bierce, whom he met only twice, but it is an entertaining if meandering picture of the California milieu of Bierce's later years. Fatout's biography (15) is certainly comprehensive (I will not say definitive), but it irks me by its unwarranted value judgments and by a general air that Bierce is not worth the bother of such detailed treatment. Fatout's subsequent study of Bierce's Black Hills expedition (16) is wondrously detailed and slightly more respectful.

Critical: Frederic Taber Cooper's early article (9)—the only significant critical work on Bierce prior to his disappearance—carefully examines Bierce's critical utterances; his analysis of the stories is unremarkable. H. L. Mencken's entertaining account (29) is perhaps the most perceptive of the early articles on Bierce; it sees "cynicism" as the focus of Bierce's entire work, from poetry to fables to journalism to short stories. Mencken also relates a charming anecdote about accompanying Bierce to a funeral. Van Wyck Brooks wrote two articles on Bierce. The first (7), a review of Bierce's letters, is a sensitive reflection on Bierce's temperamental ostracism from his time. The second (8) emphasizes the same point less intelligently. Napier Wilt (45) closely studies Bierce's Civil War experiences and writings, but draws no broader conclusion from them. Arthur M. Miller (30) studies Poe's influence upon both Bierce's critical and fictional work with great intelligence and sensitivity, acknowledging that Bierce "usually changed what he borrowed."

Edmund Wilson's relatively unperceptive piece (44) finds Bierce merely obsessed with death and seeks biographical clues for his philosophical and political attitudes. Marcus Klein (24) attempts to place Bierce in a literary and cultural context, claiming that Bierce's importance was in combating "the national propaganda for goodness and light." Bierce's stories, however, are "merely clever . . . efficient little machines." Stuart C. Woodruff's book (46) is a tedious and simple-minded analysis of the short stories in which his revulsion at Bierce's grisliness (precisely what Bierce was aiming at) repeatedly betrays him into hostile and pejorative judgments.

Mary Elizabeth Grenander's biographical-critical study (19) is a distinguished work, providing very close readings of a number of Bierce's stories and examining Bierce's other work more elaborately than most previous accounts. I find her division of Bierce's tales overly schematic, but on the whole this study may still be the best single account of Bierce's life and work, although her discussion of Bierce's philosophy is very sketchy. Daniel Aaron (1) has written an interesting study of the effects of the Civil War on Bierce's life, work, and thought; he makes the important point that "Bierce's tales of war are not in the least realistic; they are, as he doubtless intended them to be, incredible events occurring in credible surroundings." Russell Roth (35) finds a strong strain of misogyny in Bierce, particularly hatred of his mother.

B. S. Field's all too brief study (17) claims that "All of the work of Bierce . . . ought to be judged as the work of a joker and a practitioner of *humor noir*" and that comparisons to Twain or Crane are beside the point. F. J. Logan (25) somewhat hysterically defends Bierce's greatness by a very close reading of "An Occurrence at Owl Creek Bridge." John R. Brazil (6) studies Bierce's political and literary theory, particularly his rejection of realism and his scorn of political reform. I am not sure, however, that Bierce "sought to escape the social and political realities that so confused him," nor am I clear how Brazil has even arrived at this conclusion. Lawrence I. Berkove (3) is one of the few to study Bierce's Swiftian satires, finding them paradigmatic of Bierce's rejection of utopia and his political scepticism.

Cathy N. Davidson's recent book (11) is too rich for brief summary but seeks to show that Bierce is "an impressionistic, surrealistic, philosophical, postmodernist fictionalizer" where "the horror, natural or supernatural, is almost always perceived as irrational." This is not at all my view of Bierce, but no one can deny Davidson's extraordinarily close and subtle (if occasionally laborious) treatments of nearly the whole corpus of Bierce's fiction.

H. P. LOVECRAFT

Given my peculiar position in the field, it is difficult for me to write briefly of the history and development of Lovecraftian studies. I have already written a lengthy account of scholarship in the decade following the death of August Derleth (15), and much more could be written on the subject.

Bibliographical: My bibliography (18) and supplement (19) seem comprehensive and were founded upon the landmark work of George T. Wetzel (48). Some bibliographical problems still remain, and foreign work on Lovecraft is becoming increasingly voluminous and hence increasingly difficult to chart.

Biographical: It seems that nearly every associate of Lovecraft has written an account of him; of the briefer ones we can cite R. H. Barlow's and Donald Wandrei's (in Lovecraft's *Marginalia,* 1944), J. Vernon Shea's (46), and Kenneth Sterling's poignant recent memoir (47). Two men who knew Lovecraft for nearly his entire adult life have written full-length memoirs. W. Paul Cook's (8) is rapidly reaching classic status for its chiseled prose, charming anecdotes, and vividly real portrayal of the man. Frank Belknap Long's (24) is a disappointment, being rambling and insubstantial. Sonia Davis, Lovecraft's wife, has written a lengthy article (10) which, though nearly illiterate in parts, is worth deep study.

The only full-length biography—Derleth's *H. P. L.: A Memoir* (1945) does not qualify as such—is by L. Sprague de Camp (11). While bulky and full of information (some of it erroneous), the work is flawed in its very conception because of de Camp's complete ignorance of Lovecraft's philosophy and his concomitant failure to understand the sources for Lovecraft's views and actions—especially such things as his amateur stance, his association with the past, and his racialism. Kenneth W. Faig's slender book (13) may be a more satisfactory biographical account, although it is a fraction of the size of de Camp's.

Critical: Early critics Matthew H. Onderdonk (34, 35) and George T. Wetzel (49) did much to lay the foundations of Lovecraft studies by stressing Lovecraft's materialism and cosmicism. Fritz Leiber wrote a pioneering article, "A Literary

Copernicus" (1949; reprinted in 17), tracing Lovecraft's transition from super-naturalism to quasi science fiction. Peter Penzoldt's *The Supernatural in Fiction* (excerpts reprinted in 17) is a significant early work for its close study of Love-craft's style and structural complexity, although I have voiced my profound dis-agreement with the whole category of the "pure tale of horror" into which Pen-zoldt relegates Lovecraft.

Little substantive work was done in the 1950s and 1960s; but the death of August Derleth in 1971 triggered a spate of critical work. Richard L. Tierney's "The Derleth Mythos" (included in 14) began the dismantling of Derleth's erro-neous conception of Lovecraft's myth cycle, work that was completed by Dirk W. Mosig's "H. P. Lovecraft: Myth-Maker" (reprinted in 17). Mosig went on to write several significant articles (29, 30), focusing upon a Jungian interpreta-tion. Barton L. St. Armand's two principal works (41, 42) are enormously rich and difficult to summarize; both reveal a keen understanding of Lovecraft and an attempt to place him in a broader context of literature and thought.

Lovecraft's myth cycle has attracted considerable attention; much of it is of an extremely trivial and frivolous sort, as exemplified in Lin Carter's *Lovecraft: A Look behind the "Cthulhu Mythos"* (1972). Of greater interest are Robert M. Price's several important contributions (36, 37, 38, 39), showing the degree to which Lovecraft's artificial pantheon and its appurtenances resemble actual religions and myth cycles. Some recent critics—notably Will Murray (33) and David E. Schultz (44)—have questioned the very existence of the myth cycle as a discrete group of tales within Lovecraft's work, although Murray has gone on to examine interesting components of the myth cycle (31, 32).

Little real work has been done on Lovecraft's philosophy. St. Armand attempts it, but his knowledge of Lovecraft's views is not sufficiently detailed or sympa-thetic. The first chapter of my monograph (16) lays down the bare bones of Lovecraft's thought, and another article (20) discusses the relation of his meta-physics to his aesthetics. Steven J. Mariconda has also done good work in this direction (26). Maurice Lévy (23) has written perhaps the single best work on Lovecraft, and he brilliantly integrates biographical, philosophical, and thematic approaches in a highly original conception of Lovecraft the man and writer.

As I have mentioned in my chapter, much recent work on Lovecraft is of a philological nature—good examples being Jason C. Eckhardt's discussion of *At the Mountains of Madness* in the context of the Antarctic exploration of his time (12), or Donald R. Burleson's study of Hawthorne's influence on Lovecraft (3). For Lovecraft's style Steven J. Mariconda's two articles (25, 27) are essential. Paul Buhle's "Dystopia as Utopia" (1976; reprinted in 17) and my "Topical Ref-erences in Lovecraft" (22) treat Lovecraft's place in political, social, and intellec-tual history.

Of the two recent full-length studies, Donald R. Burleson's (2) is wide-ranging but too often descends to lengthy plot description instead of analysis; but he understands the central importance of cosmicism in Lovecraft's thought and also has keen discussions of some of Lovecraft's poetry. Peter Cannon's volume (5) is a perfectly competent study but breaks no new ground and also contains more paraphrase than criticism. Still, it is a reliable guide to Lovecraft and very capably integrates the newest findings in the field.

BIBLIOGRAPHY

GENERAL

Bibliographies

Bleiler, Everett F. *The Guide to Supernatural Fiction.* Kent, Ohio: Kent State University Press, 1983.

Currey, L. W. *Science Fiction and Fantasy Authors: A Bibliography of First Printings of Their Fiction and Selected Nonfiction.* Boston: G. K. Hall, 1979. (Rev. ed. in progress.)

Day, Bradford M. *The Checklist of Fantastic Literature in Paperbound Books.* Denver, N.Y.: Science-Fiction and Fantasy Publications, 1965. New York: Arno Press, 1975.

Reginald, R. *Science Fiction and Fantasy Literature: A Checklist 1700–1974.* 2 vols. Detroit: Gale Research Co., 1979.

Tuck, Donald H. *The Encyclopedia of Science Fiction and Fantasy through 1968.* 3 vols. Chicago: Advent Publishers, 1974–1982.

Tymn, Marshall B., ed. *Horror Literature: A Core Collection and Reference Guide.* New York: R. R. Bowker, 1981.

———, Kenneth J. Zahorski, and Robert H. Boyer. *Fantasy Literature: A Core Collection and Reference Guide.* New York: R. R. Bowker, 1979.

General Studies

Attebery, Brian. *The Fantasy Tradition in American Literature from Irving to Le Guin.* Bloomington: Indiana University Press, 1980.

Briggs, Julia. *Night Visitors: The Rise and Fall of the English Ghost Story.* London: Faber & Faber, 1977.

Daniels, Les. *Living in Fear: A History of Horror in the Mass Media.* New York: Scribner's, 1975. St. Albans: Paladin Books, 1977 (as *Fear*).

Heller, Terry. *The Delights of Terror: An Aesthetics of the Tale of Terror.* Urbana: University of Illinois Press, 1987.

Irwin, W. R. *The Game of the Impossible: A Rhetoric of Fantasy.* Urbana: University of Illinois Press, 1976.

Jackson, Rosemary. *Fantasy: The Literature of Subversion.* London: Methuen, 1981.

MacAndrew, Elizabeth. *The Gothic Tradition in Fiction.* New York: Columbia University Press, 1979.

Penzoldt, Peter. *The Supernatural in Fiction.* London: Peter Nevill, 1952. New York: Humanities Press, 1965.

Punter, David. *The Literature of Terror: A History of Gothic Fictions from 1765 to the Present Day.* London: Longmans, 1980.

Rabkin, Eric S. *The Fantastic in Literature.* Princeton: Princeton University Press, 1976.

Scarborough, Dorothy. *The Supernatural in Modern English Fiction.* New York: Putnam's, 1917. New York: Humanities Press, 1965.

Smith, Clark Ashton. *Planets and Dimensions: Collected Essays.* Edited by Charles K. Wolfe. Baltimore: Mirage Press, 1973.

Sullivan, Jack. *Elegant Nightmares: The English Ghost Story from LeFanu to Blackwood.* Athens: Ohio University Press, 1978.

————, ed. *The Penguin Encyclopaedia of Horror and the Supernatural.* New York: Viking Penguin, 1986.

Todorov, Tzvetan. *The Fantastic: A Structural Approach to a Literary Genre.* Translated by Richard Howard. Cleveland: Press of Case Western Reserve University, 1973. Ithaca: Cornell University Press, 1975. Originally published as *Introduction à la littérature fantastique.* Paris: Editions du Seuil, 1970.

Vax, Louis. *L'Art et la littérature fantastiques.* 4th ed. Paris: Presses Universitaires de France, 1974.

————. *La Séduction de l'étrange: Etude sur la littérature fantastique.* Paris: Presses Universitaires de France, 1965.

Wolff, Robert Lee. *Strange Stories: Explorations in Victorian Fiction—The Occult and the Neurotic.* Boston: Gambit, 1971.

ARTHUR MACHEN

Primary

Poetry

Eleusinia. Hereford, Wales: Joseph Jones, 1881. West Warwick, R.I.: Necronomicon Press, 1988 (with *Beneath the Barley*).

Short Stories

The Great God Pan and The Inmost Light. London: John Lane; Boston: Roberts Brothers, 1894. London: Grant Richards, 1913.

The House of Souls. London: Grant Richards, 1906. New York: Knopf, 1922. Freeport, N.Y.: Books for Libraries Press, 1971.

The Angels of Mons: The Bowmen and Other Legends of the War. London: Simpkin, Marshall, Hamilton, Kent, 1915. New York: Putnam's, 1915. Freeport, N.Y.: Books for Libraries Press, 1972.

The Great Return. London: Faith Press, 1915.

Ornaments in Jade. New York: Knopf, 1924.

The Shining Pyramid. London: Martin Secker, 1925. New York: Knopf, 1925.

The Cosy Room. London: Rich & Cowan, 1936. New York: Arno Press, 1976.

The Children of the Pool and Other Stories. London: Hutchinson, 1936. New York: Arno Press, 1976.

Holy Terrors. Harmondsworth: Penguin, 1946.

Tales of Horror and the Supernatural. New York: Knopf, 1948. London: Richards Press, 1949. London: John Baker, 1964. St. Albans: Panther, 1963 (2 vols.). New York: Pinnacle, 1971 (2 vols.), 1983.

The Strange World of Arthur Machen. New York: Juniper Press, 1960.

Novels

The Chronicle of Clemendy. London: Privately printed, 1888. New York: Knopf, 1926.

The Three Impostors; or, The Transmutations. London: John Lane; Boston: Roberts Brothers, 1895. New York: Knopf, 1923. London: John Baker, 1964. New York: Ballantine, 1972. (Also included in the 1906 edition of *The House of Souls.*)

The Hill of Dreams. London: Grant Richards, 1907. New York: Knopf, 1923. London: Richards Press, 1954 (with an introduction by Lord Dunsany). London: John Baker, 1968. New York: Dover, 1986.

The Terror. London: Duckworth, 1917. New York: W. W. Norton, 1965. London: White Lion, 1973. (Also in *Tales of Horror and the Supernatural.*)

The Secret Glory. London: Martin Secker, 1922. New York: Knopf, 1922. (Unpublished conclusion, Arthur Machen Papers, Beinecke Library, Yale University.)

The Green Round. London: Ernest Benn, 1933. Sauk City, Wis.: Arkham House, 1968.

Essays and Miscellany

The Anatomy of Tobacco. London: George Redway, 1884. New York: Knopf, 1926.

A Chapter from the Book Called The Ingenious Gentleman Don Quijote de la Mancha Which by Some Mischance Has Not Till Now Been Printed. London: George Redway, 1887.

Thesaurus Incantatus: The Enchanted Treasure; or, The Spagyric Quest of Beroaldus

Cosmopolita. London: Thomas Marvell [Arthur Machen and Harry Spurr], 1888.

Hieroglyphics: A Note upon Ecstasy in Literature. London: Grant Richards, 1902. London: Martin Secker, 1910. New York: Mitchell Kennerley, 1913. New York: Knopf, 1923. London: Unicorn Press, 1960.

The House of the Hidden Light (with A. E. Waite). London: Privately printed, 1904.

Dr. Stiggins: His Views and Principles. London: Francis Griffiths, 1906. New York: Knopf, 1925.

"Parsifal": The Story of the Holy Grail. London: General Cinematograph Agencies, [c. 1913].

War and the Christian Faith. London: Skeffington & Sons, 1918.

The Pantomime of the Year. London: Privately printed, 1921.

The Grand Trouvaille: A Legend of Pentonville. London: First Edition Bookshop, 1923.

The Shining Pyramid. Edited by Vincent Starrett. Chicago: Covici-McGee, 1924.

The Collector's Craft. London: First Edition Bookshop, 1924.

Strange Roads and With the Gods in Spring. London: Classic Press, 1924.

Dog and Duck. London: Jonathan Cape, 1924. New York: Knopf, 1924.

The Glorious Mystery. Edited by Vincent Starrett. Chicago: Covici-McGee, 1924.

Precious Balms. London: Spurr & Swift, 1924.

A Preface to "Casanova's Escape from the Leads." London: Casanova Society, 1925.

The Canning Wonder. London: Chatto & Windus, 1925. New York: Knopf, 1926.

Dreads and Drolls. London: Martin Secker, 1926. New York: Knopf, 1927. Freeport, N.Y.: Books for Libraries Press, 1967.

Notes and Queries. London: Spurr & Swift, 1926.

A Souvenir of Cadby Hall. London: J. Lyons & Co., 1927.

Parish of Amersham. Amersham: S. G. Mason, 1930.

Tom O'Bedlam and His Song. Westport, Conn.: Apellicon Press, 1930.

Beneath the Barley: A Note on the Origins of "Eleusinia." London: Privately printed [John Gawsworth], 1931. West Warwick, R.I.: Necronomicon Press, 1988 (with *Eleusinia*).

In the 'Eighties. Amersham: Privately printed, 1931.

An Introduction to John Gawsworth's "Above the River." Amersham: Privately printed, 1931.

A Few Letters. Cleveland: Rowfant Club, 1932.

The Glitter of the Brook. Dalton, Ga.: Postprandial Press, 1932.

Bridles and Spurs. Cleveland: Rowfant Club, 1951.

Guinevere and Lancelot and Others. Edited by Cuyler W. Brooks, Jr., and Michael Shoemaker. Newport News, Va.: Purple Mouth Press, 1987.

Selected Letters. Edited by Mark Valentine and Roger Dobson. London: Thorsons, 1988.

Autobiography

Far Off Things. London: Martin Secker, 1922. New York: Knopf, 1922.
Things Near and Far. London: Martin Secker, 1923. New York: Knopf, 1923.
The London Adventure. London: Martin Secker, 1924. New York: Knopf, 1925.
  London: Village Press, 1974.
Autobiography [*Far Off Things* and *Things Near and Far*]. London: Richards Press,
  1951. London: Garnstone, 1974.

Translations

Marguerite of Navarre. *The Heptameron.* London: Privately printed, 1886. London: George Routledge & Sons; New York: Dutton, 1905. New York: Knopf,
  1924.
Beroalde de Verville. *Fantastic Tales or the Way to Attain.* London: Privately printed,
  1890. New York: Boni & Liveright, 1923.
Jacques Casanova. *The Memoirs of Jacques Casanova.* 12 vols. London: Privately
  printed, 1894. London: Casanova Society, 1922. New York: Knopf, 1929
  (2 vols.). New York: A. & C. Boni, 1932 (2 vols.). Edinburgh: Limited Editions
  Club, 1940 (8 vols.). New York: Putnam's; London: Elek Books, 1959–1961
  (6 vols.). New York: Dover, 1961 (3 vols.).
Casanova's Escape from the Leads. London: Casanova Society, 1925. New York:
  Knopf, 1925.
Lady Hester Lucy Stanhope. *Remarks upon Hermodactylus.* London: Privately
  printed, 1933.

Collected Works

Works. Caerleon Edition. 9 vols. London: Martin Secker, 1923.

Secondary

(1) Adcock, Arthur St. John. "Arthur Machen." In *The Glory That Was Grub
  Street,* pp. 213–244. New York: Frederick A. Stokes, 1928.
(2) Carr, John Dickson. "Hammock Companions" [review of *Tales of Horror and
  the Supernatural*]. *New York Times Book Review,* August 1, 1948, p. 10.
(3) Cohen, J. M. "Books and Writers." *Spectator,* July 20, 1951, p. 100.
(4) Danielson, Henry. *Arthur Machen: A Bibliography.* London: Henry Danielson,
  1923.
(5) Gekle, William Francis. *Arthur Machen: Weaver of Fantasy.* Millbrook, N.Y.:
  Round Table Press, 1949.

(6) Goldstone, Adrian, and Wesley Sweetser. *A Bibliography of Arthur Machen.* Austin: University of Texas Press, 1965.

(7) Gorman, Herbert S. "Arthur Machen Pursues His Mystic Way." *New York Times Book Review,* January 16, 1927, p. 5.

(8) Gunther, John. "The Truth about Arthur Machen." *Bookman* (New York) 61 (July 1925): 571–574.

(9) Hillyer, Robert. "Arthur Machen." *Atlantic Monthly* 179 (May 1947): 138–140.

(10) ———. "Arthur Machen." *Yale Review* 13 (October 1923): 174–176.

(11) Jordan-Smith, Paul. "Black Magic: An Impression of Arthur Machen." In *On Strange Altars,* pp. 214–235. New York: A. & C. Boni, 1924.

(12) Krutch, Joseph Wood. "Tales of a Mystic." *Nation,* September 13, 1922, pp. 258–259.

(13) Lynch, Helen. "Arthur Machen." *Sewanee Review* 47 (July–September 1939): 424–427.

(14) Matteson, Robert S. "Arthur Machen: A Vision of an Enchanted Land." *Personalist* 46 (Spring 1965): 253–268.

(15) Miles, Hamish. "Machen in Retrospect." *Dial* 74 (June 1923): 627–630.

(16) Reynolds, Aidan, and William Charlton. *Arthur Machen: A Short Account of His Life and Work.* London: Richards Press, 1963. Oxford: Caermaen Books, 1988.

(17) Roberts, R. Ellis. "Arthur Machen." *Bookman* (London) 62 (September 1922): 240–242.

(18) Sewell, Brocard, ed. *Arthur Machen.* Llandeilo: St. Albert's Press, 1960.

(19) Shiel, M. P. "On Scholar-Artistry." In *Science, Life and Literature,* pp. 95–100. London: Williams & Norgate, 1950.

(20) Starrett, Vincent. "Arthur Machen: A Novelist of Ecstasy and Sin." *Reedy's Mirror,* October 5, 1917, pp. 631–632. Reprinted in Starrett's *Buried Caesars,* pp. 1–31. Chicago: Covici-McGee, 1923.

(21) Sweetser, Wesley D. *Arthur Machen.* New York: Twayne, 1964.

(22) Symons, Julian. "Horror in the Nineties." *Books and Bookmen* 10 (March 1965): 12–13, 37.

(23) Tierney, Myles. "The Highway to Avalon." *Bookman* (New York) 60 (October 1924): 224–226.

(24) Tyler, Robert L. "Arthur Machen: The Minor Writer and His Function." *Approach,* Spring 1960, pp. 21–26.

(25) Valentine, Mark, and Roger Dobson, eds. *Arthur Machen: Apostle of Wonder.* Oxford: Caermaen Books, 1985.

(26) ———. *Arthur Machen: Artist and Mystic.* Oxford: Caermaen Books, 1986.

(27) Van Vechten, Carl. "Arthur Machen: Dreamer and Mystic." *Literary Digest International Book Review* 1 (February 1923): 36–37. Reprinted in Van Vechten's *Excavations,* pp. 162–269. New York: Knopf, 1926.

(28) ———. *Peter Whiffle.* New York: Knopf, 1922.

(29) Wright, Cuthbert. "Far-Off Things." *Freeman,* April 4, 1923, pp. 90–92.

LORD DUNSANY

Primary

Short Stories

The Gods of Pegāna. London: Elkin Mathews, 1905. London: Pegāna Press, 1911. Boston: John W. Luce, n.d.

Time and the Gods. London: William Heinemann, 1906. Boston: John W. Luce, n.d. New York: Boni & Liveright (Modern Library), 1918 (with *The Book of Wonder*). New York: Putnam's, 1922.

The Sword of Welleran and Other Stories. London: George Allen & Sons, 1908. Boston: John W. Luce, n.d. New York: Boni & Liveright (Modern Library), 1917 (with *A Dreamer's Tales*). Norwood, Pa.: Norwood Editions, 1978 (with *A Dreamer's Tales*).

A Dreamer's Tales. London: George Allen & Sons, 1910. Boston: John W. Luce, n.d. New York: Boni & Liveright (Modern Library), 1917 (with *The Sword of Welleran*). Freeport, N.Y.: Books for Libraries Press, 1969. Philadelphia: Owlswick Press, 1976. Norwood, Pa.: Norwood Editions, 1978 (with *The Sword of Welleran*).

The Book of Wonder. London: William Heinemann, 1912. Boston: John W. Luce, n.d. New York: Boni & Liveright (Modern Library), 1918 (with *Time and the Gods*). London: Elkin Mathews, 1919.

Selections from the Writings of Lord Dunsany. Introduction by W. B. Yeats. Churchtown: Cuala Press, 1912. Shannon: Irish University Press, 1971.

Fifty-one Tales. London: Elkin Mathews, 1915. New York: Mitchell Kennerley, 1915. Boston: Little, Brown, 1917. Van Nuys, Calif.: Newcastle, 1974 (as *The Food of Death*).

The Last Book of Wonder. Boston: John W. Luce, 1916. London: Elkin Mathews, 1916 (as *Tales of Wonder*). Freeport, N.Y.: Books for Libraries Press, 1969.

Tales of War. Dublin: Talbot Press; London: T. Fisher Unwin, 1918. Boston: Little, Brown, 1918. London: Putnam's, 1922.

Tales of Three Hemispheres. Boston: John W. Luce, 1919. London: T. Fisher Unwin, 1920. Philadelphia: Owlswick Press, 1976.

The Travel Tales of Mr. Joseph Jorkens. London: Putnam's, 1931. New York: Putnam's, 1931. London: Remploy, 1980.

Mr. Jorkens Remembers Africa. London: William Heinemann, 1934. New York: Longmans, Green, 1934 (as *Jorkens Remembers Africa*). Freeport, N.Y.: Books for Libraries Press, 1972.

Jorkens Has a Large Whiskey. London: Putnam's, 1940.

The Fourth Book of Jorkens. London: Jarrolds, 1948. Sauk City, Wis.: Arkham
   House, 1948.
The Man Who Ate the Phoenix. London: Jarrolds, 1949.
The Little Tales of Smethers and Other Stories. London: Jarrolds, 1952. London:
   Remploy, 1978.
Jorkens Borrows Another Whiskey. London: Michael Joseph, 1954.
The Sword of Welleran and Other Tales of Enchantment. New York: Devin-Adair,
   1954.
At the Edge of the World. Edited by Lin Carter. New York: Ballantine, 1970.
Beyond the Fields We Know. Edited by Lin Carter. New York: Ballantine, 1972.
Gods, Men and Ghosts. Edited by E. F. Bleiler. New York: Dover, 1972.
Over the Hills and Far Away. Edited by Lin Carter. New York: Ballantine, 1974.
The Ghosts of the Heaviside Layer and Other Fantasms. Edited by Darrell Schweit-
   zer. Philadelphia: Owlswick Press, 1980.

Plays

Five Plays. London: Grant Richards, 1914. Boston: Little, Brown, 1914. New
   York: Mitchell Kennerley, 1914. London: Putnam's, 1925.
Plays of Gods and Men. Dublin: Talbot Press, 1917. London: T. Fisher Unwin,
   1917. Boston: John W. Luce, 1917. New York: Putnam's, 1918. Great Neck,
   N.Y.: Core Collection Books, 1977. Darby, Pa.: Arden Library, 1979.
If. London: Putnam's, 1921. New York: Putnam's, 1922. London: Putnam's,
   1923 (with *Plays of Near and Far*).
Plays of Near and Far. London: Putnam's, 1922. London: Putnam's, 1923 (with
   If). New York: Putnam's, 1923.
Alexander and Three Small Plays. London: Putnam's, 1925. New York: Putnam's,
   1926.
The Old Folk of the Centuries. London: Elkin Mathews & Marrot, 1930.
Lord Adrian. Waltham Saint Lawrence: Golden Cockerel Press, 1933.
Mr. Faithful. New York: Samuel French, 1935.
Plays for Earth and Air. London: William Heinemann, 1937.

Novels

The Chronicles of Rodriguez. London: Putnam's, 1922. New York: Putnam's, 1922
   (as *Don Rodriguez: Chronicles of Shadow Valley*). London: Pan/Ballantine, 1972.
The King of Elfland's Daughter. New York: Putnam's, 1924. London: Putnam's,
   1924. New York: Ballantine, 1969. London: Unwin Paperbacks, 1982.
The Charwoman's Shadow. London: Putnam's, 1926. New York: Putnam's, 1926.
   New York: Ballantine, 1973. London: Unwin Paperbacks, 1983.

The Blessing of Pan. London: Putnam's, 1927. New York: Putnam's, 1927.

The Curse of the Wise Woman. London: William Heinemann, 1933. New York: Longmans, Green, 1933. London: Collins, 1972.

Up in the Hills. London: William Heinemann, 1935. New York: Putnam's, 1936.

Rory and Bran. London: William Heinemann, 1936. New York: Putnam's, 1937.

My Talks with Dean Spanley. London: William Heinemann, 1936. New York: Putnam's, 1936. London: Collins, 1972.

The Story of Mona Sheehy. London: William Heinemann, 1939. New York: Harper, 1940.

Guerrilla. London: William Heinemann, 1944. Indianapolis: Bobbs-Merrill, 1944.

The Strange Journeys of Colonel Polders. London: Jarrolds, 1950.

The Last Revolution. London: Jarrolds, 1951.

His Fellow Men. London: Jarrolds, 1952.

Poetry

Fifty Poems. London: Putnam's, 1929.

Mirage Water. London: Putnam's, 1938. Philadelphia: Dorrance, 1939.

War Poems. London: Hutchinson, 1941.

Wandering Songs. London: Hutchinson, 1943.

A Journey. London: Macdonald, 1944.

The Year. London: Jarrolds, 1946.

The Odes of Horace (translation). London: William Heinemann, 1947. London and New York: Dent/Dutton (Everyman's Library), 1961 (as *The Collected Works of Horace;* other works translated by Michael Oakley).

Autobiography

Unhappy Far-Off Things. London: Elkin Mathews, 1919. Boston: Little, Brown, 1919.

My Ireland. London: Jarrolds, 1937. New York: Funk & Wagnalls, 1937.

Patches of Sunlight. London: William Heinemann, 1938. New York: Reynal & Hitchcock, 1938. London: Mellifont Press, 1944.

While the Sirens Slept. London: Jarrolds, 1944.

The Sirens Wake. London: Jarrolds, 1945.

Essays and Miscellany

Nowadays. Boston: Four Seas, 1918.

If I Were Dictator. London: Methuen, 1934.

The Donellan Lectures. London: William Heinemann, 1945.

A Glimpse from a Watch Tower. London: Jarrolds, 1946. (Many essays are included in *The Ghosts of the Heaviside Layer*.)

Secondary

(1) Amory, Mark. *Biography of Lord Dunsany.* London: Collins, 1972.

(2) Bierstadt, Edward Hale. *Dunsany the Dramatist.* Boston: Little, Brown, 1917. Rev. ed. Boston: Little, Brown, 1919.

(3) Bowen, Elizabeth. "Our Ireland" [review of *My Ireland*]. *New Statesman and Nation,* June 26, 1937, pp. 1050–1052.

(4) Boyd, Emma Garrett. "Lord Dunsany, Dreamer." *Forum* 57 (April 1917): 497–508.

(5) Boyd, Ernest A. "Lord Dunsany—Fantaisiste." In *Appreciations and Depreciations,* pp. 71–100. New York: John Lane, 1918. Freeport, N.Y.: Books for Libraries Press, 1968.

(6) Cantrell, Brent. "British Fairy Tradition in *The King of Elfland's Daughter.*" *Romantist* 4/5 (1980–1981): 51–54.

(7) Chandler, A. Bertram. "The Dunsany Touch" [review of *The Fourth Book of Jorkens*]. *Fantasy Review* 11 (April–May 1948): 48.

(8) Chislett, William. "New Gods for Old" and "Lord Dunsany: Amateur and Artist." In *Moderns and Near-Moderns,* pp. 171–180, 181–188. New York: Grafton Press, 1928.

(9) Clarke, Arthur C. "Dunsany Lord of Fantasy." *Rhodomagnetic Digest* 3 (November–December 1951): 16–18.

(10) Colum, Padraic. Introduction to *A Dreamer's Tales,* pp. xiii–xviii. New York: Boni & Liveright (Modern Library), 1918.

(11) De Casseres, Benjamin. "Lord Dunsany." In *Forty Immortals,* pp. 212–215. New York: Seven Arts, 1926. Reprinted in *Studies in Weird Fiction* no. 1 (Summer 1986): 33–34.

(12) Desmond, Shaw. "Dunsany, Yeats and Shaw: Trinity of Magic." *Bookman* (New York) 58 (November 1923): 260–266.

(13) Gogarty, Oliver St. John. "Lord Dunsany." *Atlantic Monthly* 195 (March 1955): 67–72.

(14) ———. "My Friends Stephens and Dunsany." *Tomorrow* 10 (March 1951): 22–28.

(15) Greene, Graham. Review of *The Curse of the Wise Woman. Spectator,* November 3, 1933, p. 638.

(16) Hamilton, Clayton. "Lord Dunsany: Personal Impressions." *Bookman* (New York) 50 (February 1920): 537–542. Reprinted in Hamilton's *Seen on the Stage,* pp. 237–248. New York: Henry Holt, 1920.

(17) ———. "The Plays of Lord Dunsany." *Bookman* (New York) 44 (January 1917): 469–477.

(18) Hammond, Josephine. "Wonder and the Playwright, Lord Dunsany." *Personalist* 3 (January 1922): 5–30.

(19) Harris, Frank. "Lord Dunsany and Sidney Sime." In *Contemporary Portraits: Second Series*, pp. 141–157. New York: Frank Harris, 1919.

(20) Heaney, Seamus. "The Labourer and the Lord." *Listener*, September 28, 1972, pp. 408–409.

(21) Lewisohn, Ludwig. "Dunsany." *Nation*, July 25, 1923, p. 95.

(22) Littlefield, Hazel. *Lord Dunsany: King of Dreams: A Personal Portrait*. New York: Exposition Press, 1959.

(23) Llwyd, J. P. D. "Lord Dunsany: Herald of the New Romance." *Dalhousie Review* 3 (January 1924): 474–482.

(24) Lovecraft, H. P. "Lord Dunsany and His Work" (1922). In *Marginalia*, pp. 148–160. Sauk City, Wis.: Arkham House, 1944.

(25) Mahony, Patrick, "Lord Dunsany's Centennial: A Memoir." *Eire-Ireland* 14 (Spring 1979): 126–130.

(26) Moses, Montrose J. "Lord Dunsany's Peculiar Genius." *Bellman*, April 14, 1917, pp. 405–409.

(27) O'Conor, Norreys Jephson. *Changing Ireland: Literary Backgrounds of the Irish Free State 1889–1922*, pp. 148–156. Cambridge, Mass.: Harvard University Press, 1924.

(28) O'Faoláin, Seán. Review of *Up in the Hills*. *Spectator*, October 18, 1935, p. 628.

(29) Paul-Dubois, Louis. "Lord Dunsany: Le Maitre du merveilleux." *Revue des Deux Mondes* 16 (August 15, 1933): 893–919.

(30) Price, Nancy. "An Aesthetic Falstaff—Lord Dunsany." In *Each in His Own Way*, pp. 89–97. London: Frederick Muller, 1960.

(31) Priestley, J. B. Review of *The King of Elfland's Daughter*. *London Mercury* 10 (August 1924): 428–429.

(32) [Russell, George William] AE. "A Maker of Mythologies." *Irish Statesman*, April 17, 1926. Reprinted in *Living Age*, May 29, 1926, pp. 464–466.

(33) Saul, George Brandon. "Strange Gods and Far Places: The Short Fiction of Lord Dunsany." *Arizona Quarterly* 19 (Autumn 1963): 197–210.

(34) Schweitzer, Darrell. "Lovecraft and Lord Dunsany." In *Essays Lovecraftian*, pp. 91–107. Edited by Darrell Schweitzer. Baltimore: T-K Graphics, 1976. Rev. version reprinted in *Discovering H. P. Lovecraft*, pp. 91–112. Mercer Island, Wash.: Starmont House, 1987.

(35) ———. *Pathways to Elfland: The Writings of Lord Dunsany*. Philadelphia: Owlswick Press, 1989.

(36) Shepard, Odell. "Lord Dunsany—Myth-Maker." *Scribner's Magazine* 69

(May 1921): 595–599. Reprinted in Shepard's *The Joys of Forgetting: A Book of Bagatelles*, pp. 30–47. Boston: Houghton Mifflin, 1929.

(37) Sturtevant, Ethel G. "Dunsany on Gods and Men." *Columbia University Quarterly* 21 (July 1919): 186–199.

(38) Waugh, Evelyn. "Five Lives" [review of *Patches of Sunlight*]. *Spectator,* July 17, 1938, pp. 1112–1114.

(39) Weygandt, Cornelius. "The Dramas of Lord Dunsany." *University of Pennsylvania Public Lectures* 6 (1918–1919): 63–82. Reprinted in Weygandt's *Tuesdays at Ten,* pp. 13–42. Philadelphia: University of Pennsylvania Press, 1928. Freeport, N.Y.: Books for Libraries Press, 1967.

(40) Yeats, W. B. Introduction to *Selections from the Writings of Lord Dunsany,* pp. [xix–xxvii]. Churchtown: Cuala Press, 1912. Shannon: Irish University Press, 1971. Reprinted in *Studies in Weird Fiction* no. 5 (Spring 1989): 27–29.

ALGERNON BLACKWOOD

Primary

Short Stories

The Empty House and Other Ghost Stories. London: Eveleigh Nash, 1906. New York: Donald C. Vaughan, 1915. New York: Knopf, 1917. London: Richards Press, 1947. London: John Baker, 1964.

The Listener and Other Stories. London: Eveleigh Nash, 1907. New York: Vaughan & Gomme, 1914. New York: Knopf, 1917. Freeport, N.Y.: Books for Libraries Press, 1971. (Included in *Selected Tales* [1964].)

John Silence: Physician Extraordinary. London: Eveleigh Nash, 1908. Boston: John W. Luce, 1909. London: Macmillan, 1912. New York: Vaughan & Gomme, 1914. New York: Knopf, 1917. New York: Dutton, 1920. London: Richards Press, 1942. London: John Baker, 1969.

The Lost Valley and Other Stories. London: Eveleigh Nash, 1910. New York: Vaughan & Gomme, 1914. New York: Knopf, 1917. London: Nash & Grayson, 1931. Freeport, N.Y.: Books for Libraries Press, 1971.

Pan's Garden: A Volume of Nature Stories. London: Macmillan, 1912. New York: Macmillan, 1912. Freeport, N.Y.: Books for Libraries Press, 1971.

Ten Minute Stories. London: John Murray, 1914. New York: Dutton, 1914. Freeport, N.Y.: Books for Libraries Press, 1969.

Incredible Adventures. London: Macmillan, 1914. New York: Macmillan, 1914.

Day and Night Stories. London: Cassell, 1917. New York: Dutton, 1917.

The Wolves of God and Other Fey Stories (with Wilfred Wilson). London: Cassell, 1921. New York: Dutton, 1921.

Tongues of Fire and Other Sketches. London: Herbert Jenkins, 1924. New York: Dutton, 1925.

Ancient Sorceries and Other Tales. London: Collins, 1927.

The Dance of Death and Other Tales. London: Herbert Jenkins, 1927. London: Pan, 1963.

Strange Stories. London: William Heinemann, 1929. New York: Arno Press, 1976.

Algernon Blackwood. Tales of Today and Yesterday. London: George G. Harrap, 1930.

The Willows and Other Queer Tales. London: Collins, 1935.

Shocks. London: Grayson & Grayson, 1935. New York: Dutton, 1936.

The Tales of Algernon Blackwood. London: Martin Secker, 1938. New York: Dutton, 1939.

Selected Tales. Harmondsworth: Penguin, 1942.

Selected Stories. New York: Editions for the Armed Services, 1945.

The Doll and One Other. Sauk City, Wis.: Arkham House, 1946.

Tales of the Uncanny and Supernatural. London: Peter Nevill, 1949. London: Spring Books, 1962. Secaucus, N.J.: Castle Books, 1974.

In the Realm of Terror. New York: Pantheon, 1957.

Selected Tales. London: John Baker, 1964. New York: Dutton, 1965 (as *Tales of Terror and the Unknown*). Harmondsworth: Penguin, 1966 (as *The Insanity of Jones and Other Tales*).

Tales of the Mysterious and Macabre. London: Spring Books, 1967. Secaucus, N.J.: Castle Books, 1974.

Ancient Sorceries and Other Stories. Harmondsworth: Penguin, 1968.

Best Ghost Stories. Edited by E. F. Bleiler. New York: Dover, 1973.

Best Supernatural Tales. New York: Causeway Books, 1973.

Tales of the Supernatural. Woodbridge: Boydell Press, 1983.

Novels

Jimbo: A Fantasy. London: Macmillan, 1909. New York: Macmillan, 1909.

The Education of Uncle Paul. London: Macmillan, 1909. New York: Henry Holt, 1910.

The Human Chord. London: Macmillan, 1910. New York: Macmillan, 1911. London: Tom Stacey, 1972.

The Centaur. London: Macmillan, 1911. New York: Macmillan, 1912. Harmondsworth: Penguin, 1938. New York: Arno Press, 1976.

A Prisoner in Fairyland. London: Macmillan, 1913. New York: Macmillan, 1913.

The Extra Day. London: Macmillan, 1915. New York: Macmillan, 1915.

Julius LeVallon: An Episode. London: Cassell, 1916. New York: Dutton, 1916.

The Wave: An Egyptian Aftermath. London: Macmillan, 1916. New York: Dutton, 1916.

The Promise of Air. London: Macmillan, 1918. New York: Dutton, 1918.

The Garden of Survival. London: Macmillan, 1918. New York: Dutton, 1918.

The Bright Messenger. London: Cassell, 1921. New York: Dutton, 1922.

Sambo and Snitch. London: Basil Blackwell, 1927. New York: D. Appleton & Co., 1929.

Dudley and Gilderoy: A Nonsense. London: Ernest Benn, 1929. New York: Dutton, 1929. Portway: Cedric Chivers, 1971. New York: Curtis Books, 1973.

The Fruit Stoners. London: Grayson & Grayson, 1934. New York: Dutton, 1935. New York: Arno Press, 1978.

Plays

Karma: A Re-incarnation Play (with Violet Pearn). London: Macmillan, 1918. New York: Dutton, 1918.

Through the Crack (with Violet Pearn). London: Samuel French, 1925.

(Other plays were produced but not published.)

Autobiography

Episodes before Thirty. London: Cassell, 1923. New York: Dutton, 1924. London: Jonathan Cape, 1934 (as *Adventures before Thirty*). London: Peter Nevill, 1950.

Secondary

(1) Ashley, Mike. "Algernon Blackwood and the Golden Dawn." *Fantasy Commentator* 5 (Winter 1984): 77–91.

(2) ———. *Algernon Blackwood: A Bio-Bibliography.* Westport, Conn.: Greenwood Press, 1987.

(3) ———. "The Cosmic Connection." *Crypt of Cthulhu* 7 (St. John's Eve 1988): 3–9.

(4) ———. "Lovecraft and Blackwood: A Surveillance." *Crypt of Cthulhu* 7 (Hallowmass 1988): 3–8, 14.

(5) ———. "The Road to *The Empty House.*" *Fantasy Commentator* 5 (Fall 1985): 166–175.

(6) Colbron, Grace Isobel. "Algernon Blackwood—An Appreciation." *Bookman* (New York) 40 (February 1915): 618–621.

(7) Compton-Rickett, Arthur. "Algernon Blackwood." In *Portraits and Personalities.* London: Selwyn & Blount, 1937, pp. 55–69.

(8) ffoulkes, Maude M. C. "Algernon Blackwood." In *My Own Past*, pp. 186–202. London: Cassell, 1915.

(9) Gilbert, Stuart. "Algernon Blackwood: Novelist and Mystic." *Transition* no. 23 (July 1935): 89–96.

(10) Hudson, Derek. "A Study of Algernon Blackwood." *Essays and Studies* 14 (1961): 102–114.

(11) Lawson, Robb. "Algernon Blackwood." *Bookman* (London) 53 (November 1917): 49–51. Reprinted in *Living Age* 296 (January 26, 1918): 228–231.

(12) Penzoldt, Peter. "Algernon Blackwood." In *The Supernatural in Fiction*, pp. 228–253. London: Peter Nevill, 1952. New York: Humanities Press, 1965.

(13) Reaver, J. Russell. "From Seed to Fruit: The Doubling of Psychic Landscapes in Algernon Blackwood's *The Centaur.*" *Romantist* 4/5 (1980–1981): 55–58.

(14) Reeves, Henriette. "Algernon Blackwood: A Writer of Mysteries." *Touchstone* 7 (May 1920): 147–149.

(15) Sullivan, Jack. "The Visionary Ghost Story: Algernon Blackwood." In *Elegant Nightmares: The English Ghost Story from LeFanu to Blackwood*, pp. 112–129. Athens: Ohio University Press, 1978.

(16) Walters, Aubrey J. C. "Algernon Blackwood and Occult Literature." *Papers of the Manchester Literary Club* 54 (1928): 47–52.

M. R. JAMES

Primary

Ghost Stories

Ghost-Stories of an Antiquary. London: Edward Arnold, 1904. Harmondsworth: Penguin, 1937. Freeport, N.Y.: Books for Libraries Press, 1969. New York: Dover, 1971.

More Ghost Stories of an Antiquary. London: Edward Arnold, 1911. Freeport, N.Y.: Books for Libraries Press, 1971.

A Thin Ghost and Others. London: Edward Arnold; New York: Longmans, Green, 1919. Freeport, N.Y.: Books for Libraries Press, 1971.

The Five Jars. London: Edward Arnold, 1922. New York: Arno Press, 1976.

A Warning to the Curious. London: Edward Arnold, 1925.

The Collected Ghost Stories of M. R. James. London: Edward Arnold, 1931, 1974. Harmondsworth: Penguin, 1984 (as *The Penguin Complete Ghost Stories of M. R. James*).

Book of the Supernatural. Edited by Peter Haining. London: Foulsham, 1979. New York: Stein & Day, 1979 (as *The Book of Ghost Stories*).

Autobiography

Eton and King's: Recollections, Mostly Trivial, 1875–1925. London: Williams & Norgate, 1926.

Secondary

(1) Briggs, Julia. "No Mere Antiquary: M. R. James." In *Night Visitors: The Rise and Fall of the English Ghost Story,* pp. 124–141. London: Faber & Faber, 1977.

(2) Butts, Mary. "The Art of Montagu[e] James." *London Mercury* 29 (February 1934): 306–317.

(3) Cox, J. Randolph. "Ghostly Antiquary: The Stories of Montague Rhodes James." *English Literature in Transition* 12 (1969): 197–202.

(4) Cox, Michael. *M. R. James: An Informal Portrait.* Oxford: Oxford University Press, 1983.

(5) Fleming, Peter. "The Stuff of Nightmares." *Spectator,* April 18, 1931, p. 633.

(6) Frazetto, Jack P. "A Study of the Preternatural Fiction of Sheridan Le Fanu and Its Impact upon the Tales of Montague Rhodes James." Ph.D. diss., St. John's University, 1956.

(7) Gaselee, Stephen. "Montague Rhodes James." *Proceedings of the British Academy* 22 (1936): 418–433.

(8) Leslie, Shane. "Montague Rhodes James." *Quarterly Review* 304 (January 1966): 45–56.

(9) Lubbock, S. G. *A Memoir of Montague Rhodes James.* Cambridge: Cambridge University Press, 1939.

(10) Penzoldt, Peter. "Dr. M. R. James." In *The Supernatural in Fiction,* pp. 191–202. London: Peter Nevill, 1952. New York: Humanities Press, 1965.

(11) Pfaff, Richard William. *Montague Rhodes James.* London: Scolar Press, 1980.

(12) Sullivan, Jack. "The Antiquarian Ghost Story: Montague Rhodes James." In *Elegant Nightmares: The English Ghost Story from LeFanu to Blackwood,* pp. 69–90. Athens: Ohio University Press, 1978.

(13) Varma, Devendra P. "The Ghost Stories of M. R. James: Artistic Exponent of the Victorian Macabre." *Indian Journal of English Studies* n.s. 4 (1983): 73–81.

(14) Warren, Austin. "The Marvels of M. R. James, Antiquary." In *Connections,* pp. 86–107. Ann Arbor: University of Michigan Press, 1970.

AMBROSE BIERCE

Primary

Humor

The Fiend's Delight. London: John Camden Hotten, 1872. New York: A. L. Lyster, 1873. Upper Saddle River, N.J.: Literature House, 1970.

Nuggets and Dust Panned Out in California. London: Chatto & Windus, 1872.

Cobwebs: Being the Fables of Zimbri, the Parsee. London: "Fun" Office, 1873. London: George Routledge & Sons, 1874 (as *Cobwebs from an Empty Skull*).

The Dance of Death (with Thomas A. Harcourt). San Francisco: H. Keller, 1877.

Fantastic Fables. New York: Putnam's, 1899. New York: A. & C. Boni, 1926 (with *The Monk and the Hangman's Daughter*). New York: Dover, 1970.

The Devil's Dictionary. New York: Doubleday, Page, 1906 (as *The Cynic's Word Book*). New York: A. & C. Boni, 1926. Cleveland: World Publishing Co., 1941. New York: Dover, 1958.

The Sardonic Humor of Ambrose Bierce. Edited by George Barkin. New York: Dover, 1963.

The Enlarged Devil's Dictionary. Edited by Ernest Jerome Hopkins. Garden City, N.Y.: Doubleday, 1967.

Poetry

Black Beetles in Amber. New York: Western Authors Publishing Co., 1892. Upper Saddle River, N.J.: Literature House, 1970.

Shapes of Clay. San Francisco: W. E. Wood, 1903.

An Invocation. San Francisco: Book Club of California, 1928.

A Vision of Doom. Edited by Donald Sidney-Fryer. West Kingston, R:I.: Donald M. Grant, 1980.

Short Stories

Tales of Soldiers and Civilians. New York: E. L. G. Steele, 1891. London: Chatto & Windus, 1892 (as *In the Midst of Life: Tales of Soldiers and Civilians*). New York: Lovell, Coryell & Co., 1895. New York: Putnam's, 1898 (rev. ed.). New York: Boni & Liveright, 1918 (from *Collected Works,* vol. 2). London: Jonathan Cape, 1928 (as *The Eyes of the Panther: Tales of Soldiers and Civilians*). Harmondsworth: Penguin, 1939. New York: New American Library, 1961. Freeport, N.Y.: Books for Libraries Press, 1970 (rpt. of 1891 ed.). (Contents of all unspecified editions differ slightly.)

Can Such Things Be? New York: Cassell, 1893. Washington, D.C.: Neale Publishing Co., 1903. New York: Boni & Liveright, 1918 (from *Collected Works,* vol. 3). London: Jonathan Cape, 1927. Freeport, N.Y.: Books for Libraries Press, 1971 (rpt. of 1918 ed.). Secaucus, N.J.: Citadel Press, 1974. (Contents of all unspecified editions differ slightly.)

Collected Works, vol. 8. Washington, D.C.: Neale Publishing Co., 1911.

A Son of the Gods and A Horseman in the Sky. San Francisco: Paul Elder & Co., 1907.

Ten Tales. London: First Edition Club, 1925.

Ghost and Horror Stories. Edited by E. F. Bleiler. New York: Dover, 1964.

Stories and Fables. Edited by Edward Wagenknecht. Owings Mills, M.D.: Stemmer House, 1977.

Essays and Miscellany

The Shadow on the Dial. San Francisco: A. M. Robertson, 1909.

Write It Right: A Little Blacklist of Literary Faults. New York: Neale Publishing Co., 1909. New York: Union Library Association, 1934. San Francisco: Grabhorn-Hoyem, 1971.

Letters. Edited by Bertha Clark Pope. San Francisco: Book Club of California, 1922. New York: Gordian Press, 1967.

Twenty-one Letters. Edited by Samuel Loveman. Cleveland: George Kirk, 1922. Folcroft, P.A.: Folcroft Library Editions, 1973.

Selections from "Prattle." Edited by Carroll D. Hall. San Francisco: Book Club of California, 1936.

The Ambrose Bierce Satanic Reader. Edited by Jerome Hopkins. Garden City, N.Y.: Doubleday, 1968.

Skepticism and Dissent: Selected Journalism 1898–1901. Edited by Lawrence I. Berkove. Ann Arbor, Mich.: Delmas, 1980.

Translation

Richard Voss. *The Monk and the Hangman's Daughter* (with G. A. Danziger). Chicago: F. J. Schulte, 1892. New York: Neale Publishing Co., 1907. New York: A.& C. Boni, 1926 (with *Fantastic Fables*). London: Jonathan Cape, 1927. New York: Limited Editions Club, 1967.

Collected Works

Collected Works. 12 vols. Washington, D.C.: Neale Publishing Co., 1909–1912. New York: Gordian Press, 1966.

Collected Writings. New York: Citadel Press, 1946.

Secondary

(1) Aaron, Daniel. "Ambrose Bierce and the American Civil War." In *Uses of Literature,* pp. 115–131. Edited by Monroe Engel. Cambridge, Mass.: Harvard University Press, 1973.

(2) Bahr, Howard W. "Ambrose Bierce and Realism." *Southern Quarterly* 1 (July 1963): 309–330.

(3) Berkove, Lawrence I. "The Impossible Dreams: Ambrose Bierce on Utopia and America." *Huntington Library Quarterly* 44 (Autumn 1981): 283–392.

(4) ———. "'A Strange Adventure': The Story behind a Bierce Tale." *American Literary Realism* 14 (Spring 1981): 70–76.

(5) Boynton, Percy H. "Ambrose Bierce." In *More Contemporary Americans*, pp. 75–93. Chicago: University of Chicago Press, 1927.

(6) Brazil, John R. "Behind the Bitterness: Ambrose Bierce in Text and Context." *American Literary Realism* 13 (Autumn 1980): 225–237.

(7) Brooks, Van Wyck. "The Letters of Ambrose Bierce." In *Emerson and Others*, pp. 149–157. New York: Dutton, 1927.

(8) ———. "San Francisco: Ambrose Bierce." In *The Confident Years 1885–1915*, pp. 201–215. New York: Dutton, 1952.

(9) Cooper, Frederic Taber. "Ambrose Bierce." In *Some American Story Tellers*, pp. 331–353. New York: Henry Holt, 1911.

(10) Davidson, Cathy N., ed. *Critical Essays on Ambrose Bierce*. Boston: G. K. Hall, 1982.

(11) ———. *The Experimental Fictions of Ambrose Bierce*. Lincoln: University of Nebraska Press, 1984.

(12) ———. "Re-structuring the Ineffable and Ambrose Bierce's 'The Secret of Macarger's Gulch.'" *Markham Review* 12 (Fall 1982): 14–19.

(13) de Castro, Adolphe [G. A. Danziger]. *Portrait of Ambrose Bierce*. New York: Century, 1929.

(14) Fadiman, Clifton. "Portrait of a Misanthrope." *Saturday Review of Literature*, October 12, 1946, p. 12.

(15) Fatout, Paul. *Ambrose Bierce: The Devil's Lexicographer*. Norman: University of Oklahoma Press, 1951.

(16) ———. *Ambrose Bierce and the Black Hills*. Norman: University of Oklahoma Press, 1956.

(17) Field, B. S., Jr. "Ambrose Bierce as a Comic." *Western Humanities Review* 31 (Spring 1977): 173–180.

(18) Grattan, C. Hartley. *Bitter Bierce: A Mystery of American Letters*. Garden City, N.Y.: Doubleday, 1929.

(19) Grenander, M. E. *Ambrose Bierce*. New York: Twayne, 1971.

(20) Hall, Carroll D. *Bierce and the Poe Hoax*. San Francisco: Book Club of California, 1943.

(21) Hayden, Brad. "Ambrose Bierce: The Esthetics of a Derelict Romantic." *Gypsy Scholar* 7 (1980): 3–14.

(22) Jordan-Smith, Paul. "Ambrose Bierce." In *On Strange Altars*, pp. 262–275. New York: A. & C. Boni, 1924.

(23) Kazin, Alfred. "On Ambrose Bierce and 'Parker Adderson, Philosopher.'" In *The American Short Story*, pp. 26–35. Edited by Calvin Skaggs. New York: Dell, 1977.

(24) Klein, Marcus. "San Francisco and Her Hateful Ambrose Bierce." *Hudson Review* 7 (Autumn 1954): 392–407.

(25) Logan, F. J. "The Wry Seriousness of 'Owl Creek Bridge.'" *American Literary Realism* 10 (Spring 1977): 101–113.

(26) Maclean, Robert C. "The Deaths in Ambrose Bierce's 'Halpin Frayser.'" *Papers on Language and Literature* 10 (Fall 1974): 394–402.

(27) McWilliams, Carey. *Ambrose Bierce: A Biography.* New York: A. & C. Boni, 1929.

(28) Martin, Jay. "Ambrose Bierce." In *The Comic Imagination in American Literature,* pp. 195–205. Edited by Louis D. Rubin, Jr. New Brunswick, N.J.: Rutgers University Press, 1972.

(29) Mencken, H. L. "Ambrose Bierce." In *Prejudices: Sixth Series,* pp. 259–265. New York: Knopf, 1927.

(30) Miller, Arthur M. "The Influence of Edgar Allan Poe on Ambrose Bierce." *American Literature* 4 (May 1932): 130–150.

(31) Nations, Leroy J. "Ambrose Bierce: The Gray Wolf of American Letters." *South Atlantic Quarterly* 25 (July 1926): 253–265.

(32) Neale, Walter. *Life of Ambrose Bierce.* New York: Neale Publishing Co., 1929.

(33) Noel, Joseph. *Footloose in Arcadia: A Personal Portrait of Jack London, George Sterling, Ambrose Bierce.* New York: Carrick & Evans, 1940.

(34) Partridge, Eric. "Ambrose Bierce." *London Mercury* 16 (October 1927): 625–637.

(35) Roth, Russell. "Ambrose Bierce's 'Detestable Creature.'" *Western American Literature* 9 (Fall 1974): 169–176.

(36) Solomon, Eric. "The Bitterness of Battle: Ambrose Bierce's War Fiction." *Midwest Quarterly* 5 (Winter 1964): 147–165.

(37) Starrett, Vincent. *Ambrose Bierce.* Chicago: Walter M. Hill, 1920.

(38) ———. *Ambrose Bierce: A Bibliography.* Philadelphia: Centaur Book Shop, 1929.

(39) Stein, William Bysshe. "Bierce's 'The Death of Halpin Frayser': The Poetics of Gothic Consciousness." *Emerson Society Quarterly* 18 (2nd Quarter 1972): 115–122.

(40) Sterling, George. "The Shadow Maker." *American Mercury* 6 (September 1925): 10–19.

(41) Thomas, Jeffrey F. "Ambrose Bierce." *American Literary Realism* 8 (Summer 1975): 198–201.

(42) Walker, Franklin. *Ambrose Bierce: The Wickedest Man in San Francisco.* San Francisco: Colt Press, 1941.

(43) Wiggins, Robert A. *Ambrose Bierce.* Minneapolis: University of Minnesota Press, 1964.

(44) Wilson, Edmund. "Ambrose Bierce on the Owl Creek Bridge." In *Patriotic Gore*, pp. 617–634. New York: Oxford University Press, 1962.

(45) Wilt, Napier. "Ambrose Bierce and the Civil War." *American Literature* 1 (November 1929): 260–285.

(46) Woodruff, Stuart C. *The Short Stories of Ambrose Bierce*. Pittsburgh: University of Pittsburgh Press, 1964.

H. P. LOVECRAFT

Primary

Short Stories

The Shunned House. Athol, Mass.: W. Paul Cook, 1928. (Printed but not bound or distributed.)

The Battle That Ended the Century (with R. H. Barlow). [De Land, Fla.: R. H. Barlow, 1934.]

The Cats of Ulthar. Cassia, Fla.: Dragon-Fly Press, 1935.

The Shadow over Innsmouth. Everett, Pa.: Visionary Publishing Co., 1936.

A History of the "Necronomicon." Oakman, Ala.: Wilson H. Shepherd, 1938.

The Outsider and Others. Edited by August Derleth and Donald Wandrei. Sauk City, Wis.: Arkham House, 1939. (Includes "Supernatural Horror in Literature.")

Beyond the Wall of Sleep. Edited by August Derleth and Donald Wandrei. Sauk City, Wis.: Arkham House, 1943.

The Dunwich Horror and Others. Edited by August Derleth. Sauk City, Wis.: Arkham House, 1963. Rev. ed. edited by S. T. Joshi. Sauk City, Wis.: Arkham House, 1984.

At the Mountains of Madness and Other Novels. Edited by August Derleth. Sauk City, Wis.: Arkham House, 1964. Rev. ed. edited by S. T. Joshi. Sauk City, Wis.: Arkham House, 1985.

Dagon and Other Macabre Tales. Edited by August Derleth. Sauk City, Wis.: Arkham House, 1965. Rev. ed. edited by S. T. Joshi. Sauk City, Wis.: Arkham House, 1986.

The Horror in the Museum and Other Revisions. Edited by August Derleth. Sauk City, Wis.: Arkham House, 1970. Rev. ed. edited by S. T. Joshi. Sauk City, Wis.: Arkham House, 1989.

Essays

United Amateur Press Association: Exponent of Amateur Journalism. [Elroy, Wis.: E. E. Ericson, c. 1916.]

Looking Backward. Haverhill, Mass.: C. W. Smith, [1920].

The Materialist Today. Montpelier, Vt.: Driftwind Press, 1926.

Further Criticism of Poetry. Louisville, Ky.: George G. Fetter, 1932.

Charleston. [New York: H. C. Koenig, 1936.]

Some Current Motives and Practices. [De Land, Fla.: R. H. Barlow, 1936.]

Supernatural Horror in Literature. New York: Ben Abramson, 1945. New York: Dover, 1973.

The Conservative: Complete 1915–1923. Edited by Marc A. Michaud. West Warwick, R.I.: Necronomicon Press, 1976.

Writings in "The United Amateur" 1915–1925. Edited by Marc A. Michaud. West Warwick, R.I.: Necronomicon Press, 1976.

The Californian 1934–1938. Edited by Marc A. Michaud. West Warwick, R.I.: Necronomicon Press, 1977.

In Defence of Dagon. Edited by S. T. Joshi. West Warwick, R.I.: Necronomicon Press, 1985.

Poetry

The Crime of Crimes. Llandudno, Wales: A. Harris, [1915].

HPL. [Belleville, N.J.: Corwin F. Stickney, 1937.]

Fungi from Yuggoth. [Washington, D.C.:] Fantasy Amateur Press Association, 1943.

Collected Poems. Edited by August Derleth. Sauk City, Wis.: Arkham House, 1963.

Writings in "The Tryout." Edited by Marc A. Michaud. West Warwick, R.I.: Necronomicon Press, 1977. (Includes some essays and stories.)

A Winter Wish. Edited by Tom Collins. Chapel Hill, N.C.: Whispers Press, 1977.

Saturnalia and Other Poems. Edited by S. T. Joshi. Bloomfield, N.J.: Cryptic Publications, 1984.

Medusa and Other Poems. Edited by S. T. Joshi. Mount Olive, N.C.: Cryptic Publications, 1986.

Miscellany

The Notes and Commonplace Book. [Edited by R. H. Barlow.] Lakeport, Calif.: Futile Press, 1938.

Marginalia. Edited by August Derleth and Donald Wandrei. Sauk City, Wis.: Arkham House, 1944.

Something about Cats and Other Pieces. Edited by August Derleth. Sauk City, Wis.: Arkham House, 1949. Freeport, N.Y.: Books for Libraries Press, 1971.

The Lovecraft Collectors Library. 7 vols. Edited by George Wetzel. North Tonawanda, N.Y.: SSR Publications, 1952–1955. Madison, Wis.: Strange Co., 1979 (1 vol.).

The Shuttered Room and Other Pieces. Edited by August Derleth. Sauk City, Wis.: Arkham House, 1959.

The Dark Brotherhood and Other Pieces. Edited by August Derleth. Sauk City, Wis.: Arkham House, 1966.

The Occult Lovecraft. Edited by Anthony Raven. Saddle River, N.J.: Gerry de la Ree, 1975.

To Quebec and the Stars. Edited by L. Sprague de Camp. West Kingston, R.I.: Donald M. Grant, 1976.

Uncollected Prose and Poetry. 3 vols. Edited by S. T. Joshi and Marc A. Michaud. West Warwick, R.I.: Necronomicon Press, 1978–1982.

Juvenilia 1897–1905. Edited by S. T Joshi. West Warwick, R.I.: Necronomicon Press, 1984.

Commonplace Book. 2 vols. Edited by David E. Schultz. West Warwick, R.I.: Necronomicon Press, 1987.

Letters

Dreams and Fancies. [Edited by August Derleth.] Sauk City, Wis.: Arkham House, 1962. (Includes some stories.)

Selected Letters 1911–1937. 5 vols. Edited by August Derleth, Donald Wandrei, and James Turner. Sauk City, Wis.: Arkham House, 1965–1976.

Lovecraft at Last (with Willis Conover). Arlington, Va.: Carrollton-Clark, 1975.

Uncollected Letters. Edited by S. T. Joshi. West Warwick, R.I.: Necronomicon Press, 1986.

Secondary

(1) Bender, Barry L. "Xenophobia in the Life and Work of H. P. Lovecraft." *Lovecraft Studies* 1 (Spring 1981): 22–38; (Fall 1981): 10–26.

(2) Burleson, Donald R. *H. P. Lovecraft: A Critical Study.* Westport, Conn.: Greenwood Press, 1983.

(3) ———. "H. P. Lovecraft: The Hawthorne Influence." *Extrapolation* 22 (Fall 1981): 262–269.

(4) ———. "The Mythic Hero Archetype in 'The Dunwich Horror.'" *Lovecraft Studies* 1 (Spring 1981): 3–9.

(5) Cannon, Peter. *H. P. Lovecraft.* Boston: Twayne, 1989.

(6) ———. "Lovecraft and the Mainstream Literature of His Day." *Lovecraft Studies* 2 (Fall 1982): 25–29.

(7) ———. "Sunset Terrace Imagery in Lovecraft." *Lovecraft Studies* 1 (Fall 1981): 3–9.

(8) Cook, W. Paul. *In Memoriam: Howard Phillips Lovecraft: Recollections, Appre-*

ciations, Estimates. North Montpelier, Vt.: Driftwind Press, 1941. West Warwick, R.I.: Necronomicon Press, 1977.

(9) ———. "A Plea for Lovecraft." *Ghost* no. 3 (May 1945): 55–56.

(10) Davis, Sonia H. *The Private Life of H. P. Lovecraft*. Edited by S. T. Joshi. West Warwick, R.I.: Necronomicon Press, 1985.

(11) de Camp, L. Sprague. *Lovecraft: A Biography*. Garden City, N.Y.: Doubleday, 1975.

(12) Eckhardt, Jason C. "Behind the Mountains of Madness: Lovecraft and the Antarctic in 1930." *Lovecraft Studies* 6 (Spring 1987): 31–38.

(13) Faig, Kenneth W. *H. P. Lovecraft: His Life, His Work*. West Warwick, R.I.: Necronomicon Press, 1979.

(14) Frierson, Meade, III, and Penny Frierson, eds. *HPL*. Birmingham, Ala.: Meade and Penny Frierson, 1972.

(15) Joshi, S. T. "The Development of Lovecraftian Studies, 1971–1982." *Lovecraft Studies* 3 (Spring 1984): 32–36; (Fall 1984): 62–71; 4 (Spring 1985): 18–28; (Fall 1985): 54–65.

(16) ———. *H. P. Lovecraft*. Mercer Island, Wash.: Starmont House, 1982.

(17) ———, ed. *H. P. Lovecraft: Four Decades of Criticism*. Athens: Ohio University Press, 1980.

(18) ———. *H. P. Lovecraft and Lovecraft Criticism: An Annotated Bibliography*. Kent, Ohio: Kent State University Press, 1981.

(19) ———, and L. D. Blackmore. *H. P. Lovecraft and Lovecraft Criticism: An Annotated Bibliography: Supplement 1980–1984*. West Warwick, R.I.: Necronomicon Press, 1986.

(20) ———. "'Reality' and Knowledge: Some Notes on the Aesthetic Thought of H. P. Lovecraft." *Lovecraft Studies* 1 (Fall 1980): 17–27.

(21) ———. *Selected Papers on Lovecraft*. West Warwick, R.I.: Necronomicon Press, 1989.

(22) ———. "Topical References in Lovecraft." *Extrapolation* 25 (Fall 1984): 247–265.

(23) Lévy, Maurice. *Lovecraft: A Study in the Fantastic*. Translated by S. T. Joshi. Detroit: Wayne State University Press, 1988. Originally published as *Lovecraft ou du fantastique*. Paris: Christian Bourgois (Union Générale d'Éditions), 1972.

(24) Long, Frank Belknap. *Howard Phillips Lovecraft: Dreamer on the Nightside*. Sauk City, Wis.: Arkham House, 1975.

(25) Mariconda, Steven J. "H. P. Lovecraft: Consummate Prose Stylist." *Lovecraft Studies* 3 (Fall 1984): 43–51.

(26) ———. "Lovecraft's Concept of 'Background.'" *Lovecraft Studies* 5 (Spring 1986): 3–12.

(27) ———. "Notes on the Prose Realism of H. P. Lovecraft." *Lovecraft Studies* 4 (Spring 1985): 3–12.

(28) Menegaldo, Gilles. "The City in H. P. Lovecraft's Work." Translated by S. T. Joshi. *Lovecraft Studies* 1 (Spring 1981): 10–19. Originally published as "La Ville dans l'oeuvre de H. P. Lovecraft." *Caliban* no. 16 (1979): 99–110.

(29) Mosig, Dirk W. "The Four Faces of 'The Outsider.'" *Nyctalops* 2 (July 1974): 3–10. Reprinted in *Essays Lovecraftian,* edited by Darrell Schweitzer.

(30) ———. "Poet of the Unconscious." *Platte Valley Review* 6 (April 1978): 60–66.

(31) Murray, Will. "The Dunwich Chimera and Others: Correlating the Cthulhu Mythos." *Lovecraft Studies* 3 (Spring 1984): 10–24.

(32) ———. "On the Natures of Nug and Yeb." *Lovecraft Studies* 3 (Fall 1984): 52–59.

(33) ———. "An Uncompromising Look at the Cthulhu Mythos." *Lovecraft Studies* 5 (Spring 1986): 26–31.

(34) Onderdonk, Matthew H. "Charon—in Reverse; or, H. P. Lovecraft versus the 'Realists' of Fantasy." *Fantasy Commentator* 2 (Spring 1948): 193–197. *Fresco* 9 (Spring 1958): 45–51. *Lovecraft Studies* 1 (Fall 1980): 5–10.

(35) ———. "The Lord of R'lyeh." *Fantasy Commentator* 1 (Spring 1945): 103–114. *Lovecraft Studies* 2 (Fall 1982): 8–17.

(36) Price, Robert M. "Demythologizing Cthulhu." *Lovecraft Studies* 3 (Spring 1984): 3–9, 24.

(37) ———. "Higher Criticism and the *Necronomicon.*" *Lovecraft Studies* 2 (Spring 1982): 3–13.

(38) ———. "Lovecraft's Concept of Blasphemy." *Crypt of Cthulhu* 1 (Hallowmass 1981): 3–15.

(39) ———. "The Revision Mythos." *Crypt of Cthulhu* 2 (Candlemas 1983): 15–19. Revised version reprinted in *Lovecraft Studies* 4 (Spring 1985): 43–50.

(40) Russ, Joanna. "On the Fascination of Horror Stories, Including Lovecraft's." *Science-Fiction Studies* 7 (November 1980): 350–352.

(41) St. Armand, Barton L. "H. P. Lovecraft: New England Decadent." *Caliban* no. 12 (1975): 127–155.

(42) ———. *The Roots of Horror in the Fiction of H. P. Lovecraft.* Elizabethtown, N.Y.: Dragon Press, 1977.

(43) ———, and John H. Stanley. "H. P. Lovecraft's *Waste Paper:* A Facsimile and Transcript of the Original Draft." *Books at Brown* 26 (1978): 31–47.

(44) Schultz, David E. "Who Needs the 'Cthulhu Mythos'?" *Lovecraft Studies* 5 (Fall 1986): 43–53.

(45) Schweitzer, Darrell, ed. *Essays Lovecraftian.* Baltimore: T-K Graphics, 1976. Revised edition reprinted as *Discovering H. P. Lovecraft.* Mercer Island, Wash.: Starmont House, 1987.

(46) Shea, J. Vernon. "H. P. Lovecraft: The House and the Shadows." *Fantasy and Science Fiction* 30 (May 1966): 82–99. West Warwick, R.I.: Necronomicon Press, 1982.

(47) Sterling, Kenneth. "Caverns Measureless to Man." *Science-Fantasy Correspondent* 1 (1975): 36–43.

(48) Wetzel, George, *Howard Phillips Lovecraft: Memoirs, Critiques, and Bibliographies.* North Tonawanda, N.Y.: SSR Publications, 1955.

(49) ———. "The Mechanistic-Supernatural of Lovecraft." *Fresco* 8 (Spring 1958): 54–60.

INDEX